P 60

DATE			

BAKER & TAYLOR

Ethical
Decision
Making
In
Marketing

◩ Sage Series in Business Ethics

Series Editor: Robert A. Giacalone
The E. Claiborne Robins School of Business
University of Richmond

◩ Editorial Board

Lawrence B. Chonko

Ethical Decision Making In Marketing

SSBE
Sage Series in Business Ethics

SAGE Publications
International Educational and Professional Publisher
Thousand Oaks   London   New Delhi

For information address:

SAGE Publications, Inc.
2455 Teller Road
Thousand Oaks, California 91320

SAGE Publications Ltd.
6 Bonhill Street
London EC2A 4PU
United Kingdom

SAGE Publications India Pvt. Ltd.
M-32 Market
Greater Kailash I
New Delhi 110 048 India

Printed in the United States of America

Library of Congress Cataloging-in-Publication Data

Chonko, Lawrence B.
    Ethical decision making in marketing / Lawrence B. Chonko
        p.   cm. — (Sage series in business ethics ; 1)
    Includes bibliographical references and index.
    ISBN 0-8039-5545-6 (C). — ISBN 0-8039-5546-4 (P)
    1. Marketing—Decision making—Moral and ethical aspects.
    I. Title.   II. Series.
    HF5415.135.C45   1995
    658.8′02—dc20   95-1876

This book is printed on acid-free paper.

95 96 97 98 99 10 9 8 7 6 5 4 3 2 1

Sage Production Editor: Tricia K. Bennett
Sage Typesetter: Janelle LeMaster

Contents

Preface

Today, you can hardly pick up your local newspaper, read a national news magazine, or watch a television news show without hearing something about ethics. Over the last two decades, the subject of business ethics has created tremendous interest in the media, among the public, and in business organizations. Accompanying all this attention is a paradox: Although we have learned much about ethics over the last two decades, the field seems to be more perplexing to marketing managers than ever before.

Although many organizations try to incorporate ethics into their employees' daily activities and many universities offer ethics courses, for many businesspeople, the study of business ethics is irrelevant. One reason for this paradox is that many ethicists are condescending in their approach. They walk in rarefied air, shouting platitudes and "thou shalt nots" without providing much in the way of substantive guidance for real-world dilemmas. All too often, they espouse an ethical absolute (which is not all bad), but they then treat their absolute as the only absolute, expecting others to instantly conform to it. However, as this text illustrates, no one absolute is currently universally accepted.

A second reason for the paradox is that many ethicists have presented harsh critiques of capitalism. Like it or not, it is here to stay (for a while), and we must work within the system. For those who feel compelled to change the system, let me recommend promoting an alternative system's positive elements rather than the negative aspects of capitalism. This approach is more professional and more educational, and it may reveal that the capitalist system, although not perfect, is not all that bad. Furthermore, any new idea that is promoted only as better than the negative aspects of an old idea might not really be a very good idea, particularly if the new idea is weaker in comparison to the strengths of the old idea.

Third, many who have dealt with the subject of ethics have taken to the promotion of abstract theories. There is nothing like a little experience to upset a theory. Now, theory can be good in that theory is based on observations of the real world. It is my contention that the difficulties with ethical theories are not the theories themselves but the manner in which the theories are presented. Theory can be presented in practical and useful ways, but it seldom is.

A fourth reason for the paradox is that many "experts" have tried to peddle "quick and dirty" solutions to ethics problems. Although some experts have provided great value to the business community, too many have "huckstered" businesspeople into thinking that ethical problems have easy solutions. Occasionally, they do; but as this book illustrates, often they do not.

Fifth, many experienced businesspeople have taken time to comment on the state of business ethics. The key word is *comment*. Although their intentions are good and their insights based on their personal experiences may be valuable, too often, they resort to pontification without really providing ethical substance to those who need it.

Ethics is more than pontification. It is more than platitudes and thou shalt nots. It is more than public relations. The study of ethics is a process of reasoning and thinking about actual problems. It is not haphazard. It is more than the statement, "When in doubt do right." Ethics is decision making. In universities, we take great pains to proclaim that decision making is a process, that it is challenging, that it invites conflicts and negotiations because different people have different points of view, and that it often yields answers that are not completely satisfactory to all. Ethics is the same. Reasonable people disagree about the course of many business decisions. Reasonable people also disagree about the course for many ethical decisions.

I have said to my students that ethical decision making is a subset of business decision making. I say this because not all business decisions have ethical ramifications. However, for those that do, the ethical component means that making those business decisions is more challenging. Just as not all business decisions are clear-cut, ethical decisions can also be very ambiguous.

Let me say a few things about this book. First, I hope you enjoy reading it. More important, I hope you learn something about ethical decision making. The book is written from a decision-making perspective and can be broken down into four parts. Chapter 1, the first part, presents an overview of ethics in business and marketing. Chapters 2 through 4 provide a look at how marketing professionals make decisions and the factors and conflicts involved in those decisions. Chapter 5 represents the third part and consists of a discussion of various ethical remedies that exist in the marketplace. Finally, Chapters 6 through 11 present materials on various marketing decision areas—information, product, price, advertising, selling, and distribution. The text of each chapter offers many decision-making situations that you will be asked to discuss. At the end of each chapter are questions that you, your friends, and your instructor can discuss.

As you read this book, keep in mind that, for each of us, there may be a "right" answer to all of the ethical dilemmas we encounter. But the right answer for you may not be the right answer for someone else. Keep in mind that ethical decision making involves and affects many others. These others may not (and are not likely to) agree with what each of you thinks is the proper thing to do. In other words, disagreement or conflict will exist in any decision-making situation in which you are involved. One reason for this conflict is that different people subscribe to different ethical theories. Furthermore, even those of us who have a firm foundation in an ethical orientation face difficulty in applying that ethical orientation in every situation we face.

This book represents an attempt to deal with one of the major concerns about ethics treatments—the unwillingness to grapple with differences between people who subscribe to different ethical orientations. However, it does not attempt to overcome this criticism with an in-depth treatment of those ethical theories. Rather, it attempts to do so by providing a text that challenges you to consider how others might view ethical situations—what decision-making rules guide them, what their religious beliefs might be, what alternative courses of action they might consider, and so on. In other words, this book attempts to "simplify" the presentation of ethical decision making by substituting a "people-are-different" approach for the in-depth theoretical treatment of ethical decision rules.

One of the realities of life in organizations and marketing decision making is the persistent reappearance of conflicts as decisions must be made. Although such persistence can be frustrating, I have found that students who develop decision-making skills can cope with such conflicts. They may not like the conflict, but at least they recognize that conflict is an inevitable part of all decision making, ethically based or not. They also recognize that conflicts stem from basic theoretical differences among those involved in the decision.

These two recognitions provide value to students in that they approach ethical decision-making situations with an awareness that others will not think as they do, and they begin cataloging how others make decisions as a way of learning how to anticipate what different individuals might say or do in certain situations. Students also realize that, as situations change, so do people and so does the information that is relevant to ethical decision making.

To this end, this text provides you with many opportunities to make marketing decisions that marketing professionals would make. Chapters 6 through 11 contain numerous scenarios to challenge your decision-making skill, both within the text and at the end of each chapter. Chapters 1 through 5 periodically ask you to stop and think about topics and ideas being discussed in the text by posing questions for you to answer. In all chapters, the in-text questions are printed in italics so that they are easy to identify. It would be well worth your time and effort to discuss these questions with your instructor, your colleagues, and your friends. Such discussions will serve to familiarize you with many aspects of ethical decision making and, I hope, encourage you to develop an ethic that will guide you as you pursue your education and your career.

Ethics, Business, and Marketing

PURPOSE

To provide an overview of ethical problems faced by marketers and an introduction to some of the issues with which marketers struggle as they engage in ethical decision making.

MAJOR POINTS

Marketing professionals struggle with many ethical issues.

The nature of marketing professionals' jobs places them in situations that have ethical connotations.

Some often discussed issues, such as (a) the purpose of a business, (b) long- versus short-term thinking, (c) the notion that businesspeople operate from more than one ethic, and (d) ethics as rules for decision making, are looked to by marketing professionals for guidance but can create difficulties for ethical decision makers.

Ethics does have a place in business and marketing decision making.

L et's start out with a question. *"Is marketing unethical?"* Today, it is difficult to pick up a newspaper or magazine that does not contain some story about questionable business and marketing behavior. In some circles, ethics is the "buzzword" of the 1990s, with some taking ethics very seriously and others viewing it as the latest hot topic for business discussion, a topic that will eventually lose its favor like many other business fads. This book takes the problems associated with ethics seriously. Business ethics is not a fad. Indeed, the subject of business ethics has been with us for thousands of years, as illustrated by the following passage from the Bible: "The wisdom of the prudent is to give thought to their ways, but the folly of fools is deception" (Proverbs 14:8). The Bible is not the only ancient source of ethical guidelines. For example, Buddhism has its eightfold path—right views, right intent, right speech, right conduct, right livelihood, right effort, right mindfulness, and right concentration—which serves as a guideline for behavior (see Smith, 1991, pp. 105-112). Many may just be discovering the seriousness of ethics, but consideration of ethics has been with us since the dawn of time—since the serpent deceived Eve about the apple.

The most recent public interest in ethics has arisen, partly, because of the media's presentation of the 1980s as the "decade of greed." The Wall Street scandals associated with hostile takeovers, insider trading, and junk bond financing give credence to this title. And such stories continue. As we move through the 1990s, the savings and loan industry has been the subject of countless stories of ethical abuse.

Many place the blame for the ethical abuses they see on the marketing profession. The claims against marketing include assertions such as "Marketing has promoted lifestyles that encourage greed, excess, and ethical misconduct." *Is the marketing profession at fault? Or is it only some of those employed in the profession who are at fault? Where would business organizations be without sound, ethical, marketing strategies? Does marketing simply reflect the values held by society? Is marketing unfairly criticized as the element of business in which unethical behavior is the norm?*

These are all good questions that I hope will provoke some discussion in your class. This book will not give you the answer to any of them. This is not an answer book. But I hope this book will lead you to think about why some marketing professionals choose to take the low ground and engage in unethical behavior. I hope it will provide you with a better understanding of the ethical decisions faced by marketers and the influences on those decisions. Finally, I hope it will provide you, through the presentation of ethical situations, with greater abilities to cope with ethical situations that you will encounter in your lives and your careers. Your behavior, however, is ultimately your own, and therefore it is your responsibility. Learn to seek counsel and advice when confronted with ethical dilemmas. but, ultimately, you are accountable for your own actions. Ultimately, you must choose. *How do you feel about your own responsibility and accountability? Where do you think our society is headed concerning responsibility and accountability?*

■ ETHICAL PROBLEMS FACED BY MARKETING PROFESSIONALS

The marketing profession has long been questioned about ethical abuses (Cox, 1965, p. 26). For example, over 30 years ago, a classic work identified eight major

Issue	Percentage of Marketing Professionals Responding	
Bribery—Gifts from outside vendors, payment of questionable commissions, "money under the table"	15%	Table 1.1 Ethical Issues in Marketing[a]
Fairness—Unfairly placing company interests over family obligations, taking credit for the work of others, inducing customers to use services not needed, manipulation of others	14%	
Honesty—Lying to customers to obtain orders, misrepresenting services and capabilities	12%	
Price—Differential pricing, charging higher prices than firms with similar products while claiming superiority, meeting competitive prices	12%	
Product—Product safety, product and brand infringement, exaggerated performance claims, products that do not benefit consumers	11%	
Personnel—Firing, hiring, employee evaluation	10%	
Confidentiality—Temptations to use or obtain classified, secret, or competitive information	5%	
Advertising—Crossing the line between puffery and misrepresentation, misleading customers	4%	
Manipulation of data—Falsifying figures or misusing statistics or information, distortion	4%	
Purchasing—Reciprocity in the selection of suppliers	3%	

SOURCE: Reprinted by permission of the publisher from "Ethics and Marketing Management: An Empirical Investigation," by Lawrence B. Chonko and Shelby D. Hunt, *Journal of Business Research,* Vol. 13, pp. 339-359. Copyright 1985 by Elsevier Science Inc.
a. Marketing professionals ($N = 1,076$) were asked to describe the most difficult ethical issue they face.

ethical problems that businesspeople wanted to eliminate (Baumhart, 1961). These problems included (a) gifts, gratuities, bribes, and "call girls"; (b) price discrimination and unfair pricing; (c) dishonest advertising; (d) miscellaneous unfair competitive practices; (e) cheating customers, unfair credit practices, and overselling; (f) price collusion by competitors; (g) dishonesty in making or keeping a contract; and (h) unfairness to employees and prejudice in hiring. Not so proudly, five of the eight ethical abuses cited above are in the domain of marketer's activities.

You might say, "Well, that was over three decades ago. Times have changed." Surely, they have. Well, in another classic look at ethics, conducted 16 years later, the same set of undesirable behaviors were identified by businesspeople (Brenner & Molander, 1977). Times may have changed, but apparently, the behavior of people had not over those 16 years. Illustrating a project focused specifically on marketing practices, Table 1.1 reveals that marketing managers face many ethical issues in the course of their daily activities (Chonko & Hunt, 1985). The continual presentation of information like this has prompted many to make statements such as the following: "The function within business firms most often charged with ethical abuse is marketing" (Murphy & Laczniak, 1981, p. 251). Although such a statement may or may not be true, the purpose of this book is not to level criticism at the marketing profession. This book is written with the goal of fostering an understanding of the difficulties faced by marketing professionals when making decisions that have ethical ramifications. Now, once again . . . *Is marketing unethical?*

▧ THE NATURE OF ETHICS AND MARKETING EXCHANGES

"What good will it be . . . [to gain] the whole world, yet [forfeit one's] soul? Or what can [one] give in exchange for [one's] soul?" (Matthew 16:26) This statement is at the heart of ethical decision making, as is the following verse from Taoism. "[One] who stands on tiptoe doesn't stand firm. [One] who rushes ahead doesn't go far. [One] who tries to shine dims [one's] own light" (*Tao Te Ching,* chap. 24). Both statements imply gains and losses from actions. Actions imply a choice between alternative courses of action. Evaluating those alternative courses of action implies weighing the pros and cons of each alternative as seen by the individual and as seen by others with whom the individual interacts. These choices form the heart of the problems associated with ethical decision making. Simply put, people will disagree about which choice is best.

Ethical problems faced by marketing professionals stem from conflicts and disagreements. They are relationships problems. Each party in a marketing transaction brings a set of expectations regarding how the business relationship should exist and how transactions should be conducted. For example, when you, as a consumer, wish to purchase something from a retailer, you bring the following expectations about the transaction: (a) you want to be treated fairly by the retail salesperson, (b) you want to pay a "reasonable" price, and (c) you want the product to be available as advertising says it will be and in the indicated condition. Unfortunately, your expectations might not be in agreement with those of the retailer. The retail salesperson may not have time for you. Or the retailer's perception of a reasonable price may differ from yours. Or the advertising of the product may be misleading.

In such situations, ethical conflict occurs as one individual believes that his or her duties and responsibilities to one group (e.g., the retail salesperson's responsibility to the store) are inconsistent with his or her duties and responsibilities to another group (e.g., the retail salesperson's responsibilities to the customer) or to himself or herself. Simply put, people will often disagree about which action is best in a given situation. In any marketing situation, the interests of many must be taken into account. For example, accurate disclosure of information about product disadvantages may be in the best interests of the customers, but some might judge it not to be in the best interests of the company. Similarly, the sales of products that have little or no benefits to the customer, have exaggerated product claims, or both all involve a conflict between the customer and the company. For the marketing professional, ethical questions often revolve around which set of interests that marketing professional attempts to satisfy—those of the company or those of the customer. Now consider a few more situations illustrated in Newsline 1.1.

Newsline 1.1

Tom Peters Ruined My Life

I used to enjoy going shopping. I also loved the whole atmosphere of eating out—the luxury of someone waiting on you, no dishes to wash. And I used to run my stroller business the regular way. Now it's gone, all ruined, and it's Tom Peter's fault.

Before I heard him, shopping was fun! Then, in 1988, Tom came to our town to give one of his talks. He spent the whole time saying how badly most businesses are run. Then he doled out a few examples of what it's like when businesses are run right. He focused on the concept of customer service: Whether you are an employee or an owner, the customer pays your wages; the customer will vote with his dollars and his feet, sooner or later; therefore, the customer is always right. Of course, there's nothing new or complex in this, except for the degree to which you devote your strategy to customer satisfaction. For me, it was a wake-up call.

At about 7 a.m. the next day, I was at my dry cleaner. I'd been going there for years. As usual, I had waited to go until I was forced to wear the weird stuff at the back of my closet. I had a meeting at my bank the next day, so I was desperate. I asked the girl behind the counter (in my nicest voice!) if I could get a rush on it. She looked startled, and said with astonishment, "Today?" I said, "Yes." She looked really miffed and mumbled something. Abjectly, I asked if they could at least do my suit and blouse. Reluctantly, she said, "Well, I suppose we could get the suit out."

She started to write it up. I searched my purse and realized my discount coupon was in my other car, which my husband had. This cleaner's prices are reasonable if you have the coupon, and near extortionary if you don't. I asked her if I could bring the coupon at 5 p.m., when I came back. "Nope," she said. "It's the rules. Company policy." (I found a new dry cleaner.)

Later that busy day, I went to my favorite restaurant for a quiet lunch. I took my usual seat by a corner window, but it was very chilly. I drank some coffee and put my coat back on. I noticed other people still had their coats on, too. I moved to a chair, same table, away from the window, but it was still cold.

Reluctantly, I managed to catch the manager's eye. I told her it was kind of cold and could she perhaps raise the thermostat a degree or two (it's a pricey restaurant). She went over to the thermostat, which is a few feet from my table and announced loudly that it said 72 degrees. I nodded and replied, "Well yes, but it still feels cold, and see how those other customers have their coats on?" She went back to the wall, shrugged her shoulders, and replied that it clearly said 72 degrees.

I gave up and tried to go back to my magazine. But then the manager and two waitresses stood near several tables away from the windows and loudly pronounced that it was warmer over there and I should move. I hate scenes in restaurants, and now everyone was looking at me. I told them I'd already moved once, and I didn't want to move. They finally left me alone. (It was a long time before I went back.)

These incidents began happening to me more and more, because once you are on the lookout for quality service, you notice how bad most service is. It was a rough couple of years. But to prevent cynicism from setting in, I took occasional soothing trips to our local Nordstrom or stayed at a Ritz-Carlton hotel—where Customer Devotion is done right.

Every year, I take my sales staff to stay at the Ritz-Carlton, Buckhead, Georgia. Every Ritz-Carlton employee I've ever met acts as if it is the high point of his [or her] day to help us.

My first night at Buckhead, I wanted a newspaper, and the gift shop was closed. As we got a late dinner (the kitchen insisted on staying open past its closing time to serve us), I asked if any customer had left a paper behind. The waiter asked for a few minutes to look and in three was back with an *Atlanta Constitution,* a *USA Today,* a *New York Times,* and a *Wall Street Journal.* When I asked if they had opened up the gift shop, he said, no, they had just checked around the hotel. No big deal! He was a little out of breath and had obviously been on the run. No charge, of course. He was beaming.

Another time, I was trying to find a special grocery store in Atlanta, so I could get goat cheese to make special pizza for my son (he's allergic to cow's milk). The Ritz-Carlton concierge found the store I needed. When there was not a taxi in sight, he summoned a doorman to drive me in a hotel car. As we drove along, the young man told me proudly that he was new and had gone through three days of training before he was allowed to open the door at the entrance for customers. Now, that's devotion to details! No charge for the ride, of course,

This degree of Customer Devotion simply cannot be displayed by your staff unless you lead the way. Every time you dish out lousy service, your staff follows your lead.

What does my business do differently now from what we did before Tom's inspiration? Anyone in our company can stop production if he [or she] thinks there's a flaw. Any employee can send a stroller that's on order Fed Ex (at $87 a pop) if he feels we have not met our delivery commitments. Beyond our lifetime guarantee for frames and one year guarantee on the wheels, our customer service people can do whatever it takes, up to $300 per customer, to make things right for the customer (we track costs religiously, so that we can keep this up). We stay in contact after each repair, and the customer gets a postcard to send that comes directly to me and lets me know if we took care of matters to the customer's satisfaction. And we keep trying, until that customer is doing great. Those postcards are an immediate report card and the best part of my day.

So, I finally have reached a point of equilibrium, where I view myself and my staff as people with a religious devotion to our customers. The annoying businesses I run into are the Heathen. If they understood this love of customers, they'd be doing it. But they just don't know any better, poor things.

SOURCE: Baechler, M. (1993, October 25). "Tom Peters Ruined My Life." *Wall Street Journal,* p. A18. Reprinted with permission of the *Wall Street Journal,* © 1993 Dow Jones & Company, Inc. All rights reserved.

On the Boundary

The situations described in Newsline 1.1 demonstrate that marketers are boundary spanners. That is, they are in positions in which they must relate to customers, suppliers, wholesalers, retailers, advertising agencies, research agencies, the media, and regulatory agencies. As a result, marketers are confronted with many demands from many individuals (sometimes referred to as *stakeholders*). These demands often conflict and put pressures on marketers to make decisions that are not satisfactory to all parties. Such decisions may require that these parties "concede" certain things, and few of us like to make concessions. *Why do you think most people do not like to make concessions?*

As marketers also engage in transactions with customers, they must represent their organizations. They must also be advocates for their customers. This dual advocacy role often places pressure on marketers to make decisions that are not to the complete satisfaction of one or the other of the parties to the transaction.

At the same time, marketers can wield considerable power in the marketplace: They can advertise in the mass media; they can allocate scarce resources; they can provide benefits to customers; they can control information. The ability to wield power, coupled with the boundary-spanning and advocacy role of marketers often puts marketers into situations in which unethical behaviors appear to be viable options. *Why do you think this is so?* As you will see in this text, those unethical options can seem to hold considerable promise in the short run.

Put yourself in the position of sales representative. You have just entered the office of a new prospect. How you view prospects will influence how you proceed. Do you view prospects as potential transactions? Or do you view them as potential lifelong customer relationships? If you seek instant reward, you view prospects as transactions, and you might do "whatever it takes" to make the sale . . . once. Sure, you may have increased your bottom line and that of the organization. But have you created a partner in business? Probably not. You visit that same customer some time in the future and express surprise when that *former* customer refuses to do business with you and you can't understand why. You overlook such things as selling a product that was not needed, not calling the customer to check on deliveries and satisfaction, not working with the customer as problems with the product were encountered. In other words, you were sales oriented, not customer oriented. You were short-term oriented, not long-term oriented.

Marketing professionals must recognize that, in exchange relationships, the key word is *relationship*—a long-term orientation. There is a relationship between bottom-line performance and the integrity associated with treating customers properly.

> When people work for an organization that they believe is fair, where everyone is willing to give of themselves to get the job done, where traditions of loyalty and caring are hallmarks, people work to a higher level. The values around them become part of them, and they think of the customer as someone to whom they owe the finest possible product and service. (Sonnenberg & Goldberg, 1992, p. 53)

Before we proceed further, it should be noted that ethics and marketing exchanges are not one-sided. That is, consumers can also behave in unethical ways. Table 1.2 presents a summary of consumers' responses to 27 ethical belief statements. The information reveals that consumers also have divergent opinions concerning the ethical nature of certain behaviors. *How do you feel about these statements? Do your classmates agree with you?*

Disagreements and Conflicts

Conflict occurs between individuals who disagree about the "best" course of action. Conflict occurs when one individual must decide which alternative courses of action "fit" with their perceptions of the ethical way to conduct themselves. Conflict exists between the short run (making a profit through unethical activities) and the long run (perhaps being less profitable in the short run but still being in business and more profitable in the long run). The nature of the role of the marketer as decision maker is such that it places the marketer in positions of conflict. Marketers are confronted with choices between conflicting alternatives reflecting different and sometimes conflicting priorities of values. *Can you think of some conflicts that marketers face?*

Some people have little conflict. They are so self-centered and self-interested that they let nothing get in the way of personal gain. Fortunately, most people are not like this. Most people experience conflict, and many agonize over "the right thing to do." Sometimes they make poor choices. Often, these poor choices are the result of a lack of thought, misunderstanding of the circumstances, or pressures placed on them by others who have power over them (e.g., the boss).

Sometimes the pressure is unintended. For example, suppose you are a salesperson and you are attending an industrywide trade show. At that show, a marketing executive from a competitive organization makes a statement about price wars and the effect they have on company profits. As a salesperson, you may feel pressure to

Activity	Percentage Believing Action Is Wrong[a]	Percentage Believing Action Is Not Wrong[b]
1. Changing price tags on merchandise in store	97%	2%
2. Drinking soft drink in supermarket without paying for it	99%	1%
3. Using long-distance access code that does not belong to you	95%	2%
4. Reporting a lost item as "stolen" to insurance company to collect	92%	3%
5. Giving misleading price information to a clerk to "save" money	95%	2%
6. Returning damaged merchandise when the damage is your fault	93%	3%
7. Getting too much change and not saying anything	87%	6%
8. Observing someone shoplifting and ignoring it	81%	5%
9. Lying about a child's age to get a lower price	82%	7%
10. Not saying anything when the waitress miscalculates the bill in your favor	85%	8%
11. Removing the pollution control device from your car to get better mileage	80%	12%
12. Breaking a bottle of salad dressing in the supermarket and doing nothing about it	78%	7%
13. Stretching the truth on an income tax return	75%	13%
14. Returning merchandise to a store claiming it was a gift when it was not	74%	14%
15. Taking a "souvenir" from a hotel or restaurant	77%	13%
16. Using a coupon for merchandise you did not buy	74%	14%
17. Using an expired coupon for merchandise	73%	13%
18. Joining a music club to get free tapes with no intention of making future purchases	70%	8%
19. Not telling the truth when negotiating the price of a new car	66%	14%
20. Moving into a new residence, finding the cable TV still hooked up, and using it rather than signing up and paying for it	66%	17%
21. Tasting grapes in a supermarket and not buying any	66%	17%
22. Using computer software or games you did not buy	37%	18%
23. Recording a tape instead of buying it	34%	46%
24. Returning an item after finding out the same item is now on sale	36%	47%
25. Returning merchandise after trying it and not liking it	22%	62%
26. Spending an hour trying on different dresses and not buying any	16%	64%
27. Taping a movie from the television	13%	67%

Table 1.2 Consumers' Responses to Marketplace Activities

SOURCE: Adapted by permission of the publisher from "Consumer Ethics: An Investigation of the Ethical Beliefs of the Final Consumer," by James A. Muncy and Scott J. Vitell, *Journal of Business Research*, Vol. 24, pp. 297-311. Copyright 1992 by Elsevier Science Inc.
a. Percentage of respondents who "believe" or "strongly believe" an action is wrong.
b. Percentage of respondents who "believe" or "strongly believe" an action is not wrong.

improve profit margins and, instead of trying to offer the usual discounts to customers, you engage in a strategy of meeting competitive prices. *Have you engaged in price fixing?* Think about this scenario throughout the book. The chapter (Chapter 8) on ethics and pricing decisions may shed some light on this situation.

Marketing professionals who face conflicting pressures often seek to rationalize. Rationalization, as further discussed in Chapter 4, is not a wise strategy—particularly if it involves a compromise of values. Nevertheless, marketers often rationalize (Vitell & Grove, 1987, p. 434):

"I didn't know it was illegal."

"This toy is harmful only if used in the wrong way."

"There is really no reason to tell customers about our product's disadvantages because the advantages are so good."

"The side effects of this drug will affect only a few people."

"I had no choice . . . my job was on the line."

"Any consumer who really believes this ad needs help beyond that which can be provided by marketing."

"Everybody does it."

"I did this because it benefited many."

▧ ISSUES THAT CREATE ETHICAL DECISION-MAKING DIFFICULTIES

We are often very quick to criticize. When we read about some marketing misdeed, we often ask, "How could they have done such a stupid thing?" Well, one reason is that all ethical decisions require human judgment. In making such judgments, individuals often seek guidelines. These guidelines may come in the form of business philosophies, long- versus short-term viewpoints, or ethical codes of conduct. Although individuals seek guidance, you will see in the next sections of this book that evaluating such guidance requires judgment in and of itself.

The Purpose of Business

What is the purpose of business? The question is deceptively simple, but the answer is not. If you believe that the purpose of a business is to make a profit, then this belief will guide your decision making. If you believe, however, that the purpose of a business goes beyond making a profit, then you have a different decision-making guide. Different perceptions of the purpose can lead to conflict.

- According to the customers, the purpose of a business is to provide us with goods and services that satisfy our needs and wants.
- According to the owners, the purpose of a business is to yield profits and appreciation of capital.
- According to the employees, the purpose of a business is to provide us with a good standard of living.

Customers, owners, and employees are all members of the business system. Each of these stakeholders contributes value to business, and each requires some return for their contributions (Sherwin, 1983). What is often overlooked is the interworking of the members of the business systems. Owners risk capital. Employees supply energy, knowledge, and imagination. Customers provide revenues that result in wages and profits. Each has a stake in the business. Each contributes to the business. Each expects to receive something in return from the business. Each is important to the proper functioning of any business.

But other stakeholders also have an interest in the nature of business. For example, public policymakers establish rules that govern the relationships between the members of the business system and between business and the larger society. Although society sets some limits on business activities, business still has much freedom in which to operate. This is so because our society, historically, has seen more potential in private enterprise than other economic systems (e.g., socialism). Our society believes that the private enterprise system will produce a greater quantity, quality, and variety of goods for the satisfaction of customers than that which would be produced under alternative economic systems. But our society also expects that resources will be conserved, prices on goods and services will be low, products will be safe, advertising about products will be truthful, salespeople will not try to manipulate, warranties will be honored, and more. With this brief look at the U.S. business system, let's take a look at the nature of business by examining two extreme viewpoints.

The Business of Business Is Profit

Many would submit the following statement about the purpose of a business: "Business must fight as if it were at war. And, like a good war, it should be fought gallantly, daringly, and above all, not morally" (Levitt, 1958, p. 43).

In essence, such a viewpoint implies that businesses are in the business of producing goods and services to make a profit. Many (not all) in this camp suggest that businesses act irresponsibly if they take on tasks relating to ethical decision making. Such endeavors are better left for other organizations or individuals. *What do you think about this?*

According to this profits-oriented view, business organizations should be evaluated only according to how well they achieve business goals. All that business needs to do is maintain price competitive markets, and the market system will ensure that scarce resources are used to optimally satisfy consumer needs. Any organization that is (a) optimally satisfying consumer needs, (b) running efficiently, and (c) maximizing profits while (d) following legal requirements and (e) adhering to standards of truth and integrity is said to be fulfilling societal requirements. This viewpoint has been stated very clearly by economist Milton Friedman (1962):

> The view has been gaining widespread acceptance that corporate officials . . . have a "social responsibility" that goes beyond serving the interest of their stockholders or their members. This view shows a fundamental misconception of the character and nature of a free economy. In such an economy, there is one and only one social responsibility of business—to use its resources and engage in activities designed to increase its profits, so long as it stays within the rules of the game, which is to say, engages in open and free competition, without deception or fraud.
>
> . . . Few trends could so thoroughly undermine the very foundations of our free society as the acceptance by corporate officials of a social responsibility other than to make as much money for the stockholders as possible. (p. 133)

The Business of Business Is Profit . . . and . . .

The opposing viewpoint is that business organizations do not run like machines (Donaldson, 1970; Goodpaster, 1970). Rules can change. Goals can change. Business organizations constantly undergo self-assessment and self-study in response to changes—changes in their markets, among their competitors, from the government. In other words, business organizations must react and change in accord with elements of the business environment. Proponents of this viewpoint argue that seeking profits is an acceptable goal, but it is not sufficient. Business organizations must assume responsibilities that go beyond things such as effectiveness, efficiency, and legality and take on ethical responsibilities with respect to its employees, stockholders, customers, and society as a whole. In other words, business organizations have a responsibility to all those who might be affected by the activities of the organization. *How do you feel about this viewpoint?* The arguments for a business responsibility are summarized by the following quotation:

> First, most industrial markets are not perfectly competitive as the argument assumes, and to the extent that firms do not have to compete they can maximize profits in spite of inefficient production. Secondly, the argument assumes that any steps taken to increase profits will necessarily be socially beneficial, when in fact several ways of increasing profits actually injure society: allowing harmful pollution to go uncontrolled, deceptive advertising, concealing product hazards, fraud, bribery, tax evasion, price fixing, and so on. Thirdly, the argument assumes that by producing

whatever the buying public wants (or values) firms are producing what all the members of society want, when in fact the wants of large segments of society (the poor and the disadvantaged) are not necessarily met because they cannot participate fully in the marketplace. (Velasquez, 1982, pp. 17-18)

Nestlé Versus Johnson & Johnson. Because this book is about decision making, let's take a look at two companies and the decision each made when confronted with ethical decision-making situations. These two organizations are often used as cases to make the point that ethics is good business. The first company, Nestlé, sought to sell its infant formula to Third World companies in Africa. Nestlé representatives, dressed in white lab coats to look like doctors, sold the product. Free samples were given out. Many mothers switched to the formula, allowing their own breast milk to dry up. Unfortunately, many of these mothers had no uncontaminated water with which to mix the formula. So the product was useless, and when the mothers ran out of money to buy the formula, many babies starved to death. Nestlé was subjected to a 10-year, worldwide boycott when these actions were published. It took Nestlé 10 years to comply with an order from the World Health Organization to stop its marketing practices. The company lost millions of dollars.

In 1982, someone put lethal poison in Extra Strength Tylenol capsules made by our second company, Johnson & Johnson. Immediately, Johnson & Johnson ordered the recall of millions of dollars of product. Hot lines were established, ad campaigns informing the public of the situation were aired, and rewards were offered for the one(s) responsible for the deaths of several individuals. The company's reputation actually improved after the incident. Later, Johnson & Johnson was able to reintroduce the product and fully recover its market share. *What do you think was the difference between the responses of Nestlé and Johnson & Johnson to their respective ethical dilemmas?*

Let's read about how one president and chief operating officer views business ethics:

During the eighties, we've heard a lot about ethics problems such as conflicts of interest, particularly in Washington. But they're minor compared to what a lack of moral leadership can mean.

As I said earlier, I'm a strong believer in the fundamental fairness and goodness of the American people. It's to our credit that there aren't more lapses in ethical behavior. But sometimes ethics is not what you do, but what you don't do—or even how long you take to do something. For example, the Exxon Valdez incident. This story isn't over yet and there are many aspects to it that I'm not qualified to judge.

But I can say this: Mr. Rawls, then CEO of Exxon, was being criticized as much for delays in responses as for the spill. He didn't quickly take the high ground. He waited a full week and then, when he finally spoke, he didn't accept responsibility. Whatever else happens as this incident unfolds, that failure to act quickly to take the high ground surely has done great damage to the company.

As others put it: "They lost the battle in the first 48 hours. Exxon's worst mistake was to respond too slowly."

Exxon is certainly not alone on the business front. The Wall Street scandals are in a class by themselves—there's Ivan Boesky, there's Dennis Levine, there are Drexel Burnham and Michael Milken. Self-interest seems to be the first concern—robbing tomorrow for the short-term gain.

Executives of Beech-Nut Nutrition Corporation, the nation's second largest baby food company, sold phony apple juice just to save their company $4.2 million. The costs of the fraud in lives and dollars, have far exceeded that amount and the fallout losses like lower market share are not yet reversed by Beech-Nut and its parent, Nestlé.

There are too many more of these—and, of course, they extend beyond business to all society. What do we have in contrast?

There are many, many good examples of ethical corporate conduct, but most don't match the bad in magnitude, cost or media interest. To illustrate the importance and the benefits of quickly taking the high ground, I could not find a better example than the Tylenol incident in 1982.

Let me just briefly give you headlines and a few sentences from the actual *Wall Street Journal* coverage of the day:

> Oct. 4, 1982—"Johnson & Johnson Seeks Quick End to the Tylenol Tragedy. Stunned by the deaths linked to Tylenol, Johnson & Johnson executives worked through the weekend with law enforcement agencies toward a quick end to the tragedy involving the company's most important product . . . Johnson & Johnson, maker of Tylenol, moved quickly to avoid more deaths . . ."

> Dec. 24, 1982—"Tylenol regains most of No. 1 share, astounding doomsayers . . . Johnson & Johnson appears to have pulled off a marketing miracle. In the days following Tylenol's link to several Chicago-area deaths, marketing experts were quick to compose elegies. But less than three months later Tylenol is close to recouping lost business."

Quickly take the high ground. James E. Burke, Chairman of Johnson & Johnson, and his lieutenants moved quickly and ethically for their company's long term benefit. There was financial loss, but a quick and strong recovery. Loyalty to the product and the company proved its value. Nobody ever said the high ground wouldn't cost. But overall, ethics is good business. (Bartlett, 1989, pp. 6-7; Reprinted with permission)

Conflict and Profits

Figure 1.1 presents an ethics-profits trade-off matrix. Ideally, a solution of high ethics and high profits guides marketing decision making. Some would argue that this is not always possible. *What do you think?* But courses of action that pursue high ethics are strongly encouraged. Such courses of action will not always produce the highest profits in the short run, but in the long run, many organizations have been very successful because they maintained high ethical standards.

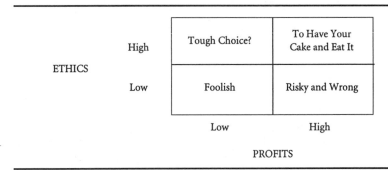

<table>
<tr><td rowspan="2">ETHICS</td><td>High</td><td>Tough Choice?</td><td>To Have Your Cake and Eat It</td></tr>
<tr><td>Low</td><td>Foolish</td><td>Risky and Wrong</td></tr>
</table>

	Low	High
	PROFITS	

Figure 1.1.
Ethics-Profit
Trade-Off Matrix

SOURCE: Goldsmith and Clutterbuck (1984).

Obviously, the many ethical concerns have focused on the high profit, low ethics quadrant in Figure 1.1. Such actions are risky in that short-term profits may be high but, in the long run, those who have suffered negative consequences as a result of the unethical behavior cease doing business with the unethical organization. As you read in the Nestlé example, the costs may be high in the long run. The classic example is the high-pressure, door-to-door salesperson. Such individuals uses strategies in which they have to sell only once to a customer because they know they will never get an audience the second time around. The actions of such salespeople are well documented. But how about the marketing manager who interviews with a competitor and uses the promise of competitive information in the negotiations for the job? The risks of getting caught are small, and the profits (higher wages and a promotion) can be high as shown in the second quadrant.

The third quadrant poses difficulty. Actions may be ethical but unprofitable. Let's look at one example. Many would consider the sale of cigarettes to be an unethical activity. According to their contention, the cigarette makers should take the ethical high road and withdraw from the industry. Clearly, such actions would not be profitable. But wait! Some of you who read this book may not even agree that the sale of cigarettes is unethical. There is conflict among you.

Because there is a fourth quadrant, we will mention it—the quadrant in which someone undertakes unethical and unprofitable actions. Such actions are foolish and do not require comment.

The Prisoner's Dilemma Analogy to Ethical Decision Making in Marketing

To illustrate choice, conflict, and consequences, many have compared decision making in ethical situations to a vignette based on game theory called the prisoner's dilemma. In the prisoner's dilemma, the police attempt to encourage either of two guilty suspects to turn state's evidence. If both suspects keep quiet (choice), both receive a shorter jail sentence (consequence). If one prisoner confesses (choice and

	Marketer One	
	Blows Whistle	*Does Not Blow Whistle*
Blows Whistle	Marketer 1 risks losing job Marketer 2 risks losing job	Marketer 1 keeps job and receives large bonus Marketer 2 loses job
Does Not Blow Whistle	Marketer 1 losing job Marketer 2 keeps job and receives large bonus	Marketer 1 keeps job and receives small bonus Marketer 2 keeps job and receives small bonus

Marketer Two

Figure 1.2. The Prisoner's Dilemma: An Illustration

conflict), that prisoner will go free and the other will receive a longer sentence (consequences). If both confess (choice), however, both will receive the longer sentences (consequences).

A sample set of choices for a prisoner's dilemma game is shown in Figure 1.2. Suppose a firm is about to introduce a product that is not safe for children. Suppose, furthermore, that two marketers in the firm know this. Each can choose to "blow the whistle" or not, with each choice resulting in certain consequences, as shown in Figure 1.2. A key element of the prisoner's dilemma lies in the fact that if one marketer blows the whistle and the other does not, the second marketer keeps his or her job and earns a large bonus, whereas the whistle-blower loses his or her job. If both marketers blow the whistle, each loses his or her job. If both marketers choose not to blow the whistle, each keeps his or her job and earns a small bonus. According to this scheme, the rational (perhaps, financial only) short-term strategy is not to cooperate and blow the whistle, but to let the other marketer blow the whistle by himself or herself. The result is substantially more gain for the non-whistle-blower.

If the prisoner's dilemma were a completely accurate representation of reality, the world of marketing would be filled with hucksters, cheats, and frauds. Fortunately, this is not the case, although there is no denying that some of these types of individuals are employed in the marketing profession. There are some similarities, however, between the prisoner's dilemma game and ethical decision making (Hansen, 1991). Organizations gain, in the long run, only when there is cooperation. Consistent mutual defection leads to consistent losses and the demise of the individual and the organization. Any marketer who seeks short-term gain for himself or herself by imposing a long-term cost on the company is acting unethically.

Long-Term Versus Short-Term Thinking

Today's marketing professional faces a prisoner's dilemma type situation. There is great pressure to take more and more short-term views. Some have called this "the search for instant gratification." Although organizations may advocate a long-term perspective as being best, what happens if the marketing professional does not cooperate and adopts a short-term perspective? The results are less than would be obtained if cooperation was achieved on a long-term basis or if the marketing professional opted for the long-term perspective, disagreeing with the short-term perspective advocated by the organization. Unfortunately, but quite realistically, the marketing professional is often pressured by such factors as loss of job, loss of promotion opportunity, and loss of rewards as being imminent if he or she does not follow the short-term approach, often advocated by the company's policies. Indeed, these situations can and do occur, but such thinking is also short-term in nature and fits right into the prisoner's dilemma situation of two defections.

Consider some of the dilemmas faced by marketing professionals. They may advocate objectives such as increasing customer service, improving product quality, and improving overall performance for the customer. Everyone would agree that these are noble objectives. Naturally, everyone would also like to cut costs, often done in the short run to ensure the company's survival; but that may mean (a) reducing the opportunities for fair and competitive earnings; (b) eliminating peoples' jobs without regard to skills and performance; (c) drastically reducing research and development, often the only forward-looking element of the organization; and (d) eliminating the audit group so that the cost-cutting measures cannot be effectively monitored. *What do you think? Can some of these short-term considerations be made consistent with the long-term perspective?*

Although short-run-oriented objectives may be useful, they often have some unintended and very serious long-term consequences for the organization if the organization's thinking is strictly short-term. Just one illustration. In the preceding example, suppose the organization that cut costs by cutting back its research and development (R&D) is the innovation leader in its industry. As a result of cutting back R&D, the company's short-term profit picture improves. But, in the long run, the organization loses its leadership position in this category and begins losing market share. This would likely take several years to occur. *How long do you think it would take to recover?*

Earlier, we discussed two polar approaches to business ethics—the view that business is in the business of profits and the view that there is more to business than profits. By now, I hope you begin to see the wisdom in the approach that adopts a long-term perspective that business is in business for profits . . . and more. Unfortunately, too may businesspeople still champion the short-term viewpoint, illustrated in the following quotation:

We live in what is probably the most competitive of the world's civilized societies. Our customs encourage a high degree of aggression in the individual's striving for success. Business is our main area of competition, and it has been ritualized into a game of strategy. The basic rules of the game have been set by the government, which attempts to detect and punish business frauds. But as long as a company does not transgress the rules of the game set by law, it has the legal right to shape its strategy without reference to anything but its profits. If it takes a long-term view of its profits, it will preserve amicable relations, so far as possible, with those with whom it deals. A wise business[person] will not seek advantage to the point where he [or she] generates dangerous hostility among employees, competitors, customers, government, or the public at large. But decisions in this area are, in the final test, decisions of strategy, not ethics. (Carr, 1968, p. 8)

Casuistry: Should Marketers Operate From Two Ethics?

History can also place pressure on marketers as decision makers. *Casuistry* is a term that was first mentioned in John Calvin's (1536/1987) *Institutes of the Christian Religion*. It was later developed into a politic ethic in the 17th century. Casuistry asserts that leaders, because of their responsibilities, have to strike a balance between (a) the ordinary demands of ethics that apply to them as individuals and (b) their social responsibility to their subjects and their kingdoms—in modern-day terms, their employees, their customers, their companies.

Casuistry was the first historical attempt to think about social responsibilities and to establish a special set of ethics for those who were in power. According to some, business ethics attempts to do the same thing as casuistry—establish a special set of ethics for those who are in control of organizations. To the casuistry proponent, the notion of social responsibility was inherent in being a leader. As such, the duty of the leader was to subordinate personal interests and behaviors to the demands of the kingdom.

The difficulty with the approach of casuistry is that it must end up being one-dimensional because, by definition, it considers social responsibility an ethical absolute. In other words, it subordinates ethics to politics because it always puts the demands of the kingdom above the "right" behavior. This does not mean that there can be no absolutes. But absolutes cannot be rooted in the demands of one individual or one group of individuals (e.g., what the boss or what the organization or what society always wants). Absolutes must be rooted in behaviors (e.g., bribery is always considered unethical and illegal in this country).

Some would argue that, today, the subject of business ethics is more political than it is ethical. Indeed, businesspeople do occupy positions and make decisions in which they must consider responsibilities to others beside themselves. But the casuistry approach insists that leaders (businesspeople) always subordinate their wants and needs, including their individual ethics, to those of others. In business terms, business is singled out for all the obligations and assigning all rights and benefits to society (Hoffman & Moore, 1982). But this implies that the rules of what is ethical for members of society are not the same as those for the businessperson. *How do you view this?*

Consider an organization that has a product that can be of benefit to some members of society but from an economic perspective can never be marketed profitably. Sound business decision making would suggest that the product be abandoned. The casuistry approach, however, would suggest that the social good to those who would benefit from the availability of the product is more important than the subsequent losses that would be suffered by the organization and, perhaps, some of its employees (the losses might be so severe that jobs would be lost). *What decision would you make?*

Before we begin our discussion of ethics as rules for decision making, let's define ethics. Ethics is the study of what constitutes good and bad conduct, including related actions and values (Barry, 1979). Ethics, as rules for decision making, differ from the notion of social responsibility. discussed earlier. Social responsibility is the set of generally accepted relationships, obligations, and duties that relate to the corporate effect on the welfare of society (Robin & Reidenbach, 1987). It is the view that marketers have responsibilities to a broad set of stakeholders. Ethics would be concerned with the nature of specific decisions made and the "goodness or badness" of those decisions in terms of the consequences of those decisions.

Ethics as Rules for Decision Making

We judge companies—and marketing professionals—by their actions, not their pious statements of intent. At the risk of invoking cliches, "talk is cheap" and "actions speak louder than words." Although we often refer to an organization as being socially responsible, it is the people in that organization who are responsible for its conduct, and it is their collective standards that make up the organization's standards. So ethics, simply stated, are guidelines or rules of conduct by which individuals make decisions. As employees of organizations, marketing professionals make decisions, and most of their decisions involve some degree of ethical judgment.

It is important for individual marketing professionals to know where they stand when they must combine business activities with ethical judgments. Therefore, it is imperative that each marketing professional know what his or her rules of conduct are. Although one person may argue that another person's rules of conduct are in error, the point is that, as individuals, we are better off if we do not declare one set of ethical principles and act from another. From my perspective, it is better to know what an individual stands for and disagree with him or her than it is to not know what that person stands for. *What do you think about this statement?* In other words, you will encounter disagreements concerning the "ethical" thing to do in many situations. Those disagreements, however, can be approached more intelligently and professionally if you know that other people will stand by their principles and they know that you will stand by your principles. You don't have to agree with their principles. Nor do they have to agree with yours. Consider, however, the difficulties associated with making decisions with those with whom your principles disagree and whose principles seem to be constantly changing.

As implied in the preceding discussion, knowing where we stand is necessary but not sufficient. It is critical that marketing professionals understand who else may be affected by their decisions and how important the interest of each of these others is concerning the process of making those decisions. Simply put, marketing professionals cannot ignore the interests of others, even if some of those others are not directly represented in the decision process.

Ethics and Absolutes

Harry S. Truman, the 33rd president of the United States stated, "The Ten Commandments and the Sermon on the Mount are all the ethical codes anybody needs." These were the principles, the absolutes, the "black and white" that President Truman attempted to follow. Most of us are probably more comfortable thinking that there are shades of gray, as illustrated in Figure 1.3, rather than taking the stand that all things are black and white, good or bad. Such thinking makes writing about ethics difficult. It also makes making ethical decisions difficult.

All of us would probably agree that cheating is wrong. If so, we have an absolute standard in this regard. But are there some gray areas? Is stealing a copy of an exam cheating? How about exchanging answers with one of your friends during the exam? Or what about the simple casual glance at another person's paper? Or trying to pry answers from your instructor during an exam? *Do all of your answers to these questions comply with the absolute that cheating is unethical, or have we discovered a gray area or two?*

How many of your friends do you know have cheated on an exam or assignment? Have you ever heard them say that cheating is wrong? How can one person say that cheating is wrong and then turn around and violate that absolute that he or she has set up? Well, as I am sure you know all too well, there is a great deal of pressure to get good grades while you are in college. If that pressure becomes too great, it might lead some to violate their absolutes (their ethics) in order to get good grades. Simply put, although ethical absolutes are, in my opinion, necessary for ethical behaviors to occur, they are not guarantees against unethical decision making.

Absolutes and Behaviors. Statements that present behavioral absolutes often cause people problems. Consider the following: "[One] who has been stealing must steal no longer" (Ephesians 4:28). Islam offers a similar perspective. The third pillar of

Personal Gray Areas

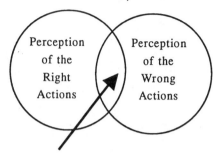

The "gray" area between right and wrong

Interpersonal Gray Areas

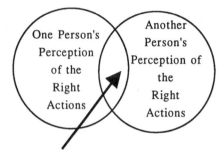

The "gray" area between right and wrong

Figure 1.3. Where Are the Gray Areas?

Islam is charity, and it invokes those who have much to help (not steal from) those who are less fortunate (see Smith, 1991, p. 246). These statements from two different traditions say not to steal. It is an absolute. In my opinion, ethics cannot exist without absolutes. But the existence of absolutes does not make anyone perfect. To illustrate the notion of absolutes, let me tell you a little about myself. I am a Christian. Specifically, I profess my Christianity as a Southern Baptist. The choice of this denomination already qualifies me to be different from other Christians who profess in other Christian denominations. Then, of course, there are many other religious denominations to which people subscribe. And there are many individuals who practice no religion whatsoever.

For me, my absolutes are in the Bible, which may answer your questions concerning the quotes from the Bible you read earlier in this chapter. The Bible teaches, however (and I know all too well), that I am not perfect. I make mistakes, I make poor judgments, I make bad decisions. In other words, I can, and do, violate the absolutes that I have taken on as my own. So one way in which ethical problems can occur is when an individual has absolutes and violates them (see Figure 1.3).

But there is another problem in dealing with ethical issues. Others with whom I work, or who are affected by my decisions, have different absolutes. Their absolutes may be in conflict with mine (see Figure 1.3). For example, I believe that one should never offer or accept a bribe. In many foreign countries, however, the offering and accepting of bribes is expected and legal behavior. If I am dealing with someone from a country where such behavior is acceptable, one of us may be placed in a position of violating one of our absolutes. Let's assume I do not wish to offer a bribe. A business agreement may not be reached. I come home to the States and my boss says, "Chonko, why didn't you make a deal?" I say, "Because I was unwilling to offer a bribe." My boss says, "You're fired."

My boss may have a different set of absolutes from mine. As you have seen from some of the citations in this chapter, there are many ethical guidelines to which individuals subscribe. My boss may be willing to ignore his or her absolutes, or my boss may not be in a position of having to actually initiate the bribe behavior; being in the situation is very different from simply knowing about it. In any event, I have lost my job and my family, which is always a primary concern, now must suffer because I did not violate an absolute. Had I violated the absolute, the deal would have been done, my boss would be happy, my kids would be eating, and . . . I would have broken the law—and, if caught, thrown in jail. By now you should recognize that, no matter which course of action I chose, there are consequences. Enough said for now. We'll get more involved in the notion of consequences and values in Chapters 2 through 4 and in the difficulties of ethical decision making throughout this book. But before we continue, from time to time you will encounter Biblical references (in addition to quotations from other religious writings). You can do with them what you like. My purpose in providing them is to present to you a person (me) who subscribes to one set of values. We all have values and we all differ. But those with differing values still find they must work together. Use these illustrations from the Bible and other religious writings as a starting point for answering the following question: *When my opinion differs from the opinion of another, how can I proceed to resolve the difference to the satisfaction of all concerned?*

The Absence of a Universally Accepted Ethical Standard. There is no universally acceptable set of standards to which every businessperson subscribes. Some people make business decisions strictly on the basis of self-interest. Others take into account the interests of others before they act. Still others act by the Golden Rule—"So in everything, do to others what you would have them do to you" (Matthew 7:12)—or by the Silver Rule of Confucianism, which states, "Do not do unto others what you would not want others to do unto you" (*The Analects,* XII:2). Then there are those who act situationally, for example, lying in one situation but not in another, similar, situation.

In practice, businesspeople can codify much of their behavior by basing it on the law. The law and ethics are not the same, however. The law is simply incapable of covering the wide variety of human behaviors that millions of businesspeople exhibit. The law does prohibit what might be called "outrageous violations" of what a society considers ethical (Barry, 1979, pp. 12-13). But what about marketing's appeals to status, prestige, sex, romance, and adventure in an effort to sell products? Are such appeals ethical? Many are legal.

Because there are no universally accepted absolute standards, even within organizations, marketers are often compelled to appeal to their own ethical standards when making decisions. Sometimes this means that marketers operate on the basis of a wealth of experience, and they can and do make ethical decisions. Sometimes, however, marketers make decisions on the basis of a "gut feeling" and, although they can make ethical decisions under such circumstances, they are treading on shaky ethical ground in doing so.

◩ DOES ETHICS HAVE A PLACE IN THE BUSINESS WORLD?

As you are undoubtedly aware, ethics seems to have become a national preoccupation. There is even a board game called *Scruples* that tests one's ability to make ethical decisions in various (and sometimes uncomfortable) situations. You might feel that there are so many unethical things taking place in business that the term *business ethics* is an oxymoron.

Some critics of capitalism argue that the system itself encourages unethical behavior. They argue that capitalism rewards selfishness, dishonesty, and greed. And if you read the newspaper, there is plenty of evidence to suggest that selfishness, dishonesty, and greed rear their ugly heads too frequently in business. These critics even cast Adam Smith as a self-interested villain based on his writings in the *Wealth of Nations* (Smith, 1776/1971). Smith did write about rational self-interest—the idea that when individuals pursue things in which they are interested they create wealth. They also create more wealth than if they were forced to pursue the interests dictated by society.

> It is not from the benevolence of the butcher, the brewer, or the baker, that we expect our dinner, but from their regard to their own self-interest. We address ourselves, not to their humanity but to their self-love, and never talk to them of our own necessities but of their advantages. (Smith, 1776/1971, p. 95)

Adam Smith (1759/1976) also wrote another book, *The Theory of Moral Sentiments*, in which he advises competitors to compete fairly and warns against violations of "fair play" (p. 83).

The lines from Adam Smith quoted earlier depict the contradiction that is at the heart of the free economy. Personal interests (sometimes selfish interests) can produce morally beneficial results. We receive the food we need from those who supply it. Some of the producers of that food may genuinely care about the well-being of those they feed. But others of those producers may be genuinely indifferent to our hunger needs. It would seem that doing things on the basis of self-interests works. It does, but it also provides the Achilles heel of the capitalist system. Many remain uncomfortable with an economic system that is motivated (at least in part) by self-interests. *What do you think? Does our market economy place too much emphasis on self-interests at the expense of the interests of others?*

Some argue that ethical issues cannot be the concern of the businessperson because business occupies a special place (i.e., business is different) and that its functions would be undermined by focusing on ethical issues. It is my contention, however, that no business can operate purely on the basis of self-interest over the long run. Businesspeople cannot subscribe to one ethical code in the office and another ethical code at home.

As part of a larger social system, marketers feel the pressures of society's concerns for truth, honesty, altruism, and respect for human beings. Business is integral to society, its activities, and its values (De George, 1986, pp. 6-7). Trust, fairness, honesty, and respect for others are critical values that are essential to business success. The free market system, with its allocation of scarce resources, can and does drive out those who serve less well the needs of customers and the society. But these things do not occur overnight. If you purchase a defective product from Company A and receive no satisfaction after voicing a complaint, will you purchase that product again? Will you buy from Company A again? When we purchase products we expect them to work "as advertised." If the marketplace's expectations are not met, the product and the company may go out of existence. Put bluntly, those individuals who serve only themselves will be replaced by others who serve the needs of the marketplace better. To survive in the long term, business and marketing must operate on ethical grounds. *Again, what do you think? Can unethical marketers survive in the long run?*

It will be the contention in this book that marketing professionals do not operate under an ethical code different from those of us in society. Businesspeople do not (or at least should not) wear one ethics hat at work, another ethics hat at home, a third ethics hat in public, and so on. I grant you, it may appear this way at times.

It will also be the contention of this book that ethics forms a vital part of our economic system. But not all societies view business ethics in the way we do. Not even everyone in this nation has the same view of business ethics. You might ask, "If ethics is that important to business, why are there so many violations?" Well, at the risk of sounding flip, nobody is perfect. Then, again, that is what this book is all about. It is about ethics. It is about everyday situations in which marketing professionals are confronted with ethical problems. It is about how people make decisions that have ethical ramifications. It is about the pressures those people experience that might lead them to choose to make unethical decisions.

CHAPTER SUMMARY

This chapter provided an overview of some of the ethical problems faced by marketers. Ethical problems can be encountered by marketing professionals simply because these professionals occupy positions that require interaction with many others who may not think alike.

Marketing professionals can seek guidelines for their ethical decision making, but even such guidelines are not without controversy. For example, disagreements even exist concerning the purpose of a business. There is much pressure to act on the basis of short-term considerations at the expense of the long-term welfare of the company and, possibly, the individual. History provides some controversy in that leaders were often judged by different ethical standards than the "common person." Finally, we all subscribe to different ethical rules and we are all susceptible to acting against the standards set by our own ethical rules.

◩ SOME QUESTIONS FOR DISCUSSION

1. Here is an assignment. Watch television this evening and pay careful attention to the advertisements you see. What do you learn from the ads about the product (service) being promoted? Would the information provided in the ad help you make a buying decision? Does the information help you learn about what the product does? Do you think any of the ads you saw violated ethical standards? Why?

2. Why do you think that the public's perception of marketing is so negative? What is your impression? What information did you use in arriving at your conclusions?

3. Comment on the information presented in Table 1.2. Are the behaviors described unethical? Why do you think so?

4. What is your opinion of the purpose of a business? How well do you think business accomplishes this purpose? Provide specific examples to support your opinion.

5. What lessons can be learned from the stories about Nestlé and Johnson & Johnson? Can these lessons be applied in all ethics-related situations?

6. Now I'll ask you to be objective about yourself. How often do you think about the long term? What long-term and short-term considerations are there in each of the following choices?

   a. Studying for an exam scheduled for next week or spending the evening in the local pub?
   b. Reading course materials as they are assigned or "cramming" for exams?
   c. Finding a copy of last semester's exam or studying?
   d. Beginning the search for employment early or waiting until the second semester of your senior year?

7. Should marketing professionals operate under more than one set of ethical rules —one for the office and one for other activities?

8. Break up into small groups. Have your instructor give each group an ethical decision-making situation (Chapters 6-11 contain many of these). Then each of the members of the group should write down (a) what he or she would do in the situation, (b) what ethical rules guided that decision, and (c) what information was considered most important. Compare answers to see what each person would do and why participants chose their respective courses of action.

2

Conflict: The Root of Ethical Problems

PURPOSE

To discuss how conflict is at the heart of all ethical problems faced by marketing professionals.

MAJOR POINTS

Perception—how we see the world—is very important to the understanding of ethical conflicts.

Each of us is guided by values, but our values may not correspond to the values of others with whom we associate.

Marketing professionals are exposed to many conflicting values as they make decisions.

One factor that seems to have intensified value conflict is the declining supply of trust in organizations.

International marketing activities pose some different ethical conflicts because of the increased diversity of values held important by individuals with different cultural backgrounds.

Differences in ethical theories can also lead to conflict, but ethical theories do provide marketing professionals with frameworks for decision making.

Individualism is a calm and considered feeling which disposes each citizen to isolate himself
[or herself] from the mass of his [or her] fellows and withdraw into the circle of family and friends;
with this little society formed to his [or her] taste, he [or she] gladly leaves the greater society to
look after itself. . . . Individualism at first only dams the spring of public virtues, but in the long run
it attacks and destroys all the others too and finally emerges in egoism . . . a vice as old as the world.

(de Tocqueville, 1840/1956, p. 98)

R ugged individualism is a cornerstone of American life. Individualism was championed by leaders such as Thomas Jefferson and Benjamin Franklin. *But has this philosophy, a basis on which America became a great nation, degenerated into one that ultimately will bring America down?* Consider the descriptions of the three decades prior to the 1990s:

1960s	"Do your own thing."
1970s	"Me decade."
1980s	"The decade of galloping greed."

According to many, the value of individualism, which emphasizes individual freedoms, personal opportunity, and upward mobility, has come into conflict with the needs of our society (Schlender, 1992). Have societal values, such as concern for the community, religious and ethnic tolerance, thrift, equality before the law, and respect for hard work, taken a back seat to individualism? Newsline 2.1 provides some thoughts regarding this question.

Newsline 2.1

What Comes After Greed?

Greed, though far from dead, seems to have gone into hibernation—like a bear in a Dunhill suit. When did it slink off? Pop historians, hunting for symbolic events to mark its passing, can choose from these: Malcolm Forbe's estimated $2 million 70th birthday bash, followed by his death. The simultaneous collapse of Donald Trump's marriage and empire. Drexel's demise. Milken's indictment. Perrier's recall. Say this much for the Eighties: When they were over, they were over.

"Greed really turns me off," Henry Kravis confided to FORTUNE in 1988. And while the world's reaction at that time was to breathe a collective, "Sure, Henry, sure," maybe Kravis, sincere or otherwise, was being prophetic. Author Tom Wolfe, 3 for 3 at catching the nation's mood (the Sixties, *Radical Chic;* the Seventies, "The 'Me' Decade"; the Eighties, *The Bonfire of the Vanities*), sees a change in values coming. Says Wolfe: "We are leaving the period of money fever that was the Eighties and entering a period of moral fever."

Already there are glimmers of what an optimist might call the New Altruism. At Christmas 1989, in San Jose, California, food kitchens for the homeless were inundated with volunteers. This Thanksgiving, yuppies ladled soup there. A marketer of luxury condominiums, age 36, explains why he chose 1990 to begin volunteering at Manhattan's Covenant House: "I spent a decade focused on my career. Now I've reached a point in my life where I want to give something back." Indeed, during the Nineties, a generation fueled by Sixties ideals and Eighties money is hitting middle age—the time most people feel their public spirit start to swell.

At Harvard business school, dean John McArthur has made ethics the centerpiece of a revamped curriculum. New graduates no longer brandish dollar bills to celebrate getting their degrees. In 1990 they waved little International flags instead. Notes Mark Pastin, professor of management at Arizona State University: "A little while ago, all my students wanted to major in finance, so they could be investment bankers. Now they all want to go into manufacturing, to *make* something. It's like they're trying to atone for the Ivan Boeskys of the world."

It is early yet to diagnose a rash of real saintliness. Greed has practical reasons for lying low right now. With recession battering the real estate and financial markets, it has fewer chances to gratify its lust. One Harvard business school student, tired of squinting into the glare of his fellows' halos, thinks money-hunger could roar back tomorrow: "If investment banks came here again offering six-figure salaries en masse, you'd see applicants lined up six deep waiting to talk to them—same way they did five years ago."

Rather than a New Altruism, we may be witnessing the birth of a New Venality. Walter Klores and Jerry Gerber, authors of *Life-Trends: The Future of Baby Boomers and Other Aging Americans,* think that enlightened self-interest explains some boomers' flirtation with good works. At companies where managements recognize the dollar cost of institutional lapses in morality, boomers see doing good as a way to advance their careers. The monied perceive that charity has the power to defuse resentment.

The unwashed now look upon the rich the way cats look at birds. What FORTUNE last year dubbed the Trust Gap is widening. Democrats and populists advocate soaking the rich as a cure for social ills. Donald Kanter, professor of marketing at Boston University and coauthor of *The Cynical Americans,* detects growing antipathy toward wealth made "too easily" or "too fast" by paper-shufflers—stock brokers, real estate promoters, bankers, and Wall Streeters generally. Some rich are naughty; others, who perspire and make things, are nice.

This attitude that one source of wealth is good, the other bad, has percolated up to Capitol Hill, where Democrat Daniel Patrick Moynihan of New York has drawn a distinction between Senators like himself whose wealth is "earned" by labor (writing, speechifying), and those whose wealth isn't (income from property or investments). When he mischievously introduced legislation in August to limit Senators' unearned income to 15% of their government salaries (the same as the limit on earned income), it passed the Senate—nays from multimillionaires Bentsen, Heinz, Kennedy, and Rockefeller notwithstanding. Since it was attached to a campaign finance bill President Bush had promised to veto, the Senators could afford to let Moynihan make his point.

Any form of preferment that can be said to be "unearned" is coming in for scrutiny, including real or imagined quotas for minorities. Populists such as Louisiana's David Duke capitalize on the resentment by sawing away at set-aside programs that benefit minorities. "Do you realize," asks Duke, "that governments are awarding contracts to firms whose bids are higher and whose work is often substandard? These programs are unfair." Scholars like Shelby Steele at San Jose State University say the unearned advantage that affirmative action programs give his fellow blacks is counterproductive.

In this darkening atmosphere of envy and suspicion, with recession under way and populism ascendant, only the foolish or the brash will flaunt advantages, earned or otherwise. Altruists and New Venals alike will find modesty an ever more becoming garment for the Nineties.

SOURCE: Farnham (1991). Used with permission.

This chapter will focus on values and what can happen when values held by individuals come in conflict. We will begin with a discussion of perception and the public's perception of marketing activities.

◿ PERCEPTION IS A KEY

Perception represents how we interpret what we "see." No doubt you have attended some sporting event, watched a movie, or listened to the same lecture with your friends. *Did you and your friends completely agree on what you saw and heard, or were there differences in what you perceived?* Perception is based on information, and we all selectively process information. At the risk of oversimplification, that means we choose to accept or reject information on the basis of how we see the world. Our selection process is not necessarily an objective one.

Consider two phenomena: scientific advances and the existing world situation. Scientific advances, which are perceived by many to hold the promise of making the world better, are held back by the perceptions of others who are concerned about the dangerous power science can wield. Which perception is accurate? Economic growth is constrained by growing environmental concerns. Many perceive that economic growth is outpaced by the growth of social problems. Now, what happens when perceptions differ? Let's ask a few more questions:

1. Are institutional constraints inherent in America's product-oriented industrial system, causing our economy to stagnate?
2. Does the decline in our balance of trade signify a decline in U.S. competitiveness?
3. Should funding for space exploration be reduced to combat poverty and urban problems?
4. Why is it that, as America becomes richer, we seem to enjoy it less?

Obviously, these questions are not easily answerable. But rest assured, you will find people who will argue, strongly, both sides of each question. And they will often cite the same set of information in their arguments. Their interpretations of that information are based on their perceptions and on the values that they hold important. Each of you probably has some thoughts about these questions, and the direction of those thoughts is influenced by your perceptions of what is important. When you discuss questions such as these, you will discover that disagreement or conflict arises because your perceptions and your values differ from those of others. As you discuss various ways of resolving questions such as these, conflict can arise about many things:

1. What information is relevant?
2. What is the "real" problem?
3. What is causing the problem?
4. What alternatives appear capable of solving the problem?
5. How should solutions be implemented?
6. Who should benefit from the solution chosen?
7. How should results be measured?
8. How should we deal with those who don't like the chosen solution?

As you continue your reading in this book, keep in mind that many of the conflicts that can occur in answering these questions will have ethical ramifications.

Before we proceed, let me say a word about compromise—a sometimes used "quick fix" to resolving conflict. We all wrestle with compromise as expressed by the familiar concept of yin/yang, which sums up life's polarities—good/evil, active/passive, positive/negative, light/dark, male/female. These polar opposites are in tension, but they can complement and balance each other. Although the yin/yang is dealt with in the Taoist, Buddhist and Zen traditions, these traditions tend to emphasize a relativist position: "Who knows what's good or bad?" (see Smith, 1991, pp. 214-216). Sometimes compromise can be good, if long-term considerations are evaluated. But when used as an easy "quick fix," there are dangers. "Food gained by fraud tastes sweet to a man, but he ends up with a mouth full of gravel" (Proverbs 20:17). There is a price to be paid for compromising one's values. Sometimes that price may be inconsequential as it relates to ethics and values. Sometimes the price of ethics compromise may seem very small, and we rationalize questionable behavior on this basis. Generally, compromise at any level makes it easier to compromise in the future. Eventually, we might even begin to rationalize to the point where we cannot distinguish between what we used to consider right and wrong.

Public Perceptions of Marketing

Because of conflict-based situations as described earlier and because marketers have made questionable decisions in the past, marketing is often perceived as a business profession filled with hucksters, cheats, and frauds who unethically manipulate consumers into buying products that they do not need or want. The existence of the so-called fast buck artist has prompted one writer to state, "What is 'visible' about marketing is not the intriguing, truly exciting research work in a variety of behavioral and technical areas. Instead, it is the picture of some pitchman selling hair spray on television" (Farmer, 1967, p. 1). The inevitable conclusion is that marketing is a profession overloaded with unethical people. Ten years later, that same author argued that the ethics of marketing was still questionable: "Marketing essentially deals with greed and selfishness and base human desires" (Farmer, 1977, p. 18).

Now consider the following information from other sources:

- A poll taken by *U.S. News and World Report* indicates that most Americans believe that unethical activity such as padding expense accounts, taking office supplies home, and using small amounts of company money for personal purposes, are frequently undertaken by businesspeople (Robin & Reidenbach, 1989).
- In a survey conducted by *Time* magazine, most Americans (76%) viewed the lack of business ethics as contributing to the decline of U.S. moral standards (Robin & Reidenbach, 1989).
- An article in the *Wall Street Journal* reported that even businesspeople (66%) feel that managers will occasionally engage in unethical behaviors (Robin & Reidenbach, 1989).
- A Gallup Poll (1983) ranked advertisers at the bottom of an "ethics and honesty" scale.

Do you agree with Farmer (1977)? With the other reports? No doubt marketing, like any other profession, has its share of questionable suspects. Let's take a look at why the marketing profession may be viewed in a less favorable way than all of us in (and about to enter) the profession deserve.

Reinforcers of the Perceptions of the Unethical Nature of Marketing Activities

It is my belief that the public's perceptions of the unethical nature of marketing activities may be overstated. A number of factors reinforce the negative image of the marketing profession. One is that the mass media can and often does exaggerate the questionable behaviors of marketers. Sensationalism about questionable behavior can do little except reinforce the notion that marketing professionals are unethical. Sensationalism is particularly effective when the public is already suspicious and attuned to the high potential for marketing misconduct. When news confirms the suspicions of the public the reaction is, "I told you so" (Saul, 1981).

A second reinforcer is that television frequently portrays businesspeople and marketing professionals as unethical. There is a growing trend in the media to "business bashing" stories (Schwartz, Washington, Fleming, & Hamilton, 1993). Stories that expose questionable (sometimes without much documentation) practices of companies are good for ratings, unfortunately, to the point where some journalists will do anything to improve ratings. For example, *Dateline NBC* aired an investigation into alleged fire hazards in older General Motors pickup trucks. A test truck was fitted with toy rocket engines to make sure that the gasoline would catch fire in a simulated crash. Jane Pauley and Stone Philips soberly read a retraction settled on by negotiators minutes before the episode aired, identifying the flaws in the test, including the finding that the fuel tank NBC had ruptured on impact had, in fact, remained intact. *But what does the public remember?*

A third reinforcer relates to the critical role that marketing plays in all our lives. As consumers, we expect responsible behavior from representatives of business organizations, and as members of society we expect businesspeople to work with us to improve our standard of living through the products and services that we purchase. When our expectations are not met, a natural reaction is "the marketing system has failed."

A fourth reinforcer of the public's attitude lies in the multitude of regulations with which marketers must contend. For example, at one time, the steel industry was subject to about 5,500 regulations enforced by 26 different government agencies (Butcher, 1978). Because business organizations have difficulty in making sure they are in compliance with all regulations, because regulations sometimes are contradictory, and because organizations cannot afford to contest every *perceived* violation, they often plead no contest. Such a plea makes business appear guilty in the eyes of the public, despite the fact that the business may have been found innocent of any violations in some cases.

A fifth reinforcer of the public's perception is the pervasiveness of marketing activities. By some accounts, we are exposed to some 3,000 marketing communications daily—television, radio, magazines, billboards, and so on. *Although we do not pay attention to most of these, are the marketing communications that are likely to gain the public's attention the ones that are done poorly, the ones that are hokey, the ones that we judge to be misleading?*

Finally, a sixth reinforcer is that the public is not very knowledgeable when it comes to what marketing is all about. When asked, many would say that "marketing is advertising." Nothing could be farther from the truth. Armed with little knowledge but a strong conviction, the public, however, tends to overstate the incidence of unethical behavior in marketing. For example, have you ever heard anyone say something like, "All automobile salespeople are crooks." This is certainly not true, but it is popular to poke fun at that profession because, probably, we all have had one or two bad experiences with members of this industry and we have all read and heard about difficulties experienced by this industry. *But how many of you are satisfied with the automobile you drive and talk about that satisfaction as freely as you might if you had a bad experience?*

▨ VALUES DIFFERENCES LEAD TO CONFLICT

Values are evident in all our behaviors. Our values represent the standards we use to guide our actions. Each of us operates from a value system that is likely to be different from the value systems of others with whom we are associated. Furthermore, our values may change over time, individually, or collectively as you will see shortly. Value changes complicate the process by which we seek agreement with others and often are at the roots of ethical conflict.

For each individual, values shape reality. Because each individual's values are unique, perceptions of right and wrong are unique. Many of us, however, operate under the assumption that others will see things in the same way we do. Sometimes this occurs. Sometimes, it does not. *When the assumption of similar values is false, do we tend to label those with different values as unethical?*

As you saw in Chapter 1, there is no set of ethical absolutes to which every individual subscribes. Individuals differ. Although it is important to recognize that individuals differ, the mere recognition of differences is an oversimplification and does not provide a satisfactory guide for ethical decision making. Perhaps the best we can hope for is that each individual establishes a set of criteria that guide his or her actions (this often happens) and that do not change (this happens less frequently). Knowing what values guide our own actions and the actions of others lends some practicality to ethical decision making. It does not eliminate conflicts, but at least decision makers know where others stand. When this is known, the search for common elements in the values of individuals can be undertaken. When some standards are held in common, we begin to approach the possibility of ethical decisions accepted by all.

Personal Values Are Areas Ripe for Conflict

Each of us has our own unique set of values—the way we see the world and react to situations. We face continuing difficulty, however. Our lives are such that we must live, work, and cooperate with others to survive as individuals, as organizations, and as a society. Although we all want to be free to pursue our own viewpoints and feelings, left to our own freedoms we would be in a constant state of conflict.

Consider Figure 2.1. The boxes in this figure represent organizations. Within each box are arrows that represent the direction of each individual's values in that

Organization A

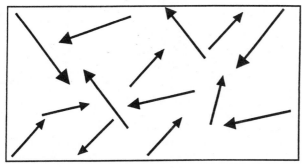

There is much conflict between the values in this organization.

Organization B

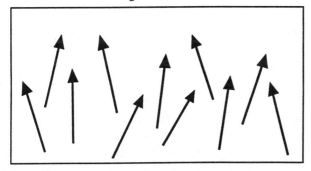

There is some conflict between the values in this organization,
but there is also some cooperation.

Figure 2.1. An
Illustration of
Values Conflict
in Organizations

organization. Without cooperation (which implies some restrictions on personal
freedoms), the individuals in Organization A are all headed in different directions.
There is conflict between values—conflict concerning how individuals view the
direction in which the organization should be headed. Now, with some cooperation,
our organization can take on the appearance of Organization B. Although all the
arrows (individuals) are not pointing precisely in the same direction, there is some
agreement as to where the organization should be headed and some latitude for
personal freedoms to be exercised.

When you begin your careers, you can expect to encounter value conflicts. *(What
conflicts of values can you anticipate?)* Such conflict can be very stressful and have
serious effects on your life and your productivity. Differences in viewpoints will skew

Table 2.1 Differences Between the Old and the New Ethic

The Old Ethic Favors . . .	The New Ethic Favors . . .
Work	Leisure
Savings	Debt
Responsibility	Rights
Competition	Protection
Sex roles	Unisexism
Sacrifice	Self-interest
Equality-inequality	Equality
Wealth accumulation	Wealth redistribution
Absolutism	Situationalism
Risk assumption	Risk aversion
Efficiency/productivity	Quality of life
Thrift/investment	Consumerism

SOURCE: Adapted from Chewning (1984). Reprinted from *Business Horizons,* April 1984. Copyright 1984 by the Foundation for the School of Business at Indiana University. Used with permission.

how people see the world. It is beyond the intent of this book to provide remedies for such value conflicts. Suffice it to say that factors such as openness, objectivity, communication, and tolerance are keys to resolving values conflicts. In fact, often-times, when they are fully understood, conflicts of values are really not value based.

Consider just one example. What is your impression of engineers? Do terms such as *product oriented, lab monkeys,* and *tinkerers* come to mind? Engineers like to build things but have little concern for their application in society, right? Wrong! Now, what about marketers? Sales oriented, smooth talking, hard-selling, fast-buck artists, right? Wrong again! Although we all have stereotypes of people based on their occupations, those stereotypes can be (and often are) inaccurate and portray a conflict of values that does not really exist.

If you look at engineering statements of philosophies, codes of ethics, and the like, you will find that satisfying societal needs is at the core of engineering philoso-phy. Sounds like the marketing concept, doesn't it? Now, are engineering and marketing values in conflict? They are to some degree, but not so much that both professions are not capable of aligning some of their values to achieve commonly held objectives. But unless marketers communicate, understand, appreciate, and tolerate (and engineers, too) what engineers do, a conflict that many perceive as inherent between the professions will continue to create difficulties.

Conflict of Values: Some Examples

The 20th century has seen tremendous changes in individuals' underlying per-sonal philosophies. Table 2.1 illustrates some of those changes, highlighting them as the old ethic and the new ethic. Both ethics grind against each other. For example, the work ethic and the leisure ethic oppose each other as do the savings and the debt ethics. But it is not as simple as that. As you read through the two lists in Table 2.1, you will probably discover that you have a foot in both camps. Every item in each list reflects values, but our society "clearly no longer has a consensus about which one is correct" (Chewning, 1984, p. 7). The result when people with different values try to work together is inevitable—conflict.

Consider just one example. Proponents of the old and new ethic accept the value of equality. But they disagree on how equality should be viewed. The old ethic suggests that one person's advantage, gained through superior performance, does not create disadvantage for another person. Inequality is viewed as results oriented, not opportunity oriented. Performance and results are rewarded. Those who perform gain rewards. Those who do not perform do not gain rewards. The new ethic, however, sees such inequality as dehumanizing. Inequality is negatively viewed. Some proponents of the new equality ethic favor a redistribution of rewards from those who perform to those who do not. They argue that no one should live in poverty. Such disagreements naturally lead to disagreements about policies and goals. *How would differences in values in Table 2.1 create difficulties for ethical decision making?*

Now, consider your future. You obtain employment with a nationally known marketing organization. You are in an entry-level sales position in a district with 12 other salespeople (ages 22-56) and a district manager who is 51. *Recall some of the conflicts you anticipated earlier.* Your new sales job requires you to work directly with customers, prospects, and individuals in your own organization (e.g., delivery, service, credit, budget, inventory) on a daily basis. Moreover, you will come in contact with others regularly (e.g., regional managers, engineering, competing salespeople, unhappy customers, the president of your firm). In short, your job requires that you undertake activities with many whose values differ from yours and who are not likely to agree with you philosophically or on day-to-day decisions.

The old and the new ethic, presented in Table 2.1, is a simple illustration of the complex set of philosophies with which one person can come into contact during the course of his or her job. Conflict is inevitable. Conflicts between individual and organizational values are not new (Cadbury, 1987). Today, however, such conflicts are more widespread as old company values clash with new individual values and more interest is being taken by outsiders in the ethical behaviors of marketing professionals as representatives of organizations. Also, ethical dilemmas go beyond one's personal rules of behavior. Marketing professionals must make decisions that affect others, all of whom have their own personal rules of behavior that may or may not be in harmony with those of the marketing professional.

Socialization and Desocialization

Socialization is a process through which an individual learns the values and behavior patterns deemed appropriate by a group or an organization. When an individual is employed by an organization, that individual has already been socialized to certain values—from his or her family, society, peers, church. All of these have an influence on what the individual believes and how the individual behaves. These individuals, already socialized, must be socialized for their roles as marketing professionals. The individual brings an ethical outlook to the organization that may be compatible with those of the organization. Often those values are not and conflict arises. *What ethical outlook did you bring to your university? Is it compatible with the ethical outlook of other students, your instructors, the university's leadership?*

When the marketing professional is confronted with organizational pressures and expectations, there are at least three basic responses (Smith & Carroll, 1984). First, the individual can reject the organization's values. Second, the individual can be selective in that he or she accepts only key organizational values. Finally, the individual can accept and conform to all organizational values. The key point is that ethical conflicts can arise when an individual's values are not consistent with those of the organization.

Three Ethics for Marketers . . . At Least

Marketing professionals have at least three ethics to look to as a basis for insight and authority in making decisions: an individual ethic, an organizational ethic, and a professional ethic, as depicted in Figure 2.2. The American concept of the individual ethic is rooted in rugged individualism, an entrepreneurial spirit, and the freedom to make our own decisions. Suppose you are calling on a department store manager and, as a token of appreciation for past business, you give her a small gift—a leather briefcase valued at $250. Your individual ethic might be that as long as such a gift is not intended to influence the store manager's decisions, it is acceptable to give a gift.

The individual ethic of autonomy, equality of opportunity, and freedom of thought often comes in conflict with the organizational ethic, which places authority, status, and small-group pressures on the individual. Organizational goals may override those of the individual. For example, standardization, specialization, and routinization—hallmarks of the U.S. organization—narrow the individual's responsibilities and can conflict with the individual's ethic. Referring to our gift illustration, suppose the organization has a strict policy against giving gifts of any value. The policy exists to prevent company representatives from becoming involved in what can be viewed as questionable situations. When you gave the briefcase to the store manager, your individual ethic came into conflict with the organization's ethic.

The professional ethic centers on individualism but tends to emphasize consensus of the group of professionals who are members of the profession. It stresses norms of the profession rather than the norms of the organization. Professional ethics are concerned with the general way of doing business but can be ambivalent, seeming to

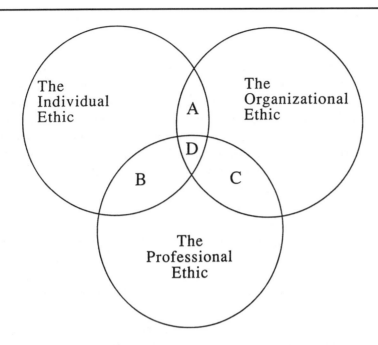

A—The individual and the organizational ethics have some common ground.
B—The individual and the professional ethics have some common ground.
C—The professional and the organizational ethics have some common ground.
D—All three ethics have some common ground.

Figure 2.2. Three Ethics for Marketers

conflict with both the individual and the organizational ethic. The standards for behavior set forth by the profession can and often do conflict with those standards set by the organization and the individual. Your profession's ethic may state that gift giving is not recommended except when such activity is customary in an industry. *What conflicts exist between the three ethics? Think about an organization in which you are a member. What values have you encountered and how have they agreed or conflicted with your values?*

A Continuum of Ethical Behavior

The preceding discussion is, in no way, to be construed as ethical relativism, which contends that no ethical guideline has any greater claim to objectivity and universality than any other. Under the tenets of ethical relativism, one would not be able to justify any value judgments at all (see Donaldson & Werhane, 1988, pp. 6-7)

—except, of course, the value judgment that there are no absolutes, which is, in reality, an absolute.

One constructive approach in understanding ethical decision making is to view ethics as a continuum in which different positions or values are represented and from which marketing decisions can be evaluated (see Smith & Quelch, 1993, p. 21). The continuum is shown in Figure 2.3. On the far left of the ethics continuum, seller interests are heavily favored. Consumer interests are heavily favored on the far right of the continuum. Implicit in Figure 2.3 is the conflict that exists between the seller's and the consumer's interests. Further implied in the continuum is the reality that marketing decisions are not solely guided by the interests of the consumer. Indeed, the customer may not even be the starting point for marketing decision making. *How do seller and consumer interests conflict with each other?*

The left side of the continuum in Figure 2.3 represents the "buyer beware" (caveat emptor) school of thought. Here, profit maximization within legal constraints is the guiding philosophy. If an action is legal and serves the purposes of the business it is considered ethical. Activities such as price fixing, deceptive advertising, and bribery are considered illegal. As you will see in this text, however, there are organizations that practice each of these. Those who engage in such practices often focus on the differences between the law and ethical behavior (the letter of the law and the spirit of the law), arguing that the law is too restrictive. Interestingly, those who are against such behaviors also point to differences between ethics and the law, arguing that the law cannot always be interpreted in a strictly legalistic fashion. In other words, the intent of the law is more pervasive than the letter of the law. The right side of the continuum represents the "seller beware" (caveat venditor) school of thought. Guided by this philosophy, marketers use customer satisfaction as the criterion against which all decisions are evaluated.

Although a few organizations may find themselves on these two positions of the continuum, most are probably somewhere closer to the middle. Industry practice represents the norms of business, and these norms are used as the basis for evaluating decisions. For such organizations, the spirit of the law takes on some importance in marketing decision making.

In the middle of the continuum is the ethics codes position. Many organizations have established ethics codes in an attempt to set standards for behavior. Such codes recognize that ethical abuses do occur and are attempts at providing guidance to marketers when ethical conflicts occur. Finally, there is the consumer sovereignty position, which is based on the notion that marketing decisions should be based on the capabilities of consumers, the consumers' rights to information, and the consumers' rights to choose. More will be said about this in Chapter 5.

Keep in mind that the positions on this continuum represent different decision-making philosophies. Five different philosophies are represented in Figure 2.3. Before

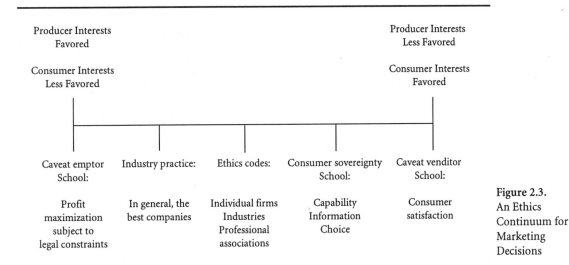

Figure 2.3. An Ethics Continuum for Marketing Decisions

SOURCE: Smith and Quelch (1993, p. 21). Used with permission.

you proceed, consider a decision to market a new drug that has been shown to have wonderful primary benefits for those who would need it but harmful side effects for a few of those individuals. *How would individuals who adopt each of the ethical philosophies in Figure 2.3 proceed with decisions concerning introduction of the product and promotion of the product?*

Values Congruence

In marketing relationships, individual decision makers interpret each others' behaviors (Frazier, 1983; Heide & John, 1988). Those involved in these relationships, however, do not always fully understand the purpose of the relationship and the processes by which the goals of the relationship may be achieved (Borys & Jemison, 1989). Such misunderstandings can become a serious source of difficulty (Dwyer, Schur, & Oh, 1987). So each partner's conjectures about other partners in a relationship can influence that relationship (Anderson & Weitz, 1992). To the extent that there is consensus or shared understanding, there is a basis for the positive development of relationships and the development of norms of behavior for those relationships (Spekman & Salmond, in press). *Before we proceed, what is your opinion about having individuals with similar values employed in an organization?*

In general, to achieve a state of values congruence, or values agreement, management must clearly communicate job expectations and values to the organization's employees. It is very difficult, however, to achieve a state of values congruence. The writings on ethics in organizations abound with materials that indicate differing perceptions of ethical problems among members of the same organization or the same profession (Harris, 1990). Similarly, a great deal of evidence suggests that individuals generally feel that they are more ethical than those with whom they work.

When individuals in a marketing relationship differ in their ethical perceptions and ethical orientations, there may be difficulty in building a high-quality relationship. Even when two individuals have the same ethical orientation, however, a quality relationship is not guaranteed. Suppose two individuals, a seller and a buyer, both have the same ethical philosophy—"look out for 'Number 1' first." Can they agree? Certainly, agreement is possible. Because both are focused on maximizing personal gain, however, either party to this arrangement may not be satisfied because the outcomes of the relationship may be judged as not maximizing personal gain.

Here's what I think. In the United States, a commonly practiced but rarely stated principle is to do what one has to do to keep customers pacified. In other words, many marketers respond to customer needs and wants according to the pressure those customers exert. As a result, many marketplace negotiations and transactions take on an adversarial nature, which can be detrimental to the relationship between the marketer and the customer. In his letter to the Philippians, Paul advised that people should consider others to be as important as themselves and to look out for the interests of others as well as their own (Philippians 2:3-4). Hinduism also speaks to helping others (*Bhagavad-Gita*, VI:1). There was a yogi sitting by the bank of the Ganges. This yogi saw a scorpion fall into the water. He grabbed for it and was stung. Again, the scorpion fell into the water; the yogi grabbed for it and was stung again. This happened two more times. Finally, a bystander questioned the behavior of the yogi, who replied, "It is the nature of the scorpion to bite. It is the nature of the yogis to help others when they can." In other words, despite obvious differences, ethical philosophies should not lead marketers into an "us versus them" attitude toward customers. It should be at the forefront of all marketing decision making that if the customer realizes "success" from a transaction, the transaction can develop into a relationship, and the development of many relationships means success for the marketing professional.

The Declining Supply of Trust

Are we experiencing a declining supply of trust in organizations? Many believe we are living in an era of mistrust among individuals and groups. Caucasians and African Americans mistrust each other. Men and women mistrust each other. Subordinates and managements do not trust each other.

There seems to be an us versus them attitude, a complex resurgence of the Hatfields and the McCoys on a national scale. Such a mentality tends to detract from innovative and productive behavior and leads individuals to focus on the self. Individual pay, advancement, and security become paramount. The concerns of others are their own concerns. The individual is looking out solely, or almost solely, for "Number 1."

Consider what might happen in a sales organization. Some sales managers may ask their salespeople to sell only products that have high profit margins. The company may even support these sales managers. Salespeople may wish to sell products with lower profit margins because they are easier to sell than the higher margin products. The sales manager and the company are not in support of these salespeople. Such an environment may lead both salespeople and sales managers to a situation of mistrust, fending for themselves. The individual ethical philosophies of each party has prevented them from seeing things from the perspective of others. The result is conflict and may lead to unethical behaviors undertaken to satisfy personal needs.

The Demand for Trust Should Increase. Many well-known businesspeople argue that, as national and international economies become more complex and unpredictable, trust is needed (e.g., Peters, 1987; Reich, 1987). Their arguments revolve around the premise that trust is more effective and efficient than laws, regulations, rules, and procedures. Consider the following comments concerning trust in organizations:

> Today's new realities (let alone common sense) require us to:
>
> —Demand total integrity . . . in all dealings, with people and systems, inside the firm and out.
> —Eliminate Mickey Mouse rules and regulations that induce cheating and game playing, which then spread to the firm's affairs.
>
> Successful organizations must shift from an age dominated by contracts and litigiousness to an age of handshakes and trust. This prescription once more reveals a paradox—namely, that the uncertainty of the environment can be swiftly dealt with only if the firm can fall back upon the certainty of relationships among people and among groups, in other words, upon trust and integrity. (Peters, 1987, pp. 518-519)

Why, then, don't people trust each other? One reason is that individuals often compromise values and rationalize behaviors. Many do this with no apparent strategy so that others hold an opinion of them such as the following: "If you want to know what Bill X is thinking, find out who was the last person in his office." In other words, Bill X is unpredictable.

◩ INTERNATIONAL MARKETING ETHICS: INCREASING THE POOL OF VALUES

Marketing professionals whose organizations market products and services internationally face additional complications in making ethical decisions. In a nutshell, those standards of ethics set forth by the organization are not likely to be the same as the ethical standards in other countries. The general ethical dilemma associated with international marketing decision making is this: If what would be considered unethical, illegal, or both in the United States is an accepted business practice elsewhere, how are marketing professionals who are U.S. citizens expected to act? How are local marketing professionals employed by the U.S. organization expected to act?

For example, one of the most common ethical issues faced by marketing professionals revolves around offering monetary inducements to others in foreign countries just to get them to do their jobs. *What payments are legitimate for marketing professionals to make to secure an order or a long-term contract? At what point do such payments become bribes?*

Can There Be Ethics Across International Boundaries?

As you have seen, ethics involves the application of rules of behavior to marketing decision making. The application of ethical principles to marketing problems involves analytical, rational, and emotional processes. You have also seen that ethical decision making can become complicated as different individuals perceive various behaviors as "good" or "acceptable" according to the values they hold important.

When discussions of values cross national borders, it is common to hear comments such as these: "Their culture is different from ours." "Their political structure is different from ours." "Their values are different from ours." Clearly, individuals born and raised in different countries and cultures think differently about certain things. They label some behaviors as acceptable when others do not, as illustrated in Newsline 2.2. They value certain things that others do not. They believe certain things that others do not. Because of these differences, many have argued that it is impossible to develop a universally accepted code of ethics. But look around at your classmates. *Do they always think the way you do? Do they believe in all the same things in which you believe? Do they hold exactly the same values as you?* Probably not. *So what is the difference between ethical problems faced by you and the ethical problems faced by international marketing professionals?* The difference does not lie in the fact that value conflicts exists. They do. The difference lies in the sheer number of different values a marketing professional encounters in an international world. Let's take a brief look at culture and its relationship to values.

Newsline 2.2

A Matter of Ethics:
Why Japan Is Not Like the United States

On February 13, it happened again. Allegations of still another political payoff surfaced. Last month, a Japanese trucking firm was accused of channeling funds to politicians.

Instantly, the charges became one more in a succession of scandals in Japan that highlight major differences in business ethics with the U.S.

In the late 1980s nearly all of Japan's leading politicians were implicated in the Recruit bribery scandal. Then last year several Japanese securities firms were revealed to have compensated their biggest customers for stock losses in 1990. And eight food-wrap manufacturers were punished for forming a cartel to raise prices.

Remarkably, so many Japanese greeted the scandals with no more than a shrug of resignation that one tends to conclude that favoritism, influence-peddling, price-fixing, and other unfair practices must be a normal part of business life in Japan.

What does this portend as more Japanese companies set up shop in the U.S. to manufacture goods and to provide financial and other services? Will the Japanese abide by U.S. ethical standards or, with their economic clout, become more aggressive and confident that they can do business anywhere on their terms?

Breaches of ethics in the U.S. are pretty much isolated occurrences—Ivan Boesky, Michael Milken, the illegal Treasury bids by Salomon Brothers. But "in Japan it's part of the system," privately confessed a director of Hitachi Ltd. shortly after his company was implicated in the 1990 securities payoffs.

Tak Wakasugi, professor of finance at the prestigious Tokyo University and codirector of the University of Michigan's School of Business Administration, blames rigid regulations for the securities-compensation scandal. The rules make it impossible for securities firms to reduce their commissions for customers who trade stocks in large lots, so the firms devise other ways to keep their customers happy.

The Japanese government is preparing new laws to outlaw compensation for stock losses. And the Japan Securities Dealers Assn. (JSDA) is promising to more closely supervise its members' activities. Leading JSDA's efforts is Shogo Watanabe, who was brought out of retirement last year to replace the JSDA chairman who resigned in a symbolic gesture of responsibility for the securities scandal. Mr. Watanabe talks of a return to higher ethical standards.

Yet Prof. Wakasugi suggests unethical behavior is a long-standing problem with origins deep in Japan's social and cultural tradition. "Loosely speaking, the Japanese think that [whether] one does business in a fair way or not is up to oneself," he observes.

Many Westerners who have lived and worked in Japan attribute Japanese tolerance of questionable practices to the nation's lack of a codifying religious morality. Japan "is not a Judeo-Christian country," remarks Thomas W. Whitson, a partner and auditor at KPMG Peat Marwick in Tokyo. "Everything [in Japan] seems pretty situational. If I would compare the countries where I've worked—the U.S., Taiwan, South Korea, and Japan—the general quality of [accounting] work is best here. On the other hand, if . . . somehow the company decides to cook the books, there's nothing that says, 'No, that's wrong.' [Rather], they say, 'Well now, what's the recipe?' "

The recipe the securities companies followed was to label customer-compensation payments as entertainment expenses to hide the facts from potentially troublesome shareholders. But the companies got into trouble when they told Japanese tax authorities that their accounts were false. Making that revelation may seem strange, but Mr. Whitson says the normally meticulous Japanese can be remarkably clumsy when they try to cheat. "Maybe they're hoping that even if people check, they'll understand somehow" why it was necessary to break the rules, he speculates.

Understanding another's "necessities" is one of the most important aspects of successfully doing business in Japan—whether the understanding is among companies belonging to the same corporate group or between companies and the government. Indeed, upon retirement many Japanese government officials take lucrative advisory posts in the companies they previously regulated. Communication between companies and the government in Japan is, not surprisingly, "very, very good," notes Prof. Wakasugi.

In fact, communication is so good on the inside that often it's difficult for outsiders to figure out what is going on. For example, although Japan's Ministry of Finance issued a directive in the spring of 1990 instructing securities companies to stop reimbursing customers for trading losses, unofficially the ministry may have verbally indicated payments could continue. For public consumption, the Ministry reacted with surprise many months later when reports of the compensation surfaced.

The fact is that blatant contradictions between *tate-mae,* the public face, and *hon-ne,* the underlying truth, are an everyday part of life and business in Japan. What seems like lying to an American is, to a Japanese, an acceptable way of avoiding an unpleasant situation. "Japanese people have an amazing capability to accept contradictions," states Mr. Whitson. "And as long as you don't rub their face in it, they're able to live with it, and things go along in a relatively placid way."

Few, if any, Japanese are fooled by the apologies government officials and business leaders usually proffer along with their resignations in the wake of a scandal. Still, they expect the ritual to be performed. The reality is that disgraced executives may be moved only sideways into advisory jobs in their companies, without any loss of salary or benefits. Politicians, too, can retain their influence—and even rebuild careers—after resigning in apparent disgrace. For example, involvement in the Recruit scandal did not keep Kiichi Miyazawa from being selected Japanese Prime Minister last October—though it had forced his resignation as Finance Minister a little more than two years earlier. Similarly, Ryutaro Hashimoto, who resigned as Finance Minister after the stock-compensation scandal, remains one of the leading candidates to succeed Mr. Miyazawa when his term as Prime Minister ends in October 1993.

Prof. Gregory Clark, who teaches comparative culture at Sophia University in Tokyo, describes Japan as a "sophisticated tribal society" in which people tend to make up rules as they go along rather than rely on a consistent moral code. "The tribal ethic has precedence. But it can't cope with all situations. So you have scandals," says Prof. Clark. "The problem [for the Japanese] is deciding what is a scandal." And more often than not, he says, the Japanese will wait for someone else to decide for them.

Prof. Clark stresses that the most important principle in Japanese business is not to rock the boat. "You've got to look after the people around you and keep them happy," he explains. KPMG Peat Marwick's Mr. Whitson believes this principle makes Japanese accountants amenable to cooking the figures. They would be inclined to obey a boss who asked them to falsify accounts because their first loyalty is to the company, not a code of ethics.

In an article in the October 1991 edition of Japan's *Usbio* magazine, Osaka University Prof. Iwao Nakatana contrasted what he called Japan's "network capitalism" with the willingness of Western people to accept a certain level of inefficiency for the sake of preserving democracy. "Whereas Japan is a society based overwhelmingly on insider relationships, the U.S. does its utmost to suppress such tendencies and create a system where all kinds of trading are entrusted to an anonymous market and [where] everyone has an equal chance," he wrote.

Japanese emphasis on personal relationships and the nation's willingness to look after its friends have given Japanese companies a major advantage over U.S. and other Western competitors in countries where bribery is a normal part of business. Prof. Wakasugi explains that Japan's history has also created a tendency to seek favors from people and companies who possess strong, centralized power. "The weaker give bribes to the stronger," he says. "It is a basic structure common to all Asian people. And [because] people think politics is a very dirty business . . . bribery is natural."

Already there are warning signs that some Japanese companies may be as unconcerned about ethics in the U.S. as they are at home. There have been complaints, for example, that the top jobs in many Japanese companies' American operations are reserved for Japanese to the exclusion of equally talented Americans, especially women. It's also alleged that some Japanese companies in the U.S. exclude Blacks and that the firms hold back high-tech supplies from U.S. customers while supplying them to Japanese companies going after the same markets as the Americans.

"They don't know the local environment so well sometimes, so they get caught doing business as usual," says KPMG Peat Marwick's Mr. Whitson. But, he adds, their damage control is extremely good, and they soon learn from their mistakes. "If morality is important to do business in the United States, then I think they would go along with it—not because it's right, but because it's good for business."

SOURCE: Whenmouth (1992). Used with permission of Penton Publishing.

Culture

Culture may be described as "that complex whole which includes knowledge, belief, art, morals, law, custom, and any other capabilities and habits acquired by man as a member of society" (Taylor, 1891, quoted in Sturdivant, 1985, p. 1). Many thinkers on culture espouse the notion of a core culture that is generally shared by the members of a society (e.g., Hofstede, 1980). These core cultural dimensions might include such values as individualism, tolerance for ambiguity, and respect for the rights of others. Naturally, difficulties arise between two cultures that place values on different things. *How many different cultures exist in the United States? Do they come into conflict from time to time? Now, how many different cultures exist in the world? What is the likelihood of conflict among the world's cultures compared to conflict among U.S. cultures?*

Complicating the understanding of culture is the fact that, within any culture, subcultures will develop. These subcultures consist of smaller groups of individuals who have adopted their own set of values, sometimes in accord with the larger society, sometimes not. In the United States, for example, we have an African American subculture, a Hispanic subculture, a variety of Asian subcultures, and many more. These different cultures foster different values, and these different values can lead people to different conclusions about ethical behavior. Now, extend the subculture to the world and consider just one country—Nigeria. In Nigeria, four primary languages are spoken, but there are over 800 dialects. If each of those dialects is represented by a different set of cultural values, it is easy to see how values conflict concerning ethical behavior can occur.

Common Values Across Cultures

Despite the almost inconceivable number of different cultures and subcultures in the world, it has been suggested that it is possible to identify common, or at least similar, values that are held by diverse cultures (Churchill, 1982). Although different cultures may have the same moral values, however, they may differ dramatically in the way they practice those values. For example, the ancient Callatians believed in honoring their dead and did so by eating the bodies. The ancient Greeks also believed in honoring the dead. But they did so by cremating the bodies (Rachels, 1986).

As another illustration, this book attempts to approach ethical problem solving from a rational, cognitive application of moral principles to marketing problems. Such an approach is decidedly Anglo-American in nature and is very different from the approach to ethical problem solving that might be taken by our colleagues in Japan or India. *What do you think? Can common ethical ground across different cultures be found?*

Understanding Cross-Cultural Ethics

Several factors are central to understanding how to contend with the difficulties of international ethical problems. These include culture, managerial values, and religion (Wines & Napier, 1992). Ethical values are embedded in each of these three elements, and those concerned with ethical problems can begin by looking at common values held across cultures.

The international marketing decision maker must also recognize that, although certain values may be held in common, they may be held with differing levels of intensity. Values that are more strongly held will be more resistant to change. Values held less strongly will be more susceptible to change (Rokeach, 1968). Putting this into a decision-making context, international marketing professionals make decisions. These decisions are affected by political, economic, personal, and other factors. Moral values and public opinion (which includes cultural elements) are also factors that affect ethical decision making.

When making decisions that span cultures, the marketing professional should look for cultural elements that overlap the two or more cultures that are represented in the decision and that will be affected by the decision (Owens, 1982).

◪ THE VALUE OF ETHICAL THEORIES

This chapter concludes with a brief discussion of ethical theories. Several ethical philosophies are briefly described in Table 2.2. As you can see, many of them fit the look-out-for-Number-1 philosophy. Often, marketing professionals who subscribe to such "individual" ethical philosophies do not worry about the consequences to others of their actions. Many times, the result is a conflict between their individual goals and the goals of the organization, the customer, or society. *Why do you think these conflicts occur?*

Many have questioned the usefulness of understanding ethical theories as a means of better understanding the ethical dilemmas that confront marketing professionals. Arguments against the usefulness of ethical theories include the following:

1. They lead to counterintuitive claims about the nature of decisions.
2. They fail to provide answers regarding what decision makers should do in certain situations.
3. They seem to condone actions by decision makers that are morally questionable.
4. They cannot tell decision makers which action to take in a specific situation.
5. They do not help decision makers resolve conflicting obligations.

Table 2.2 Selected Principles of Ethical Conduct

Kant's categorical imperative—Act in a way that you believe is right and just for any other person in a similar situation.

Carr's conventionalist ethic—Bluff and take advantage of all legal opportunities and widespread practices and customs.

The disclosure rule—Ask how it would feel to see the thinking and details of the decision disclosed to a wide audience.

The Golden Rule—Look at the problem from the position of another party affected by the decision and try to determine what response the other person would expect as the most virtuous.

The hedonistic ethic—Do whatever you find to be in your own self-interest.

Moore's intuition ethic—Go with your "gut" feeling or what you understand to be right in a given situation.

Smith's market ethic—Take selfish actions and be motivated by personal gains in business dealings.

Machiavelli's means-end ethic—Ask whether some overall good justifies any moral transgression.

Nietzsche/Marx might-equals-right ethic—Seize what advantage you are strong enough to use without respect to ordinary social conventions and laws.

The organization ethic—Ask whether actions are consistent with organizational goals and do what is good for the organization.

Garrett's principle of proportionality—Do whatever you will if there is a proportional reason for doing so.

The Protestant ethic—Do only that which can be explained before a committee of your peers.

The revelation ethic—Pray, meditate, or otherwise commune with a superior force or being.

Bentham/Mill's utilitarian ethic—Determine whether the harm in an action is outweighed by the good.

SOURCE: Lewis (1989). Reprinted by permission of Kluwer Academic Publishers.

The preceding arguments are not new. The value of ethical theories has long been the subject of debate:

> The corporate executive—like many others—finds him or herself continuously faced with mutually incompatible demands. There is no higher order criterion for or procedure available to him or her by means of which these demands can be reconciled or even rationally ordered. Those moral philosophies which have promised to provide such a criterion—and utilitarianism is perhaps the best known example—have notoriously failed to keep their promises. (MacIntyre, 1977, p. 320)

The critics seem to imply that an ethical theory should tell a decision maker what to do in every situation (Hoffman, 1984). Consider, however, the arguments concerning the nature of business: A business that is profitable is maximizing society's benefit versus the notion that a business must engage in socially responsible behaviors to maximize society's benefit. Members of both sides of this argument can defend their positions with the same ethical theory. There are often no easy answers.

Ethical theory has a number of critics who argue that ethical and moral principles are not foundational in any sense of the word (e.g., Bok, 1979; MacIntyre, 1981; May, 1987; Pincoffs, 1986). These critics argue that ethical principles are abstractions that result from relationships with ourselves and others. They argue that, as relationships deteriorate, the ethical principles no longer become enforceable. In other words, the behaviors of individuals are no longer influenced by moral principles. Certainly, there is some truth to this argument, but the fact that individuals behave unethically should not deter others from acting ethically and abiding by the ethical philosophies that the critics have reduced to a useless state. Before you read on, refer to the appendix for a brief overview of some of the more well-known ethical theories.

Conflicts Between Ethical Criteria

Suppose you are a product manager for a pharmaceutical company. You have been taking the lead on the marketing program for a revolutionary new drug. The drug can be of great benefit to many, but it has some serious side effects for some individuals.

Suppose, furthermore, that two ethical criteria are relevant to the decision to introduce the drug to the marketplace: (a) the congruence between the decision and the satisfaction of the greatest number of people and (b) the effect of the decision on individuals who have certain rights.

You are faced with a decision that, on one hand, can provide great satisfaction to many (introducing the drug). Certain individual rights, however, are violated (those who would suffer side effects). The second alternative would be to withhold introduction of the drug, respecting the individual's rights but reducing the opportunity for satisfaction for the many who would benefit from the availability of the drug.

Most of us would agree that there is merit to both of the ethical criteria relevant in your decision as product manager. There is conflict, however, between the criteria such that each criteria suggests a different decision alternative. *What would you do in this limited information situation?*

This scenario is illustrative of one of the problems cited by critics of ethical theories—there are no well-defined rules for solving ethical dilemmas (Cavanaugh, Moberg, & Velasquez, 1981). Such problems can be resolved only with judgment concerning which of the conflicting criteria should be given the most weight in the given situation. Some might say that the principle of double effect is relevant here. This principle states that it is acceptable to make a decision that has two effects, one good and one bad, provided that the decision maker's primary motivation is to achieve the good effect and provided that the good effect is important enough to allow the bad effect (Grisez, 1970).

Some of you may even be asking how I would use the ethical philosophy in Philippians 2:3-4 cited earlier. Let me assure you that it is not always easy to consider the needs of others. It is sometimes too easy to consider only self-interests. In other words, the ethical philosophy tells me what I ought to do but does not guarantee that I will do it (recall the discussion of gray areas in Figure 1.3 in Chapter 1). In most marketing situations, however, emphasizing the long-term outcome over the short-term outcome will tend to promote the customers' interests and the marketer's interests, and it seems opportune to point out that self-interests are not disdained in the Bible. "If anyone does not provide for his relatives, and especially for his immediate family, he has denied the faith" (1 Timothy 5:8). So my ethic requires that I provide for my family. But my ethic also tells me not to provide for family needs in ways harmful to others.

It is the position of this book that ethical theories are necessary for making marketing decisions regarding ethical behaviors. Ethical theories provide a framework for making ethical decisions. After all, many ethical theories are based on observed behaviors and observed characteristics such as integrity, sincerity, and honesty. The problem is that in any decision situation there are likely to be many acceptable and ethical courses of action that are dictated by the situation and the information on hand. No business rule can capture the essence of every business decision. Why should we expect any ethical theory to capture the essence of every ethical decision situation? The ethical theory may not provide an answer, but it does provide insight concerning what to consider and how to proceed in arriving at an answer. Furthermore, if it is important to interact with others, understanding of ethical theories provides decision makers with insights regarding how others make decisions—what are the key criteria as they see the situation? What constituents are considered in making the decision? Who influences them in making decisions?

Yes, there is a great deal of truth in the contention that ethical theories do not provide "black and white" answers for many. That should be of little concern to marketing and business professionals who, for centuries, have made decisions, some good and some not so good, without the availability of "the theory of how to make a profit." There is no such animal, yet business and marketing professionals still make decisions that require they deal in all of the uncertainties of predicting the future, an inescapable condition of any decision. Certainly, business decision-making guides exist (perhaps too many of them). None provides all the answers, but many provide the questions and the factors that need to be considered in making a decision. So it is with ethical theories. If you're looking for answers, you're wasting your time. If you're looking for insights, you just might learn something.

In this chapter, you read about the effects that conflict has on the ethical decision making of marketing professionals. How we perceive things can be a source of conflict. So, too, can the values held by different individuals with whom we associate. Both perceptions and values will influence what decisions are made and how they are made.

One factor that complicates ethical decision making is the declining supply of trust that seems to be prevalent in organizations. A second complicating factor is the international nature of many marketing decisions. Differences in values between countries and cultures increases the incidence of ethical conflict.

Marketing decision makers can look to ethical theories for decision-making guidelines. But even these ethical theories conflict with one another, and such conflict can also make ethical decision making difficult.

CHAPTER SUMMARY

◩ SOME QUESTIONS FOR DISCUSSION

1. Discuss the role of perception as it relates to ethical conflict.

2. Describe how values can be conducive to ethical conflict.

3. Can value differences be resolved? How would you go about trying to resolve value differences?

4. Describe some ethical conflicts that can occur as you take your first job after you graduate.

5. Do you agree that there is a declining supply of trust in organizations? If you do, how might such a situation be changed?

6. Why might two marketing decision makers who hold similar values disagree on ethical issues?

7. Discuss the influence that culture has when marketing professionals make decisions on an international scale.

8. How do you feel about ethical theories as a framework for decision making? In looking at Table 2.2 and the Appendix, do any of the ethical theories presented seem to fit your decision-making style? How close is the fit? Form small groups and (a) find out what ethical theories describe the decision-making style of others and (b) how you might proceed in making decisions with others who operate from an ethical perspective that is different from yours.

APPENDIX

Moral Theories

TELEOGICAL THEORIES

There is an ethical school of thought that argues that the moral rightness of an action can be determined by looking at its consequences. If the consequences are good, the action is good. If the consequences are bad, the action is wrong. Teleologists determine what is right by examining the ratio of good to bad that action produces. In general, the right action is the one that has produced or is intended to produce the greatest ratio of good to bad results. Three schools of thought have developed from the teleological viewpoint—egoism, utilitarianism, and situational ethics.

Egoism

Egoism suggests that an act is ethical when it promotes the individual's best long-term interests. In other words, if an action produces or is intended to produce the greatest ratio of good to bad for the individual, then the individual must choose that course of action. Egoists will make sacrifices in the short run for the purpose of long-term gain. Furthermore, egoism can be compatible with characteristics such as honesty, generosity, and self-sacrifice.

Advantages. From a marketing perspective, marketing policies and decisions are judged to be good if they promote the long-term interests of the organization. All marketing professionals must take some responsibility for evaluating their own actions. Although most organizations have codes, these codes serve only as guidelines, encouraging certain kinds of activities and discouraging others. In this respect, egoism provides an answer—an action is good if it is in the long-term best interests of the individual, the organization, or both. Egoism requires that all actions be judged solely on the basis of the "best" long-term interests.

Disadvantages. There are several problems associated with ethical egoism. First, egoism ignores blatant wrongs. When long-term self-interests are the measure, egoism takes no stand against actions that are blatantly wrong, if the results of those actions are the best in the long term. Second, egoism is not compatible with the basic nature of business. Business is part of a larger society, and as a result, business actions affect many. Egoists operate without considering the long-term interests of others. Yet others are affected by the decisions of egoists, and others have inputs into the decisions of egoists.

Third, egoism cannot resolve conflicts of interest between two or more egoists. Because each egoist would want to strive to maximize his or her self-interests, other egoists involved in the decision would have to make sacrifices. Although egoism does allow for self-sacrifice, egoists often find it difficult to engage in sacrificial behaviors when their goal is to maximize self-interests. In other words, when groups make decisions, everyone cannot maximize their gain. Any alternative selected will not be in the best long-term interests of all concerned.

Finally, egoists do not see things from others' points of view. When the best long-term interests are the evaluation criteria, the judgments of egoists are influenced only by those self-interests. Any guidance, suggestions, recommendations, or decisions will be self-serving.

Utilitarianism

Utilitarianism is an ethical philosophy that emphasizes the best interests of all concerned. As a philosophy, utilitarianism recommends that an act that is undertaken produce the greatest ratio of good to bad for everyone. There are two types of utilitarian ethics—act utilitarianism and rule utilitarianism.

> *Act utilitarianism.* Act utilitarianism is a philosophy that maintains that the right course of action is the one that produces the greatest ratio of good to bad for all concerned. The consequences for everyone resulting from alternative courses of action must be considered.
>
> *Rule utilitarianism.* Rule utilitarianism asks decision makers to consider the worth of a rule under which an action is undertaken. If keeping a rule produces more good than breaking it, we should keep the rule.

Advantages. Using utilitarian standards, a course of action is considered good if it provides more good than any other alternative. Rules, policies, and standards are not accepted blindly. They are to be tested against the criterion of the best interests of everyone. Furthermore, utilitarianism provides a way of resolving conflicts of self-interest. Individuals in organizations make decisions and evaluate their actions by examining a uniform standard— the general good. This was not the case with the egoist orientation.

Utilitarianism also recognizes the importance of others in marketing decision making. Customers, society, owners, and employees must all be considered under the philosophy of choosing the course of action that provides the greatest ratio of good to bad for everyone. Finally, utilitarianism provides latitude for marketing decision making. Decisions can be made that fit the circumstances in existence at the time of the decision. No specific action is always judged to be good.

Disadvantages. Utilitarianism, as an ethical philosophy, also suffers from several drawbacks. First, utilitarianism ignores actions that appear to be wrong in and of themselves. Both act and rule utilitarianism focus on ends rather than means. So the ends justifies the means. If this is the case, the next time a fly lands on your nose, let your friend smash it with a rock.

Under utilitarianism, it is difficult to formulate satisfactory rules. For example, suppose you were about to declare bankruptcy. Suppose also that you know that the rule "Never use privileged information for personal gain" is codified by your organization. You encounter a situation in which you have access to privileged information that will result in your receiving a large sum of money and help you avoid bankruptcy. You might reason that the harm done to others by using the information is much less than the good that will come from using the information. So you use the information. You have just changed the rule to read, "never use privileged information for personal gain . . . except in case of bankruptcy."

Situational Ethics

Situational ethics contends that the ethical action is the one that produces the greatest amount of Christian love of all the alternatives possible. Situational ethics arose because of the contention that other ethical theories were inappropriate. Specifically, ethical philosophies that are legalistic, that sought absolute laws that must always be obeyed, are overly directive. Furthermore, ethical philosophies that are existentially based, that espouse conditions of no guidelines, are nondirective. They provide no guidelines for actions. Situational ethics is proposed to fall somewhere in between these two extremes.

Advantages. According to situational ethics, rules and principles are valid only if they serve in a specific situation. Therefore, ethical decision makers must be fully acquainted with all the circumstances in a particular decision-making situation. The situational ethical philosophy humanizes business marketing decision making. The philosophy emphasizes the importance of people and their welfare in marketing decision making. Furthermore, situational ethics rejects legalism. Legalism dictates decisions and, in a strict sense, allows for no deviation—no thought. Legalists would argue that the law represents all that we need in the way of guidelines for ethical decision making. This, of course, is not true. Conformity to the law is necessary, but not sufficient, to be ethical.

Disadvantages. Situational ethics suffers from several weaknesses. First, it is not a definite decision procedure. The same motives may procure two completely different results. Let's look at the pharmaceutical industry. One marketing decision maker who wants to provide for the welfare of society might argue that introducing a drug with possible harmful side effects will maximize the amount of love for everyone concerned. A second marketing decision maker, who wants to provide for the welfare of society, might argue that the drug should not be introduced because the side effects are such that the welfare of society will not be served. The same motives produce different decisions.

Second, situational ethics really endorse the existential philosophy. Situational ethics denies general rules (e.g., telling the truth is always good.) Such rules are legalistic. Therefore, there is latitude in decisions about telling the truth. There must be certain situations in which telling the truth is not good. So individuals are left to decide for themselves under what circumstances telling the truth is good.

Finally, although situational ethics espouses Christian love in its definition, it is not a Christian ethic. Although situational ethicists use the concept of *agape* love in their reasoning—unselfish love epitomized by Christ's sacrifice on the cross—agape love is considered valid only if it serves love in every situation. In other words, such pronouncements as the Ten Commandments are reduced to the 10 suggestions by situational ethicists. They are viewed as cautious generalizations, not the absolutes espoused by Christianity, because the situational ethicist may encounter situations in which he or she, as a decision maker, will justify side-stepping the absolute.

DEONTOLOGICAL THEORIES

Deontological ethicists argue that more than the consequences of an action must be considered in making ethical decisions. Several deontological theories are presented next.

Kant's Categorical Imperative

Immanuel Kant believed that nothing was good in itself except a "good will." A good will was understood by Kant to mean the human ability to act according to the concept of law or principles. Personality characteristics such as sensitivity, talents, and so on are good and desirable only to the extent that the human will makes good use of them. Kant believed that a good will took precedence over all else.

The concept of a good will is rooted in duty, and only when an individual acts from a sense of duty does the action have any moral worth. The critical issue in following Kant's logic lies in what constitutes duty. For example, what motivates a retailer not to overcharge a customer? Does that retailer act from a perspective of serving the customer or from the perspective of avoiding legal problems if caught? According to Kant, if the action was not willed from the retailer's sense of moral duty to be honest and fair, then the action has no moral worth.

Advantages. From a marketing decision-making perspective, Kant's philosophy has some merit. For one thing, some actions (e.g., lying) are always judged to be wrong. Therefore, Kant's approach to ethics has the advantage of eliminating some uncertainty from decision making by automatically eliminating some alternatives. Second, Kant's philosophy implies a moral obligation to act from a respect for rights and recognition of responsibilities. In other words, we act ethically when we act according to our duties—that is, according to the law. The law acknowledges certain rights and responsibilities, something that marketers must consider in making ethical decisions.

Disadvantages. Kant's ethics are not without problem. First, like other ethical theories, no clear way of resolving conflict is provided. Duties come in conflict—maximizing share-holder profits versus charging reasonable prices to the consumer. How is the conflict between these two duties resolved? One might argue that serving customers' needs is in the long-term best interests of the stockholder. Although, philosophically, this is true, will serving customer's needs result in shareholder profits in the future? No one can be sure.

Golden Rule

The Golden Rule commands us to treat others as we would like others to treat us. In other words, if you want to be treated fairly, you should treat others fairly. The hallmark of the Golden Rule is impartiality. That is, we should not make exceptions for ourselves. We should not do to others what we would not want them to do to us.

Advantages. The Golden Rule offers the advantage of personalizing marketing decisions. It is difficult to think of a better directive for dealing with others than treating them as we a would like to be treated. The Golden Rule asks marketing decision makers to put themselves in other peoples' shoes, to empathize with their concerns.

Disadvantages. Unfortunately, the Golden Rule does not recognize that inequalities may exist between the parties to a marketing decision. Parties in an exchange are rarely equal. Those who argue this go on to say that because of these inequalities, parties in the exchange may not be in a position to return the behavior. But that is not what is advocated by the Golden Rule. The Golden Rule does not imply a "Scratch my back and I'll scratch yours" philosophy. Rather, it is a directive that asks individuals to treat others fairly, as they would like to be treated if the circumstances were turned around.

A second argument against the Golden Rule is that we cannot really know how others feel. Although this is true in a rigorous sense, it is my contention that this argument is also flawed. It is not necessary to know, precisely, how others feel. We do not know how to accurately predict the reactions of others to certain circumstances. There is always uncertainty. If we desired to act under conditions of complete certainty, we would never act because conditions of complete certainty never exist.

Ross's Prima Facie Duties

William David Ross held the belief that there are duties or obligations that bind us morally. Marketing decision makers using this ethical philosophy must evaluate alternatives with respect to duties involved and determine the duty that is most obligatory. The term, *prima facie,* means "on the surface" or "at first sight." For Ross, prima facie duties are those that ordinarily impose a moral obligation but under certain circumstances, may not apply. We recognize a prima facie duty at first sight as being obligatory when all other things are equal and there are no conflicting duties. According to Ross, there are six categories of prima facie duties:

1. Duties of fidelity are those that rest on prior acts of our own. Such duties include the duty not to lie, the duty to remain faithful to contracts, and the duty to keep promises.
2. Duties of gratitude are those that rest on acts of other people toward the individual. Individuals are bound by obligations that originate from relationships that we have with others.
3. Duties of justice are those that rest on the possibility of distributing pleasure or happiness in a way not in accord with the merits of those concerned. Is justice being served when the president's son or daughter, the worst salesperson in the organization, receives the largest raise?
4. Duties of beneficence are those that rely on the fact that there are people in the world whose situation we can improve. It is this duty that appears to be one of the driving forces behind the socially responsible actions of marketing organizations.
5. Duties of self-improvement are those that rest on the fact that we can improve ourselves. In other words, individuals should strive to use their talents to their fullest potential.

6. Duties of noninjury are those that do not harm others. Ross interprets the importance of not harming others as more important than the duties of beneficence.

Advantages. The Ross prima facie duties are set up in a way that leads individuals to think about those duties and to set aside those duties only when other duties have priority. The six sets of duties have clear implications for how marketing professionals should operate as they make marketing decisions. Furthermore, Ross' approach combines the utilitarian perspective of consequences with moral duties. One of the difficulties of utilitarian thinking is that it has an end justifies the means orientation. Ross recognized this weakness by remaining aware of the means by which results are achieved.

Disadvantages. The obvious disadvantage of Ross' prima facie duties lies in the question, How do we know what prima facie duties we have to begin with? Although Ross claims that these duties are self-evident, others have argued that we cannot be certain that our duties as individuals include such things as obligations to tell the truth. In other words, there are individuals who are proponents of lying if circumstances dictate such behavior. A second disadvantage concerns the relative weights and merits of the six duties proposed. In the face of conflicting duties, how is a marketing professional to decide which duty is more important?

Rawls' Principle of Maximum Justice

John Rawls (1971) published *A Theory of Justice* in which he tried to combine the merits of deontological and teleogical theories. Rawls' theory attempts to establish principles of justice. His principles rest on the notion of the "original position," a hypothetical situation in which all people are ignorant of their talents and socioeconomic status. Rawls claims that in this position, people are mutually self-interested, rational, and similar in their needs. He then proposes to ask these people what principle of justice should be followed and surmises that they would choose two such principles—the liberty principle or the difference principle.

Liberty principle. People in the original position would expect all those participating in some practice to have an equal right to the greatest amount of liberty that is compatible with a similar liberty for all.

Difference principle. People in the original position would allow for inequalities only as they serve each individual's advantage and that those inequalities arise under conditions of equal opportunity.

Advantages. Rawls' principles carry with them a respect for others. Rawls argues that it is never right to exploit even one individual for the benefit of others. Furthermore, Rawls' philosophy outlines areas of broad social responsibility for business organizations through the implementation of the liberty and difference principles. Finally, Rawls' principles require marketing decision makers to consider the preferences of individuals and groups who cannot act for themselves. For a marketing professional, the entire area of consumer-related problems fits in here. Consumers have relatively little input into marketing professionals' decisions, beginning with the conception of a product idea through to the introduction of that product to the marketplace. Because consumers are the ones who will ultimately purchase the product, however, their viewpoints should be considered.

Disadvantages. The primary disadvantage of Rawls' theory is that it is based on several questionable assumptions. One is that Rawls assumes that individuals will act rationally if they are in the original position. He further assumes that people all have similar needs, interests, and capabilities in this original position. Also, the theory conceals from those in the original position any knowledge of their interests, talents, plans, and conceptions of what is good. Finally, Rawls assumes that differences will be tolerated as long as those who are worst off see some benefit resulting from decisions.

Principle of Proportionality

Thomas Garrett's principle of proportionality has three elements: (a) what we intend, (b) how we carry out that intention, and (c) what happens. Garrett's approach brings together intentions, means, and ends. According to Garrett's philosophy, an individual is responsible for whatever he or she wills as a means or an end. So if both the means and the needs are good in and of themselves, then the individual may ethically risk foreseen but unwilled side effects if and only if there exists a proportionate reason for doing so.

According to Garrett, it is unethical to will anything bad on oneself or others. For example, a marketing manager who attempts to destroy the image of a competitive product wills something bad on that competitor and is acting unethically. Furthermore, it is unethical to risk or permit something harmful to oneself or others without a proportionate reason. *Risk* involves probabilities concerning means and ends. There is no absolute way that any one means will lead to a particular end. *Permit* means that an individual may allow something to happen but not will it to happen. A *proportionate reason* exists when the intended good result of an action is greater than the negative consequences associated with that action.

Advantages. Garrett's principle of proportionality provides a synthesis of most ethical theories. Consequences, goodness of the will, and duties are all taken into account by the proportionality principle through the employment of the concepts of intention, means, and ends. Furthermore, the principle of proportionality provides marketing professionals with flexibility while at the same time not approving of unethical behavior. This principle does not rely exclusively on consequences to judge the ethical nature of an action. Intentions and actions are also judged as ethical or unethical in this principle. So the end justifies the means only if the individual decision maker does not will something bad to happen to others.

Disadvantages. A key disadvantage of the principle is that it is vague on the subject of what constitutes bad outcomes. Furthermore, the factors surrounding proportionality are vague. Garrett uses the terms *necessary* and *useful* in his explanations of proportionality. But what is necessary and what is useful? Because deciding what is necessary and useful is a matter of some subjective judgment, the decisions concerning what constitutes proportionality are also somewhat subjective.

3

Decision Making When Ethical Considerations Are Involved

PURPOSE

To describe the decision-making process that marketing professionals go through and some of the influences on the decision-making process as they deal with ethical situations.

MAJOR POINTS

Knowledge of right and wrong is critical to understanding ethical decision making but does not always relate to why people make unethical decisions.

There are many types of unethical behavior, but they all involve some judgment by the decision maker.

In making ethical decisions, marketing decision makers are influenced by many factors. This book places these influences in five categories: (a) characteristics of the decision maker, (b) significant influences, (c) the ethical situation, (d) the decision, and (e) outcomes.

Marketing professionals are confronted with many situations in which there is no immediate or obvious solution. In these situations, there are often many alternative courses of action to consider, and evaluating these courses of action often involves assessment of intangible benefits and costs to the individual, the organization, the customer, and society. Let's begin by looking at the following decision situations (Hosmer, 1988).

Scenario 1. You are the product manager for an automotive supply organization. Your product is cast brake cylinders. Over the past 3 years, you have worked hard to improve product quality and delivery timing. Now you are receiving large orders from the Big Three automakers, and you need to expand your production facilities. You decide to request capital for expansion, knowing that your forecasts are accurate.

Scenario 2. Again, you are the product manager for the automotive supply organization. A purchasing manager from your largest customer has just called and told you that they have received a contract proposal from a foreign competitor. The contract satisfies your customer's supply needs for all of next year and does so at a price that is 17% less than your firm has been charging. Being very bright and market savvy, you anticipated this event. Instead of expanding the local plant, you have prepared a plan to move a large part of your production facility to Mexico. This move should be made easier with the passage of the North American Free Trade Agreement (NAFTA).

In each scenario, what would you do?
In each scenario, who gains and who loses?
In each scenario, what are the ethical implications of your decision?

◩ KNOWLEDGE OF RIGHT AND WRONG

Ethics decision making might be easy if we could reduce it to what is right and wrong, black and white. Each of us may have, in our own minds, an idea of what is right and wrong, but as you have seen, your concept of right and wrong is likely to be different from others' viewpoints on right and wrong. Consequently, much of the attention given to ethical decision making (and rightly so) has focused on two elements: (a) the knowledge of right and wrong and (b) the judgments that individuals make about various behaviors. The primary assumption of the knowledge of right and wrong is that the expansion and deepening of an individual's knowledge of ethics will generate improved ethical behavior. Furthermore, all of us, by nature, like to evaluate—to judge. We always seem to feel compelled to express our opinions about the actions of others, sometimes when we know little or nothing about the subject.

Many would argue that there is a strong relationship between knowing right and doing right. *What do you think?* We know that an individual's attitude toward ethical or unethical behavior does influence his or her *intentions* to engage in ethical or unethical behavior (Dubinsky & Loken, 1989). So knowledge of right and wrong and the judgments we make are, indeed, important. But by themselves, they do not explain why marketing professionals make unethical decisions. In fact, there is less correlation between knowledge of right and wrong and doing right than you might think (Chewning, 1991). Other factors come into play. As you will see later in this chapter, a person's characteristics, a person's perceptions of elements of the work situation, and a person's relations with others all influence ethical decision making.

For the marketing professional, work provides opportunities to demonstrate abilities. The financial rewards for good results can be substantial. So, too, can there be substantial rewards from things such as our associations and our acceptance by others. When the marketing professional knows what is "right," and this knowledge is consistent with needs and desires, the right alternative is taken. *However, what happens when knowledge of right and wrong and desires conflict? Do desires overcome knowledge? Does rationalizing of unethical behavior occur? Do people cheat on exams because they think it is right or because their desire to get a good grade and gain acceptance by peers is stronger than their sense of right and wrong?* Not always, but when desire overcomes knowledge of right, unethical behaviors almost always occur and justification for those behaviors is always sought.

▧ TYPES OF UNETHICAL ACTS

Before we begin discussing ethical decision making, let's take a look at one classification of unethical acts. Not all ethically questionable actions stem from the same motivations. As shown in Table 3.1, different types of ethically questionable acts have different effects (Waters & Bird, 1989).

Nonrole acts are those in which the marketing professional is acting outside his or her work role (e.g., salespeople cheating on an expense account). In such nonrole acts, the costs are borne directly by the organization and the benefits are gained by the individual. *Role failure* involves a set of activities in which the marketing professional fails to perform his or her role (e.g., conducting a poor performance evaluation). Although such actions might not yield financial gain to the individual, the organization suffers, and the individual gains something at the expense of the organization and the other individual(s) involved. *Role distortion* includes a set of actions that violate standards and are undertaken by individuals for "the benefit of the organization," although, in the long run, the actions are likely to harm the organization. The individual, however, also benefits from the ethically questionable behavior, as in the case of accepting a bribe. Finally, *role assertion* involves actions that fail to abide by generally accepted moral principles. Role assertions (e.g., withdrawing investments from nations where human rights violations exist) are often controversial because moral arguments can be used to support or criticize the actions

Type	Direct Effect	Examples
Nonrole	Against the organization	Salespeople cheat on expense account Marketing manager steals supplies Purchasing manager uses supplier in which he or she has direct interest Vice president of promotion has maintenance department paint his or her home at company expense
Role failure	Against the organization	Sales manager conducts superficial performance appraisal Sales manager does not confront salesperson who is cheating on expense account Marketing trainee criticizes boss behind the scenes Marketing researcher slants information in a favorable but inaccurate way
Role distortion	For the organization	Purchasing manager accepts bribe Product manager colludes with others to fix prices Vice president of purchasing manipulates supplier organizations Marketing manager falsifies product safety test results
Role assertion	For the organization	Vice president of marketing recommends withdrawal of investment from a foreign country that is in violation of human rights Marketing manager invests in a company that specializes in weapons manufacturing Advertising manager fails to work with regulatory agencies

Table 3.1 Types of Ethically Questionable Acts

in question. *How would you react to an organization that invested in a foreign nation in which racism was practiced?*

Judgment Calls

When faced with complex ethical decisions such as those in Table 3.1, conflicting values can make it difficult to select the right action by logic alone. In fact, almost all ethical problems are dealt with from at least a partly personal perspective. The marketing professional, using logic alone, must integrate conflicting arguments into something coherent that is satisfactory to all parties concerned. Using only logic, this may be akin to converting chaos into order. Logic is useful but it suffers from the same difficulties already discussed concerning ethics—what one person thinks is logical is not necessarily in agreement with what others think is logical. So, using only logic can actually magnify the conflicts brought on by the ethical situation.

If it sounds like reaching a consensus on ethical decision making is impossible, let me assure you, it is not. It is just difficult. When we make a decision about anything, we probably rely on some past experiences. Not only do our experiences differ from others, but our memories are faulty. When we make decisions, we attempt to forecast what the future outcomes will be based on our best interpretation of the information. Few of us are very good at predicting the future, and even if our assessment of the future is accurate, it is likely to disagree with the future assessments of others because others consider different information, place different values on information, and hold certain things more important than we do. In other words, we should not fear making ethical decisions because of the uncertainty involved. If that is the case, then you fear making any kind of decision. Decision making is future oriented, always has a variety of alternatives, always has much information to consider, and always brings out the opinions (subjective and objective) of others. In other words, ethical decision making requires judgment that goes beyond logic.

Decision making with ethical ramifications is not different from other types of decision making in terms of basic elements, such as the situation, assessing alternatives, and predicting outcomes. Of course, ethical decision making is different in that it concerns "rights and wrongs," but other types of decision making also concern rights and wrongs. Is this the best (right) action for our company to take? Have I made the best (right) decision concerning hiring this individual? Is this the best (right) product we can introduce to the marketplace? How are these decisions made? Are they based solely on logic or is some judgment used? In any decision, ethical or not, objective truth and subjective perception of many individuals must be blended to arrive at some consensus. Now, take a look at Newsline 3.1 and consider some of the ethical issues in which salespeople might be involved when dealing with customers.

Newsline 3.1

It's Hard to Be a Customer

It was while most shoppers were perusing the "back to school" circulars and I was doing my "back to home" buying that I became aware of just how difficult it is to be a customer today.

Anytime we move our earthly possessions from one castle to another, there seem to be gaps to fill in—a bookcase here, a little table there, a different-size rug, etc., etc. So with friend and friend's truck at my disposal, I set out to fill in the gaps.

I soon discovered that some furniture stores don't want to sell furniture. They prefer to sell boxes of furniture parts. If I had a B.A.—Bachelor of Assembly—degree, it is possible, though not probable, that I could transform the box of boards and bolts into a piece of furniture.

I don't have that particular degree, however, and didn't have time to seek out someone who does. So after an hour or so of the same scenario, I made my purchase from a used furniture store. There, what you see is what you get.

The next item on the list, to fight the escalating utility bills, was a roll-around fan. I found lots of them, but they were for display only. One clerk assured me that I could put it together in 15 minutes. He offered a worker who could do it for $15 (new math tells me that's $60 an hour), but he couldn't get to it for three days. Since I wanted to buy a fan, not a box of fan parts, the clerk suggested a pawn shop. That's where I went.

I had always avoided such businesses because they spoke to me of hard times and broken dreams, but they may have found a loyal customer. No boxes of parts there.

From there I went to a retail furniture outlet looking for the perfect over-stuffed chair. I figured when I found it, it would be mine. Surely, it wouldn't come in pieces in a box. I found it. Could I buy it? No.

"We can't sell you that one because it would leave a vacant spot in the display. We can order you one."

I told the salesman that wouldn't do.

Because I really liked the chair, and because I thought the whole thing was so ridiculous, I argued and persisted until he was almost ready to "let" me buy it. And then he threw out another "objection."

"Even if I let you take that one, there's no one here to load it." I assured him that my friend and I could handily lift it into the truck and be on our way, but that was not to be.

Against Store Policy

Ah, but it was against store policy to let customers load the furniture. So the salesman won the argument and the store lost a sale. I suppose the chair is still in its designated display space.

The next stop was for the bedroom wardrobe—comforter, dust-ruffle, shams, curtain, the "whole enchilada." Well, it didn't work.

After I spent an hour putting the whole thing together, I took it all apart and headed back to the store. I thought the ethical thing to do was return it as soon as possible. Wrong. I was told to take it back home, wait a couple of weeks until the check had time to clear the bank and then bring it back. I think I just don't know how to be a customer anymore.

I was beginning to see why the stock prices in home-shopping companies keep going up when I remembered it was time to call for TV cable installation in the new house.

"Aha," I thought, in my ignorance. "A business that only has service to sell will surely endeavor to please the customer."

That philosophy is probably true where there is competition. But the cable company is the only one in town. Here's how you can tell:

When I call a beauty salon, the voice says, "When would you like to come in?"

When I call the cable company I am told, "We will be able to hook you up one week from Thursday, sometime between 8 a.m. and 5 p.m. and someone needs to be there during that time. We can't be more specific because we don't know how long earlier hookups will take." Period.

That rationale is a little hard to take, given today's climate of beepers, faxes, message machines, and car phones. But to extend it to another business is to see how it really offends the customer.

"This is XYZ Beauty Salon and we can take you next Thursday sometime between 8 and 5. Not knowing how long Ms. Buttercup's perm will take, you'll just have to sit and wait until we get to you. Sorry you must take off work all day, but we are the only shop in town and you're lucky to get in at all."

During the past few years, business gurus like Tom Peters have proclaimed that we are becoming a nation of service industries, having lost our manufacturing base. In light of some revelations, CEOs have scrambled to provide training for staff members on how to provide customer satisfaction.

Under the "Total Quality Management" umbrella, these classes have spread across the country with participants from every facet of the community.

And yes, here in Waco, just down the road from the marketplace where I embarked on my shopping spree, TQM workshops were in full swing.

Now, what's wrong with this picture?

SOURCE: Falls, R. (1993, September 17). Reprinted with permission of the *Waco Tribune-Herald* and the author.

▨ ETHICAL DECISION MAKING: THE GENERIC SITUATION

Making ethical decisions is easy—if the facts are clear and the choices are black and white. Because those two conditions rarely (if ever) occur because many are involved in, or will be affected by, the decision, what conditions do exist when ethical decisions must be made? The generic ethical situation was described in Chapter 2 when eight questions that required decisions were asked. Building on these eight questions, the generic ethical situation has the following characteristics: ambiguity, incomplete information, multiple points of view, conflicting responsibilities. Therefore, as marketing professionals make decisions, their decisions will depend on the process by which they make those decisions and on their experience, intelligence, and integrity.

Ethical decision making requires that decision makers recognize the ethical implications of a decision. Ethical decision making requires that decision makers consider multiple points of view. Ethical decision making requires decision makers

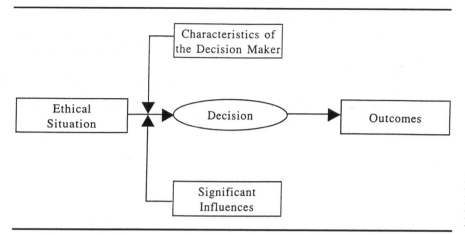

Figure 3.1. A General Framework of the Ethical Decision-Making Process

to test alternatives and balance self-interests and the interest of others. Ethical decision making requires an assessment of the long-term effects of the decision. Ethical decision making requires an examination of the decision's consistency with the values of the organization. Although this seems straightforward, the development of a consensus regarding these issues has not often occurred. Thus the qualities of the marketing professional as ethical decision maker are of paramount importance.

Ethical decisions require that marketing professionals have three qualities (Andrews, 1989). The first is the ability to recognize ethical issues (the ethical situations) and think through the consequences of alternative courses of action (outcomes). The second is a self-confidence (characteristics of the decision maker) to seek out others' points of view (significant influences) and then to decide what is right in the given situation. The third is a willingness to make a decision when all that needs to be known cannot be known and when ethical problems have no established or noncontroversial solutions (decision). These elements are shown in Figure 3.1. We'll have more to say about qualities of decision makers later in this chapter. Let's turn now to a look at a general framework for ethical decision making.

▨ A GENERAL FRAMEWORK FOR ETHICAL DECISION MAKING

Ethical decision making has been examined from many perspectives. During the past two decades, those studying ethics have proposed a number of decision-making frameworks. For example, Ferrell and Gresham (1985) proposed a model in which individual ethical decision making was influenced by the following: significant others, opportunity, social and cultural factors, and the individual's makeup. Like many of the others who proposed models of ethical decision making, their thesis revolved around the fact that many factors influence the individual confronted with an ethically related decision.

Another approach was proposed by Hunt and Vitell (1986). Their intention was to develop a model that would serve as a general theory of ethical decision making and a guide to subsequent research on how individuals make ethical decisions. In their model, four factors are proposed as influential on the individual confronted with an ethical decision: culture, industry, organization, and personal.

Still another model was proposed by Trevino (1986). This model posits that ethical decision making is a function of the individual and various situational factors, such as the individual's ego strength, locus of control, the immediate job context, organizational culture, and job characteristics. Finally, Bommer, Gratto, Gravander, and Tuttle (1987) constructed another model that attempted to capture the essence of the ethical decision-making process. They proposed six categories of influences: social, legal, professional, personal, job, and the individual.

These models, and the many others that have been developed, have captured the essence of the three qualities noted by Andrews (1989)—the ability to recognize ethical issues, self-confidence to seek out others' points of view, and willingness to make decisions. Five common elements of ethical decision making are (a) an ethical situation that requires an individual to make (b) a decision that is influenced by (c) the characteristics of the decision maker and by (d) other significant influences that influence the individual decision maker and that lead to (e) ethical or unethical outcomes (Bradley & Hatch, 1992). These five elements are shown in Figure 3.1. *Before we proceed further, what do you think about the ability of a model, like that shown in Figure 3.1, to capture the essence of all the elements of ethical decision making?*

Ethical issues can occur in any of the elements of Figure 3.1. For example, when management sets goals, it is necessary to consider the ethical implications of pursuing various directions. In evaluating alternative courses of action, it is necessary to consider the ethical outcomes of those alternatives. In implementing a decision, it is necessary to consider the ethical implications relating to the resources (human and physical) that will be affected by the decision and other nonorganizational individuals who will be affected by the decision.

As implied by Figure 3.1, and as you will see in our discussion of the various elements of Figure 3.1, marketing professionals acquire and process considerable information (related to each of the five elements of Figure 3.1) as they make decisions. This information can come from a variety of sources and relate to a variety of issues. Some of it comes from experience. Some of it is new. Some of this information is "hard," such as laws, statistics, and company policies. Some of this information is "soft," such as individuals' opinions, public opinion polls, and future projections. The marketing professional's task is to organize and analyze all of this information in an effort to make a decision that represents a profitable and ethical solution to the problem or opportunity at hand.

Before we get into a discussion of each of the elements depicted in Figure 3.1, we must keep in mind that marketing professionals suffer from some limitations (the same that we all do) in making decisions (Bommer et al., 1987). These limitations include the following:

1. *Selective perception of information.* Marketing professionals as decision makers are influenced by many individuals and many nonpersonal factors. The marketing professional may or may not elect to consider information that is relevant for a variety of reasons.
2. *Sequential processing of information.* Marketing professionals have difficulty processing a great deal of information all at the same time. Therefore, they tend to process it sequentially. The sequence in which information is processed may bias the marketing professional's judgment, limit the evaluation of related pieces of information, and prevent the marketing professional from reevaluating past information in light of new information obtained.
3. *Limited memory capacity.* Each of us is blessed with a limited memory capacity. Our limited capacity may lead us to exclude or forget certain information and restricts our access to information that may be relevant to the decision-making situation at hand.

Because of such limitations, marketing professionals may formulate decision-making rules that do not take into account all the relevant information and do not consider all the possible alternatives. New information might not be considered because the marketing professional is about to make a decision. Or the decision-making rule adopted by the marketing professional may be such that certain categories of information are automatically dismissed as irrelevant. Or information that closely fits the marketing professional's way of thinking is considered, whereas information that does not appear to fit what the marketing professional thinks is routinely not considered. The result is that decisions may be more reflective of the marketing professional's decision-making style rather than of the problem or opportunity at hand.

Characteristics of the Decision Maker

The first element of ethical decisions that we will discuss concerns the characteristics of the decision maker, shown in Figure 3.2. No two marketing professionals are alike. But it has been shown that certain characteristics of the marketing professional as decision maker are important to our understanding of decision making (Wotruba, 1990). Just as different marketing professionals are more or less prone to risk taking, various personal characteristics can also shed insight into our understanding of why people make the ethical decisions they do. For example, we've talked about the knowledge of right and wrong as influencing ethical behavior. But as previously mentioned, often overlooked in these discussions are the drives and

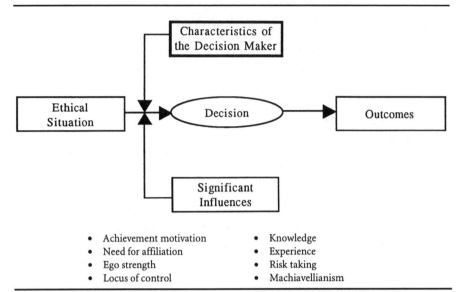

Figure 3.2.
Individual
Characteristics of
the Decision Maker
That Influence the
Ethical Decision-
Making Process

desires that lead to behavior. The discussion that follows will focus on several characteristics that can affect ethical decision making. The group of characteristics presented is not intended to be an all-inclusive list. *Perhaps you can think of others and discuss these in class.*

Achievement Motivation

Most of us have innate drives to achieve. Achievement motivation is based on the notion that an individual's achievement-oriented tendencies result from the combination of two conflicting tendencies—the motive to obtain success and the motive to avoid failure (Atkinson, 1974). Such motives manifest themselves in a number of ways, including the pursuit of status, upward mobility, and pay raises. Individuals with a strong need to achieve may tend to view certain behaviors as more ethical than their counterparts with lesser achievement desires.

In the marketplace it is hoped that we learn dignity, responsibility, and to enjoy our sense of achievement. There is little that builds our self-esteem and our self-confidence like achievement. There is truth in the adage, "success breeds success." When our efforts result in positive achievements, they provide motivation for the next task at hand.

Marketing affords those in the profession many opportunities to initiate and complete various tasks. The completion of these tasks can yield large rewards. Achievements such as these provide many opportunities to savor the moments of those achievements. Marketing professionals, however, must take care not to allow the motivation to achieve to become so important that they begin to rationalize unethical behaviors because the rewards—the achievements—are great. There is no denying the power that achievement can have over us if we are not careful. Achievement certainly is good, but it can lead to many questionable decisions if it becomes the driving force in decision making.

Need for Affiliation

Similarly, we all want to be accepted. Marketing provides many affiliation opportunities revolving around the need to develop relationships with a variety of people in order to perform one's job. Such things as attraction, anticipation of rejection, and emotional arousal are all aspects of relationship building. To the extent that the individual's need to be accepted is strong, that individual might judge certain behaviors as more ethical so that he or she can demonstrate competency and therefore gain acceptance from those who are important to him or her.

Marketing professionals, again, must be careful not to let affiliation needs be the dominant driving force in their ethical decision making. They should also be careful with whom they aspire and choose to affiliate: "He who walks with the wise grows wise, but a companion of fools suffers harm" (Proverbs 13:20). Many people will willingly provide counsel. Marketing professionals should seek counsel in the decisions they make. When such counsel runs counter to the ethics of the marketing professional, however, many problems can occur. Such problems will be discussed in Chapter 4.

Ego Strength

Ego strength is defined as an individual's ability to engage in self-directed activity and to manage tense situations (Crandall, 1973). Ego strength is related to the individual's strength of conviction. Marketing professionals high in ego strength are more likely to resist impulses and follow their convictions than their counterparts with lower ego strength. That is, those high in ego strength are more likely to do what they think is right (Grimm, Kohlberg, & White, 1968).

Locus of Control

Locus of control refers to whether or not an individual believes that his or her outcomes in life are determined by his or her own actions (internal locus of control) or by luck, fate, or others (external locus of control) (Levenson, 1974; Rotter, 1966). An individual with an internal orientation believes that outcomes are the results of his or her own efforts. These individuals are likely to accept responsibility for their actions and the consequences of their actions. Alternatively, a person with an external orientation believes that outcomes are beyond his or her control and are due to fate, luck, or destiny. Such individuals may be less likely to take personal responsibility for the consequences of unethical behaviors.

Knowledge

All individuals operate with some kind of information base. That information can be about the company, competitors, fellow employees, products, upcoming strategies, and so on. When an individual has such information, the opportunity always exists for that individual to use that information in an unethical fashion. There is an adage that states, "Knowledge is power." Some marketing professionals have access to more important information than others and may be prone to temptations to misuse that information as it places them in a position of power. *This would be a good time for you to give some thought to how a marketing professional might measure information.*

Furthermore, there are individuals in organizations who help socialize new employees into the organization. Such individuals have the opportunity to influence these new employees toward ethical or unethical behavior. For example, a trainer can have a strong influence on a new salesperson's tendencies to identify ethical situations and to take the right actions in those situations. The trainer is also in a position to suggest that actions deemed unethical by the new salesperson are "accepted business practice," providing some basis for that new salesperson to engage in ethically questionable behavior. For example, many salespeople feel that there is nothing unethical with padding an expense account, provided the level of padding stays below 10% of expenses (Krugman & Ferrell, 1981).

Experience

In some ways, experience is like knowledge. That is, marketing professionals with more experience have learned about the ethics and consequences of various alternative courses of actions. It would be nice to assume that experienced marketing professionals would be less likely to engage in questionable behaviors because they have learned a great deal over their years of employment. This is certainly true for some marketers. Other experienced marketers, however, have learned about questionable activities and have also learned that the likelihood of getting caught for the performance of those activities is small. They may also have learned ways to make those questionable activities harder to detect. Or they may have engaged in a questionable behavior so frequently they have rationalized the behavior as acceptable.

Unfortunately, experience can work for or against the promotion of ethical behavior depending on the individual with the experience.

Experience in resolving ethical conflicts accumulates. Experienced marketing professionals rely on specific sets of values to make decisions in routine situations. They can also come across situations, however, with which they have had little or no experience. Similarly, relatively new marketing professionals also have sets of values, but they are more likely to encounter ethical conflicts with which they have had little or no experience. Therefore, they consult those marketing professionals with experience for guidance concerning the proper courses of action. Those with experience can exert tremendous influence on those with less experience.

Risk Taking

Decision making involves taking some risk. When we make decisions we are forecasting that a selected course of action will provide some outcome in the future. All forecasting is risky. Each of us has different degrees to which we will take risk, and each of us has a different propensity to take risk in different situations.

Of course, we cannot talk about risk without talking about the payout from taking that risk. Let's look at a few situations:

- What is the risk of cheating on an exam and what is the reward? If the exam is worth 10% of your grade is the risk worth the reward? What about 20% of your grade? 30% of your grade?
- What is the risk of padding the expense account and what is the reward? Would you pad your expense account to obtain $25, knowing it is against company policy? How about $50? How about $100? or $500?
- What is the risk of producing an unsafe product and what is the reward? Suppose the product is inherently unsafe? Or suppose the product is safe under normal use but can cause injury if used improperly?

Now for a few more questions. *Did your assessment of the risk-reward trade-off change as the conditions of each situation changed? Do you think that your colleagues all felt the same way you do? Do you know students who cheat on insignificant exams? Why would anyone risk their job for $25? Why would anyone intentionally market an unsafe product?* The lesson here is that our assessment of risk and reward can change depending on circumstances. Furthermore, what we assess as the trade-off between risks and rewards is not likely to be the same as that of others with whom we are associated. Yet these are the people with whom you will have to reach agreement on marketing decisions.

We will conclude our discussion of risk taking with the following quote used earlier in the text, "What good will it be . . . [to gain] the whole world, yet [forfeit one's] soul?" (Matthew 16:26). There is a second part to this verse, which asks the question, "Or what can [one] give in exchange for [one's] soul?" Now let's talk trade for a moment. When a marketing professional makes a decision there is a trade-off between risk and rewards. Let's conclude by asking one more question: What reward is worth risking (a) your integrity, (b) your family, (c) spending 3 years in prison, (d) your job? Every decision has risk, a price to pay, that depends on the nature of the behaviors undertaken to achieve results. Each of us is prone to different levels of risk taking. Most of us, however, are not very good at assessing risk because we often emphasize short-term results and fail to consider long-term results. Could this be because our achievement needs or our affiliation needs are such that they dominate our thinking?

Machiavellianism

Machiavellianism is generally regarded as a measure of deceitfulness and manipulation (Hunt & Chonko, 1984; Robinson, 1973). Generally speaking, those with higher Machiavellian tendencies win through manipulation more than do those with lower Machiavellian tendencies (Christie & Geis, 1970). Also, "higher Machs" will be more successful in their manipulation (Vleeming, 1979). The interesting feature of Machiavellianism is its relationship to ethical behavior, which is summarized in the following:

> *Low Machs,* though opposed to dishonesty in principle, can be persuaded to cheat or lie given a strong, personal, and repeated inducement, especially in a face-to-face situation in which they have little time to reflect but must act, either accepting the other's wishes or rejecting them; in these situations external "rational" justification has little effect on their decisions. In contrast, high Machs, although not opposed to dishonesty in principle, will cheat less if the "rational" incentives are low or the costs (such as the probability of getting caught) are high. (Christie & Geis, 1970, p. 298)

Let's look at Machiavellian thinking in the context of "get-rich-quick" thinking. Get-rich-quick schemes prey on greed. Greed has at its core a "me first" orientation. Machiavellians do not hold in high esteem those with whom they associate. If they did, high Machs would not be as manipulative. How you value people is critical. Again, I refer to Paul's advice that people should consider others to be as important as themselves and to look out for the interests of others as well their own (see Philippians 2:3-4).

The high Mach tends to manipulate for his or her own gain. Such get-rich-quick thinking often results in consequences such as (a) getting involved in things that you cannot understand, (b) risking money you cannot afford to lose, and (c) making hasty decisions. Those marketing professionals who have Machiavellian tendencies may

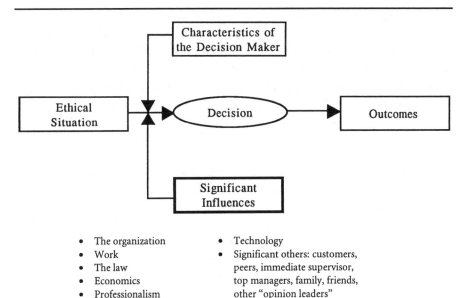

Figure 3.3.
Significant
Influences on the
Ethical Decision-
Making Process

- The organization
- Work
- The law
- Economics
- Professionalism

- Technology
- Significant others: customers, peers, immediate supervisor, top managers, family, friends, other "opinion leaders"

appear to be successful (e.g., they get rich quick) in the short run. The long run may yield different results, however: "A faithful man will be richly blessed, but one eager to get rich will not go unpunished" (Proverbs 28:20). Buddhism also speaks to overemphasis of the self. The concept of *tanha* represents a desire for private fulfillment. If this desire becomes too strong, it can led to behavior that benefits oneself at the expense of others. Buddhism teaches that once this desire becomes too strong, disharmony occurs among people.

Interestingly, marketing professionals have been found to be no more Machiavellian in nature than other occupational groups (Hunt & Chonko, 1984). Furthermore, those marketing professionals who exhibit higher Machiavellian tendencies have been found to be no more successful than other marketing professionals who exhibit lower Machiavellian tendencies. So although much is made of the Machiavellian personality, the evidence implies that it does little good to be Machiavellian and that no profession appears to attract a disproportionate share of Machiavellians to it.

Significant Influences

Many other things besides the characteristics of the decision maker affect ethics decision making. These include aspects of the organization, elements of the environment, and other individuals, summarized in Figure 3.3.

The Organization

Marketing professionals are employed by a variety of organizations in different industries having different characteristics. Some of these organizations have characteristics that are more conducive than others to ethical behavior (Raelin, 1984). For example, some organizations have top managers that are more receptive to ethical behaviors. Some organizations actively seek to hire professionals of high moral character. Some organizations have managers who have much experience in dealing with ethical situations, and that experience is transferred to other employees. Many other organizational characteristics can also influence ethical decision making. These include the organization's mission, the organization's structure, technology used in the organization, the organizational climate, division of labor, bureaucratic policies, and the way in which authority, formal and informal, is exercised (Hall, 1968). Collectively, these might all be summarized under the term *organizational culture.*

Organizational Culture. Business organizations have their own cultures just like societies do. The organization's culture is reflected in the attitudes, values, management styles, and problem solving behavior of its managers and employees. Organizational norms—accepted ways of doing things—are the results of the organization's culture.

The actions of top managers can send strong signals to marketing professionals concerning the appropriateness of certain behaviors. Top managers and supervisors have the capability of issuing rewards and punishments. In this context, such individuals become authority figures by the way they pass out rewards and punishments. Those rewards and punishments then serve to reinforce certain behaviors (those rewarded) and reduce the incidence of certain behaviors (those punished).

Most marketing organizations have policies and procedures concerning ethical behaviors. To be effective, these policies must be sufficient for allowing the detection of ethics violations. As you have seen, marketing professionals are frequently confronted with easy opportunities to act unethically. Organizational policies must provide a system of controls that decreases or eliminates such easy opportunities for unethical behavior. But as you will see in Chapter 4, policies are not sufficient to deter unethical behavior. Top management actions that support the ethical culture fostered by organizational policies must consistently reinforce those policies. *Why do you think this is the case?*

Work

The work environment is concerned with the conditions that exist in the marketing professional's job. Many factors in the work environment can affect a marketing professional's ethical decision making. One of these factors is the reward structure of the organization. Pay raises, recognition, and bonuses are generally considered to be positive reinforcers. If they are used to reward ethical behaviors that lead to excellent performance, they can be positive reinforcers of ethical behavior. If they are used solely to reward outcomes, however, they may, inadvertently, be rewarding unethical behaviors used to obtain outcomes.

The Law

The laws and regulations established by the government set the minimum standards for ethical behavior. Laws and regulations have been established to counter existing questionable marketplace behavior. A more complete discussion of some of these laws and regulations is contained in the Appendix of Chapter 5.

Laws represent the values of a society that have the force of formal authority of threat and punishment if they are broken. Because of the formal nature of laws and the corresponding punishment for breaking them, most individuals feel compelled to keep their behavior within the limits set by the law.

To be effective, the law needs to be enforced. But the law concerning business and marketing decisions is very complex, and judges, prosecutors, and investigators often find it difficult to understand the intricacies of the law. Thus actual enforcement of marketing law may be given low priority by law enforcement officials because of the difficulty of detecting infractions of the law, token enforcement and prosecution, and the relatively minor penalties issued (Geis & Stotland, 1980).

When a marketing professional breaks the law, ignorance of the law is not a legitimate defense. Although, probably, most of us will never fully understand all the subtleties of the law, the lack of knowledge does not release individuals from their responsibilities to uphold the law (Meier & Geis, 1982).

Perhaps the greatest influence on the marketing professional giving consideration to breaking the law is the likelihood of detection. Oftentimes, individuals are concerned more with the probability of getting caught than with the consequences of getting caught (Dickson, 1978). This is symptomatic of the short-term thinking that dominates much unethical decision making. The probability of detection can be a powerful deterrent. So, too, can the severity of the consequences. But the lack of aggressive prosecution for certain legal violations is also a factor that may enhance the likelihood of unethical decision making. A low likelihood that a marketing professional who breaks the law will get caught and a low probability that enforcement will be minimal are two factors that tend to enhance the individual's willingness to violate the law (Taylor, 1984).

Economics

Good, poor, or changing economic conditions can have an effect on the ethical nature of marketing decision making. In good times, certain marketing professionals may feel inclined to "take advantage of the good times" and pursue questionable marketing strategies and tactics as a means of "getting the most out of the boom times." For example, during boom times, pressures may be placed on salespeople to increase their sales as much and as quickly as possible. Similarly, some marketing professionals might use poor economic times as a rationale for "getting what they can" during times of struggle. During slower economic times, questionable promotion strategies might be used as an inducement to get customers to purchase products. Furthermore, questionable pricing strategies might be used to attract customers and to put pressure on smaller competitors. Finally, some marketing professionals might consider economic change as a rationale for unethical decision making because "who knows what the future holds?"

Professionalism

Professionalism embodies an institutionalized professional context within which marketers practice their trade. Professionalism is more than an individual simply saying, "I am a professional." Some individuals profess to be of high moral character, but their behavior is not always consistent with what they say.

The marketing profession has a professional association known as the American Marketing Association (AMA). Although not as strict in terms of membership requirements as the legal and medical professional associations, the AMA does have formal and published standards of professional conduct, which are presented in the appendix.

Some professional associations, like the AMA, have been very active in reviewing ethical problems and publishing guidelines for professionals who are confronted with similar ethical situations. Still others have been active in enforcing their ethical codes and expelling those who do not comply with the code. Also, many associations have begun the development of support mechanisms for those members who have followed codes (Broome, 1983; Unger, 1982).

Technology

Technology refers to the knowledge of how to accomplish certain tasks and achieve certain goals (Simon, 1973). Technology provides the means to improve effectiveness and efficiency of organizations that produce and market products and services that improve the standard of living enjoyed by customers. For example, technology has led to some wonderful medical advances over the past 30 years. These advances have created many marketing opportunities, and these opportunities have led to many successes. They have also led to some questionable marketplace behaviors. In general, technology affords us many opportunities to improve our lifestyles. Technology also affords us marketing opportunities. Unfortunately, like everything else, opportunity provided by technology can also attract unscrupulous individuals who seek to make their fortune by taking advantage of others who might benefit from the technology.

Significant Others

Significant others is a term used to describe those individuals who attempt to influence what the marketing professional does. Significant others include customers, peers, immediate supervisors, top management, family and friends, colleagues, and other opinion leaders. Any of these individuals may exert influence on what ethical decisions the marketing professional makes. We will present a brief discussion of customers, competitors, and other social influences here.

Customers. Customers can have a tremendous influence on the ethical decision making of marketing professionals. Little will be said about the influence of customers, who are considered professionals by this author. Suffice it to say that organizational customers and individual customers are just as much the subject of this book and just as prone to ethical conflict as those marketing professionals who are on the selling side of the exchange relationship. Also, as you saw in Chapter 1, you and I as individual consumers are not exempt from making questionable marketplace decisions and influencing marketing professionals into questionable marketing decisions.

Competitors. Ideally, competitors engage in a healthy rivalry for loyalty and revenues from consumers. Marketing professionals, however, can engage in activities that lead to their organizations' competing unfairly. For example, when competition intensifies, marketing professionals may begin to feel that their survival or that of their organization is threatened. Under such pressure, the degree to which these professionals might engage in questionable marketplace behaviors increases. *What pressures can competitors place on marketing professionals that might lead them to consider unethical activity?*

Social Influences. The social environment of a marketing professional consists of the religious, cultural, and societal values that are generally shared by members of the marketing professional's family, groups with whom the individual is involved, and society as a whole (Bommer et al., 1987). Families, churches, schools, and friends are all in a position of influence as future marketing professionals grow up and develop their own value systems.

We know that social values affect a person's behavior. Recall from Chapter 2 and the discussion of socialization that marketing professionals may be influenced by many different sets of values, including social values. But we also know that general social values can be ignored if they are not in conformity with those of the work group (Brady, 1985). There is some evidence that managers have two sets of ethics—one on the job and one off the job (e.g., Fairweather, 1980; Vandivier, 1980). That is, they apply different values on the job than they do off the job. Marketers are still influenced by values but, in certain circumstances, they subordinate social values to those of the organization, their work group, or even their own personal desires. *How can groups in which you are a member influence you to go against values that you hold to be important?*

Let's not forget the individual's family and peer groups, both of which can have a profound influence on the marketing professional's ethical decision making. Families can provide complex socialization processes that can be a powerful moral influence on the individual (Bandura, 1977), if for no other reason than that the individual has to live with the family.

Peer groups can be very influential in predicting an individual's ethical behavior (Burkett & Jensen, 1975; Grasnick & Green, 1980). As you will see in our discussion of groups in Chapter 4, factors such as "groupthink" can lead individuals to make unethical decisions (Allison, 1971; Janis, 1972). We will have more to say about significant others in Chapter 4.

Ethical Situation   A third element of the ethical decision-making process is the ethical situation itself. We will discuss two aspects of the ethical situation as shown in Figure 3.4: (a) opportunity, (b) ethical decision history, and (c) the moral intensity of the situation.

Opportunity

A marketing professional confronted with a business decision must recognize that decision making has ethical ramifications. Not every business decision has an ethical component, but many do. The opportunity for unethical behavior plays a key role. Often, such opportunity occurs because conditions of the decision-making situation are conducive to unethical behavior—perceived absence of punishment or perceived rewards (Ferrell & Gresham, 1985). Certainly, the absence of punishment provides an impetus for unethical behavior because the decision maker feels free of any negative consequences associated with the behavior.

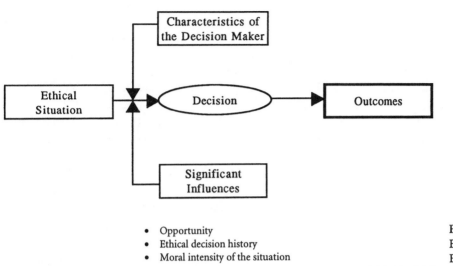

Figure 3.4.
Elements of the
Ethical Situation

Opportunity represents a set of conditions that limit unfavorable behaviors or encourage favorable behaviors. Opportunity often represents a situation that has the potential for reward. Viewing opportunity somewhat negatively, the absence of punishment for unethical behaviors opens the door for opportunities to engage in unethical behaviors. Generally, the individual, those with whom the individual is involved, and the opportunity to interact are the most influential in the individual's response to situations. As discussed in the section on risk taking, individuals will evaluate the risks and rewards associated with various courses of action and, based on inputs from others and their own ethical philosophy, a course of action will be selected that is designed to take advantage of opportunistic situations.

Ethical Decision History

Past decisions play an important role in current and future decisions. Past decisions that are reinforced will influence future decisions (Jones, 1985; Luthans & Kreitner, 1985). Therefore, as ethical decisions are made over time and reinforced, the marketing professional develops an ethical decision history. If reinforcement is regular, the tendency to make ethical decisions is likely to become relatively enduring. Of course, the opposite can also occur. If unethical decision making goes unpunished, or is rewarded, the tendency to make unethical decisions can grow stronger (Stead, Worrell, Spalding, & Stead, 1987).

Moral Intensity of the Situation

Ethical situations have their own characteristics, and these characteristics, collectively, can be called the moral intensity of the situation (Jones, 1991). Intuitively, individuals become much more concerned about ethical situations that affect those who are close to them. Individuals also seem to react more strongly to situations that have immediate effects. Situations with long-term consequences are often not given such strong consideration. An individual's moral intensity will vary from one situation to the next. In other words, individuals make judgments about different ethical situations.

Of course, for any ethical decision making to occur, the individual must recognize the ethics of the situation. This is not always the case. Recognizing an ethical situation requires two elements (Velasquez & Rostankowski, 1985). One is the recognition that a decision will have an effect on others. The second is that a choice between alternatives is involved. Moral intensity will affect the recognition of ethical issues through the processes of selective perception discussed earlier in this chapter. Issues that are important to the individual or issues that have consequences that stand out (e.g., many are affected or the risk of loss is high) will be more readily perceived as having ethical ramifications than issues that are not as important to the individual.

The Decision   A brief overview of the decision component is presented. Marketing decisions revolve around information and product, price, promotion, and distribution strategies and tactics. You will be given many opportunities in Chapters 6 through 11 to make decisions. Therefore, this section will highlight a few key aspects of the decision component of ethical decision making. As you have seen, marketing professionals will differ in their abilities to evaluate the many facets of marketing problems. They will also differ in the way they assess the effect of their decisions on others. Individual characteristics such as empathy may be related to the individual's consideration of others as he or she makes decisions (Wotruba, 1990). Despite these differences, there are several elements common to decisions. These include (a) the perceived ethical problem, (b) perceived alternatives and consequences, and (c) judgment, shown in Figure 3.5.

Perceived Ethical Problem

As has been stated before, not all marketing decisions have ethical ramifications, and individuals will differ in their assessments concerning the ethical nature of certain marketing decisions (e.g., Dubinsky & Ingram, 1984; Ferrell & Weaver, 1978). In other words, before any ethics decisions can be made, the marketing decision maker must perceive an ethical problem, and as you have already read, perceptions and

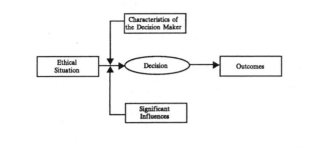

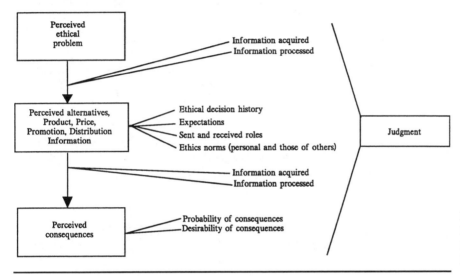

Figure 3.5.
Elements of the
Ethical Decision-
Making Process

values cause great differences in judgment concerning what is an ethical problem and what is not. Such differences will lead individuals to make decisions, based on their own value systems, that others with different value systems might consider unethical in nature.

Despite such complications, marketing professionals must still make decisions. In ethical decision-making situations, this means trying to choose an alternative that is ethically correct. How people arrive at such judgments is often influenced by the ethical theory to which they subscribe (Murphy & Laczniak, 1981; Robin & Reidenbach, 1986). As you have already seen in Chapter 2, ethical theories can be in conflict with each other and yield very different conclusions in the same situation. An alternative that is consistent with one ethic may be very inconsistent with another ethic. *Refresh your memory. How can different ethical theories lead people to reach different conclusions in the same situation?*

Perceived Alternatives and Consequences

It is unlikely that any one individual will recognize all of the possible alternative solutions to an ethical problem. In fact, the reason that individuals make different decisions in seemingly similar situations may, in part, be due to the fact that these individuals perceive different sets of alternatives from one situation to the next (Hunt & Vitell, 1986).

Referring to ethical theories for a moment, when an individual evaluates alternative courses of actions, two kinds of evaluation will occur.

The first is deontological in nature—the evaluation of the inherent rightness and wrongness of alternative behaviors. In this evaluation, the marketing professional compares alternative behaviors with a predetermined set of values that include beliefs about such things as stealing, honesty, treating people fairly, product safety, deceptive advertising, and bribery.

The individual will also undertake a teleological (focus on consequences) evaluation in which he or she will consider the following:

1. The perceived consequences of each action for various significant others
2. The probability that each consequence will occur to each significant other
3. The desirability or undesirability of each consequence
4. The importance of each stakeholder group (Hunt & Vitell, 1986)

As you can see, probabilities associated with consequences enter into ethical decision making. When any decision is made, there is rarely complete certainty concerning the consequences of that decision for one simple reason. It requires predicting the future. Moreover, individual marketing professionals will express preferences for various alternatives based on the likelihood that the alternatives will contribute to the individual's attaining personal and organizational goals (Dayton, 1979). In other words, certain consequences are perceived as more desirable than others.

Judgment

Near the beginning of this chapter, we talked about judgment. Ultimately, the individual must make a judgment about the existence of an ethical problem, the alternatives to be considered, and the action to be undertaken. Again, this is a place in which variations in decisions based on judgment occur. Some marketing professionals may choose to ignore, completely, the consequences of alternative actions. In their judgment, alternatives are evaluated strictly from the standpoint of their perceived rightness or wrongness. Other marketing professionals may ignore right and

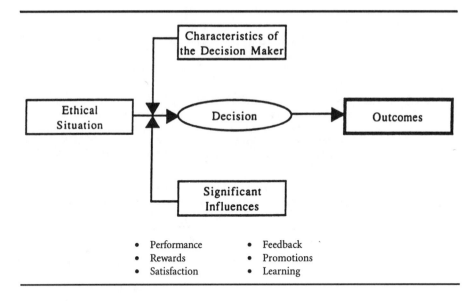

Figure 3.6.
Outcomes That Result From the Ethical Decision-Making Process

wrong and make a judgment to look solely at consequences. Still others may adopt a mixture of both kinds of evaluation. The latter decision strategy is the most likely, but decisions will still vary because of differences in individual assignments of the importance of significant others, the probabilities associated with various outcomes, and their abilities to identify all the possible outcomes associated with a particular course of action.

Outcomes

Simply put, all decisions have outcomes. These might include performance, rewards, satisfaction, feedback, promotions, or learning as shown in Figure 3.6. Outcomes are neither ethical nor unethical. It is the actions that lead to those outcomes that have ethical ramifications. As you saw in the section on ethical theories, outcomes (consequences) are often used to judge the ethical nature of an action. Although the assessment of an outcome might influence an individual to engage in a questionable act, however, the outcome is not ethical or unethical.

Keep in mind that if the result of questionable behavior is reward and that questionable behavior is not discovered (or is detected but goes unpunished), the past outcome can be a strong influence on future decisions in similar situations. Again, this discussion will be brief because you will have many opportunities to discuss the outcomes of various decisions you make in Chapters 6 through 11. Before we go to Chapter 4, however, please refer to Table 3.2 for a summary and framework for ethical decision making.

Table 3.2 A Framework for Ethical Decision Making

Step	Area	Description
1.	Context—Outside the organization	To what degree do environmental, historical, sociocultural, professional, gender, political-legal, economic, and public policy factors shape an ethically supportive external context? What are the facts and the ethical issues from this vantage point?
2.	Context—Inside the organization	What is the current level of moral development of the organization and the immediate work group? To what extent do existing policies, structures, roles, rewards, leadership, selection of salespeople and other employees, decision processes, norms, significant others, rituals, and symbols provide an ethically supportive context? What are the facts and the ethical issues from this vantage point?
3.	Ethical agents	Who are the significant others and what are their interests? What are their levels of moral development? What virtues or vices are being developed? What is their level of ego strength, independence, internal or external locus of control? What praiseworthy intentions do they indicate? What praiseworthy feelings do they exhibit? Do they inspire trust and team commitment?
4.	Ethical acts	What if everyone acted like this? Would you regard this action or these means as right in private and in public? What are your values that apply to this action? Is this action in compliance with legitimate rules? Are important contractual duties fulfilled and obligations met by this action? How would you handle potential conflicts of rights?
5.	Ethical results	Who stands to gain and lose and in what proportions? What are the costs and benefits to all significant others in the short run and long run? What future precedents will be set by the action? What action results in the greatest dispersion of positive results?
6.	Alternatives	Have you considered all the major alternatives and their combinations? What are the likely consequences of all the alternatives in the short run and long run? Have all significant others affected by the decision had a say about the situation and the recommended solution?
7.	Recommended decision and justification	What are your principle reasons for recommending this solution over others? Can you give a responsible and reasonable justification for your decision to those who may disagree with you?
8.	Implementation and control	What practical steps and timetable are needed to put your decision into effect? Who will be responsible for implementing the decision? How will you know if the recommended decision has achieved the desired result? Are there specific measures of progress toward the desired goal? What are your obligations for continued quality control?

SOURCE: Adapted with permission from Petrick, Wagley, and Von der Embse (1991), *SAM Advanced Management Journal, 56*(1), Winter 1991, Society for Advancement of Management, P.O. Box 889, Vinton, VA 24179.

This chapter provided an overview of the decision-making process of marketing professionals confronted with ethical situations. It began with a discussion of the knowledge of right and wrong, an important element in ethical decision making. But knowledge of right and wrong, by itself, does not explain why many unethical decisions are made.

All ethically based decisions require judgment on the part of the decision maker. This judgment can be influenced by many factors, including personal characteristics of the decision maker, other significant influences, the ethical situation, the decision, and the outcomes of that decision.

CHAPTER SUMMARY

▧ SOME QUESTIONS FOR DISCUSSION

1. Break into small groups and discuss the following situations: (a) cheating on an exam, (b) padding an expense account, (c) providing misleading information on a résumé, and (d) marketing a prescription drug known by some to have harmful side effects. Can you reach agreement about the rightness or wrongness of these activities? What factors might influence someone to engage in any of these activities?

2. What role does information play in ethical decision making? Will objective information always allow people to reach a consensus concerning the ethical nature of activities? Why do you think so?

3. Comment on the five common elements of ethical decision making presented in this chapter. Do you think these elements provide a solid foundation for understanding ethical decision making? If yes, why so? If not, what would you add to (or delete from) these elements and how would you adjust Figure 3.1?

4. This chapter presented several personal characteristics of the decision maker that can affect ethical decision making. Can you think of some others? How would these others influence ethical decision making?

5. Discuss why opportunity and ethical decision history can be influential in ethical decision making. What role does moral intensity play in recognizing the ethics of a situation?

American Marketing Association
Code of Ethics*

Members of the American Marketing Association (AMA) are committed to ethical professional conduct. They have joined together in subscribing to this Code of Ethics embracing the following topics:

Responsibilities of the Marketer

Marketers must accept responsibility for the consequences of their activities and make every effort to ensure that their decisions, recommendations, and actions function to identify, serve, and satisfy all relevant publics: customers, organizations, and society.

Marketers' professional conduct must be guided by:

1. The basic rule of professional ethics: not knowingly to do harm.
2. The adherence to all applicable laws and regulations.
3. The accurate representation of their education, training, and experience.
4. The active support, practice, and promotion of this Code of Ethics.

Honesty and Fairness

Marketers shall uphold and advance the integrity, honor, and dignity of the marketing profession by:

1. Being honest in serving consumers, clients, employees, suppliers, distributors, and the public.
2. Not knowingly participating in conflict of interest without prior notice to all parties involved.
3. Establishing equitable fee schedules, including the payment or receipt of usual, customary, and/or legal compensation for marketing exchanges.

---

*Reprinted by permission of the American Marketing Association.

Rights and Duties of Parties in the Marketing Exchange Process

Participants in the marketing exchange process should be able to expect that:

1. Products and services offered are safe and fit for their intended uses.
2. Communications about offered products and services are not deceptive.
3. All parties intend to discharge their obligations, financial and otherwise, in good faith.
4. Appropriate internal methods exist for equitable adjustment and/or redress of grievances concerning purchases.

It is understood that the above would include, *but is not limited to,* the following responsibilities of the marketer:

In the Area of Product Development and Management.

- Disclosure of all substantial risks associated with product or service usage.
- Identification of any product component substitution that might materially change the product or impact on the buyer's purchase decision.
- Identification of extra-cost added features.

In the Area of Promotions.

- Avoidance of false and misleading advertising.
- Rejection of high-pressure manipulations, or misleading sales tactics.
- Avoidance of sales promotions that use deception or manipulation.

In the Area of Distribution.

- Not manipulating the availability of a product for purpose of exploitation.
- Not using coercion in the marketing channel.
- Not exerting undue influence over the reseller's choice to handle a product.

In the Area of Pricing.

- Not engaging in price-fixing.
- Not practicing predatory pricing.
- Disclosing the full price associated with any purchase.

In the Area of Marketing Research.

- Prohibiting selling or fund raising under the guise of conducting research.
- Maintaining research integrity by avoiding misrepresentation and omission of pertinent research data.
- Treating outside clients and suppliers fairly.

Organizational Relationships

Marketers should be aware of how their behavior may influence or impact on the behavior of others in organizational relationships. They should not demand, encourage, or apply coercion to obtain unethical behavior in their relationships with others, such as employees, suppliers, or customers.

1. Apply confidentiality and anonymity in professional relationships with regard to privileged information.

2. Meet their obligations and responsibilities in contracts and mutual agreements in a timely manner.

3. Avoid taking the work of others, in whole or in part, and representing this work as their own or directly benefiting from it without compensation or consent of the originator or owner.

4. Avoid manipulation to take advantage of situations to maximize personal welfare in a way that unfairly deprives or damages the organization or others.

Any AMA members found to be in violation of any provision of this Code of Ethics may have his or her Association membership suspended or revoked.

SOURCE: From Smith, N. C., & Quelch, J. A. (1993). *Ethics in Marketing*. Homewood, IL: Irwin.

The Work Environment and Ethical Decisions

PURPOSE

To discuss how aspects of an individual's work environment can contribute to the challenges of ethical decision making.

MAJOR POINTS

Individuals and organizations may not always agree about ethical decision making.

Characteristics of the organization can pose threats to an individual's ethical decision making.

Other individuals ("significant others") will exert varying degrees of influence on the behavior of marketing professionals. Three of the ways they influence behavior are (a) differential association theory, (b) role theory, and (c) group processes.

Marketing professionals have many options when they are confronted with ethical situations.

In Chapter 3, a general framework for ethical decision making was presented. In this chapter, we will present some aspects of organizations that affect the marketing professional's decisions. Keep in mind the following comments about ethical decision making as you read this chapter:

1. Ethical decision making is a systematic process of reasoning and thinking when marketing professionals are confronted with ethical problems.

2. Groups of people may disagree about the ethical nature of various courses of action.

3. Not all ethical decisions are as clear-cut and easy as we would like.

4. Ethical decisions, often, are not "quick fix" decisions. They require assessment of information and scrutiny of alternative courses of action just as do marketing decisions that have no ethical ramifications.

As you will see in this chapter, many aspects of organizations and individuals can complicate the marketing professional's decision making when confronted with ethical problems.

◪ THE INDIVIDUAL AND THE ORGANIZATIONAL ETHICS

We've spent a good deal of time talking about things such as the individual's ethic, the organization's ethic, and values. How well the individual and his or her approach to ethics fits in with the organization's approach to ethics can be very influential in the quality of ethical decisions (Petrick, Wagley, & Von der Embse, 1991). Table 4.1 presents an example of two models—one of an individual's moral development and one of an organization's moral development (Petrick, Manning, & Curtis, 1989).

The first column in Table 4.1 depicts a six-stage model of individual moral development (Kohlberg & Candee, 1984). This model suggests that individuals attain successive levels of moral development. The individual moves from a very egoistic, self-centered conception of what is right to a broader understanding of the importance of considering others in the process of making decisions. In other words, the ethical theories to which an individual subscribes may change over time. Individuals at different levels of moral development, such as those shown in Table 4.1, have been found to exhibit different ethical behaviors (Penn & Collier, 1985).

The second column of Table 4.1 presents parallel stages of organizational moral development. These stages might be considered in a way similar to the organization's culture. These stages, like those for the individual, indicate success levels of moral development for the organization. Social Darwinism is similar to "survival of the fittest" and is very close to a Machiavellian orientation. The stage of organizational integrity is the highest stage of moral development presented (Petrick & Manning, 1990). The quality of the organization's ethical climate has been shown to be influential in the ethical decision making of the individuals in the organization (e.g., Barnett & Carson, 1989; Victor & Cullen, 1988).

As you can see in Table 4.1, there are many ways in which individuals and the organizations for which they work may be in disagreement about the nature of ethical decision making. Simply stated, individuals may be at a higher, lower, or the same

Stage	Personal Moral Development	Organizational Moral Development
1.	Physical consequences determine moral behavior. Avoidance of punishment and deference to power are typical of this stage.	*Social Darwinism*—Fear of extinction and the urgency of financial survival dictate moral conduct. The direct use of force is the acceptable norm.
2.	Individual pleasure needs are the primary concern and dictate attitudes toward behavior.	*Machiavellianism*—Organizational gain guides actions. Successfully attaining goals justifies the use of any effective means, including individual manipulation.
3.	The approval of others determines behavior. The good person is one who satisfies family, friends, associates.	*Cultural conformity*—A tradition of standard operating procedures and caring groups. Peer professional pressure to adhere to social norms dictates what is the right and wrong behavior.
4.	Compliance with authority, upholding of the social order, and "doing one's duty" are primary concerns.	*Allegiance to authority*—Directions from legal authority determine moral standards. Right and wrong are based on the decisions of those with legitimate hierarchical power.
5.	Tolerance for rational dissent and acceptance of majority rule become primary ethical concerns.	*Democratic participation*—Participation in decision-making reliance on majority rule become organizational moral standards. Participative management becomes institutionalized.
6.	What is right and good is a matter of individual conscience and responsibly chosen commitment. Morality is based on principled personal convictions.	*Organizational integrity*—Justice and individual rights are the moral ideals. Balanced judgment between competing interests shapes organizational character which, in turn, determines the rightness or wrongness of behavior.

Table 4.1 Models of Personal and Organizational Moral Development

SOURCE: Petrick, Manning, and Curtis (1989). Reprinted with permission.

level of moral development as their organization. Whenever they are not on the same level, conflicts can occur. Even if they are on the same level, the result is not necessarily good because both the individual and the organization can be at very low levels of moral development.

▨ THREATS TO ETHICAL BEHAVIOR

As you have already seen, ethical decision making is not always easy. Oftentimes, ethical decision making is complicated by aspects of the organization in which the

Table 4.2 Norms and Counternorms

Norm	Counternorm
Long-term relationships with customers	Selling to make short-term goals
Objectivity	Emotional involvement
Openness	Secrecy
Candor	Stonewalling
Honesty	Lying
Flexibility/adaptability	Dogmatism
Cost-effectiveness	Padding expenses
Taking responsibility	Passing the buck
Customer service	Sales emphasis
Developing young people	Looking out for "Number 1"
Team effort	Individual goals first
Consensus	Taking unfair credit
Loyalty	Criticize the company, colleagues, or both

SOURCE: Jansen and Von Glinow (1985). Reprinted with permission.

marketing professional is employed. The following discussion focuses on identifying some characteristics of organizations that pose threats to ethical decision making.

Ethical Ambivalence

An area that causes great concern for ethical behavior stems from ambivalence. In general, ambivalence refers to the experience of being pulled in psychologically opposite directions. Ethical ambivalence in organizations refers to attitudes that are shaped and maintained by organizational reward systems that conflict with the behaviors and attitudes that are consistent with the professional marketer's ethic (Jansen & Von Glinow, 1985; Mason & Mitroff, 1981). Ethical ambivalence deals with norms and counternorms that exist in an organization. Some of these are illustrated in Table 4.2.

Norms and Counternorms

Norms and counternorms such as those in Table 4.2 are shaped by the organization's reward system. For example, most organizations would be delighted to have an environment of openness and honesty. But individuals in organizations tend to develop counternorms such as secrecy and lying. Although such counternorms may be undesirable, they are often perceived as necessary to protect one's self-interests. *Can you identify any norms and counternorms at your college or university?*

Reward systems play an important role in shaping behaviors as rewards are a powerful influence in directing and motivating individuals to achieve individual and organizational goals. The organization's reward system rests on the premise that members of the organization seek information concerning behaviors and results that will be rewarded while excluding activities that will not be rewarded (Kerr, 1975).

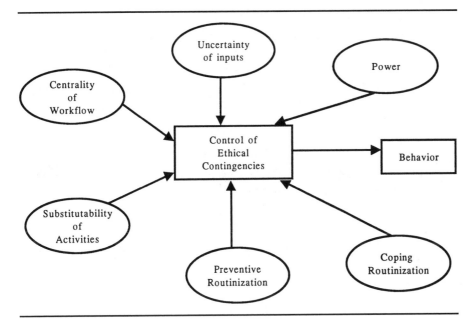

Figure 4.1.
Outcomes That
Result From the
Ethical Decision-
Making Process

Ethical ambivalence is experienced by individuals as reward systems alter the balance between norms and counternorms. *Do the reward systems at your college or university lead to ambivalence? Describe how this occurs.*

Work Setting

Figure 4.1 presents six factors that might influence the individual marketing professional's ethical decision making (Hickson, Hinings, Pennings, & Schneck, 1971). These are power, uncertainty of inputs, centrality of workflow, substitutability of activities, preventive routinization, and coping routinization.

Power. Power is the ability to influence others to act in certain ways. The marketing professional may have power to influence others or others may have power to influence the marketing professional. Power can come in a variety of forms. One power that we all often fear is the loss of our jobs. Although this fear may be more perceptual than real, it often influences marketing professionals to compromise their ethics and undertake ethically questionable behaviors. *What other forms of power exist in organizations?*

Uncertainty of Inputs. Often, marketing professionals lack information or are not sure about the availability of information concerning the performance of an ethically questionable behavior. Furthermore, marketing professionals often have uncertainty about the consequences of those behaviors, particularly in the long run. Uncertainty can be reduced in a variety of ways, including consulting with others, referring to past decisions, and examining company policies. Unfortunately, marketing professionals, too often, think in terms of the short run. As a result, they often overlook information that might lead them to pursue the higher road. But short-term thinking and the desire to "get the decision over with" and obtain whatever rewards are forthcoming can lead marketing professionals to take the lower road.

Centrality of Workflow. This represents the number of individuals with whom the marketing professional must interact in a decision-making situation. If behavior is easily observed, fewer marketing professionals are likely to take ethical risks. Alternatively, behaviors that are not easily observed can lead marketers to consider unethical activity because they think there is a low likelihood of getting caught.

Substitutability of Activities. Substitutability of activities refers to the number of different behavioral alternatives available to achieve a certain outcome. If desirable outcomes for the individual and all constituents can be achieved through ethical behaviors, unethical behaviors may be judged unnecessary. Keep in mind, however, that it is difficult for any individual to consider all possible options in any situation. Furthermore, consider that many of us are also inclined to make quick decisions, which means that we do not always give adequate thought to our decisions.

Preventive Routinization. This refers to an individual's ability to develop routine behaviors that achieve desirable outcomes. If marketing professionals can routinely solve problems or take advantage of opportunities successfully, through ethical behaviors, the inclination toward unethical behaviors can be reduced. Although recurring situations may not be exactly the same, there is often enough similarity so that routinization of behaviors is possible. *What are the advantages and disadvantages of routinizing behavior?*

Coping Routinization. Coping routinization is the ability to deal with uncertainty regarding ethical guidelines. The more clearly management can distinguish between ethical and unethical behaviors, the greater the accuracy of the guidance provided to marketing professionals as they make decisions. In other words, top management can provide firm guidelines that provide clear guidance for marketing professionals as they cope with ethical decision situations.

Annual Objectives   Setting annual objectives is a common practice among marketing organizations. They can also hamper solid performance. Take, for example, a salesperson's annual sales goal. Many activities are required before a salesperson can achieve the annual sales objective—making presentations, prospecting, follow-ups with customers, building relationships with prospects and customers, assessing customers' needs and wants, and so on. These activities often take considerable time to complete.

Those salespeople who are responsible for achieving goals might also be looked at for advancement based on their accomplishments of short-term assignments. So they may try to "hard sell" a customer at the end of the year to achieve goal. They may "sandbag" and hold late-in-the-year sales during a good year for next year's performance report. They might choose only to "sell" and not service customers to whom they have sold products. In other words, the pressure the salesperson feels to achieve the organization's short-term goals and the pressure the salesperson feels to "put up numbers" so a promotion is forthcoming may lead to short-term behaviors that can have harmful long-term effects.

Is it fair to have salespeople choose between benefits to themselves and their families (which would result from some short-term successes) and the long-term performance of the organization? You might say, "The customers' long-term interests are in the best interests of the salesperson," and I would agree with you. *However, I would respond by asking you if you study every night (in your long-term best interests) or do you opt to party at the expense of studying (short-term gratification) and hope to make it up with an all-nighter the day before the test?*

Clearly, the performance of our salesperson must be monitored regularly. But there can be conflicts of interest inherent in holding fast to short-term goals or in the advancement opportunities afforded by our organizations. Such conflicts can tend to undermine long-term performance considerations.

Performance Appraisals

In most performance appraisals, someone has agreed to achieve certain goals, and, at the end of some time period, that individual's actual performance is compared to the agreed-upon goals. Let's refer to our salesperson again. Can any salesperson, working alone, achieve all the goals set forth by the organization? The answer is a resounding "No!"

The question was loaded because no salesperson works alone. They sell products (manufacturing) that are delivered (distribution) to customers who expect them to work (customer service) long after they are paid for (credit). How often do one or more of these other functional areas of the organization contribute to a salesperson's making or not making a goal? Now, you might say, "The salesperson should not make promises that cannot be kept." I agree. But what happens if the truck breaks down or the customer cannot make payments or the product is defective? Ideally, all these problems are worked out and customers and management recognize that mistakes occur. But repairing mistakes may take time and the resolution (actual) may not occur until after the performance appraisal is conducted and the salesperson has reported that goals were not achieved.

The preceding example is a bit contrived. The point, however, is that it is difficult for performance appraisers to properly rate a person's performance. An organization whose managers adopt such a program may be violating principles of fairness in implementing performance appraisal programs. A conflict between what is being done and what could be done is created and can lead salespeople to seek ways to manipulate the appraisal process (short-term interests) so that short-term objectives are met. *What do you think about performance appraisals?*

Pyramid Politics

Typically, business organizations centralize and decentralize authority simultaneously. Power is concentrated at the top of the organization, but some responsibility for decisions is pushed down to lower levels of the organization. The reporting system used in the organization is the key to unlocking the responsibilities in most organizations (Jackall, 1993).

In the typical organization, managers set goals, formulate commitments, and report to their superiors. These superiors, in turn, take these reports and make commitments to their superiors and so on. When these commitments reach the top, they are usually sent back down in the form of objectives, to all levels of the organization. Usually, what is communicated downward is an increase over what was sent to the top. In this type of structure, subordinates usually answer to their immediate supervisors. Those subordinates must not overcommit their superiors, and they must *keep their superiors from making mistakes.* Furthermore, these subordinates must not circumvent their superiors.

One ethical problem with such a system is in the determination of who gets credit for work done. Typically, credit is pushed up the organization and blame is pushed down. The primary reason is to protect the superiors from making mistakes. Such pushing down of blame creates pressures on middle marketing managers to protect their organizations, their superiors, and themselves. Middle managers become the scapegoats when something wrong occurs. *What other ethical problems might occur in the type of pyramid system described earlier?*

The Goals of Marketing

As you know, marketing activities are undertaken with many different goals in mind—sales revenue, profits, contribution to profit margins, market share. Perhaps the goal that is most often stated for marketing is that marketing's responsibility is to improve profits by increasing the sale of products, services, or both. Marketers also talk in terms of goals such as increasing markets, opening new markets, new product development, and creating customers. These are all acceptable goals from the standpoint of the business enterprise.

Recall in Chapter 1 that we discussed differing philosophies concerning the purpose of a business. Well, these differing philosophies also have an effect on the marketing professional. Suppose we view the purpose of marketing from another perspective—that of the customer. How would the goals of marketing be changed? For one thing, the goal of marketing might be stated in terms of informing the customer about product alternatives so that the customer can make more informed choices. If the information provided about a firm's product is good, then the sales of that product might increase.

In other words, with an information-oriented goal, the marketing organization would set as a goal increasing the likelihood and frequency of free and informed transactions in the marketplace (Camenisch, 1991). This, after all, is what free market systems are all about. But does a goal stated in these terms create conflict for the marketing professional? How can this information orientation—the ideal of having a fully informed marketplace—be compromised? Other questions can also be asked:

1. How much hard information does the marketplace deserve?
2. How much relevant information are marketers obligated to provide?
3. Should potential customers be left to seek out information on their own?
4. When developing promotion strategies, at what audience level should the information be presented?
5. How much of the "policing" of marketing should be undertaken by the government and how much should be left to the industry?

The lesson to be learned here is that those with whom marketing professionals interact—their peers, competitors, customers, government, society—all have different conceptions concerning the goals that marketing should strive to achieve. Furthermore, when there may be agreement on goals, there is likely to be disagreement on the specific strategies and tactics that are acceptable for achieving those goals. Once again, marketing professionals find themselves in a conflict situation, attempting to deal with conflicting demands placed on them and the activities they perform.

There are some who profess that the marketplace, itself, is moral. Furthermore, the marketplace is an economic mechanism that operates fine without externally imposed constraints. They argue that there are moral constraints built into the way the marketplace works (Camenisch, 1991). One argument goes like this. Dishonest marketers will be unsuccessful. The marketplace will eliminate them. *What do you think? Does your answer change if you think in terms of the short run and the long run?*

Surely, bad products run their course (often quickly) in the marketplace. But many other dishonest aspects of marketing are more difficult to uncover. Products are complex, and many are offered on the basis of long-term performance. Therefore, much time must pass before their performance can truly be evaluated. Furthermore, potential negative results of using the product may not easily be discovered. For

The Marketplace Is Moral

Table 4.3 Company Threats to Ethical Behavior

A firm that routinely ignores or violates internal codes of ethics
A firm that always looks for simple solutions to ethical problems and is satisfied with "quick fixes"
A firm unwilling to take an ethical stand when there is financial cost to the decision
A firm that creates an internal environment that either encourages unethical behavior or discourages ethical behavior
A firm that usually sends its ethical problems to the legal department
A firm that looks at ethics solely as a public relations tool to enhance its image
A firm that treats its employees differently from its customers
A firm that is unfair or arbitrary in its performance appraisal standards
A firm that has no procedures or policies for handling ethical problems
A firm that provides no mechanisms for internal whistle-blowing
A firm that lacks clear lines of communication within the organization
A firm that is sensitive only to the needs of shareholders
A firm that encourages its employees to leave their personal ethical values at the door

SOURCE: Cooke (1991). Reprinted by permission of Kluwer Academic Publishers.

example, can you really describe the performance level you want in an automobile? And then are you willing to pay for that performance level? What potential side effects will occur from the extensive use of chemicals in this country? How can you assess the potential side effects from prescription drugs? Although answers to questions such as these are being developed, are marketers knowingly marketing inferior products and achieving high levels of success over the long run?

Other Threats to Ethical Decision Making

There are many other aspects of organizations that, because of their existence, place marketing professionals at ethical risk. One is an organization that normally emphasizes short-term revenues over long-term considerations. As you have seen, ethical situations are complex. They require an objective evaluation that should not be constrained by a shortsighted focus on the next quarter's earnings. Many solutions to ethical problems require a long-term commitment (Cooke, 1991). We will conclude our discussion of threats to ethical behavior by presenting several other organizational threats to ethical decision making in Table 4.3. The next section of the text will provide a discussion of how other individuals can influence the ethical decision making of marketing professionals.

■ THE ROLE OF SIGNIFICANT OTHERS

"Plans fail for lack of counsel, but with many advisers they succeed" (Proverbs 15:22). Clearly, it is important for marketing professionals to seek counsel from others. But care must be taken. Obviously, marketing professionals work with many others as they make decisions. Those others will exert varying degrees of influence on the behavior of marketing professionals. This section will deal with the role and influence of "significant others." Marketing professionals deal with many individuals who have a wealth of experience in many situations. They should seek counsel but be careful because no counselor has the right or responsibility to make decisions for someone else.

In Chapter 3, the term *significant others* was introduced in the context of discussing the influence of family and friends, customers, and competitors on the marketing professional's ethical decision making. The term is used to describe all those individuals who have some influence or some stake in the decisions of the marketing professional (Freeman, 1984). Figure 4.2 presents a framework that identifies the significant others who might be involved in an individual salesperson's exchange behavior. A quick glance at Figure 4.2 reveals that the salesperson comes in contact, directly or indirectly, with many individuals. *What do you think is the likelihood that all of these individuals can agree on all of the aspects of a sales transaction?*

A key question for the marketing professional revolves around the extent to which these significant others influence the decision making of the marketing professional. Different situations and circumstances can change the influence of significant others. The point here is that all marketing professionals make decisions in a set of relationships with others (Niebaur, 1963, 1970, chap. 1; Winter, 1966). Individuals attempt to fit their actions in response to the others who are involved in this web of relationships.

Marketing professionals can and do experience many pressures from others, both inside and outside their organizations. All too often, these marketing professionals must make decisions without much support from the organization. *Before you read on, what kind of people does the marketing professional encounter?* Suppose marketing professionals are continuously exposed to others who are dedicated to their own survival and reward? Such people are more concerned about reward than fairness. And they have the implicit support of many who would say, "Let the economic function of the organization set the ethical tone for the organization. The invisible hand of the market will moderate the negatives caused by the pursuit of self-interests." *Do you agree with this statement?*

As you read in the section on ambivalence, marketing professionals are influenced by the way they are evaluated and rewarded. If an individual's evaluations and rewards are placed in the counternorms camp, the organization is implicitly encouraging questionable behaviors. What happens when a group of individuals recognize that counternorms are the way to go? Under such pressures to get ahead, the individual may be tempted to pursue advancement at the expense of others both inside and outside the organization. The individual might engage in behaviors that can be described as cutting corners, seeking to win at all costs, making things seem

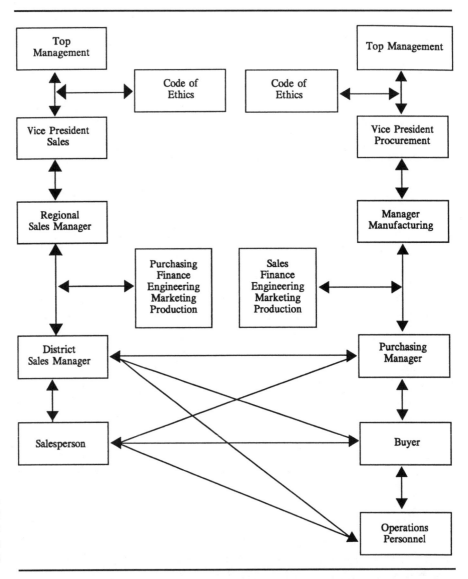

Figure 4.2. Relationships That May Affect Salespeople as Decision Makers

better than they are, or taking advantage of others. All of these reflect a myopic view of performance—a short-term view of performance at the expense of long-term implications (Andrews, 1989). Unfortunately, it is very easy for marketing professionals to fall into the trap of doing what is directly and immediately rewarded. Quantifiable and short-term results are much more visible and easy to achieve than long-term considerations of quality and future consequences of decisions.

Before we discuss how others might influence the behavior of marketing professionals, let's say a word about top management. Top managers represent a key group of significant others. Many have recognized that the activities of top management can help reduce the ethical conflicts experienced by marketing professionals (e.g., Chonko & Hunt, 1985; Hunt, Chonko, & Wilcox, 1984; Weaver & Ferrell, 1977). Proponents of top management influence usually draw three conclusions. First, top management can serve as a role model by sending unambiguous messages. In other words, top managers must practice the same set of standards that they endorse verbally and in writing. Second, top management should discourage unethical behavior by promptly reprimanding unethical conduct. Third, top management must play an active role in the development and enforcement of company, industry, and professional codes of conduct. *How do you view this? Can you think of any situations in which someone who played a role as a top manager had an influence on your behavior?*

The Influence of Top Management

There are many ways in which individuals are influenced by others. A discussion of all of these ways is well beyond the intention of this book. This section of the book will describe three influence approaches: (a) differential association theory, (b) role theory, and (c) group processes.

How Others Influence Ethical Behavior

Differential Association Theory

Differential association theory (Sutherland & Cressy, 1970) makes the assumption that ethical and unethical behavior is learned as a marketing professional interacts with others who are members of the groups with whom the marketing professional associates. If a marketing professional encounters more ethical people than unethical people, his or her behavior will tend toward being ethical. The opposite is also true. Indeed, associations with peers have been found to be more influential on ethical behavior than the individual's own belief systems (Zey-Ferrell, Weaver, & Ferrell, 1979).

As you have seen, top management and supervisors have a strong influence over the ethical behavior of their subordinates. For example, less experienced employees will tend to go along with their managers because they feel this demonstrates loyalty in matters regarding ethical judgments (Trevino & Youngblood, 1990). So a person's loyalty or a person's need to be accepted may be a more powerful influence on a person's behavior than that person's knowledge of right and wrong. *What do you think? Have you observed others learning behaviors from the groups with whom they interact?*

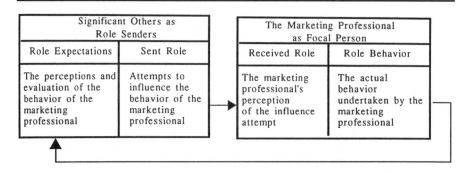

Figure 4.3. An Illustration of the Role Episode Process

SOURCE: Adapted from Katz, D. and R. L. Kahn. (1966). *The Social Psychology of Organizations.* New York: John Wiley & Sons, Inc. Copyright © 1966 by John Wiley & Sons. Reprinted by permission of John Wiley & Sons, Inc.

Role Theory

Role theory can provide some insights into how individuals make ethically related decisions. An individual's role set refers to the set of relationships that a person has that are the result of the position the individual occupies in the organization (Merton, 1957). If you recall Figure 4.2, the individuals identified would constitute the salesperson's role set. The characteristics of the members of the role set can help us gain insight into how individual marketing professionals make decisions (Miles, 1977).

Let's take a look at how role set theory can help in our understanding of ethical decision making. Figure 4.3 depicts the role episode process (White & Wooten, 1983). The role episode includes a role sender (a significant other) and a role receiver (the marketing professional). The role episode is a continuous process of sending, receiving, responding to, and sending new expectations. Four concepts are central to understanding role episodes:

1. Role expectations—Evaluative standards applied by significant others to an individual marketing professional's behavior
2. Sent role—The communications that stem from role expectations that are sent by members of the role set to influence the behavior of the marketing professional
3. Received role—The marketing professional's perception of the expectations being communicated by the members of the role set
4. Role behavior—The response of the marketing professional (Katz & Kahn, 1966, p. 88)

Although Figure 4.3 provides a concise way of looking at the influence of significant others on the marketing professional's decision making, it is a simplistic look. A variety of factors (e.g., individual and organizational characteristics) affect the relationship between the marketing professional and members of his or her role set. Figure 4.3, however, does serve to illustrate that attempts to influence individual behavior do come from many sources and that they are continuous and constantly being changed.

Group Processes

As we have discussed the influence of significant others on the individual marketing professional confronted with ethical dilemmas, it should be clear that an individual's perception of right and wrong is often not the sole determining factor in his or her decisions (Trevino, 1986). At times, an individual's beliefs interact with the beliefs of others and can shape that individual's behavioral choices. And at times, individuals can engage in unethical behavior when the culture of a group and its prevailing reward structure overwhelm an individual's belief system (Sims, 1992). As stated in Chapter 1, sometimes individuals violate their own personal ethics.

Norms. Norms are standards of behavior that groups expect of their members. They define acceptable and unacceptable behavior within the group, and, sometimes, outside the group. Norms are established in an effort to establish some degree of conformity within a group. At times, norms of a group can be in conflict with norms of the larger organization. At times, the norms of the group can be in conflict with the values of the individual. As we have already discussed, the organization's culture represents a set of norms concerning various acceptable and unacceptable behaviors. But when groups form, they sometimes engage in activities that foster questionable behavior, which serves as the basis for establishing counternorms described earlier in this chapter. One such activity, known as groupthink, is described next.

Groupthink. When a marketing professional is deeply involved in a group, "group-think" may occur (Janis, 1972). The bottom of Figure 4.4 depicts the groupthink process. Conditions that lead to groupthink are depicted in the antecedent box in Figure 4.4. When such conditions occur, the members of the group develop defense mechanisms that lead to a pattern of avoidance. Such defense mechanisms may include (a) misjudging relevant warnings, (b) inventing new arguments to support a chosen policy, (c) failure to explore the implications of ambiguous events, (d) forgetting information that would allow for challenge of selected courses of action, and (e) misperception of signals of oncoming danger.

Also shown in Figure 4.4 are the major symptoms of a group that is caught in groupthink (Van Fleet, 1991). Such symptoms may be viewed as flaws in the ethical decision-making process, such as (a) consideration of few ethical alternatives, (b) a win-at-all-costs approach, (c) rejection of dissenting opinions, and (d) selection bias in information considered in making the decision.

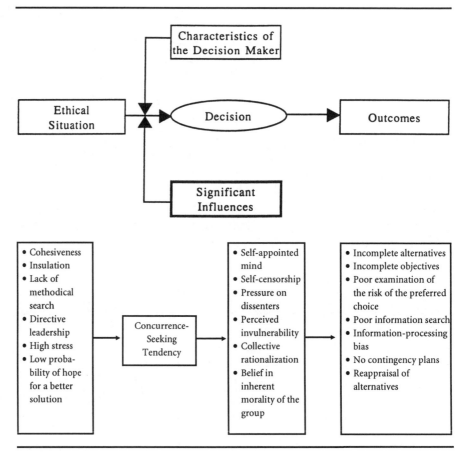

Figure 4.4. Group Factors That Influence the Ethical Decision-Making Process

SOURCE: Adapted with the permission of The Free Press, a Division of Simon & Schuster from *Decision Making: A Psychological Analysis of Conflict, Choice, and Commitment* by Irving L. Janis and Leon Mann. Copyright © 1977 by The Free Press.

Think about the times you have joined certain groups. After joining, you were probably provided opportunities to learn about and become committed to the group's goals and methods of operation. Although commitment to a group can have very positive implications, it can also lead individuals to seek continued success for the group even to the extent of being willing to engage in unethical behaviors to achieve that success.

Recalling our discussion of the need for affiliation, this need is often a major determinant in an individual's willingness to conform to the group. The approval or disapproval of an individual by group members can be a powerful motivator.

Moral Types	Descriptors	
Hedonist	Make physical pleasures the supreme goal in their lives Key question: Which course of action will yield the greatest pleasure?	**Table 4.4** A Taxonomy of Moral Types
Profit maximizer	Goal of making as much money as possible Key question: Which course of action will make the most money? All their feelings and associations can be melted down to dollars.	
Socialite	A social butterfly, a party animal Key question: Which course of action will help me best get along with the group? If you want to know what this person thinks, find out who spoke to him or her most recently. They dread being by themselves.	
Politician	Life centers around power and glory Key question: Which course of action will increase my power and glory? These people have enormous egos. These people have boundless ambitions and undertake reckless actions.	
Self-actualizer	Spiritual values predominate Key question: Which course of action will help me become a better person? These people have new insights, reform old ways, initiate new ways of thinking, strike out on new paths.	
Craftsman	A technician Positives: Creative, knowledgeable, independent, self-reliant, hardworking Negatives: Sadistic, forceful, manipulative, nontrustworthy	
Company person	Main goal in life to belong to an organization Positives: Service oriented, loyal, responsible, humble, sensitive to the needs of others, dependable, pleasant, trustworthy Negatives: Fear, worry, dependency, lacking vision, risk aversive, low drive, indecisive, change resistant	
Gamesman	Dominant goal in life to gain prestige, glory, fame Positives: Inventive, flexible, change oriented, competitive, team player, independent, risk taker, impartial, high energy, idealistic Negatives: Lack of conviction, rebellious, manipulative, lack of intimacy, lonely	

Table 4.4 presents a classification of eight moral types (Maccoby, 1978; Pattan, 1984). In dealings with others, we tend to classify or stereotype people according to the values they hold—or seem to hold. There are probably no individuals who fit any of the eight descriptions found in Table 4.4. Many, however, will exhibit predominant tendencies that lead us into classifying them as one kind of moral type or another. Most of us have to satisfy more than one need to survive.

    The values, philosophies, and leadership styles of those with whom marketing professionals interact will affect those interactions. As you have already seen, many individuals can influence the behavior of marketing professionals as they work to achieve objectives, and according to the descriptions in Table 4.4, each individual will have tendencies that are exhibited in these interactions. In other words, we learn to

**Moral Types:
Stereotyping
Significant Others**

"read" people—to anticipate "where they are coming from." The influence styles of others are reflections of their moral types.

One interesting way of looking at influence is to view it from two opposing views of human nature (Pattan, 1984). One is pessimistic. One is optimistic. According to the pessimist view, individuals ultimately act for their own self-interest. Helping others is viewed only as a means of self-advancement. This view is consistent with ethical egoist theories, which state that people should perform only those acts that benefit them. From a managerial influence perspective, the pessimist assumes that individuals are lazy, selfish, stupid, irresponsible, and immature. McGregor's Theory X, authoritarian leadership styles, and task-oriented leadership styles are all reflections of this pessimistic viewpoint of human nature. Energetic, intelligent, and independent leaders must direct others autocratically and keep them terrorized, otherwise no work will get done. *How do you feel about this pessimistic viewpoint?*

The optimistic viewpoint takes root in the notion that people are somebody. People have value. People bring something to the table. The optimist is motivated by self-interests and by the interests of others. Nonegoistic ethical theories, such as utilitarianism are consistent with the optimistic viewpoint of human behavior. According to utilitarian theory, one should always act in a way for the greatest amount of good for the greatest number of people.

Management theories such as McGregor's Theory Y, democratic leadership, and people-oriented leadership are consistent with this optimistic viewpoint of people. Leadership styles such as these work on the presumption that individuals want more than income, power, and glory from their jobs. Such leaders would strive to achieve a balance between organizational goals and needs and personal goals and needs. *Now, how do you feel about the optimist's viewpoint?*

◪ WHAT MARKETING PROFESSIONALS CAN DO ABOUT UNETHICAL BEHAVIOR

I will close this chapter with some comments concerning how marketing professionals can deal with unethical behavior. I will begin by saying that a second kind of ethical dilemma confronts marketing professionals. Oftentimes, the marketing professional faces a situation in which he or she knows that someone else in the organization is in violation of ethical principles. Table 4.5 provides several alternative courses of action, along with some pros and cons, available to the marketing professional when confronted with a situation in which a colleague is acting in a questionable way (Nielson, 1987).

Not thinking about it would do nothing to solve the problem. This is also true of the *leave* and *go along and get along* strategies. Moreover, few organizations have mechanisms that allow and facilitate an individual's rights to object to a questionable situation. Because of this, *conscientious objecting* and *protesting* are often judged to be poor alternatives, and other courses of action are sought. *Publicly blowing the whistle* is often disregarded because of the individual's fear of losing his or her job, a future reward, promotion opportunities, or all three. If the marketing professional knows how to negotiate, if there is time to negotiate, if the key people in authority are reasonable, and if there is the possibility of a positive outcome for all concerned, *negotiating* may be an appropriate strategy.

Secretly threatening to blow the whistle provides the organization with the time to change its unethical behavior without risking public damage from the revelation of that behavior. This is also true of *secretly blowing the whistle.* In both cases, the whistle blower can be discovered through the means of lie detector tests, a practice undertaken in some circumstances. Finally, *sabotage* can be effective, but many question the ethical nature of sabotage. Sabotage is a strategy of "the pot calling the kettle black." *What is your opinion of each of these approaches? Can you think of other ways to deal with unethical behavior? Is a marketing professional capable of perceiving all the alternatives that might be viable in a given situation?*

Responsibility and Accountability

Ultimately, it is the individual who is responsible and accountable for the performance of unethical behaviors. Although organizations endeavor to provide a variety of ethical guides, the individual still must decide how to behave. The individual marketing professional assesses the "right" and "wrong" of alternative behaviors. Ideally, when a behavior is judged to be wrong, it is not undertaken. But as we have already discussed, some people will violate their absolutes from time to time. Some will judge the risks associated with the wrong behavior to be such that it is worth violating their absolutes. *What factors influence the individual to select the wrong behavior?*

Clearly, the individual's ethical behavior is influenced by personal, professional, work, legal, social, religious, and peer considerations. It is the individual marketing professional, however, as decision maker, who assesses the rewards and punishments associated with various behaviors. Some judgment concerning risk, usually in the form of detection of the unethical behavior and the consequences of that behavior, is involved. To simplify, if a particular behavior is judged very risky or the payoff is judged not to be high, the individual may avoid the behavior. But as you already know, different professionals have different attitudes toward risk.

In dealing with the problems of decision making, marketing professionals must contend with the assignment of responsibilities. The term *responsibility* refers to the

	Consequences	
Actions	Advantages	Disadvantages
Not think about it	Avoids the danger of getting into a zero-sum game with colleagues	The risk of going in the wrong direction
Go along and get along	Same as "not think about it"	Same as "not think about it"
		Individuals slowly conform . . . maybe to the wrong action
Protest	Individual feels good about making effort to stop unethical behavior	Organization disregards protest Organization punishes protester
Conscientiously object	Makes clear statement that one person feels that action is unethical	Few organizations recognize individual rights to object
	Person feels good about self for making effort to stop unethical behavior	May hurt chances for rewards and advancement
Leave	Signals that organization will lose good people if unethical behavior continues	Most people are replaceable and if replacement cooperates with unethical behavior, what is gained?
	Person who leaves may join a competitor	
	Person who leaves feels better because he or she did not cooperate with unethical behavior	
Secretly blow the whistle	Can be very effective	Feelings of cowardice
	If whistle-blower remains secret, retaliation cannot occur	Creation of atmosphere of mistrust
		What will whistle-blower do if confronted by firm—tell the truth or lie?
Publicly blow the whistle	Can be effective	Organization may attack the whistle-blower
	Whistle-blower may be treated as a hero by many	It is difficult to interact with those one is criticizing
		It may be difficult to work with those who hold a grudge
Secretly threaten to blow whistle	Same as "secretly blow the whistle"	Does not permit dialogue between upper and lower managers

Table 4.5
Alternative Courses
of Action Available
in Ethical Situations

	When it works, organization is not hurt by bad publicity	Might prevent injured consumers or clients from receiving remedies
Sabotage	Can be effective	Sabotage is not dialogue
	Identity of saboteur might be protected	Retaliation might occur against the saboteur or against others
		Innocent people may be fired
Negotiate	Individual action may lead to small-group consensus that will be more effective than individual action	Does not work well in situations that are zero-sum, lose-win, in nature
		Individual who perceives ethical problem may not know how to negotiate, may lose "cool"
	Win-win solutions are possible	

SOURCE: Nielson (1987). Reprinted by permission of Kluwer Academic Publishers.

scope of tasks assigned to an individual by the nature of that individual's position in the organization. Traditionally, business responsibilities are to stockholders, employees, consumers, and society. Accountability, on the other hand, refers to blaming or praising someone for their actions. In today's business environment, work responsibilities are such that virtually everyone shares in the accountability for an action. In theory, this means that everyone should be praised (or blamed). In actuality, this means that it is almost impossible to assign accountability to anyone. This lack of accountability (the low likelihood of punishment) is one of the major catalysts for unethical behavior.

The marketing professional's work should help him or her develop a sense of responsibility and accountability. Today, many seek excuses for not fulfilling their responsibilities. Over time, such excuse making can become an accepted way of doing things to an individual to the point where the individual becomes oblivious to his or her responsibilities. Furthermore, as stated earlier, it seems that organizations have taken great pains to remove the burden of accountability from their employees. My ethic, however, teaches that there is accountability: " 'Therefore, O house of Israel, I will judge you, each one according to his ways,' declares the Sovereign Lord" (Ezekiel 18:30). The concepts of *Jen* and *Chun tzu,* from Confucianism, also speak to the issue of accountability and responsibility (see Smith, 1991, pp. 172-173). As a simple illustration, these concepts are described by the ideal host or hostess, who asks, "What can I do to accommodate my guests?" not "What can I get from them?" In short, the host or hostess knows his or her responsibilities and stands ready to be held accountable for those responsibilities.

Diffusion of Responsibility

Accountability is quite different from responsibility. For marketing professionals, accountability (blame) often has little to do with the merits of a situation. Rather, accountability has become a matter of social definition (Jackall, 1993). Because it is difficult to assign accountability for many marketing decisions, what often happens is that those who are vulnerable get blamed for the mistakes.

Marketing professionals who fear blame often set up structures that so diffuse responsibilities that someone will become the scapegoat for any questionable actions that are discovered. The scapegoat may simply be in the wrong place at the wrong time, as in the case of the person who gets promoted into an area that is, subsequently, found guilty of ethical violations. Those who wish to engage in questionable behaviors can hide behind the web of relationships that make up the structure of accountability and responsibility in large organizations—these webs are extremely difficult to untangle.

Rationalizations

Perhaps you have been asking why marketing professionals would engage in behaviors that would hurt themselves, their organizations, or others? We read, all too frequently, of behaviors that illicit responses from us such as, "How could they be so stupid?" "How could they have done that?" "Didn't they know any better?" First of all, when we read something in the paper or hear it on the news, we are not privy to all the facts and therefore must be careful about the judgments we make. Second, when individuals make decisions, they often rationalize, and such rationalizations can lead to unethical behaviors. Four commonly held rationalizations for behavior are presented next:

1. A belief that the behavior is within reasonable ethical and legal limits—that is, the behavior is *not really* immoral or illegal
2. A belief that the behavior is in the best interests of the individual, the organization, or both—the individual would somehow be *expected* to undertake the behavior
3. A belief that the behavior is *safe* because it will never be found out or punished, the classic crime and punishment issue of discovery
4. A belief that because the behavior helps the organization the organization will *condone* it and even protect the individual who engages in the behavior (Gellerman, 1986, p. 88)

The idea that an action is not really wrong goes back to Adam and Eve in the Garden of Eden. As you have seen, marketing professionals are placed in ambiguous situations. Information is lacking, alternatives are not clear. Goals conflict, peoples' expectations conflict. Put in enough situations, one might conclude that whatever behavior has not been specifically labeled as wrong must be right. This is particularly true if such behaviors have been rewarded in the past.

Top management seldom asks marketing professionals to do wrong. But it is common for top managers to leave things unsaid or take the approach that "what I don't know won't hurt me." To keep their own hands clean, they distance themselves from the marketer's decisions. But by not overtly discouraging such behaviors, they may actually be sending an implied message of support for such behaviors. Unfortunately, the marketer often does not realize a mistake has been made until it has been made and cannot be undone. Perhaps the best advice under such circumstances is the adage, "When in doubt . . . don't."

When a behavior is in the best interests of the individual, the organization, or both, the interests of others are often not considered. As we have seen, marketers who are ambitious look for ways to shine—to outperform their colleagues. Often, this approach results in choosing alternatives that pay off in the short run, but do not pay off in the long run. For example, how long can you provide poor service to a customer who has purchased one of your products? One person may get credit for the sale, get promoted, and then leave the problem of poor service to the person who replaces him or her.

Unfortunately, for those whose motivation is that they believe they can get away with unethical behavior, they often do get away with it. The only way to deal with unethical behaviors that are difficult to detect is to make them more detectable. This may simply mean promoting higher probabilities of detection. As an analogy, it has been shown that neighborhoods that post crime watch signs are less frequented by crime than are neighborhoods that do not post such signs. Although not foolproof, the sign is a sufficient deterrent to some.

Finally, some marketers believe that their organizations will condone unethical behavior if it results in profits for the organization. Most organizations have ethics codes that detail unacceptable activities. But these codes are not effective unless they are enforced by top managers. Top management must draw the line between loyalty to the organization and the violation of legal and ethical codes. To avoid serious loyalty problems, top management must continuously stress the consequences of unethical and illegal behavior. On the positive side, they must continuously stress the rewards associated with legal and ethical behavior. Top management must make it clear that organization loyalty is not above unethical or illegal behavior. Consider Newsline 4.1. What rationalizations might have been used to justify some of the decisions made concerning cigarettes?

Newsline 4.1

FDA Cites Evidence of Cigarette Makers Keeping Nicotine at Addictive Levels

Washington—The Food and Drug Administration said there is growing evidence that tobacco companies deliberately maintain the level of nicotine in cigarettes at addictive levels.

The FDA's statement marked the federal government's latest attack on the tobacco industry.

The FDA's finding, if confirmed, could provide a legal basis for FDA regulation of cigarettes as a drug, according to FDA Commissioner David Kessler. But acknowledging that such regulatory action could have "dramatic effects" on society, Dr. Kessler suggested that the agency wouldn't act without a directive from Congress. There have been various proposals for almost 20 years that the FDA regulate cigarettes, and it isn't considered likely that Congress will act now.

Several Moves by U.S.

Nonetheless, several government actions during the past 14 months have made business increasingly difficult for the tobacco industry in the U.S.

"The Clinton Administration is the first to have been willing to acknowledge the extent of the public health harm caused by tobacco," says Matthew Myers, an attorney who represents major health groups on smoking issues.

The Clinton Administration has proposed sharply raising the excise tax on cigarettes to help pay for health-care reform, and several tobacco experts said that the report that the FDA is considering regulating cigarettes as a drug should strengthen the government's hand.

"This is going to support the government's case for a tax and it's going to make it harder for the industry to fight against it," says S. Leigh Ferst, a tobacco analyst at Prudential Securities Inc. a unit of Prudential Insurance Co. of America.

Already causing major problems for the industry is the Environmental Protection Agency report issued last year that said that second-hand cigarette smoke causes lung cancer, a finding that served as a powerful tool in prodding businesses, restaurants, local governments and even sports stadiums across the country to ban or severely restrict smoking to avoid liability for subjecting people to such smoke.

Last week, Surgeon General Dr. Joycelyn Elders urged a ban on cigarette advertising directed at teenagers.

The FDA's comment, which many view as a change in position, came in response to petitions from the Coalition on Smoking OR Health, which comprises the American

Heart Association, the American Lung Association and the American Cancer Society. They are urging the FDA to regulate cigarettes as drugs.

Drugs are regulated under the Food, Drug and Cosmetic Act. A product can be categorized as a drug if it is deemed to be for therapeutic or diagnostic use or to affect the structure or function of the body. Dr. Kessler said that the FDA traditionally hasn't asserted jurisdiction over most cigarette products, although there isn't any exemption for them under the act's definition of drugs.

"Evidence is accumulating that suggests that cigarette manufacturers may intend that their products contain nicotine to satisfy an addiction," Dr. Kessler wrote in his letter.

Tobacco Institute Disagrees

Thomas Lauria, spokesman for the Tobacco Institute, assailed the FDA commissioner's statements, and said the agency's evidence isn't significant. "They have been raising this issue since the '60s," Mr. Lauria said. "The fact is tobacco isn't a drug, and is already being sufficiently regulated in every aspect."

But Scott Ballin, vice president, public affairs, at the Heart Association, said that evidence gathered by that organization and the FDA shows a "very calculated and intended effort" by the tobacco industry to control the amount of nicotine in cigarettes. He said companies are actively studying ways to extract nicotine from tobacco and pack it into cigarettes.

"The tobacco industry is in the drug business. We know it. People who are desperately fighting their addiction to nicotine know it," Mr. Ballin said. "And now the FDA knows it."

The FDA's Dr. Kessler said that while technology exists to remove nicotine from cigarettes or control its level in them, cigarettes are still marketed with sufficient nicotine to "produce and sustain addiction."

Mr. Lauria and cigarette-company officials deny that there is any deliberate manipulation of nicotine levels in cigarettes. The companies argue that cigarettes that are extremely low in nicotine have failed to catch on with smokers. A few years ago, Philip Morris Co. dropped Next, a cigarette with its lowest nicotine level to date, after "it was rejected by consumers," a company spokeswoman said.

Reps. Mike Synar (D., Okla.) and Richard Durbin (D., Ill.) have sponsored legislation that would give the FDA stronger and broader authority to regulate the manufacture, sale and promotion of tobacco products. "That piece of legislation has never made it out of committee, and I don't expect it to this time, either," Mr. Lauria said.

The Centers for Disease Control and Prevention said about 400,000 Americans die from smoking every year. About 45 million Americans smoke, and a recent study released by Dr. Elders said at least 3.1 million teenagers smoke, an increase from last year.

One excellent way for marketing professionals to deal with ethical problems is to focus on what it takes for job credibility. Obviously, there are many answers to this question. Certainly a commitment to excellence is needed. How about initiative? A positive attitude toward authority? Honesty? If marketing professionals approach their tasks faithfully and diligently, they will still encounter ethical situations. Oftentimes, ethical problems occur because marketers have shirked responsibilities; they try to play "catch up," and the result can be decisions made on the basis of incomplete and poor information.

CHAPTER SUMMARY In this chapter, elements of the work environment and their influence on ethical decision making were discussed. Organizational elements that represent threats to ethical decision making include ethical ambivalence, the work setting, annual objectives, performance appraisals, pyramid politics, the goals of marketing, and the notion that marketing is moral.

Ethical decision making is also influenced by many with whom marketing professionals are associated. Top management can be particularly influential, but so can groups to which the marketing professional belongs. Even with such influences, marketing professionals have many options when facing ethical situations. But sometimes these options are clouded by diffusion of responsibilities and rationalizations.

▨ SOME QUESTIONS FOR DISCUSSION

1. What conflicts can occur between the individual and the organization ethic presented in Table 4.1?

2. In the text, you were asked to identify norms and counternorms at your school. What were some of these? Find out what other students in your class think. Now ask your instructor for his or her opinion. What is the result of all the comparisons?

3. Describe the ethical problems that might be introduced by holding to rigid objectives in the performance appraisal process.

4. Team selling and team buying are becoming more and more common in marketing decision making. Describe how you would go about developing a reward system for such teams. What norms would be included and what counternorms might arise?

5. Do you think that the influence of top management on ethical decision making is overstated? Why do you think so?

6. Can you think of any situations in which you encountered groupthink? What were some of the things that happened? Break into small groups and share groupthink experiences. Are there common elements in the situations described?

7. Comment on the alternative courses of action described in Table 4.5. What do you think about these options? Which one(s) do you think you might consider in an ethical situation? Would your viewpoint change if the person in question was your subordinate? Your supervisor? Your company president?

5

How Marketers Have Responded to Ethical Problems

PURPOSE

To demonstrate that many marketing organizations have not ignored the ethical problems in the marketing profession. They have undertaken many programs and activities designed to eliminate or reduce the incidence of ethical problems.

MAJOR POINTS

Marketing professionals have attempted to deal with ethical problems in a number of different ways.

Codes of ethics are important elements of marketing ethics programs.

Many of the responses of marketing professionals and many of the ethical problems experienced by marketing professionals were described by President John F. Kennedy in his consumer "bill of rights."

> What has been will be again,
> What has been done will be done again;
> There is nothing new under the sun.
> Is there anything of which one can say, "Look! This is something new"?
> It was here already, long ago;
> It was here before our time.
> There is no remembrance of men of old,
> And even those who are yet to come will not be remembered
> By those who follow. (Ecclesiastes 1:9-11)

In other words, any notion of novelty is illusory. We may think some behaviors are new, but, likely, they are only new experiences for us. We often have difficulty remembering the past. Or we rarely search through the past to find guidelines concerning how to deal with the "new" situation. The novelty of ethical situations is based on our faulty perceptions or our faulty memories. True there are new ways of doing old things. Computer fraud is relatively new, but fraud is not. Misrepresentation of new facts is new, but misrepresentation is not. Disagreements between cultures concerning ethics may appear to be new, but they are not. In short, we can learn much about today's ethical problems by looking to the past for insights.

The subject of this chapter concerns marketers' responses to ethical problems. The collection of ways to deal with ethical problems presented here can be referred to as a starting point in dealing with any of the ethical problems you will encounter in this text or those you will encounter as you pursue your career. They are all based on ethical problems that have already occurred, and they are designed to act as deterrents to those problems as they arise again.

Newsline 5.1 will get you started. Note that several methods of reducing unethical behavior are recommended. As you move into Chapters 6 through 11, where you will be asked to deal with ethical problems, some of the materials presented in this chapter may serve as the starting point for recommendations you make.

Newsline 5.1

How to Make the Sale and Remain Ethical

Steve is a bright young man just starting his career in sales. He had impressed senior management during his months in the new employee training program and was quickly identified as a "fast track" young man with potential for rapid advancement into a management position.

However, after completing the company training program and being assigned to a sales representative position, he was having difficulty selling. Yes, he had gotten a few small accounts, but nothing to brag about. Finally, the opportunity to make a "big ticket" sale seemed within reach. A customer was interested in placing a major order with Steve. However, the customer demanded a kickback. Steve's manager told him that this was normal and expected, but Steve had never heard about it during his months of training. What should he do? Should he accept the order and make the payment? Should he say no and report the manager? Steve has invested almost a year in the company and this is his opportunity to shine. Also, his manager has been good to him when he hasn't been bringing in any new accounts. He likes his manager and so do most of the other sales representatives.

Thousands of young people entering the work force today face such ethical dilemmas. One might ask. "Haven't people always encountered such problems?" The answer is yes. However, in the past they were better prepared to deal with them because ethical values were taught and communicated through the family, religious leaders, and our schools. Today these institutions and groups do not have the influence they once did.

Today most people learn their ethical values from the media. What do they see and hear? They see ads and commercials that encourage materialism and deception. On the nightly news they hear of government officials who admit to lying and stealing. They hear about investment bankers who use insider information to make fortunes on Wall Street. In recent times, people in every segment of our society have been guilty of unethical practices.

In addition to the lack of deep-rooted ethical values, there are other reasons why many people act unethically when they encounter a moral dilemma at work. The prime reason is the influence of the employee's immediate supervisor. Let's go back to Steve, the new sales representative. If his manager condones the kickback, Steve more than likely will act accordingly. At this point in Steve's career he is highly dependent on his manager and will look to him for guidance. A survey by the American Management Association asked why people acted unethically at work, and the number one reason given was the influence of one's immediate supervisor.

Another reason why many employees act unethically is that they feel pressure to reach very difficult objectives. This is especially true in decentralized companies when operating units are given unrealistic objectives. If senior management one day espouses corporate ethics and the next day tells the sales managers they must increase market share by some outrageous number and by whatever means necessary, what is the message most managers get? When the pressure is on, ethics is not necessarily put on hold, but certainly many line managers view it that way.

Finally, in many companies the adherence to a strict chain of command can make acting ethically very difficult. Should Steve go over his manager's head and speak to the district sales manager or is it enough that he reported the kickback to his boss? Many people would say in a similar situation, "I told my boss I had no power to go higher. I don't report to anybody but my sales manager."

Most people want to act ethically and want to work for an ethical manager. In fact, several recent employee surveys asked what was the most important leadership ability one should possess, and the quality most frequently cited was "integrity."

Many companies are adopting codes of conduct to guide their employees. However, it takes more than writing and distributing a code of conduct. Once the code has been developed, it must be communicated and reinforced by management from the top down. Ethics must be part of every manager's training.

Most difficult business decisions are made under time pressure. Thus, by exposing managers in training sessions to potential ethical dilemmas in advance and having them apply problem-solving techniques to the issues, one increases the likelihood that managers will make the right decisions when they encounter similar dilemmas on the job.

No one, of course, can guarantee that ethics training will eliminate unethical behavior and that all managers will act ethically. No one can ensure that, anymore than one can guarantee that Steve will be a good salesperson because he completed the company sales training program. However, since most employees want to act ethically and want to work for a manager with integrity, a company must show that it truly supports ethical conduct. If a company demonstrates its support by training and reinforcing ethical behavior on the job, most employees will act ethically. Since the reputation of a company is so important for continued success, a company must demonstrate its support for ethical conduct. Not only is it doing the right thing, it's also good business.

SOURCE: Finn (1988). Reprinted with permission of *Sales & Marketing Management*, 355 Park Avenue South, New York, NY 10010-1789.

▧ GUIDES TO ETHICAL DECISION MAKING

Helpful and practical ethical guidelines exist in many organizations to help marketing professionals make ethical decisions. Ethical guidelines are not new. For example, over 3,000 years ago it was written, "Do not have two differing weights in your bag—one heavy, one light. Do not have two differing measures in your house—one large, one small" (Deuteronomy 25:13-14). Also, in Confucianism, the concept of *Li* refers to the way things ought to be done (see Smith, 1991). Confucius felt that people need models to guide their behavior, that people were not capable of determining for themselves what ought to be done. Li is a way of life provided by Confucius so that no one would ever be in doubt about how to behave. Like Confucius's concept of Li, marketing professionals use guidelines for behavior, a sample of which is shown in Table 5.1. Several advantages can be gained from the existence and use of guidelines such as these:

1. The process of setting guidelines facilitates discussion about ethical decision making. The discussion and questions posed help marketers to more clearly focus their efforts on the real problems, and it exposes marketers to various ways of thinking about ethical problems.
2. The establishment of guidelines helps build a cohesive management character as agreement occurs between individuals who thought they had different problems.
3. Marketing professionals can learn about other areas of the organization with which they have less contact.
4. The process can help to discover ethical inconsistencies in the values held by members of the organization.
5. Top management can learn how middle and lower managers think.
6. The number and quality of alternative decision strategies will improve.

Table 5.1 Ethical Guidelines Used in Examining the Ethics of Business Decisions	Have you defined the problem correctly?
	How would you define the problem if you stood on the other side of the fence?
	How did this situation occur in the first place?
	To whom and to what do you give your loyalty as a person and as a member of the organization?
	What is your intention compared with the probable results?
	How does this intention compare with the probable results?
	Whom could your decision action injure?
	Can you discuss the problem with the affected parties before you make your decision?
	Are you confident that your position will be as valid over a long period of time as it seems now?
	Could you disclose without qualm your decision or action to your boss, your president, the board of directors, your family, society as a whole?
	What is the symbolic potential of your action if understood? If misunderstood?
	Under what conditions would you allow exceptions to your stand?

SOURCE: Reprinted by permission of *Harvard Business Review*. An exhibit from "Ethics Without the Sermon," by L. Nash (November/December, 1981). Copyright © 1981 by the President and Fellows of Harvard College; all rights reserved.

What do you think? Do the guidelines shown in Table 5.1 provide the advantages just listed?

As you will see in Chapter 7, there are many ethical problems associated with the production and marketing of a product or service. Marketers have been active in setting guidelines for product-related activities. A few of these are presented here:

1. Include a formal ethical analysis as part of the product development process.
2. Provide sufficient product instructions and appropriate warning labels for all products that are produced and marketed.
3. When consumers' safety is jeopardized by a product on the market, be proactive in recalling the product from the market.
4. Develop a set of policies that deal with the removal of products in the decline stage from the marketplace (see Laczniak & Murphy, 1993, pp. 103-106).

As you have probably experienced, salespeople also face many ethical problems. These will be described in more detail in Chapter 10. Certainly, salespeople, like all other marketing professionals, are responsible for their own behaviors. Many companies, however, have taken steps to establish a climate that encourages ethical behaviors. They provide guidelines for salespeople concerning ethics in the marketplace. A sampling of these is presented next:

1. Develop and promote a detailed and explicit ethical policy statement.
2. Sales programs, including quotas, territories, compensation, and evaluation should be set and undertaken in reasonable ways by management.

Offers should be clear so that consumers understand exactly what they are buying and how much they will have to pay.

The order form should clearly describe the goods and quantity purchased, the price and terms of payment, and any additional charges.

Receipts and contracts should show the name of the sales representative and his or her address, or the name, address, and telephone number of the firm whose product is sold.

All salespersons should promptly identify themselves to a prospective customer and should truthfully indicate the purpose of their approach to the customer, identifying the company or product brands represented.

A salesperson should obey all applicable federal, state, and local laws.

A salesperson should not disparage other products or firms.

A salesperson should explain the terms and conditions for returning a product or canceling an order.

Salespersons should not create confusion in the mind of the consumer, abuse the trust of the consumer, nor exploit the lack of experience or knowledge of the consumer.

Salespersons should respect the privacy of consumers by making every effort to make calls at times that best suit the customer's convenience and wishes.

It is a customer's right to end a sales call, and salespersons should respect that right.

All references to testimonials and other endorsements should be truthful, currently applicable, and authorized by the person or organization quoted.

Product comparisons should be fair and based on substantiated facts.

Table 5.2
Ethical Standards
Salespeople Should
Follow

SOURCE: Direct Selling Education Foundation (1989). Used with permission.

3. Sales managers should encourage salespeople to seek help when they are confronted with difficult and challenging ethical problems.

4. Sales managers and top management should encourage salesperson participation in the development of policies.

5. Sales managers and top management must enforce policies concerning ethical behavior (see Laczniak & Murphy, 1993, pp. 199-202).

Trade associations can also provide help for salespeople in dealing with ethical problems. For example, the Direct Selling Association has provided some guidelines for salespeople, and these are presented in Table 5.2.

▧ SELF-REGULATION

Most organizations favor some sort of self-regulation in dealing with ethical problems (Werner, 1992). Consider the following facts obtained from a study of

Fortune 500 companies conducted by the Center for Business Ethics at Bentley College (1986):

1. Eighty percent of firms have taken steps to incorporate ethical values in their organizations.
2. Ninety-three percent of firms have written codes of ethics.
3. Forty-four percent of firms have ethics training for employees.
4. Seventy percent of firms surveyed require ethics training.
5. Forty-four percent of firms have social audits in which areas such as equal opportunity, safety, community involvement, environmental protection, and multinational conduct are covered.
6. Eighteen percent of firms have ethics committees that set ethical policies for these firms.
7. Eight percent have an individual who acts as an ethical ombudsman or ethics adviser who provides ethics counsel concerning decisions made in the organization.
8. One percent of firms have an ethics judicial board that makes judgments concerning the ethical nature of various actions undertaken by members of the organization.

The information presented here suggests that organizations are concerned with ethical behaviors. As you can see, organizations have undertaken a variety of programs designed to regulate the incidence of unethical behavior by their employees. But as you can also see from the data, there is much work to be done in the way of establishing ethical committees, ethical advisers, and ethics judiciary boards (Hoffman, Moore, & Fedor, 1986). *How effective do you think self-regulation can be? Can you envision circumstances in which self-regulation would be the only program needed to ensure ethical behavior?*

◧ CODES OF ETHICS

Corporate codes of ethics are very common. In 1979, approximately 75% of all corporations had written codes of ethics (Ethics Resource Center, 1979). A very good code of ethics has been created by Texas Instruments and is presented in Appendix A of this chapter. The following benefits are attributed to the existence and enforcement of codes of ethics.

1. Written codes allow marketers to identify what their organization recognizes as acceptable business practices.
2. Written codes help marketers to inform others that they intend to conduct business in an ethical way.

3. Written codes can be an effective internal control on behavior, which, most marketers would agree, is more desirable than having external controls.

4. Organizations with high ethical standards (a) generate greater drive and effectiveness because employees know they can do the right thing decisively, (b) attract high-caliber people more easily because these individuals prefer to work with others they can trust, and (c) develop better customer relations because customers trust them.

5. Written codes can help marketing professionals avoid confusion in determining what is ethical (see Fulmer, 1979, p. 51).

As an illustration of the efforts of marketing professionals concerning codes, several code-related suggestions have been advanced to improve the ethical decision making associated with advertising:

1. Require all businesses involved in advertising to develop specific ethical principles of operation.

2. Encourage the advertising community to push for revised association codes.

3. Consider the idea of an ethical ombudsman for the advertising community.

4. Ask more and more frequent questions concerning the ethical nature of advertisements and advertising strategies (see Laczniak & Murphy, 1993, pp. 170-173).

The American Association of Advertising Agencies' Creative Code is one illustration of an ethical code created by the advertising community. Its members have pledged not to knowingly produce advertisements that contain one or more of the following elements:

1. False or misleading statements or exaggerations, visual or verbal

2. Testimonials that do not reflect the real choice of a competent individual or group

3. Price claims that are misleading

4. Comparisons that unfairly criticize a competitive product or service

5. Claims that are not adequately supported or that distort the true meaning of statements made by experts

6. Statements, suggestions, or pictures that are offensive to the audience (see Smith & Quelch, 1993, p. 624)

Can Codes Be Effective?

There is very little information available to answer this question. One piece of evidence can be found concerning salespeople. The research of Weeks and Nantel (1993) revealed that a *well-communicated* code of ethics can help reduce the incidence of unethical behavior. The communication of the elements of the code is essential. Without communication—which might include informing employees about the content of the code, informing employees about rewards for abiding by the code, or informing employees about the enforcement of the code—the mere existence of a code has little effect on ethical behavior (Robin, Giallourakis, David, & Moritz, 1989).

Weeks and Nantel (1993) provide several additional pieces of information. One is that the sales force examined was one that performed at relatively high levels. Furthermore, members of the sales force reported high levels of satisfaction with their jobs. The sales force had even requested additional guidelines concerning proper behavior in situations that did not seem to be covered by the existing code. In other words, those things that individuals value—high performance (presumably leading to rewards) and job satisfaction—were clearly evident in an organization in which codes of ethics were communicated and enforced. Perhaps one reason for this was the fact that the codes eliminated some of the ambiguity associated with making decisions in the field (Frankel, 1989). The code provided ethics guidelines, and salespeople who followed those guidelines found they could be successful in their sales efforts.

Content of Codes of Ethics

Corporate codes of ethics tend to be somewhat legalistic in nature. This, by the way, is one reason that corporate codes of ethics will never be able to cover every single ethical situation encountered by marketing professionals. Corporate codes suffer from some of the same problems that were discussed concerning ethical theories. Despite this shortcoming, however, corporate codes contain a wealth of information and guidelines concerning various marketplace behaviors. A few of these areas are listed next:

1. *Corporate relations to employees,* which include affirmative action statements, bases for promotion, respect for the individual, training and educational opportunities, communication channels available to employees, and statements concerning privacy

2. *Interemployee relationships on ethics,* which include management responsibilities, subordinate responsibilities, and statements about honesty and integrity

3. *Whistle-blowing,* which includes the various procedures available for employees to identify and reveal unethical behaviors occurring in the organization

4. *Effect of organization on the environment,* which includes statements concerning many activities, including pollution, community involvement, and company donor policies

5. *Bribery,* which includes cash payments and the offering of excessive gifts and entertainment, and the expectation of reciprocity

6. *Insider information,* which includes new technologies, employees' changing companies, corporate espionage, and the familiar buying and selling of stock

7. *Conflicts of interest,* which include personal or financial interests outside the company that could have a negative effect on the company

8. *Antitrust laws,* which are included so that employees are familiarized with the economic problems that the company is facing

9. *Accounting,* which includes getting all information concerning transactions recorded immediately and accurate reporting of accounting information

10. *Customer relations,* which includes customer needs, customer information, handling of customer complaints, customer satisfaction, notifying customers of policy changes, fair pricing, and fair advertising

11. *Political activities and contributions,* which include holding of public office that might interfere with the employee's job performance and the type and level of contributions to political causes (see Benson, 1989, p. 311)

If you were asked to design a code of ethics for marketing professionals, what would it include? How would you state, clearly, what is ethically acceptable and what is not?

◩ TOP MANAGEMENT ACTIONS

A discussion of the influence of top management may seem redundant. It is included here to make the point that top managers can be a powerful deterrent to unethical behavior if they choose to be. Top managers have the capability of setting the ethical tone for an entire organization. This has been referred to as the establishment of an "organization ethic" (Pruden, 1971). It seems clear that any organization's policymakers must assume the responsibility for the ethical climate of an organization through a commitment to encouraging ethical behavior and to behaving ethically themselves. Ethical guidelines and ethics codes are not likely to be observed unless top management declares that supporters will be rewarded and violators will be punished.

Over a decade ago, Richard Schubert (1979), vice chairman of Bethlehem Steel wrote the following:

Management has to do more than establish codes of conduct. We have a primary responsibility to motivate and inspire employees to conduct themselves honestly and fairly. Starting at the top, we have to set the example for others to follow by acting in a morally proper way. We have to practice what we preach.

I believe strongly that what sustains this country of ours in time of difficulty and crisis is the spirit of its people. And I believe that this spirit is based on simple, old-fashioned virtues like personal honesty and fair play. Concepts like "strategic misrepresentation" or "situation ethics" or "relative morality" undermine this spirit. If students think they have to deceive each other to compete, if workers think it's okay to steal because companies are stealing on a bigger scale—then the very foundations of our society are threatened. (p. 40)

Any plan, any code of ethics for ethical behavior in organizations must start with top managers. The way top managers exercise moral judgment is accepted as the most powerful influence over the ethical behavior of employees. For example, a company president who makes a decision to immediately recall a defective product sends a different message than does the company president who withholds information about the potential harmfulness of the defective product.

Ethical codes do help. Codes can make the ethical aspects of many marketing decisions clear. But the influence of codes is negligible if the behavior of the top managers in an organization is not consistent with the organization. Remember the cliche, "Actions speak louder than words."

Establishing an Ethical Organizational Culture

Many organizations provide ethics training for their employees. We'll discuss training programs a little later in this chapter. For now, suffice it to say that for training to be effective, a corporate culture must exist that makes the training messages understandable and believable.

Establishing an ethical corporate culture is more than providing ethics training. Ethical decision making must be integrated into the day-to-day decisions undertaken by marketing professionals. Establishing an ethical corporate culture might include the following:

1. Ensuring that a code of ethics is in place and enforced
2. Ensuring that a whistle-blowing or ethical concerns procedure (or both) is established for internal ethical problem solving
3. Involving marketing professionals in the identification of ethical issues to gain understanding and resolve those issues
4. Determining the relationships in which marketing professionals are involved and making them known to all those who are involved in those relationships
5. Integrating ethical decision making into the performance appraisal process
6. Publicizing, in all organization communications, top management ethical priorities (Harrington, 1991, p. 28)

A culture does not appear suddenly. The development of a culture requires countless individual events, attitudes, policies, and beliefs (Hyman, Skipper, & Tansey, 1990). Every marketing decision made in the organization, no matter how trivial, becomes a part of the organizational culture. So developing a culture of ethical behavior is a long-term process. No single action can turn a culture around. Every day, each marketing professional must endorse the culture through his or her actions. If the culture is not supported, actions that go against the ethical culture will destroy it. Table 5.3 provides a checklist that can be used to evaluate the ethical culture of an

Does the decision treat me, or my company, as an exception to a convention that I must trust others to follow?	**Table 5.3** Checklist for Assessing the Underlying Ethical Structure of a Decision
Would I repel customers by telling them?	
Would I repel qualified job applicants by telling them?	
Have I been cliquish?	
Is my decision partial?	
Does my decision divide the constituencies of the company?	
Will I have to use coercion (pull rank) to implement my decision?	
Would I prefer to avoid the consequences of this decision?	
Did I avoid any of the questions by telling myself that I could get away with it?	

SOURCE: Adapted from Hyman, Skipper, and Tansey (1990). Reprinted from *Business Horizons*, March-April 1990. Copyright 1990 by the Foundation for the School of Business at Indiana University. Used with permission.

organization. *What do you think of these guidelines? Are they better than the ones presented in Table 5.1?*

▧ ETHICS TRAINING PROGRAMS

Ethics training and seminars have been used by some organizations to assist them in dealing with ethical problems. For example, the National Association of Purchasing Managers has an ethics committee that offers opinions on ethical questions and provides educational seminars on the subject of ethics (Cummings, 1979). Training and seminars have the objective of training marketing professionals to examine the ethical nature and implications of their decisions. Organizations must provide for the education of marketing professions in specific ethically related practices.

The two most common reasons for establishing an ethics training program are (a) developing employee awareness of ethics in business and (b) drawing attention to ethical issues to which the employee may be exposed (Center for Business Ethics, 1986). By raising awareness, organizations hope to aid decision makers in the following ways:

1. Establishing the recognition of the ethical components of business decisions
2. Legitimizing the consideration of ethics as part of decision making
3. Avoiding variability in decision making caused by the lack of awareness of rules and norms

4. Avoiding ambivalence in decision making caused by an organizational reward structure in which a person experiences being pulled in psychologically opposite directions

5. Avoiding ambivalence in decision making caused by confusion as to who is responsible for misdeeds, particularly when an employee has received an order from a superior

6. Providing decision-making frameworks for analyzing ethical issues and helping employees to apply such frameworks (Jansen & Von Glinow, 1985)

In most companies, ethics training is a communications device used by top managers to emphasize the importance of including ethical considerations in decision making. Codes of ethics are reviewed and a case study approach is often used. But few organizations really seek to raise the level of ethical thinking among employees (Harrington, 1991). Employees must sense that top management is sincere before any real influence is accomplished. So once again, we see the imperative that top management must establish an ethical culture supportive of the messages being conveyed in ethics training.

Training programs have been shown to lower the extent to which employees perceive they have to engage in unethical behaviors to get ahead in their organizations. Furthermore, when ethics training programs exist, employees tend to refuse to take unethical actions when faced with serious ethical dilemmas (Delaney & Sockell, 1992). So although the jury is still out, the existing evidence speaks in favor of the ability of ethics training programs to reduce the incidence of unethical behavior. *Recall the code of ethics you were asked to design earlier. How would you develop a training program to "teach" marketing professionals about following the guidelines you specified in your code?*

Problems With Ethics Training Programs

Despite the good news presented in the preceding section, organization ethics training programs can and do fail. One reason for this is that such programs can operate under the misconception that their primary focus should be to ensure the ethical behavior of marketing professionals (Rice & Dreilinger, 1990). When this is the focus, the training program tends to become little more than a series of "thou shalt nots." In other words, marketing professionals learn what they *should not do* in certain situations, but they do not learn what they *should do* in those same situations. Most marketing professionals have a pretty good idea of what not to do. Where they need help is in the area of what the company expects them to do in those situations. In other words, the primary reason for the failure of ethical programs is that they do not take a proactive approach to solving ethical problems by making recommendations that will work in practice.

Ethics Training and Long-Term Strategies

As you have seen, many companies have implemented ethics training in the belief that it is an integral feature in the development of an ethical company culture. But few of these companies have extended their ethics training toward strategic issues—in other words, toward the long run (Harrington, 1991). To have a long-term perspective, companies should seek to answer questions such as the following:

1. How can ethical considerations be incorporated into long-term planning?
2. How can we identify ethical issues in which the company may or may not be involved?
3. How do each of these ethical issues affect the company?
4. What is the likelihood of occurrence of each of these ethical issues?
5. What is an appropriate response(s) to each ethical issue?
6. How can individual, departmental, and company performance be monitored regarding each of these ethical issues (Harrington, 1991, p. 29)?

Ethics training, like all other ethics programs, is really a part of a larger effort to instill an ethical behavioral culture in the organization. Furthermore, it is just one of many parts of the puzzle designed to instill an ethical culture that will benefit the company in the long run. Ethics training will be effective only if the larger ethics-oriented effort of the company (e.g., codes, top management actions, ethics advisers) are effective.

▨ ETHICS ADVISERS

Just as organizations use consultants for solving business problems, they can also use ethics advisers. These advisers could occupy staff positions in the organization, their major function being to oversee ethical concerns (Keichel, 1979). Individuals occupying such positions would review decisions for their ethical content in an attempt to improve the overall ethical climate of the organization.

Ethics advisers come by a variety of titles and in a variety of forms. These include ethical officers, ethical ombudsmen, ethical devil's advocates, and special audit committees (Werner, 1992). Whatever they are called, their purpose is to seek out unethical behaviors taking place in the organization. Although their specific responsibilities vary from one organization to the next, most agree that the ethics adviser must maintain a central position in the organization. That is, he or she must have access to everyone in the organization, at all levels of the organization.

Although it is imperative that ethical advisers have direct contact with top management, this contact is also the source of one of the problems associated with ethical advisers. They become "associated" with top management. When this happens, ethics advisers can lose their effectiveness with people at lower levels of the organization. This occurs because lower-level employees feel that the ethical adviser is simply someone whom top management has assigned as a "watchdog." In actuality, the ethical adviser is charged with trying to instill behaviors that will work for the long-term good of the organization and the individuals in that organization.

◣ ETHICS COURSES

Many colleges and universities have also added ethics-related courses to their curricula. Much is being said and written about the effectiveness of such courses in promoting ethical behavior in marketing situations. They range from a segment in a "typical" business course (e.g., 3 weeks on ethics in the course, Principles of Marketing) to those that make up an entire semester and include an examination of ethics across all the functional areas of business. Rather then offer a detailed description of ethics courses, I'll leave the evaluation of their effectiveness to you. *What have you learned in your ethics course? Has it caused you to change your behavior? Has it led you to adjust your way of thinking about marketing activities? Has it led you to more long-term thinking than short-term thinking?* These are just a few of the questions that can be covered in an ethics course. You, no doubt, can think of many more.

◣ BROADENING MARKETING'S RESPONSE

This chapter closes with a brief historical look at the pressures placed on marketers to engage in ethical activity. Although much progress has been made, marketing continues to face many challenges posed by those who feel compelled to judge marketing activities. Society will continue to expect marketers to provide a high standard of living, and it will continue to challenge marketers to justify their actions. How well marketing will be able to satisfy its critics will be a function of whether organizations are successful in profitably satisfying customer's needs and wants and doing so in an ethical fashion.

The quality of life represents the demand that businesspeople make concern for **Quality of Life** society central to the conduct of business operations. It is a demand that the quality of life become the business of business (see Drucker, 1969, p. 77). Clean air, good housing, crime prevention, racial equality, and equal employment opportunity are all quality-of-life factors for which many feel business organizations bear tremendous responsibility.

Today, there is a large gap between society's expectations of quality of life and its perceptions of marketing activities. This gap is not new. Consumers have expressed concern for the quality of life for decades. Indeed, the most recent consumerism movement had its roots in 1962 when President John F. Kennedy declared that consumers were entitled to a new "bill of rights," which included the rights to choose, to safety, to be informed, and to be heard (Kennedy, 1962). The Kennedy bill of rights is at the heart of many of the ethical problems faced by marketing professionals.

Since the declaration of this bill of rights, the decades of the 1960s, 1970s, 1980s, and now the 1990s have seen a tremendous proliferation of brand and product alternatives in the marketplace. Moreover, self-service shopping and in-home shopping have taken on greater importance. Such trends would seem to satisfy the consumer's right to choose. For some products, however, there are dozens of alternatives. Many are unsafe (not satisfying the consumer's right to safety). Comparing value between all these alternatives is virtually impossible and the consumer's right to know is left unsatisfied. Furthermore, because of the trend toward self-service and in-home shopping, consumers are now placed in positions of identifying and comparing product characteristics. In many cases, information contained on packages is such that brand comparisons are difficult, if not impossible.

What exists is a situation where one set of consumer expectations (the right to choose) apparently is satisfied. But another set of consumer expectations (the right to know) is left unsatisfied. Nevertheless, consumers expect to be able to exercise all of the bill of rights in the marketplace. When these expectations are not met, quality of life suffers, and dissatisfaction with the activities of marketers occurs. *What do you think about the rights of consumers? Have these rights been better satisfied in the marketplace, or have factors such as brand proliferation, price discounting, and intense promotion actually reduced the ability of consumers to make choices in the marketplace?*

Marketers' Response to Consumerism

As you read in this chapter, marketers have responded to the pressures that have arisen from this most recent consumerism movement. Many organizations have adjusted their marketing programs in response to the demands of consumers. Organizations have established many different programs to improve ethical activity and

Consumer Policy	Consumer Rights			
	1. Choose Freely	2. Be Informed	3. Be Heard	4. Be Safe
Education	Decision making, budget, nature of market economy, rights and responsibilities	Generic product and materials data, information sources	How to assert consumer rights	Importance of health and safety, user manuals and training
Information	Buying criteria, buying advice	Models and brands data, independent consumer information programs	Market research, two-way market dialogue	Safety certification, care and maintenance data
Protection	Maintain open markets, antitrust, stop high-pressure and deceptive tactics	Truly informative advertising, product claims substantiation	Complaints-handling machinery	Minimize health and accident risks
	Choose Wisely	Keep Informed	Sound Off	Safety First
	Consumer Responsibilities			

SOURCE: Thorelli (1972, p. 195).

some have even established high-level management positions to respond to existing consumer problems and identify potential problems. Other organizations view consumerism as a marketing opportunity and have attempted to create marketing strategies designed to improve their relations with customers.

The Government's Response to Consumerism

The three most important responses to consumerism are consumer protection, consumer education, and consumer information. Table 5.4 shows the relationships between these government responses, the four rights of consumers, and consumer responsibilities. As shown in Table 5.4, government policy can be focused on protecting, educating, or informing consumers. But if marketing is to function effectively, consumers cannot simply claim certain rights. They, too, must act in a responsible way. Consumers must be careful as they make decisions because no outside agency can guarantee that consumers will choose wisely, keep informed, sound off, or protect themselves.

Companies operate under certain legal guidelines when they are dealing with customers. For example, it is imperative for companies to communicate to salespeople what these legal requirements are. A few of these legal requirements and their implications for salespeople are briefly described next:

1. Sherman Act (1890)—prohibits price collusion. Salespeople who exchange price information with competitive salespeople are called into question under the terms of the Sherman Act.

2. Clayton Act (1914)—prohibits price discrimination that tends to lessen competition. Salespeople who offer one customer (e.g., a retailer) a price discount may be subjected to legal redress under the provisions of the Clayton Act because such actions are almost always considered to lessen competition. The Clayton Act also prohibits a practice known as "full-line forcing." A salesperson cannot threaten a retailer with withdrawing some of the company's products if the retailer does not carry the salesperson's complete (full) line of products.

3. Robinson-Patman Act (1936)—prohibits customers (e.g., retailers) from pressuring salespeople to offer special deals. Such special deals can be very tempting because they go a long way to helping salespeople reach goals.

4. Wheeler-Lea Act (1938)—prohibits unfair trade practices. Such unfair trade practices include misrepresentation, deception, and high-pressure sales tactics.

5. Foreign Corrupt Practices Act (1978)—prohibits the offering of bribes to foreign government officials. This is a particularly difficult issue for salespeople because many foreign officials simply refuse to conduct business with anyone who does not "offer them something under the table."

6. Uniform Commercial Code (UCC)—guidelines adopted at the state level that concern sales contracts, warranty terms, shipping terms and other business arrangements. Salespeople who misrepresent products or overpromise product performance are subject to guidelines set forth by the UCC.

7. Cooling-off laws—Customers who purchase a product from a door-to-door salesperson have 3 working days in which they can rescind the contract. Salespeople may use questionable sales tactics to make a sale, but the customer can bow out legally from the contract anytime within 3 days of the signing of the contract.

Appendix B presents a more detailed look at how the government has attempted to ensure marketplace fairness.

An outgrowth of consumerism is that consumers no longer judge marketing activities solely on the basis of products. Consumers also consider the social costs involved in the production and sale of products. These considerations have been so broad that business organizations must consider the effect their decisions will have on many constituents, not just customers and the shareholders. The classical view of such social responsibilities suggests that business organizations are acting in a socially responsible way if they attempt to use, as efficiently as possible, the resources at their disposal in producing the products that society wants and needs and provide them at a fair price.

Today, the concept of social responsibility is much broader. The substance of today's social responsibility arises from concerns for the ethical consequences of the actions of marketing professionals because they affect the interests of many others. Thus social responsibility is concerned with the actions of individuals and focuses on the ethical consequences of the decisions that they make. For marketers to be socially

Table 5.5	It is the policy of this company to . . .
Suggested Guidelines for Socially Responsible Actions	1. Think carefully about its social responsibilities 2. Make full use of tax deductibility laws through contributions, when profits permit 3. Bear the social costs attendant upon its operation when it is possible to do so without jeopardizing its competitive financial position 4. Concentrate action programs on a limited set of socially responsible objectives 5. Concentrate action programs on areas strategically related to the present and prospective functions of the business 6. Facilitate employee actions that can be taken as individuals rather than as representatives of the company 7. Search for product and service opportunities to permit the company and other companies to make profits while advancing social interests 8. Take actions in the name of social responsibilities but not at the expense of the required level of rising profits needed to maintain the economic strength desired by management 9. Take socially responsive actions on a continuous basis 10. Examine carefully, before proceeding with socially responsive action, the needs that the company wishes to address, the contributions that the company can make, the risks involved, and the potential benefits to both the company and society

SOURCE: Steiner, George A. (1975). *Business and Society.* New York: McGraw-Hill, Inc., pp. 192-194. Reprinted by permission of McGraw-Hill, Inc.

responsible, then, their decisions must reflect the interest of the organization, consumers, shareholders, and society as a whole, one of the arguments presented in Chapter 1.

Many organizations have taken steps to develop policies to serve as guides for socially responsible actions. Table 5.5 provides a sampling of some of these policies. The effectiveness of such policies depends on their acceptance by members of the organization, particularly top management.

Not everyone, as you also saw in Chapter 1, supports this broadened social responsibility concept. Economist Milton Friedman has long since been an opponent of social responsibility (Friedman, 1970). He argues that free, unrestricted markets are the most effective way to optimize a society's allocation of resources. Managers are employees of stockholders and therefore responsible to them. Friedman argues that managers who act in socially responsible ways are being irresponsible to stockholders. For example, socially responsible activities are expensive, driving up prices and resulting in declining demand and profits. Friedman repeatedly questions how an executive can really know what is in the best interests of society. Moreover, Friedman questions executives' abilities to determine if socially responsible actions can achieve socially responsible goals or do they actually contribute to the destruction of the organization's economic power. *Now that you have read five chapters on ethics, what do you think? Should business adopt Milton Friedman's viewpoint of social responsibility?*

CHAPTER SUMMARY

Marketers have responded to ethical concerns of the marketplace in a number of ways. These include guides to ethical decision making, self-regulation, codes of ethics, ethical actions by top managers, establishing ethical organization cultures, ethics training programs, ethics advisers, and ethics courses. Many of the ethical issues faced by marketers have roots in President John F. Kennedy's consumer's bill of rights, which addresses consumers' rights to choose, to safety, to be informed, and to be heard.

◪ SOME QUESTIONS FOR DISCUSSION

1. Of all the responses to ethical problems made by marketers, which do you think are the most effective? Least effective? Why?

2. How would you rate the ethics course or ethics component taught at your school? What should be included? Deleted? Do you feel that such courses are effective in reducing ethical problems?

3. If you were asked to write a code of ethics for the classroom conduct of college students, what would you include? Do you think it would be effective? Under what circumstances could it be effective?

4. Do you feel that training programs designed to make marketing professionals aware of ethical problems are effective? Why do you think so?

Texas Instruments Code of Ethics:
The TI Commitment*

Ethical decision-making depends upon your understanding of personal and TI values and principles coupled with good personal judgment. You, the individual, play the most important role in the ethical decision-making process and, therefore, in the ethical standards of TI. "The TI Commitment" will aid you in this process by describing our mission, our basic principles, and our values.

THE TI COMMITMENT

Mission

Texas Instruments exists to create, make, and market useful products and services to satisfy the needs of customers throughout the world.

Principles

We will accomplish this with "Excellence in everything we do."

- Perform with unquestionable ethics and integrity
- Achieve customer satisfaction through total quality
- Be a world-class technology/manufacturing leader
- Provide profitable growth/fair return on assets
- Achieve continuous improvement with measurable progress
- Be a good corporate citizen

Values

We expect the highest levels of performance and integrity from our people. We will create an environment where people are valued as individuals and treated with respect and dignity, fairness and equality. We will strive to create opportunities for them to develop and reach their full potential and to achieve their professional and personal goals.

---

*Reprinted by permission of Texas Instruments.

ETHICAL DECISION-MAKING

TI policies and procedures have been developed over the years and are revised as required. Although a real effort has been made to cover the questions that might be raised in the area of business ethics, no set of policies and procedures can begin to cover every situation that might arise.

Regardless of the job we do at TI, ethics and integrity are always critical in our everyday decisions:

. . . when reporting time worked

. . . when using TI resources

. . . when interacting with customers, suppliers, and competitors

. . . when confronted with a difficult deadline

. . . when required to sign off that an item of work has been properly done

. . . when deciding whether to raise an ethical issue

All TIers have not only the right but the personal responsibility to resolve any doubts or uncertainties relating to ethical questions in the course of their duties at TI.

WHERE TO GO FOR ANSWERS

All TIers are encouraged to ask questions and to keep asking questions until satisfied that their questions are answered. If you have any doubts as to whether a decision you are making is the right one, then get advice from any of the following recommended sources:

1. The best and most convenient source for information is your supervisor. The supervisor is generally closest to your situation and understands how you fit into the overall program.

2. If for any reason you cannot resolve an issue with your supervisor or local managers, you should contact your Personnel Administrator. TI Human Resources people are there to help you resolve many issues, including ethics issues. You may counsel with them any time.

3. If there are other ethical issues that you wish to discuss, you can contact the TI Ethics Director in confidence or even anonymously.

4. For questions regarding contracts, pricing practices, or anything with a legal orientation, TI Legal can help you find the answers. You should also send our lawyers copies of any unfamiliar documents you receive which appear to have a legal significance to TI. This booklet covers many legal issues on which you should contact TI Legal for more information.

5. Standard Policies and Procedures (SP&P), various manuals, and other information can be obtained through TI Human Resources or can be accessed through an IMS-connected terminal.

6. The "Open Door" process allows any TIer access to higher levels of the management chain.

7. This booklet can provide you with much information on ethical issues, as can the Cornerstone series of booklets. All of these are available through your supervisor, TI

Human Resources or the TI Forms Warehouse, international stationery stores, or the equivalent.

There may be other sources depending upon the situation, but remember, keep asking until you are satisfied that you have a proper answer. It may not be the one you wanted or expected, but you must feel confident that it is consistent with TI policy.

TI ETHICS DIRECTOR

The TI Ethics Director serves the TI employee in several different ways. It is here that TI policies and procedures are closely examined for real-world applications. To be credible, our policies must be relevant, must effectively address the issues, and must be up to date. Most important, Ethics Office communication and education efforts help keep all TIers aware of what is expected and required of them . . . and we all perform our tasks better and appreciate our endeavors more fully if we understand those expectations and requirements.

To close the communications loop, TIers can contact the Ethics Director confidentially or anonymously to ask questions and voice concerns.

These open lines of communication are vitally important to TI, because we need to stay aware of employee concerns and questions. TIers around the world can report potential problems and the possible need to revise policies and procedures. The TI Ethics Director reports directly to the chairman of the TI Ethics Committee, a high-level steering body of senior TI managers who are available to review issues of major significance and take appropriate actions.

SUPERVISOR RELATIONSHIP

The supervisor-to-TIer relationship at all levels of the organization is an absolutely vital interface at TI. It is the interface that must permit and promote candid discussion of problems. It is the interface where aggressive goals must be set with the understanding that they must be achieved with the highest standards of conduct. It is this interface that must provide for the recognition of both integrity and goal attainment.

GOVERNMENT LAWS AND REGULATIONS

It is TI policy to abide by both the letter and the spirit of the laws in the countries where we operate. But when we believe these laws need revision, we will seek to inform appropriate agencies and representatives of our position on matters affecting our corporate welfare and that of our employees.

IN THE MARKETPLACE

Quality

For every product or service we offer, we will understand the requirements that meet the customers' needs, and we will conform to those requirements without exception. To achieve customer satisfaction through total quality, we must maintain relationships based on integrity and trust. Supplying products and services that meet customers' expectations is more than a quality obligation. It's our ethical commitment.

Statement in Sales, Advertising, and Publicity

TI's reputation for integrity is a priceless asset and the result of continuous effort by all of us. The truth, well told, must be the objective of all of our promotion efforts.

A momentary advantage gained through even slight misrepresentation or exaggeration can jeopardize our future success. This applies to our personal discussions with others about TI as well as to our promotional efforts. TI's reputation is completely in our hands, to be enhanced or damaged by the nature of our actions.

Customers and Suppliers

Customers deserve, and we will provide, factual information regarding prices, capabilities, and schedules. It is never acceptable to underestimate problems or to exaggerate benefits in order to obtain business. If we encounter unforeseen problems or developments that will affect our customers, we will tell them and work earnestly to minimize the impact or provide relief as appropriate. We must assure that customers obtain value from TI and that they are dealt with fairly and honestly.

We shall also treat our suppliers fairly and honestly. TI suppliers deserve and will be provided clear instructions and accurate and timely feedback. In turn, we expect and will demand quality, integrity, and competence from them.

Competition

In many countries, it is unlawful to collaborate with competitors or their representatives for the purpose of establishing or maintaining prices. TI's policy goes beyond the letter of the law. Our policy holds it to be unethical to discuss prices with competitors at any time, except when dealing with competitors as suppliers or customers, or as associates in teaming or other legally permitted business relationships. Even then, we will discuss prices only to the extent necessary to accomplish a lawful and proper objective. It is also unethical and unlawful to collaborate with competitors or their representatives to restrain competition in other ways, such as by dividing markets or customers, or by restricting production. In many countries, it is unlawful to require a customer to charge a certain price upon resale of a product.

Anyone having any doubt about whether a contemplated action might restrain competition or amount to unfair competition must immediately consult TI Legal.

Reciprocal Dealing

It is TI policy to sell its products and services by serving the customers' needs, not by using our purchasing power as a threat—real or implied. We at TI shall under no circumstances require our suppliers to buy from TI under any kind of coercion, expressed or implied, nor shall we agree to purchase products or services from any customer under any circumstance that implies or amounts to reciprocal dealing, that is, an agreement to purchase based on the supplier's commitment to purchase from TI.

Estimates Must Be Reasonable

In the normal course of business, it is necessary to provide financial estimates to government procurement personnel, taxing authorities, and audit agencies, as well as to other customers and suppliers. Such estimates also are involved daily in TI's internal operations. An estimator should know, in good conscience, that the basis for the estimate is reasonable. Here, "reasonable" means based upon known facts in instances where facts exist, or upon the estimator's sincere and honest judgment in the absence of facts.

GIFTS AND ENTERTAINMENT

It is TI Policy that TIers may not give or accept any gift that might appear to improperly influence a business relationship or decision. If we receive any substantial gift or favor, it must be returned and our supervisor notified. This policy does not apply to items of small value commonly exchanged in business relationships, but even here, discretion and common sense should be our guide. In commercial business, the exchange of social amenities between suppliers, customers, and the TIers is acceptable when reasonably based on a clear business purpose and within the bounds of good taste. Excessive entertainment of any sort is not acceptable. Conferences accompanied by a meal with suppliers or customers are often necessary and desirable. Whenever appropriate, these meals should be on a reciprocal basis. Payment for meals of government employees (if permitted) should be handled in accordance with appropriate agency regulations.

TIers must scrupulously observe government laws and regulations relating to gifts and entertainment for public employees in the countries involved. TI policy is to avoid even the appearance of an improper action. Kickbacks are not to be given or accepted in any form under any circumstances. Kickbacks are anything of value provided directly or indirectly to another party for the purpose of improperly obtaining or rewarding favorable treatment.

TIers and family members may not accept any discount on personal purchases that may be construed to be offered because of a supplier's relationship with TI, unless the same discount is available to all TIers.

Your organization may choose to establish gift and entertainment guidelines that are more restrictive than those described above. Check your Group's policy.

IMPROPER USE OF CORPORATE ASSETS

TI directors, officers, and other TIers may not use company assets for personal gain. Such a practice not only violates TI policy and ethical standards, but may also violate tax or other legal requirements.

TI's equipment, tools, materials, and supplies have been purchased for the specific purpose of conducting company business. Each of us must recognize that purposeful misapplication or waste of these items is an ethical violation, and their unauthorized removal from TI's facilities is a violation of TI policy and may be a violation of the law.

Personal use of office equipment and secretarial time is permitted only on an incidental or occasional basis and it should never interfere with the conduct of TI business.

Additionally, it is TI policy that no TI employee may do work during non-TI time for the personal benefit of any corporate, corporate staff, group, division, or subsidiary officer, even if the officer pays the employee personally.

POLITICAL CONTRIBUTIONS

It is TI policy that no company funds or assets may be used for making political contributions of any kind to a political candidate or holder of an office of any government—local, regional, or national—in any country. This is so, even where permitted by local law.

For purposes of this policy, the term "political contribution" includes direct or indirect payments, loans, advances, deposits or gifts of money, or any services. It also includes gifts, subscriptions, memberships, purchase of tickets, purchase of advertising space, furnishing of supplies, and payment of expenses and compensation of employees performing services for a political organization, candidate or public official.

PAYMENTS IN CONNECTION WITH BUSINESS TRANSACTIONS

Every action taken by TI as an institution and by employees in the performance of our duties will measure up to the highest ethical, moral, and legal standards. Compliance with this policy is the responsibility of each of us. Employees with knowledge of irregularities involving corporate assets or funds that may represent a questionable payment should report the matter to their supervisor, the TI Ethics Director, TI Corporate Tax, or TI Legal. If the irregularity involves suppliers, report the matter to your purchasing manager or group material manager.

No bribes of any type may be paid to anyone. This prohibition is without limitation. A bribe is defined as a payment made to influence someone to do something that should not be done or to omit something that should be done under the rules of that person's employer or the laws of the country involved.

Payments to Suppliers

Payments for goods and services received for TI use will be made only to suppliers who have been verified as legitimate sources by the appropriate TI purchasing organization.

Payments to Government Employees

No payments may be made to any government officials or employees in any country where such payments are illegal under the laws of that country.

Payments to government officials that are legal in the country where made must conform to written company procedures.

Payments to Consultants, Distributors, or Agents

Payments of fees to consultants, distributors, or agents will be at rates consistent with the value of the services expected or performed.

Payments to Commercial Customers

No payment may be made, either directly or indirectly, to an employee of a TI customer or prospective customer for the purpose of influencing the employee into taking an improper action.

Payments to Other Persons

Payments for other than normal commercial purposes to persons who are not employees of governments and are not customers, that are legal in the country where made, may be made only in accordance with company procedures.

Payments in a Country Other Than Payee's Residence

Requests for payment of fees or salaries to an account in a country other than payee's residence or place of business (sometimes referred to as "split fees") may be honored if no violation of law is involved and there is nothing in the total transaction that would compromise TI's high standards of ethics.

Falsification of Records

No payments or receipt shall be approved, made, or accepted with the intention or understanding that any part of such payment or receipt is to be used for a purpose other than that described by the documents supporting the transaction. "Slush funds," or similar funds or accounts where no accounting for receipts or expenditures is made on the books of TI, are strictly prohibited.

CONFLICT OF INTEREST

Service on Other Boards

TI requires that each director, officer, division manager, department manager, or TIer with an organizational assignment equivalent to that of division or department manager (job grades 34 and up) obtain prior approval of the TI Board before accepting appointment as a member of the board of directors or as an officer of any other company, trade association, charitable or educational institution, or similar organization, not including religious or social organizations. Similarly, each officer of a TI subsidiary must obtain approval of any such appointments from the board of directors of the subsidiary. This policy is not intended to prevent service on such boards, but is intended to avoid a conflict of interest between TI and the other organization.

Professional Consultants Employed by TI

TI, in the normal course of its business, employs an independent certified public accounting firm to perform statutory audits and employs outside law firms to assist TI in litigation and other matters. TI also employs investment bankers, management consultants, advertising agencies, and other similar firms and individuals. The performance by these firms and individuals of similar services for companies in competing businesses must be carefully considered to prevent disclosure of TI proprietary information and, in general, the perform-ance of such services for competing companies will be discouraged. Inquiries received from such firms and individuals concerning services to other companies normally will be referred to the TI General Counsel and, when appropriate, will be referred by the TI General Counsel to the TI Board.

Outside Commercial Interests

Ownership by TIers of stock or other financial interests in an outside concern generates an important ethical consideration. Such a situation could have, or create the appearance of having, an adverse influence on judgments, decisions, or actions regarding their responsibili-ties to TI.

Always consider whether outside interests of any kind create, or appear to create, obli-gations to other organizations that could come into conflict with responsibilities to TI. For example, a TIer whose job is selling should not hold an interest in any company with which TI competes if this interest is of such importance that it could influence that individual's performance as a TI employee. Nor should a TIer in a purchasing function, or in a position to recommend or influence purchasing from any specific supplier, hold an interest in any company from which TI makes purchases if this interest is of such importance that it could influence the TIer in making purchasing decisions.

In summary, we should not have any responsibilities to an outside concern that could not be fulfilled honestly without influencing the performance of our TI responsibilities.

With prudent consideration of these principles, it is ethical and permissible, of course, for TIers to invest in broadly distributed, publicly traded stocks, since conflict of interest rarely exists in those situations.

Employment By Non-TI Companies

Although a TIer may engage in part-time employment during non-TI working hours, the work should never be in competition or association with any of TI's businesses. For example, a TIer should not work for a TI customer, supplier, or competitor unless a group level officer has determined it to be in TI's best interest to do so. The work should not involve the use of TI time or resources, nor should it adversely affect the TIer's judgment, decisions, or ability to meet TI work assignment responsibilities. TI prefers that this type of work be done with the full knowledge and approval of the supervisor.

INVESTMENT IN TI STOCK

TI encourages its employees to invest in TI stock, but not to speculate in TI stock by in-and-out trading. In order to avoid any appearance that a TIer is speculating in TI stock, no employee should engage in short sales of TI stock or trade in "puts," "calls," or other options on TI stock. If unusual circumstances appear to make a transaction in an option on TI stock appropriate, the transaction should be cleared with the TI General Counsel in advance.

We often have information about TI that is not known to the investing public. Sometimes, this inside information may also be "material" in relation to the stock market. TIers with material inside information are prohibited by law in many countries from buying or selling TI stock. The penalties for violating the prohibition are severe.

Examples of events that would ordinarily involve material inside information include a change in the dividend, a stock split, a merger, acquisition of a sizable company, or financial performance substantially different from that in relevant prior periods unless previously indicated in public statements or generally expected on the basis of publicly known factors.

The courts say that information is material if there is a substantial likelihood that a reasonable investor would consider it important in making an investment decision. Deciding if information about a future event is material or not requires a balancing of the probability that the event will actually occur with the expected magnitude of the event in the totality of the company's activities.

A practical approach to materiality is to ask: "If the information I have were made public right now, what are the chances that the market price of TI stock would rise or fall?" The higher the chances of a market price change, the higher the chances that a court will hold the information material.

If a TIer does have material inside information, the TIer should not trade in TI stock until the information has become public or obsolete. At the same time, the TIer may not "tip" others to trade in TI stock.

Directors and officers are also subject to other restrictions in addition to those involving material inside information.

TI PROPRIETARY INFORMATION

TI's trade secrets, proprietary information, and much other internal information are valuable assets. Protection of this information plays a vital role in TI's continued growth and in our ability to compete.

Under the laws of most countries, a trade secret is treated as property, usually in the form of information, knowledge, or know-how, the possession of which gives the owner some advantage over competitors who do not possess the "secret." A trade secret must be secret, that is, not generally or publicly known; but a secret need not be patentable subject matter to qualify as a trade secret. Our obligations with respect to proprietary and trade-secret information of TI are:

1. Not to disclose this information to persons outside of TI by conversations with visitors, suppliers, family, or others, except where an approved, written nondisclosure agreement (NDA) has been executed with the recipient.

2. Not to use this information for our own benefit or for the profit or benefit of persons outside of TI.

3. Not to disclose this information to other TIers except on a "need-to-know" basis, and then only with a positive statement that the information is a TI trade secret. TIers who have the "need to know" are those who can do their jobs properly only with knowledge of the proprietary or trade-secret information.

TI's trade-secret and proprietary information is not always of a technical nature. Typical of such important information are TI business, research, and new product plans; objectives, strategies, and tactical-action programs; divisional and department sales, profits, and any unpublished financial or pricing information; yields, designs, efficiencies, and capacities of TI's production facilities, methods, and systems; salary, wage, and benefit data; specific employment levels for sites or organizations; employee, customer, and supplier lists; and detailed information regarding customer requirements, preferences, business habits, and plans, except where such information is publicly available. This list, while not complete, suggests the wide scope and variety of TI proprietary information that must be safeguarded. While failure to mark does not destroy the trade-secret and proprietary nature of the information, for greater security, TI trade-secret and proprietary information should be marked "TI Strictly Private" or "TI Internal Data." Most of what we know about our own jobs and the jobs of others should remain in the plant or office when we finish the day's work.

A special category of proprietary information is TI software. Software created and owned by TI may be TI proprietary information. All proprietary TI software should display the TI copyright legend and should be marked and identified as "TI Strictly Private" or "TI Internal Data." All TI software that is distributed outside of TI must be subject to a software license agreement approved in writing by TI Legal and TI management.

If we leave TI, our legal obligation is to protect TI's trade-secret and proprietary information until the information becomes publicly available or TI no longer considers it trade secret or proprietary. We should remember also that TI correspondence, printed matter, documents, records of any kind, specific process knowledge, procedures, and special TI ways of doing things are all the property of, and must remain at, TI.

TRADE SECRETS AND SOFTWARE OF OTHERS

Do Not Reveal or Use Trade Secrets of Former Employers

It is TI policy and practice to respect the trade secrets of others. This is particularly pertinent if a TIer has knowledge of trade secrets of a former employer. Thus, no TIer is to reveal any information to TI that might reasonably be considered a trade secret of a former employer.

Software of Others

Much of the software used at TI was created and copyrighted by other companies and may be subject to nondisclosure restrictions. TI does not usually own software created by other companies, but receives and uses the software under a license agreement. It is TI policy to comply with license agreements which govern the use of software. Reproducing software without authorization may violate these agreements and be illegal. We must never make copies, resell, or transfer software created by another company, unless it is authorized under the applicable software license agreement.

Receive Information From Outside TI
Only on a Nonconfidential Basis

It is also TI policy and practice to refuse to receive or consider any proprietary data or trade-secret information—for example, ideas, inventions, confidential internal data, and patent applications—submitted to TI from companies or persons outside of TI without written approval by TI Patents and the appropriate group president, unless the submitting party agrees in writing that the submission is made on a nonconfidential basis in accordance with TI's "Suggestions Submission Agreement" form. This agreement form (copies of which are available from TI Patents), when properly signed by the submitter, prevents the possible creation of a confidential relationship between TI and the submitting party. Any TIer who has a question in this area should contact TI Patents.

Respect Trade Secrets of Others

TIers may, through an approved written agreement, become familiar with proprietary designs, processes, or techniques of suppliers, customers, competitors, and others, or gain other information which has been designated as proprietary or as trade secrets. We must take care to respect the proprietary nature of this information and not use it or reveal it without proper authorization. TIers are not authorized to accept such information without an approved written agreement explaining the rights and obligations of all parties, usually in the form of a nondisclosure agreement (NDA). Most NDA's restrict the proprietary information to people within TI who have a need-to-know for a specific purpose, such as preparing a proposal or qualifying suppliers.

TRANSACTIONS WITH GOVERNMENTAL AGENCIES

Good business ethics, quality products, and integrity in meeting commitments are important to both our government and commercial businesses. But suppliers to government agencies have additional requirements not usually found in standard commercial transactions. Since the laws and regulations that govern business with governmental agencies vary widely from country to country, contact TI Legal for specific requirements in a particular country.

AUDIT PROGRAM

An ongoing audit program is conducted throughout TI by its Corporate Internal Audit function. Audits include (but are not limited to) evaluating compliance with policies, procedures, and regulations (including government procurement regulations), reviewing the quality and integrity of financial statements, evaluating the economical and efficient use of resources, and reviewing internal controls of new and existing management systems. Results of these audits are presented to management and the Audit Committee of the Board of Directors as appropriate.

Group or division personnel may also perform audits as directed by their management. Our candid and cooperative participation in these audits is essential.

DISCIPLINARY ACTION AND VIOLATIONS OF THE LAW

Any employee who violates TI's ethical standards is subject to disciplinary action, which can include oral reprimand, written reprimand, probation, suspension, or immediate termination.

All employees should also be aware that certain actions and omissions prohibited by TI policies and local governments may violate the criminal laws of these countries and could lead to individual criminal prosecution and, upon conviction, to fines and imprisonment.

OUR RESPONSIBILITIES

To Other TIers

Ethical and moral responsibilities go far beyond the specific situations described in these statements. These responsibilities are involved in everything we do, both on and off the job. We all want to be proud of TI and the people with whom we work. The basic virtues of kindness, courtesy, and integrity are the elements that provide the framework for a pleasant working environment.

The hours we spend at work are more satisfying and rewarding when we demonstrate respect for all associates regardless of gender, age, race, religion, handicap, national origin, or status in TI's organization. TI is committed to being an equal opportunity employer. It is TI policy to support this objective through hiring, promotion, transfer, and all other terms and conditions of employment.

To Good Government

Every TIer should take an active interest in local, regional, or national government. Consistent with applicable law, each of us is encouraged to qualify as a voter, know the issues, platforms, and the capabilities of candidates, work in support of the candidate of our choice, and vote in every election. Freedom of choice in political viewpoint and party affiliation is a basic right. It is TI policy not to interfere with the exercise of this right but to encourage all TIers to participate voluntarily as individuals in political activities consistent with applicable law, including making personal contributions in support of the candidates or political organizations of their choice.

To Our Community

We all expect TI to be a good neighbor and to do its part in developing and maintaining wholesome surroundings for us and our families, just as each of us wants to be a good neighbor and to contribute to our communities. The practice of good ethics in our personal lives, together with the practice of good ethics by TI as a corporation, will do much to help ensure that we are fulfilling our obligations to the communities in which we live and work.

APPENDIX B

The Political/Legal
Environment of Marketing

Laws, government agencies, and consumer interest groups all work to motivate, influence, and constrain the activities of marketers. Over the years, political and legal activity has greatly increased, making it necessary for marketers to evaluate their activities more closely so that they stay in accord with national, state, and community legislation and agencies.

THE ROLE OF GOVERNMENT

The legal activity of the government, as it applies to business, is intended to be of benefit to two groups—consumers and business organizations. Consumers benefit through the reduction or elimination of marketing practices that are misleading, harmful, or illegal. For example, in several deregulated industries (e.g., airlines, trucking, telephone, banking), costs of purchasing have declined. Similarly, rulings by government agencies such as the Food and Drug Administration have eliminated many harmful products from grocery stores and drugstores.

Business organizations have also benefited from political and legal activity. Although many organizations complain about the hundreds of restrictive laws that they must follow, such laws also prevent competitors from engaging in unfair and deceptive practices that have the potential to destroy competition. Such laws have also forced organizations to discover new and more efficient ways of doing business, which, in the long run, have proven very beneficial.

Fundamentally, the goal of government legislation is to promote a healthy competitive environment through the regulation of certain activities. Governments at all levels attempt to develop "rules of the game" that are fair, competitive, and free of questionable activities. The intended result is satisfied consumers who can purchase reliable products at a reasonable price.

LAWS THAT AFFECT COMPETITION: THE ANTITRUST FRAMEWORK

In attempting to encourage free competition and discourage activities aimed at reducing competition, the government has enacted a series of laws. These include (a) the Sherman Act, (b) the Clayton Act, and (c) the Federal Trade Commission Act. Each of these is discussed next.

The Sherman Act

The Sherman Act was passed in 1890. The need for the Sherman Act arose because of a large number of mergers and other forms of business agreements that ultimately resulted in the formation of monopolies in the 1870s and the 1880s. Supporters of the Sherman Act wanted to preserve free competition by preventing business from unfairly accumulating market power. The act has two basic provisions. First, it prohibits "every contract, combination, or conspiracy in restraint of trade" (Section 1). Second, it prohibits "monopolies or any attempts by firms to monopolize."

Originally, the Sherman Act was interpreted as meaning that all restraints of trade were illegal. In 1911, however, this interpretation was relaxed to refer only to restraints of trade that were "unreasonably restrictive of competition." This latter interpretation is known as *the rule of reason concept*. That is, it became the task of the courts to interpret the nature of restraints of trade in order to determine their legality.

The Clayton Act

The Sherman Act was discovered to have shortcomings in preventing certain business practices, and the courts found a need for more specific guidelines. The result was the passage of the Clayton Act in 1911. The Clayton Act allows the courts to declare marketing practices illegal if those practices have a "probable" effect of substantially lessening competition or creating a monopoly. A key term is *probable effect*. Under the provisions of the Sherman Act, business practices were legal unless the courts could specifically show that competition had been adversely affected. Under the Clayton Act, the courts have far more latitude in interpreting what constitutes a restraint of trade.

The Clayton Act prohibits certain practices "where the effect of the practices may be to substantially lessen competition or tend to create a monopoly in a line of commerce." Included among these practices are the following:

1. Price discrimination—Section 2.
2. Tying agreements and exclusive arrangements—Section 3.
3. Acquisition of stock of other firms—Section 7.
4. Individuals sitting on boards of two or more firms whose sales volume exceeds $1 million—Section 8.

The Federal Trade Commission Act

In the same year as the Clayton Act, Congress also passed the Federal Trade Commission Act. The Federal Trade Commission Act had two primary objectives. First, it declared unfair methods of competition to be illegal. Second, it created the Federal Trade Commission (FTC), an agency whose primary responsibility is to protect businesses and consumers from unfair, deceptive, or anticompetitive practices. To do this, the FTC was given authority to define and prohibit unfair methods of competition. The FTC has the flexibility to investigate business practices such as advertising, pricing, and distribution. Specifically, it has been given the authority to regulate credit, labeling, packaging, warranties, and advertising.

The Robinson-Patman Act

During the 1930s, supermarket chain stores grew into prominence. These stores were capable of purchasing items in large quantities. As a result, they had significant power and were able to influence sellers into offering them special prices and service not available to smaller food grocers. Small grocers were placed at a considerable disadvantage because of these discriminatory practices. Congress passed the Robinson-Patman Act in 1936 to prevent these discriminatory practices between sellers and large buyers. Essentially, the Robinson-Patman Act prohibits any nonretail seller from selling goods of like grade and quality at different prices to different buyers if the result would be to substantially lessen competition.

The Wheeler-Lea Act

This act was passed as an amendment to the Federal Trade Commission Act in 1938. Specifically, the Wheeler-Lea Act allows the FTC to prohibit deceptive acts and unfair methods of competition. The FTC was given the following additional powers:

1. Initiate investigations against firms without waiting for formal complaints
2. Regulate activities and practices that deceive consumers
3. Issue cease and desist orders
4. Fine firms that do not comply with cease and desist orders

A cease and desist order is a ruling made by the FTC. It is a request that a company stop a particular practice that the FTC believes to be illegal. When a firm complies with the order, it will usually not hear from the FTC again. But if the firm does not comply with the order, the FTC can prosecute for violation of antitrust laws. Firms can appeal cease and desist orders within 60 days of the date they are issued.

The Celler-Kefauver Act

This act, passed in 1950, amends Section 7 of the Clayton Act. The Celler-Kefauver Act prohibits one firm from purchasing the assets of another firm when the effect would be to lessen competition or create a monopoly. Prior to 1950, only the acquisition of stock was illegal.

The Federal Trade Commission Improvement Act

Increased consumer orientation by the FTC, along with additional rule-making and regulatory power were provided by the Federal Trade Commission Improvement Act of 1975. The FTC Improvement Act expanded the power of the FTC in the following ways:

1. It gives the FTC the right to designate specific marketing practices as unfair or deceptive.

2. It allows the FTC to support (monetarily) the participation of consumer groups and other interest groups in rule-making procedures.

3. It permits the FTC to fine companies that violate trade rules.

4. It declares that cease and desist orders against one firm could serve as the basis for penalizing other companies that engage in the same practices.

5. It allows the FTC to obtain restitution for consumers that have been deceived. The FTC can change deceptive company contracts, force companies to refund money, force companies to pay damages, or force companies to make public their deceptive practices.

The Hart-Scott-Rodino Antitrust Improvement Act

This act was passed in 1976 and again, strengthens Section 7 of the Clayton Act. The Hart-Scott-Rodino Act requires a company to notify the FTC of its intentions to merge with another company. The purpose of this act was to give the FTC more time in preparing its case against the proposed merger.

CONSUMER PROTECTION

As indicated earlier, the government is actively involved in protecting consumers from unfair business practices. Toward this same end, a number of consumer protection laws have been passed. Consumer protection goes beyond the powers of the FTC and is not a new concept. For example, the Food and Drug Act was passed in 1906, before the Federal Trade Commissions Act. Consumer protection represents attempts by the government to make consumer buying less risky and consumer buying mistakes less costly.

A less formal type of consumer protection emerged during the early 1900s. Known today as consumerism, it began when production and distribution capacity ran ahead of effective demand and the competition for customers became intense. At the same time, a vast array of new and more complicated products made buying more difficult and confusing. General consumer frustration appeared in the form of fairly well organized protests in the 1920s. One outcome of these protests was the development of a nonprofit testing agency known as Consumers Research, Inc., which, today, publishes *Consumer Reports*.

The depression and World War II and the Korean War diminished the importance of consumerism until the early 1960s when Ralph Nader published *Unsafe at Any Speed,* Rachel Carson published *Silent Spring,* and Jessica Mitford published *The American Way of Death.* These publications, and others like them, indicted marketing organizations for the damage caused to consumers and society by their products and methods. The movement was spurred on by President Kennedy's famous consumer bill of rights speech in 1962. His speech included the following consumer rights:

1. The right to safety—to be protected against the marketing of goods that are hazardous to health or life.

2. The right to be informed—to be protected against fraudulent, deceitful, or grossly misleading information, advertising, or labeling or other practices and to be given the facts needed to make an informed choice.
3. The right to choose—to be assured, wherever possible, access to a variety of products and services at competitive prices.
4. The right to be heard—to be assured that the consumer interest will receive full and sympathetic consideration in the formulation of government policy.

Since this speech, literally hundreds of consumer interest groups have formed, all interested in preserving the rights of consumers to be protected from certain products or marketing policies and strategies. This trend has seen a resurgence in the early 1990s, and marketers are paying more and more attention to the needs and wants of these consumer interest groups as well as the needs and wants of the individual consumer.

GOVERNMENT REGULATORY AGENCIES

Congress has established several government regulatory agencies that are responsible for enforcing consumer protection laws. Regulatory agencies can have a great effect on an organization's marketing performance. The agencies have the power to administer laws by enforcing rules and regulations. In some cases, agencies even have the power to determine what the rules will be in the future and how they will be enforced.

SELF-REGULATION

As you saw in the ethics chapter, self-regulation is increasing in importance as a substitute for government regulation. Industry trade associations, organizations such as the Better Business Bureau, and industries capitalizing on other industries' inability to respond to consumer needs and wants all represent potential ways of improving the responsiveness of marketers to consumers.

Three of the more successful self-regulation activities of marketers are (a) the regulation of advertising by the National Advertising Review Board (NARB), (b) the work of the Better Business Bureau (BBB) at the local level, and (c) the work of the National Association of Broadcasters (NAB). The NARB has had many successes in monitoring deceptive advertising. Similarly, the BBB has been very effective in monitoring and publicizing unfair and deceptive marketing practices. The BBB, supported by local businesses, investigates complaints and attempts to convince the offender to stop questionable practices. It can seek legal remedies, if necessary. NAB sets standards for television stations. Standards are established for both commercials and programming.

6

Ethics and Marketing Information Decisions

PURPOSE

To describe some of the ethical issues faced by marketing professionals that are related to marketing research and the use of marketing information.

MAJOR POINTS

Accurate and timely market information is important to marketing professionals for many reasons.

Information is communicated to the marketplace, information is collected by marketing organizations, and information is communicated to the marketing organization.

Ethical issues concerning market research and information can occur (a) in the way the research is conducted, (b) in using information in relationship with clients, and (c) in gathering information about competitors.

We live in an age of information. In fact, we are probably overwhelmed with information. Marketing organizations engage in considerable information-gathering activities to develop and guide their marketing programs. Of interest in this chapter are ethical issues associated with information as it relates to three groups—customers, clients, and competitors. Before discussing these issues, please refer to Newsline 6.1, which will give you some idea of the scope of the ethical problems concerning information.

Newsline 6.1

Computer "Cracking" Is Seen on the Rise

NEW YORK—Tomorrow is the fifth anniversary of the Internet's most celebrated security lapse. The Internet is vastly bigger now, and, as one Internet provider just learned, so are the opportunities for computer mischief.

Public Access Network Corp., a commercial service known as Panix that sells its customers access to the Internet, was penetrated by an unauthorized system "cracker," who obtained high-level access to the system, forcing it to shut down for three days in late October. But many other Internet-connected networks may have been affected.

The globe-spanning Internet, which some estimate is growing by up to 8 million users a month, comprises thousands of individual computer networks. The intruder stole the secret passwords of Panix users who were using the service to connect to other networks. Panix says it has about 3,000 customers. In an electronic message to more than 175 other networks on the Internet, Panix's system administrators warned that "a security incident of very large proportion" had occurred.

The magnitude and consequences of the breach are unknown, because the cracker's programs were hidden in the Panix system, collecting information for some time. "For all I know, this cracker has passwords to hundreds, maybe thousands of locations," says Alexis Rosen, co-owner of Panix.

Crackers Are Better Organized

In November 1988, a Cornell University graduate student, Robert T. Morris, made computer security front-page news when he launched an electronic "virus" that crashed some 6,000 computers on the Internet. Mr. Morris, who became the first person charged with violating the federal Computer Fraud and Abuse Act, did not realize that his rogue program could be destructive. (He was fined $10,000 and served 400 hours of community service.) But now, warn industry experts, the "cracking" community is much better organized and sophisticated. What's more, as a chain of networks, the Internet is only as strong as its weakest, or most unsecured link; once a cracker has broken into one network on the Internet, others are vulnerable.

"We're seeing a tremendous increase" in cracking, says Dain Gary, manager of the Computer Emergency Response Team (CERT), which helps network administrators cope with break-ins on the Internet. "The trend directly corresponds to the growth in the Internet."

Mr. Gary says that his group, which is funded by the government and was started after the Morris incident, logs three to four security breaches a day. This year, Mr. Gary expects a 50% increase over last year's 773 reported security breaches. But fearing embarrassment and loss of public confidence, businesses rarely report break-ins; experts estimate that only 15% of breaches are reported to law-enforcement authorities.

Consequently, the cost and impact of such breaches are hard to assess. Mr. Rosen of Panix, which is based in New York City, estimates that the incident cost $4,000 in credit to users who couldn't use the system for the three days it was down. That amount, he adds, doesn't take into account the 22-hour days he and his system administrators spent rebuilding their software.

Breaches Are Costly

At Columbia University, one of many academic sites whose security may have been compromised by the Panix break-in, system administrators estimate that they pay $50,000 each year in overtime spent coping with security breaches. "We have account break-ins routinely," says Alan Crosswell, Columbia's manager of computing systems. "It's a big deal."

James Settle, supervisory special agent of the FBI's National Computer Crimes Squad, says most networks connected to the Internet are potentially at risk. That includes "telecommunications computer networks, stock markets or any kind of computer network that doesn't have secure systems. You can be connected to someone else who is connected (to the Internet) and become vulnerable," he says. Like using a stolen credit card, crackers can run up thousands of dollars in charges to unsuspecting users. In fact, since some users give networks credit-card numbers for billing purposes, these too could be revealed. Crackers with proper access could also tap into electronic mail and other confidential personal files.

As security measures have improved since the 1988 Cornell incident, so have the crackers. The teenage hacker testing system limits for the thrill of it, says Mr. Settle of the FBI, "has grown up." Now in his mid-20s, the typical cracker is in it for monetary gain, including charging for industrial espionage, Mr. Settle says, while declining to discuss past cases.

Crackers probe for weaknesses in a network's operating system, the program that manages all other software programs. Once a loophole is found, the news gets spread in underground publications, at cracker conventions, and on computer bulletin boards. Cracker-designed programs that exploit these defects and search for crucial information are distributed in much the same way.

In the case of Panix, administrators eventually found the "sniffer" program that the cracker had installed to watch and take notes as Panix's users logged onto other computer networks. By monitoring those activities, the cracker stole the passwords to those other networks.

In May, The Village, a Cambridge, Mass., Internet access provider, spotted a cracker. "It wasn't a mild prank by any stretch of the imagination," says Brendan E. Quinn, the system administrator who spent three days rebuilding his network. When the cracker sensed administrators were tracking him, he deleted a crucial system file, paralyzing Village's network.

Security-conscious companies with sensitive information that are tied to the Internet usually try to build a "firewall," a combination of hardware and software measures that make cracking much more difficult. Commercial on-line services are less at risk because they only offer gateways to the Internet—essentially doors that open periodically to allow electronic mail to pass both ways. "We built enough checkpoints into the system that it's virtually impossible to crack," says a spokeswoman for American Online Inc. Since the Internet is not closely governed but rather operated by a loose confederation of its users, Internet-wide security measures are difficult to implement.

SOURCE: Sandberg, Jared. (1993, November 1). "Computer 'Cracking' Is Seen on the Rise." *Wall Street Journal,* p. B5. Reprinted by permission of the *Wall Street Journal,* © 1993 Dow Jones & Company, Inc. All rights reserved worldwide.

ETHICAL ISSUES IN GATHERING INFORMATION FROM CUSTOMERS

Marketing research has received considerable attention in the ethics literature (e.g., Tsalikis & Fritzche, 1989). Developing good relations with consumers is vital for the undertaking of marketing research. Marketers rely on information from consumers to make decisions concerning their marketplace offerings. Indeed, marketers cannot survive without information from consumers. Figure 6.1 depicts the importance of consumer information to marketing decision makers. As shown in Figure 6.1, the marketing organization makes decisions concerning products to be offered to the marketplace and how those products will be priced, promoted, and distributed. Consumers respond to parts of the market offering in different ways. These responses are typified by the consumer decision process shown in Figure 6.1. Consumers' responses are translated in the organization's ability to achieve various objectives. Finally, complicating this process is the fact that environmental factors can and do influence the organization's decisions concerning its market offerings and how consumers make decisions in the marketplace. So as you can see, marketing organizations must gather and analyze considerable information to make good marketplace decisions.

One source of market information comes from the consumer. Without consumer goodwill, consumers will not respond to surveys issued by marketing researchers. So consumer goodwill is essential for the quality of research and perhaps even the survival of the industry. Nevertheless, there have been many ethical abuses associated with the process of gathering information from consumers. One reason for this is that research is done with at least some motivation for profit. Like other marketing activities, the lure of profit can often be so tempting that it leads decision

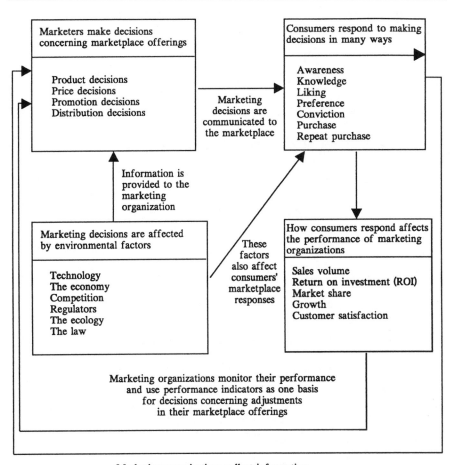

Figure 6.1.
Information and
Marketing Decision
Making

makers in making questionable decisions or using questionable tactics to reach a desired goal (Schneider, 1982, p. 591). Table 6.1 provides a summary of the ethical issues that have arisen when consumers are asked to be respondents in the marketing research process.

You might ask, "What's the big deal about anonymity?" Well, one reason for promising anonymity is that consumers will respond more readily to market surveys

Respondent Anonymity

Table 6.1 Ethical Issues
Involving Respondents

Ethical Issues	Rights Violations
Respondent anonymity	Right to privacy
Exposing respondents to stress	Right to safety
Use of special equipment and techniques	Right to privacy, safety, choice
Participants have prior knowledge	Right to be informed, privacy
Deceptive techniques	Right to be informed
Coercive techniques	Right to choice
Selling disguised as research	Right to be informed
Embarrassing/offensive	Right to respect

SOURCE: Adapted from *Marketing Research: Methodological Foundations*, Fifth Edition by Gilbert A. Churchill, Jr. Copyright © 1991 by The Dryden Press, reproduced by permission of the publisher.

if they believe their anonymity is preserved (Tybout & Zaltman, 1974). Greater response means better quality information for the research firm and its client. Furthermore, greater response presents other opportunities for the research firm and its client. It is these other opportunities where ethical issues concerning anonymity arise.

Most research that is conducted is done so with a promise that each respondent's comments will be kept anonymous. Many organizations have provisions in their codes of ethics designed to protect the consumer's right to privacy. For example, the American Marketing Association Code of Ethics (see Appendix in Chapter 3) contains the following statement concerning anonymity:

> If respondents have been led to believe, directly or indirectly, that they are participating in a market research survey and that their anonymity will be protected, their names shall not be made known to anyone outside the research organization or research department, or used for other than research purposes. (p. 1)

One reason for this is that any consumer's responses to a survey could be used by the research organization or the research organization's client for the purpose of obtaining sales leads. The use of the customer's information in this way represents a violation of the customer's right to privacy. Furthermore, it will serve to discredit the research organization that made the promise of anonymity.

Information about consumers can also be obtained in other ways. For example, credit card companies have sold information about card holders without the permission of the cardholders or without providing compensation for the cardholders. Such practices violate the Code of Fair Information Practices of 1973, which states, "There must be a way for individuals to prevent information about themselves obtained for one purpose from being used or made available for other purposes without their consent" (Senn, 1990, p. 724).

Problems with anonymity have been exacerbated by the recent growth in tele-marketing practices of many organizations. Consumers do not make the distinction between telemarketing for the purpose of making sales and marketing research being conducted over the phone (Honomichl, 1991). As a result, there is greater skepticism about respondent anonymity in marketing research. There is also greater reluctance on the part of consumers to participate in legitimate marketing research projects because consumers fear they are being set up for a sale.

There have been times when respondents in a research study have experienced stress because they believe that they have to know the answers to certain questions (Day, 1975). Or they may feel that they are being put "on the spot" because they may not be able to distinguish their proclaimed favorite brand from other brands. Creditable research organizations take the responsibility to make their respondents feel comfortable with the research process. Among other things, their interviewers are instructed to provide a relaxed environment, to work with respondents to make them feel comfortable and to provide statements such as, "There are no correct responses— we are only interested in *your opinion.*"

Respondent Stress

Other recommendations to reduce stress include allowing respondents to ask questions during and after interviews. Such practices are in keeping with the consumer's right to be heard and the right to safety. Many research companies also debrief respondents, letting respondents know something about the nature of the project and how the results will be used after the interview is complete.

Most codes require researchers to identify themselves and the research organizations for which they are employed. But client confidentiality is permissible because respondents may have a bias against the client that would lead them to providing biased information. The respondent has certain rights to information concerning the research process. The divulging of certain information, however, such as the identity of the client, may lead to poor results and render the entire research undertaking useless from quality of information perspective. For this reason, many organizations that wish to do research employ the services of an outside firm. The research is then conducted using the outside firm's name.

Deceptive Practices in Research

Any respondent has the right to withdraw from an interview or refuse to answer certain questions contained in the interview. Some codes even go so far as to state that in the case of respondent withdrawal, any information obtained up until that point in time should not be used by the research organization. In essence, such provisions recognize the voluntary nature of the respondent's participation.

Coercion in the Research Process

Although provisions such as these exist in many codes, ethical violations still occur. For example, interviewers work hard at setting up interviews and may feel pressured to use persuasive techniques to induce a participant to continue with an interview out of a sense of obligation. Another form of coercive behavior may exist in situations in which there is a captive audience (e.g., surveys of employees) in which the individuals may believe that certain penalties may occur for nonparticipation.

The potential for coercive techniques in telephone interviews is very high because the interviewer may feel that he or she has nothing to lose if the respondent refuses to answer questions. In actuality, the interviewer may lose much because respondents answering under duress may be prone to bending the truth or lying, which will distort the results of the survey. When survey results are distorted, clients using them can make incorrect and costly marketplace decisions. In general, it is always a wise practice for researchers to obtain the informed expressed consent of any respondents when conducting interviews (Frey & Kinnear, 1979). This helps ensure that compliance is voluntary and helps to improve the quality of information obtained.

Using Research as an Entry to Sell

Many codes of ethics specifically state that selling under the disguise of research is an unethical practice. Such codes state that if the research procedure requires selling or a simulated selling situation, then the nature of the situation must be explained to respondents after the research has been completed. Moreover, any money that has changed hands must be reimbursed to the participants.

"Sugging," as it is called, is an illegal practice in the United States (Frey & Kinnear, 1979). One form of sugging occurs when respondents are asked to answer questions about some subject and then are told they have won a prize. When they attempt to collect their prize they are required to sit through a sales presentation ("We Woz Sugged," 1991). Today, because of pressures associated with the telemarketing boom, many research firms tell respondents "up front" that they are not selling anything. Nevertheless, selling disguised as research still occurs and there is growing resentment on the part of consumers (Schlossberg, 1991).

The European Society for Opinion and Marketing Research (ESOMAR) has undertaken a program calling for self-regulation among telemarketers (Coleman, 1992), the major issue being sugging. One of the recommendations includes the clear distinction between selling and research activities when both are conducted by the same organization. *How do you feel about this? Is selling under the guise of research unethical? Should telephone researchers be required to inform respondents that no form of selling is involved? Should respondents be given the opportunity to obtain information about the research organization at no cost to themselves?*

Embarrassing and Offending Respondents

Typically, respondents receive nothing in return for their participation in marketing research. At least they are entitled to respect. Researchers should respect the respondent's time, feelings, dignity, and voluntary nature of the research process.

The research process should be made as positive an experience as possible for the respondents. This, of course, simply represents treating others properly. From a financial perspective, however, such treatment of participants is recommended because the quality of information from poorly treated respondents is suspect and therefore so are the decisions made using that information.

Although the preceding discussion has focused on situations in which surveys may lead to embarrassment for respondents, there are other ways in which the collection of information may pose embarrassment for consumers. For example, car rental companies are creating "black lists" of bad drivers (Hirsch, 1993). Some car companies are checking motor vehicle department records to screen out high-risk drivers. Two large companies, Hertz Corporation and National Car Rental Systems, Inc., place rejected drivers on "do-not-rent" lists that prevent them from renting a car anywhere in the country. Avis is looking into developing a similar list. The rental car people argue that such lists improve safety on the road. But critics argue that the lists might be abused and are subject to error. *What do you think? Is the development of so-called black lists for drivers an ethical practice? What issues would you consider if you were asked to make an ethical judgment concerning this situation?*

As you have already read, researchers should operate under conditions of voluntary cooperation of respondents, informed consent of respondents and the consumer's right to information. Codes of ethics require that statements used to secure respondent cooperation in marketing research must be factual and must be honored by the research organization.

Involving Participation Without Prior Knowledge

An ethical issue concerning prior knowledge can occur when research is conducted using observation techniques. Some research involves observing consumers while they shop, and the consumer is often unaware of the fact that he or she is being observed (Churchill, 1991). This is a difficult issue because informing consumers prior to observation may alter their behavior. Several suggestions have been advanced to handle the ethical problems associated with observation techniques, including (a) posting a notice in the store area that behaviors are being observed, (b) asking permission of the shoppers after the information has been collected, and (c) providing the opportunity to refuse to participate.

Influence peddling can occur at any level of the organization. In fact, questions about influence peddling have even been raised about the highest position in the country, the president of the United States. Although at the time of this writing, the allegations have not been proven, there are many questions concerning the diversion of funds from a savings and loan institution to politicians seeking reelection (Ingersoll & Barrett, 1993). In particular, the U.S. attorney's office is investigating whether checks drawn on a savings and loan institution went into a campaign fund for President Clinton. Although the jury is still out and I hope that the president is cleared of any wrongdoing, the case serves to illustrate that there is always the possibility that anyone in marketing can seek to influence others through the issuing of cash payments. *What do you think should be the strategy when someone tries to peddle influence by paying another? What types of information needs do you think might prompt such influence attempts? Can you think of ways in which such information can be obtained in an ethical manner?*

The Use of Equipment and Research Techniques   Some marketing research requires the use of certain kinds of equipment or the use of special research techniques. Codes of ethics require that participants have prior knowledge of the use of various equipment, such as videotape recorders or other monitoring devices. At times, respondents are observed and recorded in places where their behavior can reasonably be expected to be observed (e.g., in a store). For such circumstances, ethics codes usually specify that all reasonable precautions be taken to ensure anonymity and that individuals are told immediately after shopping that their actions have been observed and recorded. Furthermore, these individuals should be given the opportunity to see the recordings or the information that was obtained and, if so desired, withdrawn from the research process.

Some of the controversy revolves around the argument that the use of unobtrusive research techniques (i.e., the respondent does not know he or she is being observed) violates the respondent's right to choose. One choice involves participation in the research. A second choice might involve the participant's avoidance of stores in which such research is undertaken, thereby restricting the respondent's store and (possibly) brand choice. Before we proceed to the next section, Table 6.2 provides a brief summary of some data protection principles that ethical marketing researchers will follow.

▧ ETHICAL ISSUES AND CLIENTS

Recently, Lotus Development Corporation, a $200-million software marketer sued Rossin, Greenberg, Seronick & Hill, a $26-million advertising agency. The basis for the suit was a flyer that was given Lotus by rival software company, Microsoft Corporation. Microsoft had received the flyer from the advertising agency pitching the $10 million plus Microsoft business. The flyer sent to Microsoft read as follows:

"You probably haven't thought about talking to an agency in Boston. . . . But since we know your competition's plans, isn't it worth taking a flyer? The reason we know so much about Lotus is that some of our newest employees just spent the past year

Personal data held by data users

Table 6.2 Data
Protection Principles

1. The information to be contained in personal data shall be obtained, and personal data shall be processed, fairly and lawfully.

2. Personal data shall be held only for one or more specified and lawful purposes.

3. Personal data held for any purpose or purposes shall not be used or disclosed in any manner incompatible with that purpose or those purposes.

4. Personal data held for any purpose or purposes shall be adequate, relevant, and not excessive in relation to that purpose or those purposes.

5. Personal data held for any purpose or purposes shall not be kept for longer than is necessary for that purpose or those purposes.

6. An individual shall be entitled

   a. at reasonable intervals and without undue delay or expense

      i. to be informed by any data user whether he [or she] holds personal data of which that individual is the subject; and
      ii. to access to any such data held by a data user, and

   b. where appropriate, to have such data corrected or erased.

Personal data held by data users or . . . computer bureau

7. Appropriate security measures shall be taken against unauthorized access to, or alteration, disclosure, or destruction of personal data.

SOURCE: Bell (1984). Reprinted with permission of Personnel Publications Ltd.

and a half working on the Lotus business at another agency. So they are intimately acquainted with Lotus' thoughts about Microsoft and their plans to deal with the introduction of [Microsoft's] Excel." (Horton, 1986, p. 9)

How aggressively can an advertising agency promote its past experience with a competitor when going after a new client? What do you think of Microsoft's reaction? Does Lotus have a justifiable lawsuit? The advertising agency plans to countersue Lotus. What charges do you think they can bring?

Consumers as participants in research are not the only individuals who are confronted with ethical problems in the information-gathering process. Table 6.3 provides a summary of responses by marketing researchers who were asked to identify their most difficult ethical issue, many of which concern the relationship between the research agency and the client, including research integrity, treating outside clients fairly, and research confidentiality (Hunt, Chonko, & Wilcox, 1984).

Research integrity issues include deliberately withholding information, falsifying data, altering research results, misusing statistics, ignoring important and relevant information, compromising the design of the research process (i.e., collecting information in the wrong way), and misinterpreting the result of research with the objective of supporting a predetermined "goal" of the client.

Table 6.3 Ethical Issues in Marketing Research[a]

Issue	In-House Researchers Frequency (n = 196)		Agency Researchers Frequency (n = 99)		Total Frequency (n = 295)	
	Number	Percentage	Number	Percentage	Number	Percentage
1. Research integrity	62	31	37	37	99	33
2. Treating outside clients fairly	15	8	16	16	31	11
3. Research confidentiality	15	8	12	12	27	9
4. Marketing mix social issues	17	9	6	6	23	8
5. Personnel issues	14	7	6	6	20	7
6. Treating respondents fairly	17	9	2	2	19	6
7. Treating others in company fairly	11	6	1	1	12	4
8. Interviewer dishonesty	1	1	9	9	10	3
9. Gifts, bribes, entertainment	6	3	2	2	8	3
10. Treating suppliers fairly	8	4	—	—	8	3
11. Legal issues	8	4	—	—	8	3
12. Misuse of funds	5	3	1	1	6	2
13. Other	17	9	7	7	24	8

SOURCE: Hunt, S. D., Chonko, L. B., & Wilcox, J. B. (1984). "Ethical Problems of Marketing Researchers." *Journal of Marketing Research, 21*, pp. 309-324. Reprinted by permission of the American Marketing Association.
a. Response to open-ended question: "In all professions (e.g., law, medicine, education, accounting, marketing, etc.), managers are exposed to at least some situations that pose a moral or ethical problem. Would you please briefly describe the job situation that poses the *most difficult* moral or ethical problem for you?"

One of the researchers made the following comment:

It is tough to be in a position where you criticize management. Much marketing research is only "eye wash" for the wholesale buyers to convince them that the product is indeed needed and will sell in volume—almost a "fraudulent" situation.

A second client-related ethical issue concerned the fair treatment of clients. The predominant issue here concerned prices charged for marketing research. Ethical problems included passing on hidden charges to the client, cutting corners on making sure that the research was valid in an effort to keep costs down, and the use of more expensive retainer-type contracts as opposed to less expensive, fixed-price, one project contracts.

Confidentiality issues arose as researchers struggled to balance the interests of different clients. Another confidentiality issue concerned the use of information received by a former (and unethical) employee of a competitive organization. This is, indeed a difficult issue. When individuals change companies it is often difficult to separate background information and knowledge from information and knowledge developed specifically for the employee's former organization. Table 6.3 provides a

Overstating the value of the conclusions	Not informing clients of the limitations of research	**Table 6.4** Ethical Problems That Can Occur Between Clients and Researchers
Reporting what the client "wants to hear"	Overbilling the client	
Conducting research that is not needed	Failure to reveal certain findings	
Using specialized language that the client does not understand	Failure to maintain client confidentiality	
Misuse of statistical analysis to obtain "desired" results	Failure to avoid possible conflicts of interest	
Use of shortcuts to save on expenses	Changing research procedures after proposal has been approved without consent of client	
Using the wrong research approach to collect information needed by client	Client solicits research proposals for purpose of gaining information with no intention of employing services of proposers	
Using individuals with insufficient expertise to conduct the research project	Client cancels project for no reason	
Fitting the client's research needs to the type of research in which the research organization specializes	Client refuses to pay for project	

brief summary of some more of the possible ethical problems that concern researchers and their clients.

Before we leave this section, keep in mind that clients are not perfect either. Table 6.4 lists several ethical abuses initiated by clients. As you can see, more than half of the respondents indicated that they are "fairly or very often" asked to bid on projects they have no chance of securing because of client purchasing policies. Furthermore, and something you should be aware of, over 60% of the respondents reported that clients distort research findings when communicating them to the public (Laroche, McGown, & Rainville, 1986).

▨ ETHICS AND COMPETITIVE INTELLIGENCE

Marketing decision making requires that an organization keep pace with what is happening in the marketplace. This means that knowledge of competitive offerings and strategies is needed to maintain a competitive edge in the marketplace. Information about competitors is highly valued, and there is nothing inherently wrong with collecting it. Competitive information forms one of the bases for positioning an organization's marketplace offerings. Furthermore, it forms the basis for one organization's gaining advantage over others in the marketplace. Unfortunately, although competitive intelligence is important, it is also prone to questionable marketplace behaviors.

Theft of and misappropriation of competitive information has grown considerably over the last several years ("Information Thieves," 1986). One reason for such corporate espionage is that legitimate research can be very expensive. It is often cheaper to get ideas from a competitor than to invest in research. Of course, allegations are often difficult to prove as there is so much information available, and much of it can be obtained from a variety of legitimate sources. Nevertheless, controversies such as searching trash in the casket industry (Johnson, 1987), cookie recipe espionage (Neiman, 1984), and piracy in the rental car industry (Lewin, 1984) continue to arise.

As competition intensifies, the pressure to maintain competitive advantage in the marketplace grows. Traditionally, competitive information was used as a means of trying to determine how one company's market offerings fit in the marketplace. Today, however, the use of competitive information has become much more negative. Competitors make disparaging comments about each other in advertising. Salespeople talk down about competition. Retailers continually claim they have better prices than their competitors. In other words, the trend is toward using competitive information to undermine the competition.

Because of competitive pressures, companies provide incentives for their employees to obtain competitive information. On the downside, such practices can provide the incentive for engaging in questionable intelligence-gathering approaches. In general, questionable intelligence-gathering techniques are used to gain access to information that a competitor has chosen not to make public. Although no one questions the value of such information to a competitor, there are many who question the techniques used to gain access to information that competitors do not wish to publicly divulge.

Misrepresentation   Misrepresentation occurs in many forms—conducting phony job interviews, hiring students to gather information under the disguise of student projects (Ansberry, 1987), students gathering information and after graduation using that information to open up a competing business, posing as a potential capital supplier. Each of these activities represents an unethical means of obtaining information about competitive activities. Unfortunately, many organizations condone the use of such questionable strategies. In one study, 46% of the respondents reported that they approved of posing as students to gather information about competitors (Cohen & Czepiec, 1988).

In the Bible, Zaccheus, the famous tax collector, became a follower of Jesus. Prior to this time, Zaccheus had collected far more taxes than were warranted from many of the people. He willingly misrepresented the amount of tax they owed. After he became a follower, he went directly to those he had wronged and made restitution. In fact, he was so eager to correct his ways that he said he would be willing to give half of his possessions to the poor and that if he had defrauded anyone, he would repay them fourfold (see Luke 19:8).

Do things such as Zaccheus' situation happen today? Let me relate a personal story. When I was studying for my Ph.D., I would do jigsaw puzzles until 4 or 5 in the morning for sanity. Implied with every puzzle is the promise that "all the pieces will be in the box." One night, I completed a 3,000-piece puzzle, except for the missing piece. I wrote a very nasty letter to the company. The company's response? A new box of the same puzzle—and two new puzzles! The company made restitution. I was in shock. I've told every class I have ever taught this story (for about 17 years).

Influence Peddling

At times, questionable research techniques might be used in an effort to influence potential informants in ways that cause them to violate the confidentiality of their employers. One common means of influence is the offering of inducements (bribes) in exchange for company information that is considered to be confidential. Inducements commonly come in the form of cash payments but can also come in other forms, such as promotion opportunities. Although the practice of influencing people in exchange for information may seem obviously unethical, many executives have stated they would use the practice (Brenner & Molander, 1977). Furthermore, many executives will tell you that they hire employees away from competitors and expect those employees to reveal competitive secrets (Wall, 1977).

Influence-peddling approaches erode the relationships of trust and confidence that employers should have with employees. Using such approaches, those seeking information create a conflict in the minds of the person from whom they are seeking interest. Of course, the information seeker has only his or her own self-interest in mind, but this is not communicated to other parties. The other party is approached with a "deal" that leads to possible reward. The lure of the rewards is the factor that can lead to the conflict concerning whether or not to reveal confidential information. The information seeker's logic is that the information being sought cannot be obtained because it is confidential or can be obtained through influence peddling less expensively than through other ethical approaches.

One of the difficulties surrounding information confidentiality is answering the question, What information is confidential? Many employees, suppliers, and customers really do not know the answer to this. And there may be differences of opinion.

For example, suppose a salesperson provides a customer with some information that the salesperson feels is provided in confidence. If the customer does not know this or does not think it is confidential, that customer may reveal that information to others, unknowingly violating the original seller's confidentiality. Like many other ethics questions, it is very easy for those who reveal confidential information to plead "I didn't know" in many cases.

Surveillance—How Much James Bond Is Acceptable?

Few of us would argue that technology has provided many positive benefits for organizations and for consumers. Technology, however, has also increased the ability of one organization to engage in surveillance activities of other organizations' information and activities. Today, electronic surveillance, bugging offices, and aerial photography are used to obtain information that otherwise might be confidential.

When surveillance involves the use of technology, it is akin to trespassing or theft and is subject to legal redress. But what happens when one person happens to eavesdrop on a competitor at a social function? Well, the prevailing legal opinion is that corporations have no legal right to privacy, but many organization representatives still feel that there is a right to privacy and that they should be able to assume that they will not be observed or listened to in certain situations.

Regardless of the method used, surveillance techniques fall right out of the James Bond novels. They represent ways for someone to obtain information that otherwise could not be obtained because the owner of the information does not wish to reveal it. But where does one draw the line? For example, how would you evaluate the ethical nature of the following surveillance techniques?

1. Placing an electronic bug in a competitors' office
2. Having a salesperson observe and count the number of grocery store shelf facings commanded by competitors in order to estimate their sales volume
3. A vice president of marketing attending an opera overhearing two competitors discussing information that is considered confidential
4. Using aerial photography to monitor a competitor's construction progress on a new manufacturing facility
5. Having employees or nonemployees sit outside a competitor's distribution centers and count the number of trucks leaving in an effort to estimate sales
6. Carrying a mini tape recorder so that you can record all of your conversations at a trade show that many customers and competitors will be attending

Suppose you are interested in buying a piece of road maintenance equipment at a cost of $275,000. You call Caterpillar, Inc. to inquire, but you reach a voice mail system. You leave a message for a salesperson to contact you in the morning. The next morning, a salesperson calls you, but you quickly discover that this salesperson represents a competitor of the company you called yesterday. You inquire about how this salesperson knew to call you and the response given to you is that it was just a coincidence. What do you think? Later in the day the salesperson from Caterpillar calls and you relate your call from the competitor. The CAT salesperson says that such calls are a regular occurrence, that stealing business leads from voice mail systems is reaching epidemic proportions. The CAT salesperson tells you that Caterpillar monitors voice mail theft by placing false messages from fictitious customers (actual calls in response to these false messages made by competitive salespeople have shown that about 75% of all of their false messages result in a call from a competitor). *Now what do you think? Is the competitor acting in an ethical fashion? How about Caterpillar? Do either or both of these activities fall into the practice of espionage?*

We'll make one more comment about espionage. When Linda Paris opened up the phone bill for her company, Philadelphia Newspapers, Inc., she discovered over 6,000 calls made to Pakistan, Egypt, and the Dominican Republic (Lewyn, 1991). These were places the Philadelphia reporters rarely called. The bill for these calls was over $90,000, nearly one fourth of the Knight-Ridder, Inc. unit's entire phone bill. Philadelphia Newspapers was a victim of a relatively new type of crime called PBX fraud. Thieves can steal a password and tap into a PBX and then dial anywhere in the world, "free of charge." Often the thieves are drug dealers who place hard-to-trace calls. PBX thieves are hard to catch. Oftentimes, they break into one PBX and make their call, but instead of dialing their final destination, they also break into a second PBX to complete the call. This makes it even more difficult to track the caller. *Although the preceding scenario might not exactly fit your conception of espionage, if a person can "steal" phone time through the use of computers, what other information might be stolen in a similar way?*

One of the difficulties involved in marketing is keeping trade secrets. For example, if you were a competitor, how would you like to know the formula for Coca-Cola, or the programming code for Microsoft's Windows, or the subscriber list for the *Wall Street Journal*? Each of these is a trade secret. To be a trade secret, the information must not be generally known, and it must provide a competitive advantage (Lans, 1993). But a trade secret can be used by anyone who discovers it through honest means. This means that a person who works with the Coca-Cola formula, for example, has acquired that knowledge through honest means. If that person was to work for a competitor, the Coca-Cola formula could be learned by that competitor. To protect trade secrets, companies use confidentiality statements in their employment contracts for those who have access to trade secrets. They also implement plant security procedures designed to exclude the general public from access to trade secrets. Suppose you are an employee of a company that has trade secrets. That

Unsolicited Intelligence Gathering

company goes through a period of downsizing in which you lose your job. Prior to leaving, you reproduce copies of trade-secret documents and then go into business for yourself as a competitor of your former employer. *What do you think about the ethics of this situation? Did the company have trade secrets and were those trade secrets taken under false pretenses? Who would you decide for in a court of law? What issues would you consider?*

There are times when someone might come across confidential information that was not solicited in any way. This commonly occurs when an employee who is unhappy, leaves his or her former organization and gains employment with a competitor. As a means of retaliation, the unhappy former employee begins revealing proprietary information about his or her former organization.

Or suppose a salesperson unknowingly leaves a new price list on a customer's desk and the customer does not realize this. When a competitor enters the customer's office and sees the list, what should the competitor do? Should unsolicited information be respected as private by the competitor? The prevailing view and that expressed in the Uniform Trade Secrets Act suggests that confidential information that was not unsolicited should not be examined or used, although there is some disagreement on this issue. The basic argument against privacy is that any organization has the responsibility to be careful with its information. If information is lost due to carelessness, it is not unreasonable to expect that organization to suffer some consequences. *What do you think?*

Planning is important, and information is needed to plan effectively. We each have some inner drive that leads us to engage in planning—for college, for a career, for marriage. Marketing professionals plan to predict the future, to identify new markets, to develop new products. Planning is good but only if information is accurate and priorities are in order.

CHAPTER SUMMARY Marketing professionals rely on accurate and timely information as they make decisions. As information is collected and used, ethical problems can occur. There are many ethical problems related to gathering information from customers. There are also ethical problems concerning information use and clients. Finally, there are ethical problems associated with obtaining and using information about competitors.

▧ INFORMATION SCENARIOS

1. You have just been hired as a partner in a marketing consulting firm. After just a few weeks, you realize that this firm uses the experience and education of its partners as a key feature in its sales presentations to clients. But you have also seen that these individuals are not the ones primarily responsible for carrying out projects once they are obtained. Younger, less experienced associates assume these responsibilities. Some of these have graduated from college less than a year ago. Comment on this incident. What are the ethical issues in this situation? How would you handle these issues?

2. You are good friends with the sales vice president of one of your clients. Your research firm has just completed an attitude survey of all the salespeople in your friend's company. In analyzing the results of that survey you discover that several of the salespeople are having difficulties with their supervisors. You provide this information to your friend who promptly uses this information to conduct an "impromptu" performance review of all the sales supervisors. Comment on this incident. What are the ethical issues in this situation? How would you handle these issues?

3. You are the project director for your firm's research department. The marketing vice president wants you to provide supportive information for a product that is experiencing some difficulty in the market. You collected information from over 1,500 customers 2 years ago and their response, at that time, was positive toward this product. But something has changed and no one in your firm knows what. The marketing vice president has a great deal of his career invested in this product and informs you that it would be acceptable to use the data that was collected 2 years ago as supporting documentation for the product. Comment on this incident. What are the ethical issues in this situation? How would you handle these issues?

4. During a sales call with one of your better customers, your customer begins discussing some problems that her firm is having with one of their competitors. It seems that your customer is losing sales to this competitor. You inform your customer that you have some information about that competitor that will help your customer recover those lost sales. You also inform your customer that you will be willing to divulge that information if your customer increases the size of her company's order. Comment on this incident. What are the ethical issues in this situation? How would you handle these issues?

5. You are the promotion director for a large consumer product firm. Your company is about to launch a multimillion dollar advertising campaign for a new product that has taken 4 years to develop and test market. One week before the scheduled introduction, you discover the results of a lab test that have been hidden away in company files. These tests show that, under certain conditions, the product may inflict some harm on users. You discover this information about 2 hours before the final meeting set up to discuss the details of the new product introduction. Comment on this incident. What are the ethical issues in this situation? How would you handle these issues?

6. You are a sales representative and are making a sales call to a new customer. One of your leading products is about to be replaced by another one that is technologically superior but slightly more expensive. The customer does not know this but is interested in the older product. During the course of the conversation, the customer asks you about a disadvantage of the older product that will be eliminated by the newer version. Because you are in the middle of a sales contest and you need sales to win, you choose not to tell the customer about the upcoming improvements. Furthermore, the newer version of the product is not scheduled for marketing until next year, too late to do you any good in the current contest. Comment on this incident. What are the ethical issues in this situation? How would you handle these issues?

7. On April 1, you accepted a new position as product manager with one of your current firm's competitors. Your new job will not begin until June 1. Your present company requires 2 weeks minimum notice when employees quit. In the case of employment by a competitor, however, immediate resignations are demanded. You decide not to tell the company about the change in jobs until May 30. You need to be paid for the 2 months because you support a family and have one child in college and you rationalize that you might learn something interesting about your old company while you're still on the job (Dabholkar & Kellaris, 1992). What are the ethical issues in this situation? How would you handle these issues?

8. Mr. Kameswar R. Ati is an employee of AT&T. AT&T is seeking to bar him from moving to rival Fujitsu, Inc. The reason is that AT&T is trying to prevent Fujitsu from gaining access to confidential information to which Mr. Ati, a $47,500-a-year employee, has access (Cody, 1993). According to trade-secret specialists, pursuing a case against an employee so far down the corporate ladder is unusual. Do you think that AT&T's behavior is out of line? Do you think if the court decides for AT&T that other such actions by other companies would occur? At what corporate level do you think an employee should be immune from such actions as those taken by AT&T?

9. In a series of recent actions, the government has accused law firms of complicity in the failures in the savings and loan industries (Stevens, 1993). One of the key issues concerns the obligations of a law firm representing a savings and loan institution to the regulators. Should lawyers report suspected wrongdoing by a client's top officers to the client's directors? Some lawyers have complained about the immense amount of time spent creating excessively detailed information about what they have told their clients—just in case they are questioned later. They end up billing their clients for this practice. What do you think? Is it ethical for the law firm to bill clients for activities not required by regulators but undertaken "just in case" regulators inquire? Should an attorney representing a savings and loan be required to disclose to regulators that the savings and loan officials misled regulators?

10. You graduated from "Your University" just over 8 months ago. Your research firm has landed a client who has paid $350,000 for a marketing plan. The client relationship was developed by your firm's president and several of the principle researchers, each of whom has been with your firm for at least 20 years. They have assigned you to the project, telling you that the fee paid by the client is one of the largest ever received by the firm. It is your responsibility to take the lead on the project and design the plan. But you do not have to worry. The president and other "experienced" firm personnel will present the plan to the client. What do you think about the nature of this practice? How would the client react if it was revealed that someone with only 1 year of "research" experience was actually developing the marketing plan that they had paid $350,000 for?

11. You are employed by XYZ Strategic Marketing Consultants. Your firm has just completed a research project in which 2,000 customers of a client organization were polled for their opinions concerning the product quality of your client firm's offerings. Unfortunately, the results are not very favorable to your client's firm and your boss has told you to "massage" the results so that they appear to imply that your client's customers are positive about their marketplace offerings. How would you deal with this situation? What would you say to your supervisor? Suppose this was a regular client who paid your firm over $100,000 annually to conduct research on their behalf?

12. You have just completed a customer satisfaction study for your firm's largest customer. In that study you found that 8% of the client's customers were very satisfied with the client's products, 21% were satisfied, 35% were somewhat satisfied, 24% were somewhat dissatisfied, and 12% were very dissatisfied. You are instructed to report that 64% of the client's customers are satisfied with their

marketplace offerings. Is this an accurate reflection of the information obtained? How would you present the preceding results to a client in a way that would provide the most objective and usable information to the client?

13. Acme Research Corporation belongs to a trade association that has an active marketing research subgroup. At meetings of this subgroup, the marketing research directors routinely exchange confidential price information. Your firm's research director then turns this information over to the sales department but is careful not to let your firm's marketing executives know about the source of the information. The result is that your firm's sales and profitability are enhanced and top management is informed that the results are due to sales strategies and tactics. What ethical violations are occurring here? If you became aware of this situation and knew that the potential long-term consequences of such behavior were negative what course of action would you take? What circumstances might exist that would encourage you or discourage you from "blowing the whistle" on this practice (Akaah, 1989)?

14. You are the marketing research director for a large research company. Your firm frequently makes extensive studies of the retail climate in several large cities. You are approached by a federally supported minority group that is interested in getting a mall built in a minority area of one of these cities. They have asked you for access to the retail information your firm has obtained. Your firm has a policy of not sharing this information with trade associations. What would be your response to this group? How would you respond if they threatened you and your firm with a discrimination suit (Crawford, 1970)?

15. Your firm has contracted to conduct in-depth interviews with several hundred customers of a new client organization. The vice president of your firm wants to impress your client, so he instructs you to train interviewers to carry tape recorders in their attaché cases and not inform the clients that their interviews are being recorded. Does such a practice violate any ethical principles? How would you respond to the vice president's request? What recommendations can you make regarding the research procedure (Crawford, 1970)?

16. Your firm has signed a contract with a retailer to conduct a national mail survey of 25,000 of their customers. The retailer instructs you that the customers should be informed that their responses are to remain anonymous. But your superior directs you to code each questionnaire with ultraviolet ink so that respondents can be identified in case there is any need of following up with them. Your superior is in line for promotion to vice president, and she tells you that if the

response rate to this project and the results of the project are favorable to the retailer, her promotion is all but ensured. How would you handle this situation?

17. You are the marketing vice president for a manufacturer of high-tech products. You have just learned that a competitor has made an important scientific discovery that will result in a competitive advantage over your firm in the marketplace. You are good friends with one of your competitor's key technical people, and your president is aware of this relationship. Your president makes a "tongue in cheek" comment about hiring your friend, which you ignore. Several days later, however, the president asks you if you have talked to your friend about switching companies. How would you respond to this situation (Vitell & Festervand, 1987)?

18. You are the marketing research director for a local television station. You are asked by the station's general manager to conduct a survey that would justify a rate increase of 20% for advertising space during your station's programming. How would you respond to this request (Kelley, 1992a)?

19. You are a new employee at a marketing research firm. Your firm has a long-term contract with a client who wants to produce and market a "state-of-the art" fax machine. While conducting a project for your client, you learn that a competitor has plans to launch a new fax machine. The competitor's product seems to be of higher quality than the one your firm's client is considering. The marketing research director of your firm comes to you and tells you to pose as a potential buyer for the competitor's fax machine so that you obtain information about their intended offering. Should you accept this role (Artz, 1992)?

20. At-Home Gourmet Video Dinners have captured the interest of young affluent consumers who wish to entertain but do not want to spend hours laboring in the kitchen. Meanwhile, your company has invested $3 million in R&D on its own version of this product. Your company's menu is varied and has tested out as superior to the menu offered by At-Home Gourmet. Your company plans a national roll-out in 2 weeks. Late one night, you are watching TV and you see an ad for video dinners marketed by a third competitor. You are in shock. You, and no one in your company, had any idea that a third competitor was interested in this market. The product they are advertising looks exactly like your company's product. The menu is remarkably similar, and the packaging is almost identical to that planned for your company's products. What are your options (Bennett & Snell, 1988)?

INFORMATION MINICASE

XYZ Marketing Research

Greg is in the second month of employment with XYZ Marketing Research. The firm is a large, well-known, highly respected, very successful supplier of marketing research. Its clients include major companies in many different industries throughout the world.

Routine procedure is for Ms. Jordan and Mr. Collins to secure business in the form of research projects. Each project ends with an analyst preparing a written report with marketing strategy recommendations based on his or her interpretation of the data. This report is given to Elizabeth, who gives it to Ms. Jordan and Mr. Collins, who then deliver the written report, complete with a verbal presentation, to the client.

Projects are assigned to one of the 16 research analysts by Elizabeth, depending on the workloads of the different analysts. Given the volume of projects and the similarity of most projects, different analysts usually work on different parts of a project. For example, different analysts are used to plan the sample, construct the questionnaire, and interpret the data. Data collection and computer processing of data are conducted by separate companies contracted with the XYZ Marketing Research Company.

Greg's responsibilities are to interpret the data and write a report with marketing strategy recommendations. He has completed about 20 such projects, for which the co-owners have praised his work. On Wednesday afternoon, he completed this project. Following regular procedures, he gave the completed report to Elizabeth to give to Ms. Jordan and Mr. Collins. Thursday morning when Greg arrived at work, he found the original computer data printouts by his door with numerous numbers in the tables changed with red ink. There was also a note to see Elizabeth.

Elizabeth explained that Mr. Collins thought the findings should have been different and the client would probably not agree with the actual findings and related recommendations. He has therefore taken "research license" and changed a few numbers in the computer data printouts. Now he wants you (Greg) to rewrite your report accordingly. Elizabeth explained that because clients are provided with a copy of these summary printout sheets, she has called the outside computer firm to send new printouts with the revised numbers.

1. What are the relevant facts?
2. What are the ethical issues?
3. Who are the primary stakeholders?
4. What are the possible alternatives?

5. What are the ethics of the alternatives?

6. What does each stakeholder have a right to expect?

7. What rights do the owners of XYZ Marketing Research have?

8. Does Greg benefit more or less by speaking up?

9. Is there a difference between long- and short-term consequences if Greg speaks up?

10. What action should Greg take?

SOURCE: Patzer, Gordon L. (1992). "Falsification of Data" (Minicase 10). *Business Ethics Program.* Arthur Andersen & Co. Copyright © 1992 by Gordon L. Patzer. Minicases developed by the Arthur Andersen & Co., SC Business Ethics Program. Printed with permission of Arthur Andersen & Co., SC.

7

Ethics and Product Decisions

PURPOSE

To describe ethical problems that can occur as marketing professionals make product-related decisions.

MAJOR POINTS

Ethical problems can occur at any stage of the product development process.

Marketing professionals face a variety of ethical issues concerning product design and safety.

Misleading information on product labels is also a key area of ethical concern for marketing professionals.

Other product-related ethical issues include product counterfeiting, socially controversial products, environmentally incompatible products, and planned obsolescence.

This chapter concerns ethical issues related to the product strategies planned and implemented by marketing professionals. Almost all marketing organizations who introduce products to the marketplace go through some sort of planning process. Regardless of the type of organization, there are some elements that each of these organizations have in common as they endeavor to plan and implement product strategies and tactics (Hisrich & Peters, 1991).

▧ THE PRODUCT DEVELOPMENT PROCESS

Before we begin our discussion of ethical issues related to product strategies, a brief review of the product development process is presented. This review is presented with the intention of sensitizing you to some of the circumstances that exist at the various stages of the process that can lead to ethical questions.

Step 1: New Ideas Are Generated

New products that reach the marketplace begin as ideas. The watchword for those who participate in the generation of ideas is *creativity*. Often, idea generators are given no-holds-barred license to think of creative ideas that might serve some needs or wants in the marketplace.

Key Ethical Issues

1. Legal counsel is frequently given no role to play at this stage of the product development process, yet they are often in the best position to identify potential legal or ethical violations or both early in the product development process.
2. Critique of ideas and those who originate ideas is often prevented until after all ideas have been listed. As a result, the task of critiquing ideas appears to take on monumental proportions and, therefore, may not be performed as thoroughly as needed.
3. There is a perception that any attempt to discuss legal or ethical issues or both related to ideas would hinder the creativity of those involved in generating ideas. When cautionary statements are made, they may be interpreted as impeding progress. Furthermore, careful people can be ridiculed as being conservative "sticks-in-the-mud." Consequently, many who feel that critique is needed may be reluctant because they do not want to be critiqued themselves.

Step 2: Screening New Product Ideas

In the screening stage, the emphasis is on reducing the number of ideas generated that are, at this point, judged to have some likelihood of success to some manageable number. Legal counsel is consulted at this stage in an effort to identify any legal problems that might be associated with the production and marketing of each of the product ideas being considered.

Key Ethical Issues

1. Safety considerations are often not discussed at this time. Rather, the focus is on factors such as profitability, materials costs, and other economic concerns. A user's perspective is often not considered.

2. Historically, viewpoints of members from other functional areas of the organization are often not considered at this point in the process, although this is not the case with all organizations (McGuire, 1972). Sometimes, opinions are not sought because those with a product idea have a vested interest in that idea and do not want to hear "bad news."

Step 3: Product Development and Evaluation

Ideas must eventually be developed into physical products, and product uses and benefits must be given careful consideration. Product development and evaluation also involves determining the target market for the product(s) being examined. At this stage, many organizations have found great value in taking products to customers and asking customers to explain how they might use the product and what benefits would be derived from that use.

Key Ethical Issues

1. To avoid litigation related to product liability, marketing professionals must assess, completely, all the ways in which consumers might use a product (Lawless & Fisher, 1990). More commonly, however, questions such as "Will it sell?" and "How can we promote it?" are discussed. Consumer usage is treated as an afterthought.
2. Marketing professionals must also try to anticipate any others who might come into contact with the product. Some products, when used, affect nonusers. We see more and more of this as the environmental effect of various products is debated in the news media.

Step 4: Planning the Marketing Program

No product can be successfully marketed without strong promotion, pricing, and distribution strategies. Promotion programs must inform customers about products and encourage their use. Prices must be competitive and perceived as providing fair value to customers. Distribution must make the product available in places in which the customer elects to shop.

Key Ethical Issues

1. Does advertising accurately portray the product's features and benefits?
2. Do salespeople provide adequate instruction concerning correct usage of products (see Boedecker, Morgan, & Stoltman, 1991)?
3. Do product labels accurately describe all warnings concerning product use (see Boedecker et al., 1991)?
4. Is the product packaged in such a way as to reduce the risks of tampering?
5. Are product labels, instructions for use, and so on communicated in such a fashion that they can be understood by all customers (see Jacoby & Hoyer, 1989)?

Many organizations choose to do a complete or partial test of their product and accompanying marketing program before they roll the product out on a national scale. The purpose of test marketing is to uncover any problems with the product and the marketing program and to try to obtain some information about the viability of the product in the marketplace.

Step 5: Testing the Product

Key Ethical Issues

1. Does the test provide adequate information on product use and misuses so that the marketing professionals can evaluate safety considerations?
2. If the test uncovers some questionable aspects of the product, the marketing program, or both, will the organization make the needed changes or simply say that they have reached their limits on the financial and human resources invested in the project?

Finally, the product and accompanying marketing program are fully introduced to the marketplace. In the early stages of product introductions, marketing professionals should monitor sales, market share, customer reactions, and problems and opportunities that might occur that were not anticipated prior to the introduction of the product.

Step 6: Introduce the Product to the Market

Key Ethical Issues

1. Are consumers being exposed to unfair risks that should have been corrected prior to introduction?
2. When should a product be recalled and under what circumstances should it be recalled (see Jackson & Morgan, 1988)?
3. Are all marketing promotions portraying accurate representation of the features and benefits associated with the product?
4. Do labels and instructions accurately describe potential dangers associated with product misuses?

Eventually, all products lose their appeal to the marketplace and must be withdrawn or modified. Such decisions are among the toughest for marketing professionals. Consider the marketing professional who has devoted 10 years to the development and marketing of a product that is no longer strongly accepted by the marketplace. How easy is it for that individual to make the decision to change or withdraw the product? How readily will that same person accept that decision if it is made by others in the organization?

Step 7: Managing Products in the Decline Stage

Key Ethical Issues

1. Is information concerning a declining product purposefully withheld to prolong the life of the product?
2. Are product withdrawal decisions made by others with the intention of making the professional who was responsible for the product look bad in the eyes of top management?

▨ ETHICAL ISSUES RELATED TO PRODUCT DECISIONS

Before you read about product-related ethical issues, please read Newsline 7.1. *How many of the key ethical issues cited in the product development process are relevant here?* All marketing organizations should produce and market good products. There is more to be considered than making a profit. Consider this saying from the Christian tradition: "A good name is more desirable than great riches; to be esteemed is better than silver or gold" (Proverbs 22:1). Hinduism also teaches that worldly success cannot satisfy us completely because wealth and power do not survive, as illustrated by the expression, "You can't take it with you."

Newsline 7.1

A Wonder Offer From Herbalife

The health-product outfit has new stock to sell, but questions abound.

Need to shed a little cellulite? Bothered by a sluggish intestinal tract? Mark Hughes has just the thing for you. Last year, the 37-year-old founder of Herbalife International, Inc. sold $405 million worth of herbal cellulite busters and other such products.

These days, Hughes is gearing up with a different pitch. Herbalife has filed a registration statement for a secondary offering of 5 million shares. Some 75% of the company's 26.5 million outstanding shares are held by insiders. The new issue will include 2 million new shares and some 3 million shares held by Hughes and former sales chief Lawrence Thompson. With its shares now trading near 14 over the counter, Herbalife's portion of the proceeds will be about $28 million. Management says it will use that to fund a catalog business.

Big Sales. Is Herbalife a buy? On the surface, things look rosy. Retail sales—dollars taken in by distributors who sell Herbalife products door-to-door—doubled, to $337 million, in the first half of 1993. Net income came in at $20.2 million, vs. $8.6 million in 1992's first half. Distributors such as Betty J. McGregor of Lakewood, Calif. says Herbalife's hot-selling new weight-loss product, Thermojetics, is ringing up big sales in the U.S. Overseas sales are booming, too, and the stock is up from $.50 in 1991. "It's not easy to find a growth stock like this that is selling at only 10 times earnings," says Fred Astman of First Wilshire Securities Management, which owns 280,000 shares.

The boom comes after a big downturn for Herbalife. Founded in 1980, the company agreed in 1982 to reformulate at least one herbal treatment that included traces of mandrake and pokeroot after the Food & Drug Administration questioned the safety of those herbs. After 1985 congressional hearings on natural treatments generated negative publicity for Herbalife, its sales fell from $427 million in 1985 to $177.7 million in 1986.

Now, Herbalife could be heading for trouble again. It acknowledges that possible new FDA rules for dietary supplements could force it to change or drop some products. And Thermojetics—which accounts for 40% of U.S. sales—is already under fire. The FDA is investigating reports from doctors that Ma huang, a Chinese herb used in Thermojetics, may have serious side effects such as hypertension. Earlier this year, Herbalife reformulated Thermojetics for sale in Canada after a similar probe.

California is also monitoring Herbalife. In 1986, without admitting fault, the company agreed to pay the state $850,000 to settle charges it had made unproven claims about the benefits of certain products. Herbalife says it instructs its sales force not to make such claims. But distributors contacted by BUSINESS WEEK said their customers report everything from the disappearance of tumors to the elimination of chest pains after using Herbalife products. Testimonials so close to implying the products can cure diseases "would be of concern," says California Deputy Attorney General Albert N. Shelden.

Foreign Affairs. Herbalife says its products are safe. And David R. Addis, the company's chief counsel, contends the new FDA rules will probably only require some simple label modifications. Thermojetics, he says, could be easily reformulated without Ma huang, as it was in Canada.

The final big question: how long can Herbalife's foreign sales keep booming? Sales surged, then fell off, in new markets such as New Zealand and Mexico partly because of inconsistent distribution. In Spain, Herbalife's second-largest market in 1982, sales dropped 23% in this year's first quarter, partly because of regulatory restrictions. Herbalife says a beefed-up marketing staff and a better flow of new products will solve such problems. But Hughes may need lots of salesmanship to convince the market that Herbalife is a safe investment.

SOURCE: Barrett (1993). Reprinted from September 13, 1993, issue of *Business Week* by special permission. Copyright © 1993 by McGraw-Hill, Inc.

Organizations are known by the quality of their products or the quality of their services. The value of high-quality products is difficult to measure. We know that positive word-of-mouth advertising can be a very powerful force in the marketplace. When a friend buys a product and the product "delivers," that friend tells other friends. Does your friend have credibility? Do you trust your friend's judgment? Are marketing promotions more believable than your friend's testimony? We also know that unsatisfied customers will also freely describe their experiences to friends—and anyone else who will listen. We do not know how to measure the influence of this negative word-of-mouth advertising, but it can safely be said that *it costs a lot to produce a bad product.* With that said, let's explore some of the ethical issues related to product strategy.

Product Design and Safety

Product design is concerned with the way in which a product is put together. Faulty product design has been responsible for some of the most well-known and tragic product failures. Both the Ford Pinto and the space shuttle, *Challenger,* were involved in incidents that were caused by poor product design.

As customers, we expect safe products, but we rarely actively use safety as a key purchase criterion (Nelson-Horchler, 1988). One reason for this is that other product features and benefits may be more important to us. A second reason is that product safety is not often discussed in the promotions aimed at influencing our purchases. A third reason is that we are all aware that the government has enacted considerable legislation designed to ensure product safety. Because of this, many of us may simply assume that the products we purchase are "guaranteed" to be safe.

One of the key ethical issues facing organizations is the extent to which they are responsible for designing safety into a product. Many companies can do much more to design safety features into their products. But such safety designs would raise the price of those products, and there is some question about whether or not consumers are willing to pay higher prices for those products.

A second ethical issue related to product design and safety is that consumers often do not use safety as a key to making purchase decisions. For example, Sears unsuccessfully attempted to market a line of "safe" children's pajamas. They learned the hard way that purchase decisions were still made on the basis of traditional features, such as price, color, softness, and attractiveness. They learned this even in the face of strong consumer sentiment for using nonflammable fabrics in children's clothing.

A third ethical issue facing organizations is the misuse of products by consumers. What constitutes misuse is open to debate in the courts. Clearly, organizations must provide clear labels and instructions regarding how to use products. But not all of us read labels and instructions. Who is responsible for product misuse when the

1. Finding the right repair shop
   a. What should you look for when choosing a repair shop?
 	
2. Finding the right technician
   a. Is one technician better than another?
 	
3. Repair charges: Unlocking the mystery
   a. What should be included in an estimate?
   b. When would you get a second opinion?
   c. After your repair is done, what do you need?
   d. What should you know about the parts to be repaired or replaced on your vehicle?
 	
4. Preventive maintenance
   a. What are the consequences of postponing maintenance?
   b. What maintenance guidelines should you follow to avoid costly repairs?
 	
5. Protecting your auto repair investment
   a. What warranties and service contracts apply to vehicle repairs?
   b. How do you resolve a dispute regarding billing, quality of repairs, or warranties?
	Table 7.1 Federal Trade Commission Guidelines for Consumers Needing Automotive Repairs

SOURCE: *Taking the Scare Out of Auto Repairs* (1993).

consumer does not read enclosed instructions? Who is responsible for misuse when the consumer uses a product for purposes not intended by the manufacturer?

Several product areas have been particularly susceptible to ethically related issues. One such area is children's toys. Toys with jagged edges, toys with small parts that can be swallowed, and toys that fire projectiles that could lead to eye injury represent products potentially harmful to children. Although toymakers openly abide by the ethical principle that they have a special responsibility to youngsters, a surprising number of unsafe products reach the marketplace each year ("Danger Is Lurking," 1989).

Product Liability Legislation

The American Automobile Association, the Federal Trade Commission, and the National Association of Attorneys General have allied to produce consumer guidelines for auto repairs. Table 7.1 provides an overview of the kind of information contained in those guidelines.

The law concerning warranties requires that a product's performance be of a certain quality level. Liability can arise from manufacturer's defects or from inadequate provision of warnings or from design defects. Tort law provides additional protection for the consumer. Tort law is based on the principle of negligence and holds sellers liable if a product is proven defective and causes injury (Stern & Eovaldi, 1984). That is, marketing organizations can be held liable if they are judged to have failed to take reasonable safety steps in the product development process.

Furthermore, *strict liability* was established in 1963 and holds that marketing organizations can be held liable for injuries caused by products that were in defective condition or are judged to be potentially dangerous (Jacobs, 1988). That the seller knew the product to be defective or dangerous does not have to be established. In other words, marketing organizations are responsible for compensating injured people even if those injured cannot prove that the marketing organization was careless in the product development process.

Regulation by Federal Agencies. In addition to the law, products are also regulated by several government agencies. These agencies regulate products in an effort to ensure safety, quality, and performance. Following is a brief listing of several regulatory agencies and the products over which they have jurisdiction.

1. The United States Department of Agriculture (USDA)—agricultural products, including meat, vegetables, fruit, poultry, and eggs. The USDA can inspect manufacturing and processing facilities and take action against manufacturers and distributors in the case of spoiled products reaching the marketplace.
2. The United States Treasury Department—tobacco, firearms, and alcohol products. One of the primary responsibilities of the Treasury Department is to contend with the social problems related to products under its jurisdiction.
3. The Food and Drug Administration (FDA)—drugs, medical devices, and cosmetics. The FDA approves new drug applications and certified drugs as being safe and effective. Similarly, with the other products in its jurisdiction, if the FDA finds them to be unsafe, the FDA can seize these products through a court order.
4. The Department of Transportation (DOT)—automobile safety. A division of the DOT, the National Highway and Traffic Safety Administration is the agency that conducts tests of automobiles, including the famous "crash tests" you may have seen on television.
5. The Consumer Products Safety Commission (CPSC)—consumer products. The CPSC can develop safety standards for products. It conducts research that investigates products that have led to injury, illness, or death. The CPSC also works with consumers to assist them in making product safety evaluations.

Westinghouse, since the 1930s, has been one of the biggest purchasers of polychlorinated byphenyl (PCBs) as fire retardants and coolants in capacitors and transformers. Many other large companies have also been heavy buyers of PCBs, including General Electric, McGraw Edison, and National Cash Register (NCR). It is estimated that tens of thousands of workers have handled PCBs (Schroeder, 1991). PCBs have been the focal point of lawsuits concerning health risks that companies who purchased PCBs did not disclose to their employees. These companies argue that there has never been any link between PCBs and health problems other than skin rashes. In 1977 and 1985, the National Institute for Occupational Safety and Health conducted two studies and reported no link between PCBs and current medical ailments, and in 1988, after a study of the medical literature, the director of health and risk capabilities of the Environmental Protection Agency concluded that exposure to PCBs does not lead to clearly demonstrable negative effects on health. *Should companies openly discuss the potential health hazards of chemicals or technologies and risk exposing themselves to financially crippling liability lawsuits? Or should they keep quiet until all the evidence is in? How much knowledge should a company have about health risks before it is held liable for those health risks? Suppose research discovers that a product is harmful in some way in 1995. Prior to this time, however, scientific tests were not capable of discovering the "now discovered" health risk. Should a company that has been using that product for many years be held liable for the health risks? How should that company proceed in the face of the new data?*

When a marketing organization attempts to create an image for its product that is different from the image of competitive products, it is using a product positioning strategy. Positioning involves many considerations. First, a product may be positioned on the basis of unique features and benefits offered. Second, a product may be positioned by the way it is depicted in advertisements. Third, a product may be positioned because it carries the same brand name as other products used by consumers.

Product Positioning

Ethical considerations for marketing professionals involve the basis for positioning a product. Oftentimes, consumers can be misled by the way in which a product is used in advertising. For example, ads that depict vehicles climbing up or down the side of a mountain may suggest more about things such as product safety, traction, horsepower, and the like than is actually provided by the product. Or consider image advertising in which an advertisement might imply that the product is for "cool" people only. *What ads can you think of that fit this category? Is positioning a product in such a way unethical?*

Ideally, products should be positioned in such a way that consumers can rationally make decisions based on information concerning product features and benefits. Unfortunately, we all make decisions on the basis of some less than rational motivations. For example, we all buy products for things such as prestige, status, and convenience. And there is nothing wrong with that. The ethical issue is how far should marketing professionals go in communicating such intangibles and positioning their products on the basis of such intangibles?

In the last decade, the marketplace's concern about misleading and inadequate information on product labels seems to have grown exponentially. This is particularly true of food and other consumable products. A number of things have contributed to this growing concern: (a) some tragic incidents in which products were tampered

Misleading Information on Labels

with, (b) consumers becoming more concerned about what they are buying, (c) consumers becoming more health conscious, and (d) consumers becoming more concerned about the effect of products and packages on the environment. Many organizations have been accused of providing misleading health information on products (Miller, 1989).

Listed next are some questions that focus on the difficulties in dealing with the ethical issues associated with product packaging and labeling:

1. What is nutritional and how do we, as consumers, know it?
2. What is good for the environment, and how do we, as consumers, know it?
3. In the face of conflicting evidence concerning things such as nutrition and environmentally compatible products, how do we as consumers decide on what is nutritional or is environmentally compatible?
4. Does the mere provision of a list of ingredients really provide "usable" information for the average consumer?

Many consumers depend on labels to determine what they buy. But shoppers must be careful or else they can easily be deceived (Gorman, 1991). For example, consider the following:

1. Budget Gourmet Light and Healthy Salisbury Steak, which is labeled "low fat," derives 45% of its total calories from fat.
2. Diet Coke contains more than the one heavily advertised calorie per can (so does Diet Pepsi).
3. There is no real fruit—just fruit flavors—in Post Fruity Pebbles.
4. Honey Nut Cheerios provide more sugar than they do honey and more salt than found in salted peanuts.
5. Mrs. Smith's Natural Juice Apple Pie contains artificial preservatives. The word *natural* refers to the fruit juice used to make the pie.

As many as 40% of consumers are skeptical about labels, and doctors see a danger in messages such as these, particularly for consumers with chronic heart disease, hypertension, or diabetes, who can be misled by the current labels (Gorman, 1991). Stouffer's Lean Cuisine boasts that it contains "never more than a gram of sodium." Although the claim is true, nutritionists usually measure salt content in milligrams, not grams. Stouffer's products contain almost half the sodium allowed daily for someone on a typical salt-restricted diet. The relabeling of all products with currently misleading information will cost manufacturers $600 million during the next two decades. *Should consumers have to pay for this as manufacturers pass these costs down? Or should manufacturers simply be asked to bear the cost because it was their action that led to the misleading labels in the first place?*

Warning Labels

Warning labels are used to call attention to dangers that might exist with certain products. Warning labels provide information that allow consumers to use products in a safe manner. Warning labels also reduce the organization's risk of liability. For example, I have high blood pressure and have taken medication for that condition for over 10 years. This condition has sensitized me to read warning labels on many over-the-counter medications that are safe to use for most people but that can have some serious side effects for people who take blood pressure medication. Clearly, over-the-counter medications are safe to use under most circumstances and if used in the right dosages. My situation makes me an exception, and I have learned to read labels on over-the-counter drugs so that I reduce the risk of side effects.

Many products contain warning labels. Clearly, it is in the organization's and the consumer's best interests to have clearly printed and easily understood warnings on inherently dangerous products (Bettman, Payne, & Staelin, 1986). But some concern exists over the sheer number of warning labels being used. They may become so commonplace that consumers ignore them and therefore remain unaware or ignore the risks associated with certain products (Driver, 1987; Schwartz & Driver, 1983). Also, as consumers use a product more frequently, they tend to become complacent and be less concerned with product safety information (Goldhaber & De Turck, 1988).

There is a federal law that requires cigarette makers to place warning labels on cigarette ads. Now cigarette marketers are dressing for success—outfitting customers with caps, T-shirts, and other merchandise that carries among other well-known smoking images, the Joe Camel logo (Shapiro, 1993). Antismoking activists and some legislators charge that such marketing exploits a loophole in the labeling law. *What do you think? Are the cigarette companies creating millions of walking billboards as the Rev. Jesse Brown of Philadelphia complains? Are they trying to get around regulations that require health warnings? Do hats and T-shirts fall under the same legislation as cigarette pack labels? Is it ethical to produce items so small (e.g., pocket knives, stop-watches, and money clips) that they are exempt from labeling requirements?*

Packaging

Our society has become more and more concerned about the waste associated with packing of products. These concerns revolve around the following issues:

1. Packaging is excessive. The use of excessive packing depletes resources and raises prices at the consumer level.
2. Shortages of paper, aluminum, and other packaging materials put pressure on companies to reduce the amount of packing used in products.
3. Many products now have packaging that is difficult to tamper with (Crossen, 1986). Often, such packages appear to use excessive amounts of materials.

Benefit	Example	Representative Ethical Issue
Theft protection	Bubble packs used on many hardware products	How much would theft increase if small products (e.g., nuts and bolts) had less packaging or no packaging? What would be the impact on price at the marketplace?
Stackability	Containers in which consumer products are shipped in bulk to retailers	If large containers that allow products to be stacked for transport are not used, how much more will it cost at the marketplace because of the increase in transportation costs associated with not being able to carry as much product in each truckload or carload?
Protection	Containers in which styrofoam or other packing materials are used	What are the cost trade-offs of damaged goods to the consumers versus those associated with the packaging necessary?
Identification/ information	Packages that contain information, logos, and pictures that allow them to be easily identified on the shelf	Is the information accurate? Does the information contain puffery? Is the information deceptive?
Quality connotation	Products that have packages designed to promote a quality image (e.g., cosmetics)	Does the consumers' perception of fair value become distorted by the perceived quality associated with a package? Can the consumer assess the "real" value of the product when packaging is used to communicate high quality?
Reduction of consumers' time cost	Any product that is packaged, the alternative being the consumer has to package it himself or herself	Should consumers be made aware of the costs of packaging that are included in the final price of the product?

Table 7.2 Benefits Provided by Packaging

The issue of how much packaging is absolutely necessary and how much is used is not easily resolvable. For example, consider the benefits that packages provide in the marketplace, as shown in Table 7.2. Not all packages provide for all of the benefits in Table 7.2. Clearly, consumers want these benefits and have often expressed a willingness to pay for such benefits. But many consumers now complain about the waste associated with excessive packaging. What is excessive? Can manufacturers provide lesser packaging that provides the same benefits as those illustrated in Table 7.2? To reduce packaging waste, are consumers willing to give up some of these benefits? Will products sell as well if their packing is drastically changed? These and other questions form the basis of the ethical issues surrounding product packaging.

Product Recalls

Many organizations have undertaken serious efforts to design and market safe products. No one is perfect, however, and occasionally, some inherently dangerous

Is the product flawed?	**Table 7.3** Questions to Ask in a Recall Decision Situation
If so, is the flaw dangerous to customers, the organization's reputation, or both?	
If so, is the flaw removable and can the cost of removing the flaw be covered?	
If not, can the customer be educated to use the product safely?	
If not, withdraw the product.	

SOURCE: Kotler and Mantrala (1985). Reprinted with permission.

products do reach the marketplace. Harm to consumers can occur because of product defects, product tampering, product misuse, or in unanticipated ways. When organizations ignore product safety issues, they risk serious and costly product liability damages. The financial costs associated with product liability can be astronomical. So, too, can the damage to the organization's image.

Recalling products has been an effective way for organizations to deal with product safety issues. For example, in 1986, someone tampered with Tylenol capsules in retail outlets. As you read earlier in this book, Johnson & Johnson chose to recall all capsules and destroy them at a cost of about $150 million ("A Hard Decision," 1986). Similarly, Procter & Gamble recalled its Rely tampon after it was discovered it was linked to toxic shock syndrome. This was done at a cost of $75 million (Davidson & Goodpaster, 1983). Both organizations acted quickly and decided that consumers' safety was much more important than the costs associated with the recall procedures used. Although both organizations had their critics, the criticisms disappeared rather quickly.

As you can see, recalling products is an expensive proposition—in the short run. The expense can make it a difficult ethical issue because marketing professionals must gauge both the short-term and long-term reactions of the marketplace to various alternative course of action, including, but not limited to, recalling the product immediately on one end of the spectrum and doing nothing on the other end of the spectrum. As one piece of information available to decision makers, the effect on product demand that results from recalls is usually short-term in nature (Reilly & Hoffer, 1983).

Although there are no absolute guidelines for marketing professionals to follow when dealing with a recall decision situation, the sequence of questions shown in Table 7.3 is suggested.

If you read the list in Table 7.3 closely, you will probably have identified some ethical issues inherent in using this list. First, what is a dangerous flaw as described in the second question? Second, what ethical guidelines are provided to reconcile the conflict between the cost to customers and the costs to the organization? Third, this same conflict must be resolved when dealing with the costs associated with removing a flaw that is judged to be removable. No one ever said that decisions involving ethics were easy.

Ford Motor Company and Chrysler Corporation are wrestling to correct quality glitches in new products ("Ford, Chrysler Move to Correct," 1993). Ford halted production of the 1994 Mustang after discovering a bad weld in the wiring harness. Chrysler is recalling some Ram pickup trucks to check a bolt on the front suspension bar. *How do you feel about these actions? Do such actions help or hurt the images of these companies? Suppose you knew that Ford discovered the need for recall on fewer than 200 cars and Chrysler recalled only about 2,000 trucks. Does the number of products recalled matter? Do you think that the cost of a recall has an effect on the recall decisions of organizations?*

Product Warranties

A warranty is a guarantee of product quality and of product safety (Udell & Laczniak, 1981). Express warranties describe the specific obligations of the seller concerning the performance of a product. A second type of warranty, an implied warranty, is intended to guarantee that the product will perform in a safe manner when used for ordinary purposes. One element of the implied warranty is that it sets minimum product performance expectations that the seller cannot legally avoid. Express warranties add extra obligations to the seller from a legal perspective.

We always hear about warranties. But do you know the difference between the two major types of warranties used by marketers? As just mentioned, one is an express warranty. Express warranties are explicitly communicated to the consumer. For example, if an ad claims that a watch will operate underwater, the seller is liable for damage or replacement if the watch stops while the owner is swimming. Any affirmation of fact or promise creates an express warranty (Sack, 1986). An implied warranty makes a promise about the condition of a product at the time it is sold. It does not have to be explicitly stated. Implied warranties imply that a product is fit for use, is packaged properly, is labeled properly, and conforms to the promises made on the label. For example, if you purchase a lawn mower, you can expect it to cut the grass without damaging the grass. *Is a warranty statement an expression, on the part of the seller, that the seller will stand behind the product? What ways do marketers use to avoid the terms of warranties, expressed or implied?*

Product Counterfeiting   The unauthorized copying of patented products, trademarks, and copyrights is called *product counterfeiting*. Counterfeit products cost U.S. businesses billions of dollars every year (Harvey, 1988). The essence of counterfeiting is that one producer will produce a product that looks just like that of another manufacturer. Sometimes, the counterfeit product is cheaper because it is inferior in quality to the original version of the product. Oftentimes, the counterfeit is sold at the same price because neither the retailer nor the consumer can tell the difference. Products that have been counterfeited include watches, shampoos, basketballs, sunglasses, and liquors. Pirate cassettes and videotapes are also examples of counterfeit products.

Counterfeiting is both unethical and illegal in the United States. The primary reason is that the counterfeiting firm is judged to be unfairly capitalizing on the reputation of the original manufacturer and the brand of products it produces. Furthermore, counterfeits confuse the consumer by making them think they are purchasing one brand of product when, in reality, they are actually purchasing another, often inferior brand, unknowingly.

Some health care experts say that the proposed Clinton health care plan, with its mandate that employers pay for workers' health care coverage, could make it more profitable for business to skirt the law than to comply by it (Gupta & Tannenbaum, 1993). These experts feel that parallel, clandestine plans (counterfeits) that cater to the uninsured, will grow and that health care fraud could increase. *What do you think about counterfeit products and services? Will such health care counterfeits merely be creative ways of providing health care service or will there be violations of the law? Is it possible for an organization to prevent the appearance of counterfeits for its products?*

Socially Controversial Products

How do you feel about cigarettes, firearms, and alcohol? Do your friends feel the same way? Because of some strong public sentiment, cigarettes now contain health warnings, and cigarette advertising has been eliminated from television. Alcohol has been attacked in some circles as a health hazard and as a causal factor in many crimes. It has certainly been a factor in the automobile-related deaths of many people.

The strongest critics of such products favor the complete elimination of their sale in the marketplace. Still other critics call for restrictions on how these products should be marketed to the general public. The debate concerning such socially controversial products will likely continue for a long time. One key ethical issue in the debate concerns the obligations of marketers who produce and promote such products.

Within one week of the bombing of the World Trade Center, many companies rushed to produce products and services designed to help people cope with the disaster (Selz & Emshwiller, 1993). Many of the products were safety oriented. These companies ran advertising on radio and television and set up toll-free hot lines calling on high-rise tenants and seeking media interviews. *Does a disaster such as the bombing of the World Trade Center produce a legitimate marketing opportunity? Can tasteful marketing strategies be developed that are based on such disasters? Do such disasters open windows of opportunity that might not otherwise be there or that will close up in a short period of time?*

Environmentally Incompatible Products

Environmentally incompatible products include those that create some problem for the physical environment. Aerosol spray cans, nonbiodegradable packaging, chemicals and detergents that pollute, and medical wastes are all products that have come under fire because of the consequences of their use to the physical environment.

We live in a "disposable society," with the average person throwing away about 3.5 pounds of garbage daily. Approximately 30% of this garbage comes in the form of product packages (Brown, 1989). The issue of products and the environment is one that affects everyone. Although most of us were probably not affected when McDonald's switched from polystyrene cartons to paper wrappers for their hamburgers, many of us might be affected by the challenges to such often used products as plastic trash bags, disposable diapers, and plastic food wrap.

As you know, many companies have introduced products that are supposed to be compatible with the environment. These so called "green" products are marketed on the basis of their compatibility with the environment in an effort to gain a competitive edge over "nongreen" competitors. The Federal Trade Commission (FTC) has pursued many of these companies and has put a halt to many of the green claims made by marketers. One company, Mr. Coffee, claimed that its coffee filters were manufactured with a chlorine-free process that eliminates the release of harmful by-products. Furthermore, they claimed that their filters were made from recycled paper and that their paperboard packaging was recyclable (Gatty, 1993). The FTC charged that some chlorine was evident in the filter bleaching process and that some, although fewer, harmful by-products were released. The FTC also said the filters were not made from recycled paper. Furthermore, although the packaging was recyclable, only a few collection facilities existed nationwide that accepted this type of material. *Was Mr. Coffee justified in making its green claims? Was the FTC too harsh in its judgment of the claims of Mr. Coffee? Do you think that consumers are more susceptible to green claims or health claims? Why do you think this is so?*

Planned Obsolescence

When a manufacturer produces a product with an intentionally limited life, that manufacturer is building obsolescence into the product. The result is that we purchase more of such products than we would if these products had longer lives. Obsolescence is sometimes a difficult issue. For example, companies have the capability of producing a battery with lifetime working potential. Instead, they produce batteries that have a limited life. Surely, we purchase more limited-life batteries than we would lifetime batteries. But the limited-life batteries are much less expensive per unit than the cost of the lifetime battery.

In theory, products with limited life would seem to bring on competitors with similar products that last longer. Indeed, there are many such examples and many more examples of advertising claiming longer lasting life. The presumption is that products seen as substitutes by consumers will be purchased if they are judged to be of better quality than those products currently purchased by the consumer.

Another type of obsolescence is illustrated by fashion type products. Examples are designer jeans and this year's styles from Paris. Such products receive heavy promotion as trendy, upscale, and in style. But they go out of style the next year when the same promoters promote next year's fashions in the same way. In other words, advertising is used to socially outdate products that are otherwise still in good working order. The ethical question here is whether consumers dictate fashion preferences or fashion availability and promotion dictate consumer preferences.

Finally, another form of obsolescence exists in the high-tech industry. This year's generation of microcomputers will be implicitly advertised as out of date, slower, or having less memory when next year's models arrive and are advertised as faster and having more memory. Although, in fact, such claims may be true, there is some ethical concern about whether consumers need all of the extras provided by the next generation of computers. Many consumers purchase computer upgrades because of pressures to have the latest in technology, whether or not a real need is being satisfied by that technology.

CHAPTER SUMMARY

This chapter described some of the ethical problems that can occur as marketing professionals produce and market products. Ethical problems can occur at any stage of the product development process. Six ethical issues related to product development and marketing were highlighted in this chapter. These included product design and safety, misleading information on labels, product counterfeiting, socially controversial products, environmentally incompatible products, and planned obsolescence.

◙ PRODUCT SCENARIOS

1. You are the marketing director for a $115 million dollar manufacturing organization. Your company's president is excited about a new product that has been developed by the vice president of design, who is a longtime employee of the organization and the president's best friend. The president tells you to make the product a marketing success.

While you are out soliciting bids from international suppliers, you accidentally discover that the product is unsafe and will not pass the standards of the Food and Drug Administration. But you are also aware of a loophole in FDA regulations that would allow your company to market the product in the United States without FDA approval. What ethical issues are evident in this situation? How would you resolve these issues?

2. Your company sells a water purification system whose filtering mechanism contains contaminants, one of which is a possible carcinogen. The product contains a filtration system sealed with a methylene-chloride-based glue, which seeps into the water. Your company's engineers were immediately aware of the problem, but it is the judgment of your company's marketing vice president that the risk to individual consumers because of the leakage is minimal (Murphy & Laczniak, 1981, p. 255). What ethical issues are evident in this situation? How would you resolve these issues?

3. You work for a tobacco manufacturer, a company in an industry that has been heavily criticized in the United States concerning the safety of cigarette smoking. You have been asked by the marketing vice president to look into the possibilities of Third World nations as a source of growth for your company and its tobacco products.

Currently, the cigarette market generates about $200 billion in sales, of which these Third World countries are responsible for about $65 billion. You know that many of the cigarettes sold in these Third World nations contain more tar and nicotine than those cigarettes sold in the United States. You also know that your company and other companies have arrangements with many of these Third World nations' governments to collect a substantial portion of the product's price in the form of sales taxes (Murphy & Laczniak, 1981, p. 258). What ethical issues are evident in this situation? How would you resolve these issues?

4. Your company has produced a product that has been declared unsafe by U.S. regulatory agencies. You company has invested millions in research and development for this product. Your supervisor asks you to look into international markets, telling you that "dumping" of products declared unsafe in the United States is accepted business practice because many foreign nations have not made the "unsafe" designation on the product. What ethical issues are evident in this situation? How would you resolve these issues?

5. You are employed by an automobile dealer and you have sold a car to a customer. The car carries a 1-year warranty. About 6 months after the car was purchased, the customer experiences transmission problems. The customer brings the car to your dealership where some minor adjustments are made. The problem continues, and

each time your dealership's service department makes minor adjustments. Finally, after the 13th month, the customer brings the car in again and the service department completely replaces the transmission at the customer's expense (Henthorne, Robin, & Reidenbach, 1992, p. 851). What ethical issues are evident in this situation? How would you resolve these issues?

6. You are a senior editor for a large publishing company. You have just received a manuscript from one of your most successful authors. It provides the most authoritative account, to date, of the history and development of the atomic bomb. In reading through the manuscript, you discover that one of the chapters contains a detailed description of how the bomb is made. You try several times to convince the author to eliminate the chapter, noting your concerns about making such information available to the mass market. The author believes that the chapter is critical to the success of the book and does not agree to its elimination (Fritzche & Becker, 1983, p. 293). What ethical issues are evident in this situation? How would you resolve these issues?

7. An artificial sweetener, Sugarsub, has been linked to cancer in laboratory rats. The validity of these findings has been the source of much heated debate among medical experts. The FDA has ordered products containing Sugarsub banned from sale in the United States. You work for a company that distributes a soft drink that uses Sugarsub as a sweetener. Your superior has informed you of your company's plans to market that product in Europe where there is no ban on Sugarsub (Laczniak, 1983, p. 9). What ethical issues are evident in this situation? How would you resolve these issues?

8. You are a salesperson employed by Childrens Togs, Inc., a manufacturer of children's sleepwear. You have been with the company for a little over a year. Consumer pressures have required that your company treat all sleepwear with a fire-retardant chemical. Subsequent research, however, has shown that this chemical may cause cancer in those who wear the clothing treated with the chemical. As a result, all sleepwear treated with this chemical has been banned in the United States. The ban has left your company with over $3 million in inventory. Your company's marketing vice president has asked for suggestions concerning the inventory and has offered a promotion and significant raise for the suggestion that is accepted (Harris, 1990, p. 745). What ethical issues are evident in this situation? How would you resolve these issues?

9. You are the marketing director for a direct-sales organization that has built its reputation by selling quality merchandise at moderate to high prices. You sell through independent contractors who are expected to present the line to poten-

tial customers, take orders, and make sure that the merchandise is delivered. The success of your organization is highly dependent on its reputation. Recently, one of your independent contractors has purchased a less expensive line of merchandise and is offering it along with your company's products. This contractor is not telling potential customers of the difference between the two product lines, and the independent contractor is making considerable income from the sale of the lesser quality merchandise (Reidenbach, Robin, & Dawson, 1991, p. 84). What ethical issues are evident in this situation? How would you resolve these issues?

10. You are the product manager for an auto parts manufacturer. Your firm received a large contract to manufacture axles to be used in a new line of front wheel drive automobiles made by a large automaker. The contract is very important to your company, which has recently experienced some market share erosion. Prior to receiving the contract, a large number of your company's employees had been scheduled to be laid off one month before Christmas.

Final testing of the axles was completed last week and the first shipments are scheduled for 3 weeks. As you examine the reports, you discover that the axles failed when loaded at 20% over the rated capacity and subjected to strong torsion forces. Conditions could occur in a heavily loaded vehicle braking for a curve down a hill. The auto manufacturer's specifications called for the axle to carry 130% of its rated capacity without failing. You show the results to your boss and to the marketing vice president, both of whom indicate they know of the report. Both say that the conditions for failure are low in likelihood and there is not time to redesign the axle and meet the first delivery date. Failure to deliver would result in the loss of the contract and the loss of many jobs (Fritzche & Becker, 1983, p. 293). What ethical issues are evident in this situation? How would you resolve these issues?

11. According to some officials, lead poisoning is a child's most devastating environmental disease. The Environmental Defense Fund argues that lead hurts one child in six, lowering IQ and inducing hyperactivity (Stipp, 1993). But according to one pediatrician at the Columbia Presbyterian Medical Center in New York, lead poisoning is no longer a serious problem Another pediatrician at the Kaiser Permanente Medical Center in Oakland, California, pointed out that children have problems with malnutrition, homelessness, abuse, lack of immunization, violence, and AIDS; however, no children have experienced lead poisoning for years (Stipp, 1993). Suppose you are a homeowner and a housing inspector found lead paint in your home (it's an older home). You are ordered to abate

the lead paint from any child-reachable surfaces. You agree but cannot get a bank to lend you the needed $10,000 because your house's value has fallen and because of the threat of possible lead poisoning lawsuits. How would you handle this situation? On a national scale, it is estimated that it would cost at least $300 billion to abate all the lead paint surfaces in the United States, a demand being made by some activists. How can such issues be decided? Is someone who has lead-based paint behaving in an unethical manner if he or she chooses not to remove it? Ideally, what information would you like to have in making decisions concerning lead paint and lead poisoning?

12. Your firm has recently been given the results of a study in which it was discovered that many of your customers are misusing your firm's products. Although no health dangers were involved, the customers' misuse was causing them to use much more of your product than necessary if used correctly. Your firm has spent several hundred thousand dollars in R&D modifying two of its products. Unfortunately, neither modification compensates for the customers' misuse of the products. Indeed, in one case, customer misuse seems to be encouraged. How would you deal with this situation knowing that the "new products are close to being introduced to the marketplace and the advertising campaign introducing the product changes is set to begin in one week" (Akaah, 1989, p. 376)?

13. You are the director for your state's lottery. Your boss asks you to develop a new lottery game targeted toward lower-income households because many of these are known to be frequent lottery players. Your boss is a member of a minority group, and her father is a compulsive gambler. She has some reservations about the new lottery game. But she also knows that the governor has promised to use proceeds from the new lottery sales to enhance statewide education. Would you agree to develop the new lottery game? Are there ethical issues inherent in a lottery? What are they (Kelley, 1992b)?

14. You are the sales representative for a furniture retailer. You have just returned from leave due to surgery. While you were gone, your sales department and purchasing department collaborated to buy an inferior brand of furniture. Their intention is to market this furniture as a high-quality brand, similar to those that your store is known for selling. You know that your store is experiencing pressure to make profits and that the new line of furniture can help you achieve your sales goals. But you also know that inferior-quality products can damage your store's reputation in the long run. Should you sell the new furniture? What, if anything, should you say to your boss (Fritzche, 1992a)?

15. You are the buyer of ethnic art works. You work with a Native American group to sell their woven baskets. Over lunch, your boss and a new client approach you with a proposal to change the symbols and colors of the woven baskets. The client will place a large order for the baskets after assurances that the changes will be made. You know that cultural symbols are important to the Native Americans you represent. Should this change be approved by the Native Americans who weave the baskets? How would you handle this situation if the Native American groups told you that the proposed changes were unacceptable (Cohen, 1992b)?

PRODUCT MINICASE

Elite Furniture

Jan Smith had planned on spending 6 months at home before returning to work after the birth of her first child. However, she and her husband had recently purchased a new home and the high mortgage payments dictated an early return.

Jan worked for Elite Furniture, a manufacturer of quality furniture. She had recently been promoted to assistant product manager for upholstered furniture after serving as a sales rep in the Eastern Region for 3 years. After returning to work, Jan discovered that the purchasing manager had recently started buying an inferior grade of padding for use in upholstered furniture. The padding would last about half as long as the regular padding, but the lower quality could not be detected by the buyer.

When Jan revealed this information to her boss, she was told that the purchasing manager was following orders from top management. The company was having financial difficulties and had to cut costs. The change in padding quality was a quick and safe way to do so. Jan argued that selling inferior merchandise as quality product was no way to solve budget problems, but she got nowhere.

Elite Furniture projected an image of quality that Jan had stressed to her retailers when she was calling on the Eastern Region. She could envision that image eroding rapidly as consumers began to experience premature wear in the expensive furniture. Not only would Elite's reputation be damaged, but the reputation of the retailers carrying Elite's products would also likely suffer.

1. What are the relevant facts?
2. What are the ethical issues?
3. Who are the primary stakeholders?
4. What are the possible alternatives?

5. What are the ethics of the alternatives?

6. Does the consumer have the right to know?

7. What are the practical constraints?

8. What action should be taken?

SOURCE: Fritzche, David J. (1992a). "Elite Furniture" (Minicase 18). *Business Ethics Program*. Arthur Andersen & Co. Copyright © 1992 by David J. Fritzche. Minicases developed by the Arthur Andersen & Co., SC Business Ethics Program. Printed with permission of Arthur Andersen & Co., SC.

Ethics and Pricing Decisions

PURPOSE

To discuss some of the key ethical issues with which marketing professionals are concerned as they make pricing decisions.

MAJOR POINTS

Price represents the value placed on the product or service by both the buyer and the seller.

A key pricing issue concerns the setting of prices that are viewed as fair by both the buyer and the seller.

The following ethical pricing issues are discussed in this chapter—nonprice price increases, price discounting, price advertising, price fixing, predatory pricing, resale price maintenance, discriminatory pricing, unit pricing, and misleading pricing.

P rice represents the value placed on a product by both the seller and the customer. From the seller's standpoint, price represents what that seller feels the customer will view as fair value for the product or service purchased. The seller is in business to make a profit because profits are what keep organizations producing products into the future. From the customer's viewpoint, price represents a measure of perceived quality and value of the product or service being purchased. If the product is successful, some would argue that the good of society is being served (see Bowie & Duska, 1990, pp. 25-27).

From the consumer's viewpoint, price also is the means by which choice is exercised. That is, consumers have limited resources to allocate among various products and services. When the consumer makes a decision to purchase a product or service, he or she is actually purchasing a combination of product features that will provide benefits (utility) over the life of the product that are, in the consumer's judgment, worth the price paid for that product or service. Determining price on the basis of benefits received by the consumer is one recommended strategy for setting prices (Williams, 1982).

Because consumers often use emotional criteria (e.g., status, prestige, convenience, luxury, exclusivity, fashion) in making decisions, it is very difficult to assess the value of products in terms of price. One reason for this is that, although the economic law of supply and demand suggests that demand for products will increase as the price of those products declines, this does not always occur in the marketplace. In fact, there are many products for which the demand would decline if the price declined because consumers would not realize the emotional or intangible benefits such as those mentioned earlier.

▨ FAIRNESS

In Japan, the chairman of a leading construction company was arrested in a bribery scandal. It is alleged that the chairman bribed government officials to obtain preferential treatment for his company's bids on public works projects ("Executive Arrested," 1993). *How can a distinction be made between a bribe and a campaign contribution or donation to a government program? Evaluate the possible consequences related to bribery activities.*

A key issue concerning pricing, then, is fairness. What is a fair price to the consumer and the seller? Oftentimes, we encounter situations in which the price charged depends on the negotiating ability of the buyer. This is the basis for haggling used by street merchants, such as those found in Mexico. If buyers know the real cost of items, they can get good prices. Unfortunately, this rarely occurs so the buyer must place trust in the seller to offer a fair price. One approach for such situations is "Love your neighbor as yourself" (found in Matthew 22:39). From this principle comes the Golden Rule "So in everything, do to others what you would have them do to you" (Matthew 7:12).

Generally, consumers accept price increases if they are related to the cost of producing and selling products and services (Kahneman, Knetsch, & Thaler, 1986).

But consumers do not expect sellers to pass on cost savings if the costs of production or selling decline. Consumers, however, do perceive price increases brought on by shortages to be unfair (Conte, 1990). One very questionable set of behaviors concerns price gouging—charging exceptionally high prices for products because of extraordinary circumstances. For example, some firms charged excessively high prices for products such as bottled water, milk, and building materials in the aftermath of Hurricane Andrew in Florida. These firms took advantage of an unusual, and often desperate, situation to charge extraordinarily high prices and make large profits in the short run.

Fair Value

Implied by fairness is that manufacturers should attempt to set prices in a way that communicates fair value to resellers and consumers alike. But this is easier said than done. Suppose, for example, a manufacturer produces a product and sells it to wholesalers for $10.00, a 100% increase over the cost of making the product. Suppose, furthermore, that the manufacturer has determined that $29.95 is the optimum price at the marketplace. Above that, demand for the product will decline quickly. The wholesaler who buys the product for $10.00 may need a margin of 100% to cover all wholesale costs and make a reasonable profit. So that wholesaler prices the product at $20.00 to retailers.

Now the retailer is also in business to make a profit and may require a markup of 100% to cover costs of retailing the product and make a reasonable profit. The final price to the consumer is now $40.00—the consumer will not buy the product in the quantities forecasted by the manufacturer. Therefore, one or more of the members of the channel must reduce the price (and the profit) to reach the projected optimum retail price of $29.95. But $40.00 is not likely to be perceived as fair by the final consumer. Because each of these channel members is likely to feel that its price is fair, how can the final price to the consumer be reduced in such a way that the retail price is perceived as fair to the consumer? Although common sense says that the product should sell for $29.95, the fairness issue makes the implementation of that $29.95 price recommendation difficult.

The preceding illustration also serves to point out one of the major problems associated with pricing—the pressure for profits. Many examples of unethical behavior have been undertaken in the name of making profits. As you saw in the first chapter, there is a strong school of thought that argues that the only purpose of a business is to make a profit. When marketers lose sight of the principle of reasonable profits (fair prices), they open themselves up to many questionable behaviors, including advertising deception, manipulative selling, and using substandard materials in products. Now, read Newsline 8.1. *What do you think? Is unethical pricing behavior evident here?*

Newsline 8.1

Kodak Announces It Won
a Round Over Fuji Paper

The International Trade Commission made a preliminary determination yesterday that Eastman Kodak Co. was "materially injured" by low prices of photographic paper sold in the U.S. by Fuji Photo Film Co., Kodak said.

The ITC, a U.S. agency, couldn't be reached for comment late yesterday. In a statement, Fuji, which is based in Tokyo, said preliminary rulings "are common and not necessarily indicative of the final outcome. . . . Fuji is confident that Kodak will not be entitled" to tariffs.

The ITC preliminary determination was made in response to a petition that the Rochester, NY, photography, health-care and chemicals concern filed in August, alleging that Fuji uses profits from "monopoly-like" sales in the Japanese market to subsidize dumping of paper in the U.S. The color paper in question is made by Fuji in Japan and the Netherlands. It is used to make prints of photographs.

Before tariffs can be imposed on the Fuji paper, the U.S. Commerce Department would have to make a preliminary determination that Fuji sold the paper in the U.S. at prices below fair market value. A Kodak spokesman said he doesn't expect such a ruling until about next February. Once both the ITC and the Commerce Department make their preliminary rulings, tariffs could be imposed. The ITC and the Commerce Department would then make final rulings, which could result in an adjustment of the tariffs.

In its antidumping petition, Kodak alleged that Fuji sold the paper in the U.S., at prices as low as one fourth of what it charges in Japan.

When Kodak filed its petition, Fuji issued a statement saying that because Kodak dominates the color-paper market, Kodak is the pricing leader. Fuji also said that its own paper offers consumers "alternatives, in both quality and price."

Tariffs on the Fuji paper would be a significant plus for Kodak, which has been suffering from pricing pressures—mainly from Fuji—on its film and color negative paper. One month before the Kodak board disclosed in early August that it had asked for his resignation, Chairman Kay R. Whitmore said that a pricing strategy would be a major part of a Kodak restructuring plan. However, in light of Mr. Whitmore's pending departure, such a strategy will probably be left up to Kodak's new chief executive, who is expected to be named before the end of the year.

Kodak made the announcement after the markets closed. In composite trading yesterday on the New York Stock Exchange, Kodak shares closed at $59.125, down 12.5 cents.

SOURCE: "Kodak Announces It Won a Round Over Fuji Paper." (1993, October 13). *Wall Street Journal*, p. B5. Reprinted by permission of the *Wall Street Journal*, © 1993 Dow Jones & Company, Inc. All rights reserved worldwide.

Recently, some auto dealers have gone to a one-price selling strategy (Crain, 1991). The local dealer sets a price, which is almost always lower than the manufacturer's list price. This price is not negotiable. *What do you think of this practice? Do consumers get as good a price with one-price selling compared to negotiating? Is one-price selling simply a way for auto dealers to obtain higher prices and profits?*

◪ ETHICAL PRICING ISSUES

Within the area of pricing, there are also many questionable practices that can be implemented by marketers. Some of these are described in Table 8.1.

Nonprice Price Increases   Most of you are probably too young to remember the nickel candy bar. The nickel candy bar is one example of downsizing the quality, quantity, or both of a product without reducing the price. Many years ago, you could buy a candy bar for a nickel. Over time, as the price of ingredients rose, candy bar manufacturers faced a dilemma—to raise prices or to reduce the size of the candy bar. Initially, many opted to reduce the size of the bar. But as ingredient prices continued to rise, eventually the candy manufacturers were compelled to raise prices, and some increased the size of the bar. However, the price of ingredients continued to rise, and the candy bar manufacturers again faced the same dilemma—increase the price or reduce the size of the bar?

When costs increase, sellers often pass those costs on to the consumer in the form of price increases. In certain instances, however, the customer expects to pay a certain price. So when costs increase, the only way the seller can maintain the expected price at the marketplace is to reduce costs by reducing the quantity or quality of the product. This practice has occurred in many products, including reducing the number of sports cards per pack, eliminating the bubble gum from the baseball card pack, and reducing the number of disposable diapers per package.

Sellers typically defend such practices by arguing that reducing quantity, quality, or both is a convenient way to respond to cost increases when changes in price are not advisable or not easily implemented (e.g., sales in vending machines). Sellers also argue that modern technology allows them to reduce the size of packages while maintaining the original integrity of the product. They also often argue that nonprice price increases represent a way that they can bring product and packaging costs more in line with that of competitors. Regardless, the use of nonprice price increases does

Predatory pricing. In times past, a firm might sell its products for less than their cost for a period of time, in hopes of driving a competitor out of business. Such practices are regulated at the national level by antitrust legislation (Sherman and Clayton Acts), and several states have unfair trade practices acts.

Horizontal price fixing (collusion). Agreements among direct competitors to charge an identical price are generally held to be illegal per se under the Sherman and Clayton Acts. However, agreements under the supervision of government agencies are legal. Collusion on prices is difficult to prove because identical or very similar prices may also result from legal tactics, such as (a) extremely competitive markets where prices are generally equalized (e.g., gasoline and beer) or (b) the industry following a price leader and engaging in parallel pricing.

Price discrimination. Selling a product of like grade and quality to different consumers for different prices is illegal under the Robinson-Patman Act "where the effect of such discrimination may be to substantially lessen competition or may tend to create a monopoly in any line of commerce." Price discrimination litigation under the Robinson-Patman Act is perhaps the most complex and time-consuming (and criticized) of all marketing litigation. The Robinson-Patman Act provides for bona fide efforts to meet competition and cost differences (e.g., quantity discounts), and it covers promotional allowances.

Price deception. Posted prices for some products, particularly consumer goods, sometimes bear little relationship to the actual price of the product. Bait-and-switch tactics (advertising a product for a low price to get consumers into the store and then pressuring them to buy a higher priced model), "buy one get one free" promises, and "going-out-of-business sales" are examples. Laws, such as the Automobile Information Disclosure Act, Truth in Lending Act, and unit-pricing statutes have been enacted to combat deceptive advertising. The Federal Trade Commission also has issued "Guides Against Deceptive Pricing."

Markup pricing. There are state laws that set the minimum amount that any product must be marked up. For example, some grocery products must carry a 6% markup. Therefore, supermarket chains may not sell these products for less than 6% above their cost. These statutes are sometimes controversial because retailers do not always follow them, and they tend to take away efficiency advantages of chain stores and other mass merchandisers.

Vertical price fixing (resale price maintenance). "Fair-trade laws" used to allow the manufacturer to control prices at all levels in the channel of distribution. Currently, this type of price fixing is not allowed. The Consumer Goods Pricing Act of 1975 repealed earlier statutes in this area. Despite the absence of these laws, some manufacturers exert substantial control over pricing their products. They argue that this is justified to maintain a quality image. The future of resale price maintenance is uncertain.

SOURCE: Adapted from Patrick E. Murphy and Ben M. Enis. (1985). *Marketing*, p. 415. Glenview, IL: Scott Foresman. Reprinted by permission of the authors.

Table 8.1 Legal Issues Affecting Pricing Decisions

not change the fact that consumers get less product and, very often, sellers can increase their profit margins ("Critics Call Cuts," 1991).

Price Discounting

We live in an age in which price discounting seems to be the only way in which retailers think they can move products from their shelves. During the last 10 to 15 years, we have seen a revolution in price-discounting approaches, including rebates, warehouse stores, discount outlet malls, deep price cuts, and price clubs. These developments have led to a number of ethical problems:

1. Are goods from an outlet store really cheaper? If they are cheaper, is the consumer purchasing first-line merchandise, or are "seconds" or damaged goods being bought?

2. Do "sales" by retail outlets really represent reductions in price or are they disguises for the prices the retailer would normally charge if we were not seemingly locked into this "discount mentality"?

3. What do words such as *sale, clearance,* and *discount* mean to the consumer? Are consumers' expectations being met when they shop under these sale conditions?

4. Are products really less expensive at a warehouse store or price club?

Price discounting would appear to be good news for consumers. Retailers make all sorts of promises concerning low prices, competitive prices, matching prices, and so forth. But such price discounts, when combined with advertising, actually work to the benefit of the retailers (sometimes) but often give customers a false sense of security. Prices advertised are not always the "lowest in town," although many consumers arrive with that expectation. Furthermore, many retailers fully expect that once customers are drawn into the store, they will buy much more than the low-priced advertised item.

The discounting trend has made consumers more aware of discounting practices. It has also led consumers to devote shopping time to those times when sales are advertised. Consumers have always been "deal prone," and the age of the discount has just heightened that sensitivity toward "getting the good deal." When consumers are sensitized to getting good prices, they are often susceptible to discounting pricing practices that promise products at cheaper prices but that really do not deliver on those promises.

In Proverbs 11:1, we are told, "The Lord abhors dishonest scales, but accurate weights are His delight." The principle of differing weights occurred in times past when it was common for street merchants to have two sets of weights that hung in a bag around their waists. When they sold grain to the poor community, merchants would use the lighter weights to measure out grain portions because the poor could not afford to have their own weights. In more affluent areas, however, the merchants used the proper weights because if they were caught they would be invited to spend some time in the rock quarry. *How does the principle of differing weights apply to pricing strategies today?*

In France, discount pricing approaches, such as markdowns and clearance sales, have come under government control ("France Aims to Regulate," 1990). The new rules were implemented after random checks found about one fourth of 6,000 stores inspected were guilty of faking price reductions. Now, sales are limited to two periods annually, not lasting more than 2 months each. *Do discount price approaches trick customers? What thoughts come to mind when you hear phrases such as "clearance sale" or "50% off"? How can you protect yourself from practices such as those now regulated in France?*

Price appeals are frequently used in advertising. One of the ethical issues dealing with price advertising concerns the difference between what the consumer understands the price of an advertised product to be and what that price actually is. For example, you may see an ad for an airline that advertises round trip fares to some destination for an advertised price. But many of these ads contain small print somewhere near the bottom that describes all the restrictions that accompany the advertised price. Such practices can be misleading and can also be judged to be deceptive if all of the restrictions are not disclosed in the ad (Wise, 1989). **Price Advertising**

Price discounting and price advertising are often seen together. Many retailers advertise "lowest price" or "everyday low price." For these statements to be true, the retailer making the statement must know what all of its competitors are charging for the advertised item. This is rarely, if ever, the case. Unfortunately, for consumers to recognize the truth in the ad requires that they know what all competitors are charging for the advertised product. This, too, is also very unlikely. JCPenney, Sears, and Montgomery Ward have all been reprimanded by the Better Business Bureau for advertising prices such as those just described (Johnson & Koten, 1988).

In the early 1980s, the Dauphin Deposit Bank & Trust Corporation, in Harrisburg, Pennsylvania, advertised variable-rate individual retirement accounts (IRAs) with a guaranteed minimum interest rate of 10%. Consumers were told that accounts were automatically renewable every 18 months (Myers, 1993). Many customers continue to hold these IRAs because interest rates on alternative investments have declined (e.g., 3% on certificates of deposit). To counter losses on the 10% IRAs, Dauphin began charging a 1/2% service fee on the 10% IRA accounts with balances over $35,000. They also assess a 3% service fee for moneys rolled into these 10% IRA from other accounts. *Do the service fees represent misleading price advertising? Do the fees represent unfair trade practice? Are consumers who add outside funds to these automatically renewable accounts acting ethically?*

Section 1 of the Sherman Act stipulates that any efforts by competitors to collude on price (fix prices) are anticompetitive and therefore illegal. Explicit agreements between competitors are considered illegal. Usually, such agreements occur in the form of a contract or conspiracy. There are many instances, however, in which competitors exchange price information or engage in parallel pricing in which one competitor sets a price and the others (to remain competitive) charge similar prices. These types of practices are subject to the rule of reason, which requires an inquiry into the nature, purpose, and effect of any agreement before a decision concerning its legality can be made (see Stern & Eovaldi, 1984, p. 257). **Price Fixing**

The difficulty with most competitive arrangements is that they are difficult to prove. One competitor may act as a signal to others to adjust their prices. Under such circumstances, an implicit agreement exists but is very difficult to prove. Evidence of motive to collude must be presented, and the courts cannot rely solely on the existence of uniformity of prices across competitors to determine if a price-fixing agreement exists.

Price leadership represents one example of parallel pricing that has been judged acceptable. Under some circumstances, small competitors follow the lead of larger competitors. The usual motivation for such followership is that, to stay competitive, smaller competitors must match the prices of industry leaders.

Questions about compact disc (CD) price fixing are being raised in the United States and England. Even though CD sales have risen sharply over the last decade, retail prices have remained the same or even increased (Reilly, 1993). The Federal Trade Commission, as a reaction to these circumstances, is investigating price fixing by companies such as MCA, Sony, and Warner Music Group. *What information would you like to have before you decided if price fixing existed? Why do you think the prices of CDs have not gone down even though the demand has greatly increased?*

Predatory Pricing

Predatory pricing involves one organization's reducing prices to a low level (often unprofitable) in markets in which competition exists in an effort to drive that competition out of those markets. The price cutter expects and accepts losses because the price cutter also expects profits in the long run to increase when competition is lessened. The ultimate goal of the predator is to secure a monopoly position in the marketplace.

Such predatory pricing behavior is illegal according to Section 2 of the Sherman Act. Nevertheless, predatory pricing is difficult to prove under certain circumstances. For example, one competitor may be dominant and may be able to reduce prices to low levels because economies of scale (not enjoyed by smaller competitors) still allows the large competitor to make a profit.

A key issue in the determination of predatory pricing is the definition of unreasonably low or unprofitable prices. One rule of thumb is based on cost and is known as the Areeda-Turner test. According to this rule, predatory prices are those in which the price charged is set below average variable or marginal cost (Ortmeyer, 1993). But it may be difficult to determine the relevant costs associated with a product. Furthermore, this rule does not take into account situations in which one organization must set an unprofitable price in reaction to the low price set by a competitor. Another standard involves the intent of the organization that sets the low price and the actual prices charged relative to costs. But these two standards are often difficult to enforce because the first involves determining motive and the second requires assignments of costs that may, indeed, be arbitrary.

Many of us have grown accustomed to not paying regular prices for items such as airline tickets, clothing, and tools. Our expectations are that prices will be reduced in the future. Recently, American Airlines ran a program of discount air fares and two financially weaker companies, Continental Airlines and Northwest Airlines charged that American was trying to run them out of business (O'Brien, 1993). *How would you decide if American was engaging in predatory practices? What do you think is the effect on demand of across-the-board price cuts? Can price cuts be predatory if they are good for consumers?*

Resale Price Maintenance

Resale price maintenance is also known as vertical price fixing. The practice occurs when a manufacturer specifies the minimum and maximum prices that a wholesaler or retailer can charge for a product. Resale price maintenance practices are governed by Section 1 of the Sherman Act.

Prior to 1975, state fair trade laws exempted vertical price agreements from antitrust legislation. The purpose of the state regulations was to protect small retailers from price competition by larger retail chains and discount stores. By 1975, only 22 states still carried fair trade laws, so Congress repealed the Miller-Tydings and the McGuire Acts, which had provided for the exemption. Today, explicit agreements between manufacturers and members of the channel of distribution are illegal because they are viewed as lessening competition.

Some interesting ethical questions occur in this area. Suppose a manufacturer has an agreement with its dealers to terminate any dealers who are viewed as price cutters? Does terminating a low-price dealer inhibit competition between dealers of that manufacturer's brand? Do consumers suffer from a lack of service provided by the dealers who offer such low prices? Does the offering of such low prices lead other dealers to compete on service, thereby improving the competitive environment to the benefit of consumers? Such questions are often raised in the legal battles associated with vertical price fixing.

Discriminatory Pricing

The Robinson-Patman Act concerns price discrimination as it applies in business-to-business situations. In essence, Robinson-Patman declares it unlawful for one organization to discriminate in selling or purchasing a commodity "of like grade and quality." Goods of like grade and quality can also include consumers' perceived differences that result from promotional efforts of the selling organization. There are two exceptions to the Robinson-Patman Act. One is that price differences are justified if they reflect differences in manufacturing, selling, or delivery costs. The second is that price differences are acceptable if they exist to meet competitive prices.

In applying the Robinson-Patman Act, the rule of reason applies. That is, if there is evidence of price differentials in the marketplace, the effect on competition must be determined. Competition between sellers is examined, although such cases generally fall under the jurisdiction of predatory pricing practices. Generally, price differentials that affect competition among buyers are more commonly investigated under the Robinson-Patman Act. When a seller offers a better price to a buyer, that buyer may be given an unfair advantage in the marketplace. Such influences on competition can also occur at the buyer's level. In other words, manufacturers who differentiate prices to wholesalers who sell to retailers may, indeed, be providing the basis for unfair competition at the retail level.

Originally, the intent of the Robinson-Patman Act was to prevent larger organizations from gaining unfair advantage over smaller competitors by obtaining lower prices from suppliers. But does such protection really protect the large organizations, and not competition, as many critics argue? When one or more competitors is hurt, is competition really hindered?

Unit Pricing   Unit-pricing regulations require that prices for products must be provided on a per-unit weight or volume basis. Unit pricing is common in grocery store retailing and other forms of retailing in which packaged goods are sold. The purpose of unit pricing is to make it easier for consumers to compare prices across products of different weights and sizes.

There have been two issues raised with respect to unit pricing. One argument surrounds the cost incurred in implementing unit pricing. The argument is that these costs are such that small retailers and independent retailers are placed at a disadvantage when compared to larger retailers' abilities to install unit pricing systems (Carman, 1972-1973). Evidence suggests, however, that the costs of installation are the same across all kinds of stores (Monroe & LaPlaca, 1972).

A second issue centers around the ability of consumers to process the additional price information. Retailers use different labeling approaches and different terminology, making it difficult for consumers to assimilate all the pricing and product information. Again, however, some research refutes this because value-conscious consumers demonstrated the ability to determine the most economic product alternatives when unit prices were available (Houston, 1972).

More recently, scanner technology has led some retailers to reduce or eliminate marking the prices on individual items. They argue that, because unit prices are available, the individual marketing of products provides redundant information. Others have argued, however, that providing only shelf prices reduces the available information needed by consumers to make intelligent shopping decisions (Zeithaml, 1982). One additional problem with scanner technology is that some stores mark products with a certain price, but the scanner price on the bar code is actually set slightly higher than the marked product price. Thus the consumer actually pays more for the product than is marked on the product and often never discovers it.

Suppose you work for an automobile dealership that has an arrangement with a local finance company. The finance company gives the dealership a $250 rebate on any installment contract recommended by the dealership. Unsuspecting customers who used this finance company often paid higher interest rates and fees than they would have paid had they used a local bank. You did not know this at the time of your employment. But after learning that customers were being misled you approach your manager who says, "Don't be stupid! These people will never find out. Just do what I say." In my viewpoint, complete honesty is the minimum acceptable standard for marketer's making price decisions. **Misleading Pricing**

Sale pricing, price comparisons, and manufacturer's suggested retail prices have all been points of concern when it comes to retailers' misleading consumers with price information. Practices such as the "sale every day" and clearance sales have come under scrutiny as misleading consumers into thinking they received bargains, when, in fact, they did not. Table 8.2 describes some of the Federal Trade Commission's regulation of commercial prices.

One particular misleading strategy is "high-low" pricing in which a retailer sets a price at an artificially high level for some brief period of time. Soon, the retailer drops the price from the original, artificially high price to the price that the retailer wanted to receive all along for that product. Accompanying the drop in price is the fanfare associated with a "was-is" sales or some other form of promotion designed to emphasize the new low price. The ethical issue concerns whether or not the consumer recognizes that the new price is the regular price. Or is the consumer being misled into believing that the product is now priced at a bargain level?

Retailers use other price strategies such as "manufacturer's suggested retail price," "list price," or "reference price" strategies. Although evidence suggests that consumers are skeptical of such approaches, consumers have also demonstrated that they are influenced by such strategies (Blair & Landon, 1981; Fry & McDougall, 1974; Urbany, Bearden, & Weilbaker, 1988). Retailers using such strategies counter that consumers are knowledgeable, having been exposed to these strategies for a long period of time. Therefore, consumers are able to understand what they are buying when they buy on sale. *What do you think?*

Still another form of misleading pricing is comparative pricing. Comparative pricing occurs when one retailer compares its prices to those of other retailers. Supermarket basket comparisons are one form of comparative pricing. Ethical issues involved here include how items are selected for the basket. Any supermarket can usually find some items that are less expensive than those of competitors. Does the basket test give consumers the impression that one store's products are all less

Table 8.2 Federal
Trade Commission
Guidelines
Concerning
Misleading Pricing

1. Many advertisers offer reductions from the advertiser's own former price for a product. If the former price is the actual, bona fide price at which the product was offered, and it was offered on a regular basis for a reasonably long period of time, then the advertiser has a legitimate basis for advertising the price comparison. Under circumstances where the former price is genuine, a true bargain is being offered to consumers.

   Alternatively, if the former price is not the bona fide price but represents an artificially inflated price established solely for the purpose of seeming to offer a large price reduction, the bargain being advertised is judged to be a false bargain. The buyer is not receiving the "unusual value" expected under such advertised conditions.

2. A former price is not judged to be fictitious only because no sales at the advertised former price were made. The advertiser's responsibility, however, is to ensure that the former price is one at which the advertised product was made available to the public for a substantial period of time. Moreover, the advertiser must be careful about the language used in an advertisement. If no sales were made at the former price, the phrase, "Formerly sold at . . ." can be construed as misleading.

   Here is an example. Acme office supply sells a desk set for which Acme pays a wholesaler $25. Acme's usual markup is 100% over cost, leading to a retail price of $50. To offer a "substantial" bargain, Acme decides to mark up the desk set 200%, resulting in an artificially high price of $75. Acme will sell few desk sets at this price. However, Acme keeps the desk sets priced at this level for only a few days. Then, the advertising special hits. "Desk Sets—Were $75, now $50 . . . Great Savings!!!!" The advertised sale is not genuine.

3. Advertisers use false price comparisons in other ways. One way is to employ a price that was never offered at all or that is infrequently used in the regular course of business. Similarly, a price that was used way back in the past might be offered as the comparison price. Under these circumstances, the "sale" is not genuine unless the advertiser discloses the truth about the comparison price.

4. Often, advertisers use such terms as *regularly, usually,* and *formerly* in their price comparison advertising. When using such terms, the advertiser must make certain the price comparison is a real one. If the former price or the amount of percentage of the reduction implied by the sales is not stated in the advertisement, the advertiser must be certain that the actual reduction is a significant one. It should be large enough such that if the consumer knew what the former price was, that consumer would be able to say that he or she was receiving a true bargain by paying the revised price. Obviously, such a criterion is subjective, but an advertiser who claims a sale price of $19.95 on a product originally priced at $19.99 is offering no real bargain.

expensive? Do consumers take the percentage of savings reported by the low-price store as applicable to all products?

A cash value insurance policy creates savings that you can withdraw or borrow against. The cash values also keep insurance coverage in force. Although many cash value policies were built to last, some have fallen on hard times, because cash values have not grown as fast as forecasted. In one example, a $150,000 "vanishing premium" policy was sold under the terms that only 5 years of premium payments would be required and the insurance would be paid for life. After 5 years, however, the buyer was told that the $1,388 annual premium would have to be paid for 4 more years (Quinn, 1992). *Was the buyer misled? Do economic circumstances justify changes in price arrangements such as this one?*

This chapter presented a number of ethical issues related to pricing decisions. Price represents the value placed on a product or service by both the buyer and the seller, but it is often difficult to assess value because consumers employ emotional buying criteria as they make purchase decisions.

A key issue in pricing decisions is fairness. But marketing professionals often face tremendous pressure for profits, and this pressure can lead them to make questionable or unethical pricing decisions or both. The following ethical price issues were discussed in this chapter: nonprice price increases, price discounting, price advertising, price fixing, predatory pricing, resale price maintenance, discriminatory pricing, unit pricing, and misleading pricing.

CHAPTER SUMMARY

▨ PRICING SCENARIOS

1. Your company has just completed the design of a power tool that will remove the glazing material from windows easily and quickly. The target is the home market for use in replacing broken windows and loose glazings. You are faced with the choice of two design possibilities. The first is a light and compact design that is scheduled to retail for $29.95. When used correctly, it will do a fast and efficient job. If used incorrectly, however, it could inflict serious injury to the user's hand. The second design is more bulky and not as easy to use. It retails for $79.95 but carries no danger of injury (Fritzche & Becker, 1983, p. 293). What are the ethical issues in this situation? How would you resolve these issues?

2. You are the store manager for a large grocery store chain. Your store is located in a low-income area. Independent studies have shown that prices tend to be higher and that there is less product selection in your store than in other stores in the city. Furthermore, your grocery store chain has enacted a practice of raising prices on all merchandise on the day welfare checks are received (Reidenbach, Robin, & Dawson, 1991, p. 84). What are the ethical issues in this situation? How would you resolve these issues?

3. You are the vice president of sales for a large spice manufacturer. You recently joined a business venture with your company's president to import black pepper from India. Your new company is about to sign a 5-year contract with your original company to supply their black pepper needs. The contract is set at a price

of 3 cents per pound above the current market price for black pepper imports (Fritzche & Becker, 1983, p. 293). What are the ethical issues in this situation? How would you resolve these issues?

4. You are responsible for approving the final design of a new corporate office building to be located in Washington, D.C. The final specifications submitted by the architect contain an option to install special automatic window shades that would raise when the sun was providing heat through the glass and would lower when heat was lost through the glass. The shades would add 5% to the $40 million cost of the building. The payback on the shades in fuel savings is estimated to be 9 years. You are counting on the successful completion of the building, along with several other accomplishments, to lead you to a substantial raise and promotion. But you also know that the board of directors of the company purchasing the building has approved no more than $40 million for the project (Fritzche & Becker, 1983, p. 293). What are the ethical issues in this situation? How would you resolve these issues?

5. You are the advertising director for an agency developing a promotional campaign for one of your clients. Your client is in the hardware business and wants to promote an electric circular hand saw at a price of $49.95. The client wants you to advertise a suggested manufacturer's retail price of $69.95. This was the price at which the saw was originally advertised 3 years ago when it was introduced to the marketplace. But, today, the saw can be purchased in most retail outlets for $55.00 (Fritzche & Becker, 1983, p. 293). What are the ethical issues in this situation? How would you resolve these issues?

6. You are the purchasing director for a major hospital. Your hospital has solicited bids from companies that specialize in waste disposal. You note that one of the bids is 25% below any of the other six bids. You feel that this bid is too low to cover the costs of waste disposal effectively. You are also keenly aware of the problems associated with medical waste being washed up on some local beaches. Nevertheless, you follow your hospital's guidelines and accept the lowest bid. You do this partly because you are eligible for a substantial raise and possible promotion if you contribute to the control of medical costs (Nelson, 1992, p. 318). What are the ethical issues in this situation? How would you resolve these issues?

7. You are the purchasing manager for a large industrial supply company. You have been asked to provide your expertise on the purchase of a new building that will

allow your company to double its capacity. The estimated cost of the new building is $3,500,000. The two lowest bids for the building were received from reputable contractors. The two bids were quite similar in content, and both met your company's specifications. One of these bids, however, came in about $150,000 higher than the other bid. At a meeting, your company's president informs you of a call made by the president of the construction company that tendered the higher bid. In that conversation the construction company stated that he expected to receive the bid because he does much business with your company. Your president is leaning to accepting his company's bid (Fritzche & Becker, 1983, p. 293). What are the ethical issues in this situation? How would you resolve these issues?

8. Your company has just received an exclusive patent from the U.S. Patent Office. The patent has been awarded to a product that can increase the average car's gas mileage by about 30%. The vice president of marketing knows that your company is protected from competition by this patent. She has recommended a price to auto parts dealers of $65 on the new product. Your company can produce and distribute this new product for less than $2.00 (Harris, 1990, p. 745). What are the ethical issues in this situation? How would you resolve these issues?

9. Your company is a parts supplier in a highly competitive industry. Because of the competitiveness, it is difficult to maintain the loyalty of your customers. Your sales vice president has recently recommended a plan in which customers are given points for every $1,000 of merchandise they purchase throughout the year. At the end of the year, purchasing agents employed in these customers' organizations will be awarded all-expense-paid vacations for two to various locations, depending on their purchase volumes. Unfortunately, you are aware that your products' prices are increased to cover the travel expenses (Harris, 1990, p. 745). What are the ethical issues in this situation? How would you resolve these issues?

10. You are aware that your firm is considering raising its prices by 10%. You are in the office of one of your better customers, and you decide not to mention the price increase to them. You justify this on the grounds that this company has been a good customer of yours for several years. You also rationalize that you can go to some of your smaller and newer customers and make up the difference by warning them of the upcoming price increase and mentioning that other increases might be forthcoming in the not-too-distant future. What are the ethical issues in this situation? How would you resolve these issues?

11. You are a sales representative for a company that has a standard discount policy for certain volume sales. You are in the office of a new prospect who holds the promise of making a large purchase. You present the discount schedule to this prospect and promote it as a special discount schedule for new customers. You know that it is near the end of the quarter and that this sale will result in a large bonus for you. You are also looking at other sales companies for better job opportunities than the one currently provide by your company. What are the ethical issues in this situation? How would you resolve these issues?

12. Recently Wal-Mart Stores were found to have illegally engaged in predatory pricing by selling pharmacy products below cost (Ortega, 1993, p. A3). The ruling was that Wal-Mart's policies, as carried out in one of its local stores, had the intent of "injuring competitors and destroying competition" as defined in Arkansas' Unfair Trade Practices Act. What evidence would you like to have before deciding if predatory pricing has occurred? Should such cases be decided on the basis of one product or a "market basket" of products, as argued by Wal-Mart? Is the sale of a product below cost always an indication of predatory pricing?

13. You have just been hired as a salesperson by a firm that manufactures wood products. It is your third week on the job. You have been asked by your sales manager to review a list of materials requested by a contractor. Your firm is preparing to bid for the provision of these materials to the contractor. As the meeting ends, your manager gives you two envelopes that contain the bids of two of your competitors. Your manager explains that your firm wins many bids because of an "inside person" employed in the contractor's organization. Your manager further explains that this is the only way to succeed in the construction industry. Would you keep this job? If not, what would you say when you tell your manager that you are quitting? What ethical principles are relevant here (Fritzche, 1992b).

14. You have been hired to work for a nonprofit organization. One of your responsibilities is to initiate and process membership renewals. The cost of memberships ranges from $25 to $150. You discover that many members who were recruited in the summer months are being asked to pay annual dues again, in January. When they became members, they paid a full year's dues. Is such a procedure fair to the new members? Should you make your supervisor aware of this practice (Cohen, 1992a)?

PRICING MINICASE

Incredible Shrinking Potato Chip Package

Julie has been concerned about the profitability of the various items in her line of potato chips. According to her potato suppliers, the recent drought caused a 35% reduction in the potato crop compared to 1 year ago, resulting in a 25% hike in potato prices to large buyers such as Julie's company. Potatoes account for almost the entire content of her chips (which also consist of vegetable oil, one of three different flavoring spices, and salt), plus packaging costs. To hold the line on margin, which of late had been slim at only about 5% due to fierce competition from several other local and regional brands, Julie needs to raise potato chip prices about 15%. On her most popular 7.5 oz size, which had a price spot of $1.59 on the package, this would require a price hike of $.24, bringing the price up to $1.83.

Julie wondered what would be the appropriate strategy to deal with this unfortunate circumstance. She was very reluctant to raise the price to maintain the margin. First, she feared losing the goodwill of her loyal customers; it wouldn't be perceived as fair by them. Moreover, she was worried about competitive responses; her other larger competitors might be willing to incur a loss in the short run to keep their customer bases and to attract price-hiking rivals' customers. Julie couldn't afford such a strategy because she was evaluated solely on the basis of monthly net profits. Historical data in this industry revealed another possible competitive maneuver in the face of rising ingredient costs: Hold the line on prices and package size while reducing the net weight of the package.

Julie was concerned that this might be a deceptive practice. She recalled from a consumer behavior course she had taken in college a concept known as the "just noticeable difference." This said that relatively small changes in a stimulus (such as a price hike or a content shrinkage) go unnoticed by consumers. Julie felt intuitively that the price increases necessary to maintain margins would be noticed, given the price sensitivity of buyers for snack foods. The past industry data suggested, however, that perhaps buyers might not notice the package size reduction needed to sustain profits, which in this case would be 1.1 ounces.

Julie asked her boss, Dave, the marketing director, about the advisability of reducing the net weight of the potato chips. Dave said that this was a practice known variously as "downsizing" and "package shorting." It was a very common practice among packaged goods manufacturers. For instance, he said, candy bar manufacturers are subject to constantly fluctuating ingredient prices, and because there are expected ("fair" or "reference") prices for candy bars, package sizes are frequently adjusted without informing consumers. Jim said that was a nonissue since marketers have been aboveboard in labeling products accurately as to weight, serving size, price, and quantity. Furthermore, the Food and Drug Administration had no laws against the practice. Dave recommended downsizing the potato chips, but made it clear to Julie that the ultimate decision was up to her.

Julie still had her doubts. After all, it would seem that consumers who are in the habit of buying a particular product size generally don't scrutinize the net weight label on subsequent purchases. If this were true, it would seem that downsizing would be a deceptive practice.

1. What are the relevant facts?
2. What are the ethical issues?
3. Who are the primary stakeholders?
4. What are the possible alternatives?
5. What are the ethics of the alternatives?
6. How would you measure costs in this situation?
7. Do the benefits of maintaining profits outweigh the costs of losing customer goodwill?
8. What are the practical constraints?
9. What action should be taken?

SOURCE: Lantos, Geoffrey P. (1992b). "Incredible Shrinking Potato Chip Package" (Minicase 4). *Business Ethics Program*. Arthur Andersen & Co. Copyright © 1992 by Geoffrey P. Lantos. Minicases developed by the Arthur Andersen & Co., SC Business Ethics Program. Printed with permission of Arthur Andersen & Co., SC.

9

Ethics and Advertising Decisions

PURPOSE

To discuss some of the ethical issues faced by marketing professionals as they communicate to customers through advertising.

MAJOR POINTS

Ethical advertising decisions are often complicated because company, advertising agency, and media representatives can be involved in the those decisions.

A key issue facing marketing professionals is how far to go in attempting to be persuasive in an advertisement.

Pressure to persuade can lead to deceptive advertising practices, which may occur in the form of deception or puffery.

Other ethical issues presented in this chapter include advertising to children; demonstrations; mock-ups; endorsements and testimonials; coupon fraud; and sweepstakes, contests, and games.

A dvertising is communication by some identified sponsor. Its intent is to inform or persuade customers by presenting messages in one or more forms of mass media. Three characteristics make advertising particularly susceptible to ethical questions. First, typically, advertising messages are one-sided: They rarely say anything about the deficiencies of the product or service being advertised. Second, advertising is usually biased beyond one-sidedness. When company X says something about its products, it is expected that the message will be positive. In this respect, advertising is much like walking into a restaurant and asking the waiter or waitress, "Is the food good?" What response do you expect? And what had the answer better be if the waiter or waitress expects to keep his or her job? Finally, advertising is intrusive. It interrupts our television shows. It splits articles in magazines and newspapers. It interrupts music.

Ethical issues associated with advertising are complicated because most advertising decisions are made with the input of three groups of decision makers (see Laczniak & Murphy, 1993, pp. 170-171). Advertising agencies employ people such as account executives, copywriters, and media planners, all of whom have some influence on the way an ad finally appears in public. Then, there is the organization whose product is being advertised. Often, product managers, sales managers, and top marketing executives are involved in the approval of the advertisement before it reaches the public. Finally, there are people in the media, such as salespeople, media managers, and TV or radio station executives, who influence decisions concerning whether to carry the ad. If you will recall the discussion from earlier chapters concerning significant others, you already know that having many people involved does not necessarily prevent questionable ads from reaching the marketplace because of such factors as "groupthink" and other pressures that might influence individuals at various stages of the decision process.

▧ HOW FAR SHOULD ADVERTISING GO IN ATTEMPTING TO BE PERSUASIVE?

Much of the criticism of advertising revolves around advertising's attempts to persuade the marketplace that it should purchase one brand of product over another. Figure 9.1 describes the problems associated with persuasion. As you move to the right in the figure, the ethical difficulties associated with the nature of advertising increase. At the far end, deception, advertisers have clearly crossed over legal boundaries.

On the left side, some advertising is designed to provide information. Although such advertising can, indeed, be unethical, it is perceived as having fewer ethical problems than those forms of advertising that are listed to the right of information on the continuum on Figure 9.1. As one moves to the right on the continuum from persuasion to embellishment to deception, the likelihood of encountering advertising that has some puffery increases.

The Institute Bilingue Internacional, a language school in Dallas, Texas, offers classes in English to Spanish-speaking students, charging as much as $998 per course.

Complete Truth			Total Lie
Probably ethical	Possibly unethical		Illegal
Information	Persuasion	Embellishment	Deception

Figure 9.1. How Persuasive Should Advertising Be?

SOURCE: Gene R. Laczniak and Patrick E. Murphy, *Ethical Marketing Decisions: The Higher Road.* Copyright © 1993, p. 154. Reprinted by permission of Prentice Hall, Englewood Cliffs, NJ.

The course materials include phrases such as the following: " 'Avoid having a day of pleasure turns into nightmare for you and your family.' " " 'You were few.' " " 'Whose are those sheeps?' " " 'I'll tell you good words' " (Gerlin, 1993, p. B1). In response to more than 30 complaints from the school's students, the Texas Attorney General, Dan Morales, has filed suit seeking to bar deceptive advertising practices. *What do you think? Is the preceding evidence indicative of deception? What other information would you like to have? How would you determine if a school such as this was keeping its promises?*

Many on the side of advertising argue that advertisers should be allowed to express some pride in their products (embellishment, puffery).

Their argument is sometimes based on the premise that "all advertisers do it" or that consumers are intelligent enough to determine for themselves what is "best" or "number one" in the marketplace. Furthermore, they argue that most embellishment and puffery is harmless exaggeration, something each of us does daily even in our personal lives. Despite these arguments, there is still the potential for unethical or even illegal materials to be placed in ads that fit in the embellishment or puffery portion of the continuum in Figure 9.1 (Richards, 1990).

Deception

Webster's dictionary uses terms such as *fraud, subterfuge, double-dealing,* and *trickery* as synonyms for deception. According to Webster's, fraud always implies guilt and often criminality in a practice. Double-dealing suggests treachery or at least some action that is contrary to a professed attitude or behavior. Subterfuge involves the telling of a lie to gain something. Trickery is the use of ingenious acts to dupe or cheat. None of these terms suggests legitimate or ethical behavior.

Deception in advertising is difficult to prove, and the following discussion will provide some reasons for this difficulty. One approach to the nature of deception is presented in Figure 9.2. The three items in the center of Figure 9.2 are three areas of evidence needed to prove deception (Preston, 1993). First, there is the question of the explicit advertising claim. This item concerns the explicit content of the ad. Second, there is the question of what the ad conveys in the minds of the consumers

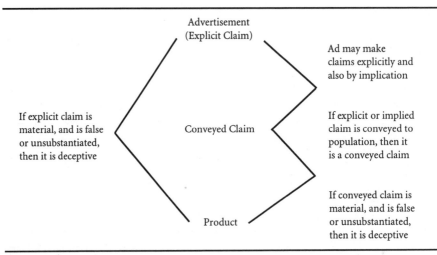

Figure 9.2. Factors Considered in Evaluating the Deceptive Nature of an Advertisement

SOURCE: Preston (1993, p. 665). Used with permission.

who see the ad. In other words, how consumers interpret the ad is considered in evaluating the deceptive nature of an ad. Finally, the facts about the product or service advertised are evaluated for their relevance to the conveyed claims.

It would seem that the left side of Figure 9.2 would lead to an automatic judgment of deception. But this side of the figure concerns only the explicit portion of the advertisement. If the explicit content of the ad is inconsistent with the product, there can be a judgment of deceptiveness. But this analysis involves only specific claims. It does not involve conveyed or interpreted claims. Therefore, the right side of Figure 9.2 represents a superior means of evaluating deception because it includes how consumers who are exposed to the ad interpret what they see and hear. Although this may sound like the best approach to evaluating deception it has some problems. *What do you think those are?*

One of the better ways to evaluate a claim made by an advertisement is to study the language of the advertiser. The *claim* represents the part of an advertisement that makes some statement for the superiority of the product in the ad. One of the reasons for the examination of advertising claims is to discover if the claim is really providing any useful and truthful information or whether pseudo-information is being provided.

Consider the use of words such as *better* and *best.* Now consider the common advertising claim, "No other brand tastes better." Does "better" mean better than all other similar products? If so, then the advertised product is the "best." But is it best overall or simply best in only one aspect of the product? And is that aspect of the product really meaningful to the customer? Furthermore, there are many situations in which brands are seen as identical by consumers. In these cases, the use of the term best simply means that the advertised product is just as good as competing alternatives.

If a product is truly superior, do you think that an ad would state the point of superiority clearly? For example, if one brand of gasoline gave you 5 more miles to the gallon than competing alternatives, such a claim would appear in advertising. Instead, we see claims such as the following:

1. Better mileage per gallon (better than what?)
2. The detergent gasoline (all gasolines are)
3. The gasoline with additive X (most gasoline brands have the same additives)

Do such ads create an illusion of superiority? What useful information is being provided? Are such claims deceptive? Table 9.1 provides an overview of several types of claims; the information value of each is questionable.

Puffery

Before we begin our discussion of puffery, let's take a look at the legal definition of puffery. Puffery is advertising or other sales representations that praise the product or service with subjective opinions, exaggerations, or vague and general statements with no specific facts (Preston, 1975). To be legal, the characteristics of products and services that are embellished or "puffed" must actually exist. Statements that claim something exists when it does not go beyond puffery.

Does puffery contain any relevant information that consumers can use in making a decision? Judge for yourself by looking again at the statements in Table 9.1.

Let's see how others feel. One author states that "the 'puffing' rule amounts to a seller's privilege to lie his head off so long as he says nothing specific" (Prosser, 1971, p. 723). Do the statements in Table 9.1 say anything specific? Does that make those statements unethical? Another author calls puffery "soft core" deception and argues that its "continued existence in the mass media shows that advertisers think it effective with a substantial portion of the public in obtaining reliance and altering purchase decisions" (Preston, 1975, p. 664).

In opposition to these critics, the Federal Trade Commission (FTC) has generally ruled that puffery is acceptable. The FTC uses the distinction between falsity and deception in making its decisions. You might ask, "What's the difference?" According to the FTC, falsity is an objective characteristic that may or may not be deceptive or illegal. Deception is a characteristic that is subjectively interpreted as injurious to consumers and, therefore, it is considered illegal. Still not convinced of the difference? Join a large group who are on your side. By now, I hope, you are beginning to see some of the difficulties in dealing with ethical issues in advertising. Even the experts

Table 9.1 Advertising Techniques That Create the Illusion of Superiority

Technique	Explanation	Illustrations
Weasel claim	Modifier that practically negates the claim that follows Weasels suck out the inside of an egg giving the appearance that the egg is intact. The egg is actually hollow.	Leaves dishes *virtually* spotless Only have the price of *many* sets *Tastes* just like its name *Fights* bad breath *Best* against mouth odor
Unfinished claim	Ad claims the product is better but does not finish the comparison	_____ gives you more Twice as much of the pain reliever doctors recommend most _____ gives you more body, more flavor You can be sure if it's _____ _____ makes it better for you
We're different and unique claim	States there is nothing else quite like the advertised product Uniqueness is to be interpreted as superiority by consumers	There's no other _____ like it Only _____ has this unique feature _____ is like nobody else's car _____ with TCP
Water is wet claim	Something is said about the product that is true for any brand Usually a statement of fact, but not an advantage	_____ the detergent gasoline _____ the natural beer _____ smells different on everyone
So what claim	A claim that is true but provides no real advantage Similar to water is wet, except that an advantage is claimed when none exists	_____ has more than twice the iron of ordinary supplements _____ gives you tasty pieces of chicken and not one but two chicken stocks _____ strong enough for a man but made for a woman

Vague claim	Unclear—uses words that are colorful but meaningless Uses emotional opinions that defy verification	Lips have never looked so luscious For skin like peaches and cream The end of meat loaf boredom _____ tastes good like a cigarette should _____ makes sensible eating delicious
Endorsement or testimonial	Use of celebrity or expert who lends his or her stellar qualities to the product	Michael Jordan for McDonald's Bill Cosby for Jell-0 Candace Bergen for Sprint
Scientific or statistical claim	Uses scientific proof or experiment, specific numbers, or impressive-sounding mystery ingredient	_____ helps build bodies 12 ways _____ has 33% more cleaning power than another brand _____ contains a sparkling drop of Retsyn _____ created by a research scientist who actually gets sinus headaches
Compliment the consumer claim	Flatters the consumer	You've come a long way, baby. The lady has taste. We think a cigar smoker is someone special.
Rhetorical question	Demands response from audience Audience answer affirms product's goodness	Isn't that the kind of car America wants? Shouldn't your family be drinking_____?

SOURCE: From *Deception Detection*, by Jeffrey Schrank, pp. 10-15. Copyright © 1975 by Jeffrey Schrank. Reprinted by permission of Beacon Press.

cannot agree on some of the terms used in judging the ethical nature of advertising. Does this sound like different value systems and conflict?

The FTC views puffery as nondeceptive using the following rationale. First, they make the assumption that consumers do not rely on such positive exaggerated statements when making purchasing decisions. Second, because such statements are not relied on by consumers, they have no capacity to deceive. Third, there is no accepted way to determine if the "puffed" statements are false (Stern & Eovaldi, 1984).

The stance taken by the FTC puts the burden on consumers to be careful (caveat emptor—"let the buyer beware") in the marketplace. Furthermore, their stance seems to be one that says, let free market, competitive forces work. Of course, the FTC has many backers when using this logic that competition is healthy and ultimately good for consumers because it leads to better quality market offerings.

At one point, Jesus said to his followers, "I am sending you out like sheep among wolves. Therefore be as shrewd as snakes and as innocent as doves" (Matthew 10:16). In other words, buyer beware. As consumers, we can all learn to be less gullible. We should be shrewd, constantly examining and judging the truth content in the messages presented by marketers. Typically, marketers present their viewpoint but do not present the other side. For example, automobile advertising always portrays a wonderful picture of the car being featured. But that car often comes with a thick payment book, never mentioned in the ad.

The Food and Drug Administration (FDA) made some decisions related to health products that became effective on July 1, 1994 (Karr, 1993). Among these were the following:

1. Folic acid in early pregnancy can reduce the threat of certain birth defects.
2. Dietary fiber and antioxidant vitamins such as beta carotene or Vitamin C cannot be represented as preventing cancer or cardiovascular disease.
3. Fish oils can prevent heart disease.

How do you view these actions? Is the FDA trying to block consumer access to health supplements or simply trying to reduce unsubstantiated claims? When can health-related information be truthfully put on labels? What constitutes significant scientific and medical agreement concerning the effects of supplements on health?

Making Promises That Cannot Be Kept

Deuteronomy 23:23 states, "Whatever your lips utter you must be sure to do." Simply put, when we give our word to do something, we ought to do it. When we make a promise, we ought to keep it. Unfortunately, many advertisers seem to think that such statements are conditional. "I'll keep my word if I profit from it," or "I'll keep my promises only if someone forces me to do so." In other words, they assess whether or not keeping a promise is to their advantage, and, if it is not (e.g., it costs money), they'll break the promise.

Many product advertisements promise more than the product can deliver. Consider, for example, fruit juices that have come under fire for misleading the public about the amount of real fruit juice contained. The product, itself, might lead us to believe that fruit juice is as stated—juice. But advertisements and packages, although highlighting the word *juice* in a variety of ways, often contain small print that reads something such as "contains 10% real juice."

This is a difficult issue, made more difficult by the fact that the product itself can cross ethical boundaries, and advertising associated with the product can also cross ethical boundaries. The difficulty relating to the product is how far does the product have to go before it is considered to be deceptive to a majority of consumers? Take the example of products that are packaged with what is called *slack packaging*. Many products come in containers that are only partially filled. Does such a practice lead consumers into thinking they are getting more product than they actually receive? Cereal manufacturers, chip manufacturers, and others who sell products that "settle" in the package use slack packaging. How much settling is acceptable before the product crosses ethical boundaries?

A variation on this is the coffee industry that has slowly moved from 16 ounces to 13 ounces and 12 ounces of coffee still packaged in a 16-ounce-sized can. The coffee makers' defense has been that roasting methods have allowed consumers to brew as many cups of coffee with 13 ounces as they previously had with 16 ounces. Do the coffee companies cross ethical boundaries with this logic?

▧ OTHER ETHICAL ADVERTISING ISSUES

Deception is not the only ethical issue confronting marketers. Other ethics issues related to advertising include advertising to children; demonstrations; mock-ups; endorsements and testimonials; coupon fraud; and sweepstakes, contests, and games. Each of these provides many problems for marketing professionals.

One particularly volatile ethical issue that advertisers have faced has concerned the advertising aimed at children. Please read Newsline 9.1 to get some idea of why advertising to children is such an intense issue. In general, groups that have voiced opposition to advertising to children have voiced four major concerns: **Advertising to Children**

1. Children are exposed to advertising of products that could be harmful to them if the products were misused (e.g., cereals with heavy sugar content).
2. Some television techniques may be deceptive because children lack the ability to evaluate them properly (e.g., program hosts or cartoon characters selling products).
3. Advertising to children is inherently bad because it exploits children (children have little sense of value, time, money).
4. Long-term exposure to advertising may have adverse effects on the development of the children's values, attitudes, and behaviors. (Smith & Quelch, 1993, p. 613)

Newsline 9.1

TV Advertising Aimed at Kids Is Filled With Fat

ATLANTA—The number of commercials for high-fat foods on children's television shows has jumped sharply despite recent federal recommendations that children follow a low-fat diet, a team of New York researchers reported.

The researchers said spot checks of Saturday morning television commercials earlier this year found that 41% of the foods advertised contained a third or more of their calories in fat. Similar spot checks in 1989 and 1990 found only 16% of the foods advertised on Saturday morning were high-fat foods. The researchers defined "high-fat" as food with 30% or more of its calories coming from fat.

"It would be wrong to say that *because* the guidelines came out there are more high-fat foods advertised," Thomas J. Starc, a pediatric cardiologist at Columbia Presbyterian Medical Center, told the American Heart Association meeting here. Instead, he suggested, issuance of the federal guidelines for children coincided with marketing changes in the food industry. "In 1989-1990 there were very few pizza ads on Saturday morning," he explained. The Saturday morning hours are now heavily loaded with commercials for Pizza Hut and Little Caesars pizzas, he noted. In previous years, he said, packaged meals like canned spaghetti were the type of high-fat food usually advertised to children.

Dr. Starc also singled out McDonald's, Burger King and Wendy's for promoting high-fat foods in their Saturday morning commercials. "It isn't that [the fast food chains] aren't trying to offer healthier foods," said Lisa C. Cohn, the nutritionist on the research team. "You walk into Pizza Hut or McDonald's and look at their actual menus, and you'll see [low-fat items]," she said, citing low-fat milkshakes at McDonald's, salads at Wendy's and baked potatoes at Pizza Hut. "But if you view Saturday morning children's television you wouldn't know" these healthier foods were available, she said.

"How the fast-food chains define a kid's meal isn't a salad," Dr. Starc added. "For six-year-old kids, the foods advertised on Saturday morning are all they see as the options for foods." He urged the food marketers to begin showing commercials that depict other healthier foods that are available.

In September 1991, the federal National Cholesterol Education Program issued guidelines urging that the diets of children more than two years old contain less than 30% of total calories in fat, as part of a long-term program to fight heart disease. The latest national nutrition survey, now several years old, showed that children get an average of 34% of their calories from fats.

Dr. Starc said the researchers counted commercials broadcast on the morning of April 24, 1993, by three network affiliates in New York. During the 15 hours of children's programming, he said, there were 423 commercials, of which 47% were for foods and 16% for toys. Of the food commercials, 38% were for cereals, considered to be low-fat foods, and 38% were for fast-food chains and packaged meals, almost all of which were high-fat foods. Snacks like cookies and candy accounted for 10% of the commercials, but 40% of the snacks advertised were high-fat products, he reported.

The researchers compared their 1993 count with similar but less extensive checks made in October 1989 and April 1990. In those years, Dr. Starc said, children saw an average of two commercials an hour for fast foods and packaged meals. The average jumped in this year's check to five commercials an hour for the predominantly high-fat fast foods and packaged meals, they reported.

"The current recommendations for low-fat foods for children are being ignored," said Dr. Starc.

SOURCE: Bishop, Jerry E. (1993, November 9). "TV Advertising Aimed at Kids Is Filled With Fat." *Wall Street Journal*, p. B1. Reprinted by permission of the *Wall Street Journal*, © 1993 Dow Jones & Company, Inc. All rights reserved worldwide.

Historically, the FTC has been of little help in resolving the ethical issues associated with children's advertising. The debate has been kept alive by activist groups who feel strongly about the four issues just cited. For example, in the late 1960s, a group of mothers in the Boston area formed Action for Children's Television (ACT) and has lobbied against children's advertising since that time. The Council on Children, Media, and Merchandising (CCMM) has focused on food products advertised to children.

Groups like this kept up public pressure and, as a result, two industry groups formed—the National Association of Broadcasters and the National Advertising Division of the Council of Better Business Bureaus. Although these two groups identified specific practices as unethical (e.g., selling of products by a show host), generally, they have taken the stance that advertising to children is a legitimate economic activity.

By 1990, the Children's Television Act was passed (Waters, 1990). Commercial television licensees and cable operators are now required to limit advertising in children's programming to no more than 10.5 minutes per hour on weekends and 12.0 minutes on weekdays. The bill also requires the Federal Communications Commission to ascertain how well each television station has served the educational needs of children as a condition of license renewal. The Federal Communications Commission is also charged with determining how to treat program-length commercials, shows based on popular toys like G.I. Joe and He-Man. To provide some idea of the scope of this last problem, by 1990 there had been 70 programs that were based on commercial products (Sheridan, 1990).

In 1991, Hasbro, Inc. advertised a G.I. Joe Battle Copter to children. The ads featured the helicopters flying, hovering, and colliding in combat. The poles and wires used to "hover" the helicopters were not shown, and the battery-operated motors, installed for the ads, that kept the rotors turning during flight were not mentioned ("G.I. Joe Surrenders," 1993). *Is this ad deceptive? How should ads aimed at children be evaluated—by adults or by children? Do you think that children are capable of making such judgments?*

Demonstrations

Often, what you see in an advertisement may not be what you think it is. When a company runs an ad in which a product is demonstrated, that company is attempting to show that, in some way, their brand is superior to the brands offered by competitors. Many advertisements contain such demonstrations. One of the earliest, and most well-known, demonstrations was undertaken by Colgate-Palmolive in which a brand of shaving cream was touted as being superior. In this ad, the shaving cream was applied to sandpaper and then the sandpaper was shaved off, supposedly demonstrating the superior moisturizing capability of the product. In reality, sandpaper was not used. Instead, the advertisement used sand sprinkled on plexiglass. It was this ad that led the FTC to determine that for any ad that created an impression that the consumer was seeing a real product demonstration, that demonstration must be real or the ad would be considered deceptive.

Mock-Ups

A mock-up is an artificial alteration of a product so that a very appealing photograph of the product may be taken. Is the ice cream in the ad really ice cream . . . or is it mashed potatoes? Is the foamy head on a beer really foam . . . or is it soapsuds? Is the soup really that chunky . . . or are there marbles in the soup so that the vegetables rise to the top?

Because of the ability to create very appealing products with mock-ups such as those just mentioned, mock-ups have been tightly regulated. A mock-up may be considered acceptable, depending on the purpose of the substitution and the product characteristics being demonstrated. Let's look at our mashed potatoes example. Real ice cream cannot withstand the heat of the lights needed for proper photography. Therefore, mashed potatoes, which can stand the heat, are substituted. This substitution is acceptable if the purpose of the ad is to demonstrate the enjoyment of eating ice cream. But if the purpose is to emphasize the texture of the ice cream or to claim that the ice cream melts at a slower rate than that of competitors then the substitution is likely to be considered deceptive.

An endorsement is defined as an advertising message that "consumers are likely to believe reflects the opinions, beliefs, findings, or experience of a party other than the sponsoring advertiser" (FTC Guides Concerning Use, 1982). A testimonial, on the other hand is an ordinary recommendation of the sponsor's product by unfamiliar people who will, most likely, be perceived as communicating the sponsor's viewpoint.

Endorsements and Testimonials

Generally, testimonials consist of ordinary consumers talking about favorable experiences with a product. The testimonial content must represent what a typical consumer would experience in using the product. The experience communicated cannot be an exception to the normal use of the product. Testimonials should use actual consumers unless a disclaimer is presented that the actors in the ad are being paid to provide the testimonial.

Endorsements, on the other hand, are usually provided by celebrities or experts. If the endorser is a celebrity, the ad must reflect the honest experience or opinion of the endorser. Furthermore, the endorser must not make claims that cannot be substantiated by the advertiser. Third, if the endorser is presented as a product user, the advertiser must have reason to believe that the celebrity will continue to use the product when the ad is run. In other words, the celebrity cannot simply try the product for the purpose of appearing to be a legitimate user in the ad. Finally, if the celebrity endorser has some financial or other interest in the product, that interest must be disclosed in the ad.

An expert as an endorser represents "an individual, group, or institution possessing, as a result of experience, study, or training, knowledge of a particular subject, which knowledge is superior to that generally acquired by ordinary individuals" (FTC Guides Concerning Use, 1982). Typically, such experts communicate the results of tests, surveys, or other studies. Such experts must meet three requirements:

1. The product qualities being endorsed must be within the expertise of those doing the endorsing.
2. The endorsement must be based on features and benefits that are available to the typical consumer.
3. The endorsement must be based on the expert's use or knowledge.

Retin-A, a Johnson & Johnson product, has Food and Drug Administration approval as an acne medicine. Several years ago, Retin-A was promoted as a wrinkle prevention ointment (Stout, 1991). In a press conference, Johnson & Johnson announced research to substantiate this claim. The study was published in the *Journal of the American Medical Association*. The FDA had not approved Retin-A as a wrinkle preventative. Furthermore, the FDA accused Johnson & Johnson of paying doctors to go on talk shows to talk about Retin-A. It was also alleged that Johnson & Johnson sponsored medical conferences in which the benefits of Retin-A were discussed. There has been at least one occurrence of negative side effects from using the ointment too close to the eyes. *How would you decide if the information presented was proper and ensured that balanced, medically accurate information was presented to the public? What do you think about the practice of paying for endorsements and testimonials?*

Coupon Fraud

Coupons are a tactic used frequently by consumer products marketing organizations. Coupon redemption is a complex process involving retailers forwarding coupons to a clearinghouse, a redemption agency, or directly to the manufacturer. Fraud or misrepresentation occurs when coupons for a product are not accepted during the retailer's course of business. Fraud can occur at any point in the life of a coupon from printing to redemption by consumers.

Most coupon fraud or misrepresentation requires the participation of retailers or their employees (Blakey, 1987). One example is the cashier who exchanges the coupon for cash when the product for which the coupon is issued is not purchased. Another example is the individual who steals coupons and sells them directly to the store or who submits them for redemption in the name of the stores.

Over 500 retailers in Michigan were implicated in a scheme to defraud manufacturers by illegally redeeming coupons (Smith, 1992). Losses were estimated at $50 million over a 5-year period. Much of the money had been sent to stores that did not exist or that had been closed for some time. Typically, manufacturers reimburse coupons only after they have conducted a store check in which such information as the number of checkout lanes and square footage of the store is obtained. This information is used to estimate the number of coupons that should be redeemed by a store. If a retailer submits more coupons than the size of the store would suggest, a coupon redemption agency should be alerted by the manufacturer. It is the manufacturer's decision to continue or stop redeeming coupons. *What factors might lead to coupon redemption fraud? Why do you think it took 5 years to uncover this incident of coupon fraud?*

Sweepstakes, contests, and games of chance are used to generate excitement for a product or to get consumers involved in the product in some way. Unethical behavior can include such things as rigging the awarding of prizes or promising prizes that are never awarded. The FTC requires all game operators to disclose the exact number of prizes being awarded, the likelihood of winning each of those prizes, the total number of outlets that are participating, the geographic scope of the contest, game, or sweepstakes (e.g., regional, national, local), the date of termination of the contest, any unredeemed prizes, and revised odds of winning.

The FTC considers all lotteries to be unfair or deceptive unless allowed by state law (Stern & Eovaldi, 1984). Lotteries (including sweepstakes and games) are considered illegal if (a) a prize is offered, (b) winning the prize depends on luck rather than skill, and (c) the participant is required to give up something of value in order to participate (e.g., requiring a purchase). The "no purchase necessary" clause in most sweepstakes and games makes them legal even if they have the first two characteristics. One of the reasons for the FTC requirements is that sweepstakes, contests, and games can become very addictive, and consumers are easily taken advantage of because of the excitement surrounding game circumstances (Enscoe, 1990).

Sweepstakes, Contests, and Games

◪ REGULATION OF ADVERTISING

As you have seen, advertising has many critics. It also has many supporters. In response to the criticisms, the advertising industry has taken on a program of self-regulation in an effort to reduce the amount of questionable advertising that reaches the marketplace. In addition to self-regulation, a number of government agencies exist with the charge of regulating advertising. A few of these regulators are described next:

1. *National Advertising Division (NAD) of the Better Business Bureau:* Set up by the media and advertising agencies, NAD investigates approximately 200 advertising cases annually. Unfortunately, most of the ads have finished running by the time they get to NAD, so the effects of the advertising have already occurred and the decisions made by NAD are often inconsequential.

2. *National Advertising Review Board (NARB):* This board consists of about 50 members of the advertising industry and the general public and handles the cases that NAD cannot successfully resolve. Like NAD, NARB has no real power except to threaten to take a case to the government agencies, most likely the FTC.

3. *Federal Trade Commission (FTC):* The FTC is charged with regulating false and deceptive advertising. Established in 1914, the FTC can require an advertiser to provide substantiation for the claims made in its ads. The FTC can also issue a cease and desist order in which an advertiser must pull its ad from the marketplace. Finally, the FTC can require an advertiser to engage in corrective advertising in which the deceptive part of an ad is corrected, overtly, in a new ad put out by the advertiser (Murphy & Wilkie, 1990).

4. *Federal Communications Commission (FCC):* The FCC can influence advertising content even though it has no direct power over advertisers, advertising agencies, broadcast media, or print media. It has power because it grants licenses to all television and radio stations and reviews those licenses periodically for possible broadcast violations. Some of those violations can occur in the choice of programming (including advertising) made by the media decision makers.

5. *Food and Drug Administration (FDA):* The FDA regulates advertising of pharmaceuticals to the medical profession. The FDA requires that certain content be contained in every advertisement. This content includes warnings and side effects. The FDA, however, has no regulations concerning how such content is presented.

◣ THE ADVERTISING DILEMMA

How can the ethics of advertising be evaluated? There are many differing opinions. For example, the ethical nature of an ad, according to one school of thought, should be based on the usefulness and essential nature of products and services (Leiser, 1979). Advertisements for products and services not considered essential or useful are judged unethical. Many consumers use this as the basis for their judgments concerning lottery, alcohol, and tobacco advertising.

Of course, there are difficulties in judging exactly what constitutes the harmful nature of a product. Furthermore, there are difficulties in assessing whether or not a product or service satisfies needs. For example, does anyone really need a BMW? An expensive stereo? A large house? Are not less expensive alternatives adequate? A more philosophical question concerns the legitimate satisfaction of wants versus needs. Is there anything unethical about marketing a product or service that is wanted but not absolutely needed?

A second school of thought argues that the ethics of advertising should be determined by the truthfulness of the message (Santilli, 1983). This argument attempts to separate the message communicated by advertisers from the product or service being advertised. Using alcohol or tobacco as an example, this school would accept truthful advertising about such products, even though many using other judgment criteria would judge these products to be harmful to users. In other words, the ethics of the advertisement are based on the style and content of the advertisement.

A third approach would be to differentiate between the information and persuasive aspects of advertising. According to this school of thought, persuasive ads are those that take away freedom of choice, in that persuasive ads take away the individual's decision-making autonomy. In other words, individuals would be acting on the basis of someone else's desires, not their own.

At times, it may be difficult to distinguish between information and persuasion. Many ads contain some of both. Second, persuasion may not always be bad. Consider ads that try to persuade young people to practice safe sex or even abstinence or to keep from doing things such as drinking and driving.

There is a new service that allows companies to screen its competitors' commercials within 36 to 48 hours after the ads run on television. Typically, companies are not in a position to monitor all their competitor's advertising in 75 top markets as quickly, or even at all. Competitive Media Alert is testing the service free of charge, with companies such as Coca-Cola and AT&T (Goldman, 1993). The companies participating are all in heated competition with their major rivals. Aggressive ads and aggressive responses are commonplace events when competition heats up. *Is such a spy service, as the service has been called, ethical? Will such a service really help companies respond to competitors? If responses speed up, costs will likely rise. Will such costs be passed on to the consumer? Will consumers realize any benefits from this service?*

CHAPTER SUMMARY

In this chapter, some ethical issues related to advertising decisions were presented. Persuasiveness is one of the hallmarks of advertising, and a key ethical question facing marketing professionals is how far to go in being persuasive. But marketing professionals often face tremendous pressures to be persuasive, and these pressures can lead them to engage in deceptive advertising practices.

In addition to deception, marketing professionals are confronted with other ethical advertising issues. These include advertising to children; demonstrations; mock-ups; endorsements and testimonials; coupon fraud; and sweepstakes, contests and games.

▧ ADVERTISING SCENARIOS

1. You are the marketing director for a company that is a leading manufacturer of breakfast cereals. Your firm has been a leader in reacting to consumer preferences that have shifted to healthy foods, and your company has added a line of all-fiber cereals. Your company has directed your advertising agency to take advantage of the consumer trend and prepare a campaign stressing that the all-fiber cereal helps prevent cancer among regular users of the cereal. This has been done despite the fact that there is no scientific evidence to prove this claim (Harris, 1990, p. 745). What are the ethical issues in this situation? How would you resolve these issues?

2. You are the sales representative for a local advertising agency in a large city. You work with all the dealers of a certain brand of automobile. Recently, you suggested that they use the following slogan in their ad campaign, "Is your family's life worth 45 mpg?" The ad campaign is a reaction to the fact that this brand of subcompact car is not as fuel efficient as some made by foreign manufacturers. But your client's brand has been shown to be a safer automobile by government-sponsored crash tests. Your purpose in selling the campaign is to ask responsible parents if they feel they should trade off fuel efficiency for safety (Laczniak, 1983, p. 9). What are the ethical issues in this situation? How would you resolve these issues?

3. You are employed by an ad agency. One of your clients produces and markets color television sets ranging in price from $300 to $1,200. In general, your client's prices are higher than those of competitors. Recently, you discovered that this client has substituted several less expensive components that, according to some engineers, will reduce the quality of the final product. But the savings of approximately $100 can be passed on to the final customer. Your agency has recommended a price-oriented advertising campaign that does not mention that the later model televisions are of lesser quality than the earlier-model televisions (Laczniak, 1983, p. 9). What are the ethical issues in this situation? How would you resolve these issues?

4. The American tobacco industry is continuously criticized about the legitimacy of the products it offers to the marketplace. The bad publicity your industry has received is on the increase. For example, local action groups have been successful in securing bans against smoking in certain public places, and they continue to

strengthen their efforts. Smoking is also banned on all airline flights of 2 hours or less. Your industry recognizes that this is a critical issue for their survival. Consequently, the tobacco trade association has doubled its budget for lobbying in an effort to fight for a reversal of some of the rules that ban smoking (Harris, 1990, p. 745). What are the ethical issues in this situation? How would you resolve these issues?

5. You are the promotion director for a department store chain that operates six different stores in your city. You are also the largest advertiser in the local newspaper. Recently, that newspaper has been running a series of articles about consumer education, focusing on how consumers can protect themselves in the marketplace. You hear through the grapevine that an upcoming article will be very critical of your store's credit policies. You contact the editor of the newspaper and threaten to pull all of your advertising if the story is run (Harris, 1990, p. 745). What are the ethical issues in this situation? How would you resolve these issues?

6. You are employed as a sales representative for a travel agency. One practice that occurs in your agency is the participation of several other sales representatives in sweepstakes sponsored by the airlines or rental car companies. These sweepstakes allow salespeople to improve their chances of winning based on the amount of business directed toward a particular airline or rental car company. When such practices occur, customers may not always receive the lowest cost option or the most convenient schedule because they are unknowingly directed by sales representatives seeking to win contests. You know that another of these sweepstakes is about to occur. You also know that your agency is about to undertake a local advertising campaign that promises customers the "best arrangements possible" (Murphy & Laczniak, 1981, p. 258). What are the ethical issues in this situation? How would you resolve these issues?

7. You work for a cereal producer. Your company has recently run an advertising campaign that claims nutritional benefits for those who consume your company's cereal products. One of the features of the ad campaign was the claim that certain ingredients help fight against cancer. You know that there has been some statistical linkage between the consumption of this ingredient and cancer prevention. But there is still considerable debate in the medical community concerning this linkage. Furthermore, an overconsumption of this ingredient can lead to other medical difficulties (Murphy & Laczniak, 1981, p. 258). What are the ethical issues in this situation? How would you resolve these issues?

8. You work for an organization whose advertising budget for the year has not been completely spent. Several of your vendors have asked you to create false invoices so that they can be paid with monies dated this year. There is not enough money left in the budget to satisfy all the vendors. Their combined requests, however, allowed you to obtain a 10% increase in your budget for the upcoming year, your intention being to use this increase for legitimate purposes in the upcoming year. What are the ethical issues in this situation? How would you resolve these issues?

9. General Motors Corporation Cadillac division has been a recipient of the Malcolm Baldridge Award for quality. The Baldridge Award recognizes companies for quality improvement efforts in developing and delivering products and services. Subsequently, they used this award in their advertising. In their ads, GM stated that 167,000 companies applied for consideration to win the award. In actuality, fewer than 100 companies applied (Mitchell, 1991). How would you evaluate the use of this information in the ads? Are consumers aware of the Baldridge Award? What significance does it have for consumers? Should such questions be considered in evaluating ads that use the Baldridge Award as a selling point?

10. The Federal Trade Commission is considering whether or not to bring suit against R.J. Reynolds Tobacco Company. At issue is the question of whether the company's "Old Joe" ad campaign appeals unfairly to children. The campaign is credited with reversing the fortunes of Camels, the nation's oldest cigarette brand ("FTC to Decide," 1993). Is a cartoon character used to advertise a cigarette brand unfairly targeting children? How would you determine the effect of such an ad on children if you were representing the FTC? R.J. Reynolds?

11. As the media director for a local television station, you are asked to work on an ad campaign for a local real estate company. The real estate company is about to begin the development of a new subdivision in a low-lying area that has flooded in the past. The company has recently done some work to reduce the danger of flooding in the future. The preliminary statement in the advertising notes that the flooding problem in this area has been solved. Is this statement deceptive? Suppose you knew that, if a flood occurred, some of the houses in this area could have as much as a foot of water standing in their yards. Would you run the ad as requested (Hansen, 1992, p. 525)?

12. A copywriter for an advertising agency has been asked to work on a campaign that presents the competitor's product as dull and boring. The copywriter feels that this form of advertising is unprofessional and the research findings con-

cerning comparative advertising are mixed. The FTC supports the use of comparative advertising if claims can be substantiated. But the copywriter would rather focus on the positive attributes of the product being advertised. Do you agree with the copywriter? How would you support claims of "dull" and "boring" about a competitor's product? Is it ethical to employ comparative advertising and do nothing but criticize a competitor's offering (Lantos, 1992a)?

13. The food service manager for a large hotel chain has been asked to develop a strategy that influences guests' choice of pizza. It seems that many guests call outside pizza parlors for delivery to their hotel room. The hotel manager wants to increase sales of the hotel's brand of pizza. The food service manager consults with the hotel's marketing director and they develop a strategy in which each hotel room will contain a brochure describing pizza. The brochure is to be designed in such a way that guests think they are ordering pizza from an outside restaurant rather than from the hotel's room service. Is this a deceptive practice? Are any consumer rights violated by the proposed strategy? Are hotel guests who order food from outside the hotel behaving ethically (Miller, 1992b)?

14. The product manager for a consumer products company has been approached by the marketing vice president. It seems that the ad campaign used to promote a laundry has been criticized as being offensive to some women. The crux of the complaints is that the campaign shows no men doing laundry. Only women are portrayed as doing laundry, and such a portrayal is viewed as demeaning to women. The marketing vice president would like to see the campaign changed. But you know that the promotion vice president is responsible for the campaign and sales of the product have increased substantially since the campaign started running. How would you handle this situation? Are the rights of women an issue here? If the campaign is stopped, what would be the effect on the product's sales (Sethna, 1992)?

15. A young couple has received an invitation to visit a real estate development over a weekend. The advertising states that they are under no obligation to buy anything. The couple must simply spend 2 hours with a developer sometime during the weekend. Toward the end of the weekend, and after they have spent time with the developer, the developer expresses her frustration that the couple has shown no interest in buying. Are sales promotions such as this ethical? What are the obligations of the people who accept offers for free weekends or other such prizes (Pandya, 1992)?

ADVERTISING MINICASE

Washing Dirty Laundry

Bruce Seth, a project manager at a consumer products company, was wondering how he should proceed with his recommendation for the Endirt commercials. Endirt had been doing well in the market, but not a week went by without a customer (or former customer) writing to complain about the commercial.

There were variations of the commercial, but the central theme was "Dirt on your shirt." It typically featured a woman saying, "Dirt on your shirt!" in a taunting voice to a man whose shirt was soiled. The man looked at another lady (presumably his wife), who was very embarrassed at the entire situation. Later shots showed her washing the shirt after rubbing Endirt into it, and the other woman (or women) saying, "No more dirt on your shirt!" The complaining letters, almost exclusively from women, expressed objections to the commercial because it was demeaning to women and otherwise offensive as well. On the one hand, the brand was doing well; it was the brand leader in a growing market, although a much larger competing company was quite capable of beating Endirt with its brand. On the other hand, were the rights of women being infringed? All the letters seemed to imply that. Bruce was a believer in the profit motive, but not at the cost of condoning unethical behavior. He had been asked to make a recommendation for the commercial for the next TV season. After reviewing the sales data and reading the letters of complaint, Bruce was contemplating his next move.

Marketing research managers and project managers worked along with brand managers on specific brand issues research. Bruce reported to Priscilla Wheeling, a marketing research manager, and would provide recommendations to her and to the brand manager responsible for Endirt. Priscilla was a capable, promising executive with excellent graduate degrees. She was supporting her husband through his Ph.D. in history. She did not like the Endirt commercial and made no secret of it. She proclaimed that she would never buy the brand because the message was offensive and because of the role of the woman in the commercial. Bruce was pursuing a graduate degree while working and putting his wife through college; he certainly needed the job and the income. He was a recent recruit and was in his probationary period.

Bruce had reviewed all the letters, practically all of which were from women and strongly negative. Many of them said, as Priscilla did, that they would not buy the brand because of the offensive commercial and because it was demeaning to women. Secondary data showed that the primary decision makers and purchasers of the product were women. Part of the reason for Endirt's success was believed to be the advertising message, which not only had a high level of recall but a high level of association with the brand. Bruce wondered if, in spite of its apparent success, it was ethical to continue with the advertising message if it infringed on the rights of women, the major buyers of the brand.

1. What are the relevant facts?
2. What are the ethical issues?
3. Who are the primary stakeholders?
4. What are the possible alternatives?
5. What are the ethics of the alternatives?
6. What are the practical constraints?
7. What actions should be taken?

SOURCE: Sethna, Beheruz N. (1992). "Washing Dirty Laundry" (Minicase 28). *Business Ethics Program*. Arthur Andersen & Co. Copyright © 1992 by Beheruz N. Sethna. Minicases developed by the Arthur Andersen & Co., SC Business Ethics Program. Printed with permission of the Arthur Andersen & Co., SC.

10

Ethics and Selling Decisions

PURPOSE

To present some of the ethical issues faced by marketing professionals as they make selling decisions.

MAJOR POINTS

Salespeople are confronted with ethical problems that often occur because of the nature of the sales job as they serve the needs of their own organization and the needs of customers, simultaneously.

Ethical issues related to salespeople and customers include high-pressure persuasion, customer discrimination, misrepresentation, gifts and entertainment, and purchasing.

Ethical issues related to salespeople and competitors include exclusionary behavior, interfering with competitive offerings, criticizing competition, and "James Bond" tactics.

Ethical issues related to salespeople and the sales organization include recruiting salespeople, compensation, promotion and evaluation, supervision, sales territories, co-workers, and company assets.

With the exception of advertising, perhaps no other area of marketing has been criticized for unethical behavior like the area of selling. Salespeople are the front line of any business. They come into direct, personal contact with customers. They represent the individuals whom customers "know" from a marketing organization. Before we get into a discussion of ethical issues faced by salespeople, let's take a look at the position that salespeople occupy inside and outside their organizations.

◩ THE SALES POSITION

Some characteristics inherent in the salesperson's position in the organization can place ethical pressure on the salesperson. A few of these are discussed next.

Salespeople Are Boundary Spanners

The salesperson's task requires that he or she work with members of the marketing organization and with customers. Salespeople are on the boundary. On the one hand, they are advocates of the products and services offered by the organization. On the other hand, they are advocates of customers in that they attempt to match up their organization's products and services with customer needs and wants. Both customers and members of the marketing organization expect some degree of loyalty from the salesperson (Belasco, 1966). The organization and customers are likely to have different expectations for the salesperson, and these differences often manifest themselves in the ethical dilemmas that salespeople face.

Salespeople Are Independent

Salespeople can act in a much more independent fashion than most others employed in organizations. Because they work outside the organization, salespeople receive very little direct supervision in comparison to other employees. They also receive less communication and oftentimes are not up-to-date on changes that have taken place with respect to the organization's marketing program. The independence has advantages and disadvantages, but from an ethical perspective, one of the disadvantages is that the independent nature of the sales job often leads salespeople into ethically suspect situations.

Salespeople Work Under Pressure

Most salespeople work under the pressure to "make goal." That is, they are expected to sell certain numbers of or dollar amounts of product in a given time period. If their performance is lagging, they face pressure to raise their level of performance to "meet goal," particularly when meeting goal means that the salesperson earns some form of incentive compensation. You might say that top managers are also under pressures to achieve goals, and I do not disagree with you. But top management can, and often does, transfer that pressure down to the sales force.

Salespeople can transfer that pressure to no one else except themselves and their customers. Such pressures lead salespeople to adopt a "sell at any cost" approach and are often catalysts for the "hard sell" and high-pressure closes that we all have experienced from time to time.

The Sales Role

There are some who argue that selling is inherently unethical. Their argument is that salespeople are required to promote what they are paid to believe rather than what they truly believe. In other words, these people are arguing that all salespeople sell things that do not necessarily perform as promised. Those advocating this argument, however, claim that real trust between the salesperson and the customer cannot be established under these circumstances (Gowans, 1984; Oakes, 1990). *What do you think? Do all salespeople communicate things in which they do not believe? Do all salespeople bend the truth? Are no salespeople to be trusted? What does this argument imply for those of us who are trying to "sell" our sorority or fraternity? Our professional organization? Our school? Our church?*

▧ THE SALESPERSON, THE CUSTOMER, AND ETHICS

Salespeoples' interactions with customers is the easiest area for most of us to identify with the ethical problems associated with the selling job. We all, at one time or another, have encountered the high-pressure, plaid-jacketed, slick-talking salesperson who tells us little about the product but pressures us to buy. Snake Oil! Hucksters! Charlatans! Buffoons! All of these terms, and many others (some less kind) have been used to describe the selling profession. Such terms abound because there is probably no one who has not directly experienced some questionable behavior by salespeople.

High-Pressure Persuasion

Selling has often been criticized in much the same way as advertising. Selling is persuasive. Salespeople pressure customers into buying products they do not need. Selling is manipulative. Selling is devious. Selling is Machiavellian. Part of this criticism stems from human nature. None of us likes to be "sold." Yet few of us like to make decisions because decisions involve risk and change. Therefore, we, as customers, often need some encouragement to make decisions—take risks and accept change. When such encouragement is of the high-pressure variety, however, selling crosses into the unethical arena.

Clearly, many of the products we have purchased, even those when some pressure has been applied have greatly benefited us. But does this imply that the "ends justify the means"? Does this mean that it is acceptable for salespeople to use questionable tactics because the product will provide benefits? Some might argue for this.

When salespeople and customers interact, ethics become relevant when the customer is denied the opportunity to choose on the basis of objective criteria. For example, a common ploy of salespeople is to close the sale by using the *standing room only technique.* Using this approach, the salesperson creates the impression that there is limited opportunity for the customer to purchase under the circumstances portrayed. A product shortage might be used. An impending price increase might be presented. If such circumstances are real, then there is no problem with the salesperson presenting this factual information to the customer. If this approach is used only to place pressure on the customer, however, then the technique is unethical.

All closing techniques used by salespeople have a basic goal of placing the customer in a situation in which he or she must make a decision. The customer can always say, "No." However, many of the closing techniques used by salespeople do not explicitly offer "no purchase" as an option to the buyer. Buyers will be asked if they like Option 1 or Option 2. Or they will be asked if they want to pay cash or use credit. But they are rarely, if ever, asked to not purchase. Some have argued that such practices raise clear ethical concerns (Gowans, 1984; Oakes, 1990).

Customer Discrimination

Sometimes, salespeople provide more favorable treatment for one customer than another. As an aside, this practice is not only limited to salespeople. In Newsline 10.1, you can see that favorable treatment can impact an entire nation. Some customers might receive more prompt delivery. Some customers might receive lower prices. Some customers might receive higher discounts. Some customers might be made aware of changes in the seller's organization; some might not.

Newsline 10.1

Brazil Is Tested by Fresh Graft Scandal— Fallout Could Further Delay Economic Reforms

RIO DE JANEIRO—Only one year after ousting its president on corruption charges, Brazil's young democracy is once again being put to the test by a new graft scandal that threatens to further delay long-overdue economic reforms.

Having cleaned up its executive branch last year by removing President Fernando Collor de Mello on charges that he benefited from a kickback scheme mounted by a close ally, Brazil's legislative branch is now engulfed in a kickback scandal of its own. And it appears to involve many of those who voted to remove Mr. Collor in the name of morality.

Meanwhile, as if to show that he's now in good company, one of the main figures of the Collor scandal re-emerged—in London—after 113 days on the run. Paulo Cesar Farias, the treasurer of Mr. Collor's victorious presidential campaign and the presumed organizer of the alleged corruption ring mounted during his presidency, claimed in a television interview that he fled because he felt "persecuted" by a Brazilian judge's imprisonment order and said he chose England because it has no extradition treaty with Brazil.

This confluence of past and present scandals is posing a challenge to Brazil's democracy, already undermined by run-away inflation of over 2,000% a year and steadily worsening urban violence. The current scandal shows how deeply the country's political system is ridden with corruption. The re-emergence of last year's scandal shows that for all the efforts at moralization, impunity for the powerful still reigns in Brazil. The side-by-side scandals are resulting in political paralysis and a sense of outrage that have translated into plunging stock markets. Last week Sao Paulo's stock market fell by 18.4%, and it fell a further 6.4% Monday before rebounding 5.26% on Tuesday and gaining another 9.4% yesterday.

"The national crisis has exceeded all limits," former President Jose Sarney said over the weekend. "It requires heroic decision."

President Itamar Franco last week said he was prepared to step down if Congress decided that the best way out of the crisis would be to call early presidential, congressional and gubernatorial elections, currently scheduled for a year from now. But the idea is largely viewed here as a cop-out, and many say the only way for Brazil's political class to regain credibility is to sponsor a domestic version of Italy's *mani pulite,* or "clean hands" crackdown on corruption.

"Either we follow Italy's example, or it will be very difficult to avoid [the circumstance] that public opinion buries representative democracy," says Sen Jarbas Pasarinho, the president of the congressional investigative committee that was set up to look into the latest scandal.

In its first week, that committee has already come up with some startling testimony. And investigators yesterday said they would examine the bank accounts of dozens of Brazilian legislators accused of diverting millions of dollars into their personal accounts. Investigators also plan to look into tax histories and phone bills, searching for evidence of illegally obtained funds.

The scandal was touched off by a former director of the federal budget office, Jose Carlos Alves dos Santos, who was arrested as a suspect in the disappearance of his wife. Asked to explain the origin of more than $1 million in cash in his possession, Mr. dos Santos said the money came from kickbacks paid by construction companies to include projects favorable to them in the budget. Testifying before the committee, he implicated

26 congressmen, three governors, three former ministers and two current ones as being part of the ring, which also included eight construction companies.

The politician he identified as the ring-leader, Joao Alves, denied everything. But asked to explain how the former head of Congress's budget commission came to own a slew of apartments and houses and lease a Lear jet, Mr. Alves, a diminutive 74-year-old with dyed black hair, said, "God helped me." He then said most of his fortune came from lottery wins. He first claimed to have won 13 times, but in subsequent interviews, said he won over 200 times. Skeptical that anyone could have such luck, even with divine intervention, government officials think Mr. Alves was laundering illicit money through a ring set up to buy winning lottery tickets at a premium from their original owners, and then cash them in.

Congress's credibility is being further eroded by a parallel investigation involving a small party that's accused of offering payments of as much as $50,000 to recruit deputies from other parties. This would allow it to reach the quorum of 15 deputies needed to present a presidential candidate and gain free television and radio time. One of the deputies implicated, Itsuo Takagama, caused an uproar when he defended himself by saying: "If a soccer player can receive a transfer fee, why can't a deputy receive money to switch parties?"

Riveted by these scandals, Congress has little time for anything else. Among the victims of this paralysis are a long-planned revision of Brazil's constitution, whose nationalistic and socialistic provisions are felt by many to contribute to Brazil's inflation and slowness in carrying out reforms. Congressmen say the reform will go on, but so far there has been no action.

Another victim is a stopgap tax increase the government was hoping to implement to stanch a projected 1994 budget deficit of as much as $25 billion. Finance Minister Fernando Henrique Cardoso said Tuesday that the tax package will be less ambitious than envisaged, and analysts say congressmen will have a hard time approving higher taxes at the same time as they're being investigated for mismanaging funds.

In addition to such preferential treatment, reciprocity is an unethical practice. Reciprocity occurs when a customer, who is also a supplier to the selling organization, is given favorable treatment. All of these actions are serious and are considered questionable business practice because they violate the natural competitive nature in an industry and detract from customers' abilities to make optimum choices in the marketplace.

Rent-A-Center has 25% of the $2.8 billion rent-to-own market. Renters, who make weekly payments, usually for 78 weeks, become owners of appliances, furniture, and other assorted products (Freedman, 1993). About 50 employees and company executives left Rent-A-Center in 1992-1993, saying that high-pressure sales tactics used in the company are oppressive and abusive. Unsophisticated, often low-income, customers are often encouraged to buy more than they can afford. If payments are not made, Rent-A-Center repossesses products and re-rents them. If all payments are made, the total may far exceed the item's retail value. For example in Utah, a customer paid $1003.56 over 18 months ($55.75 per month or $12.86 per week) for a VCR with a suggested retail price of $289.98. The effective interest rate paid was 231%. *Comment on the ethical issues raised here. Do the facts that most Rent-A-Center customers do not buy the product and can cancel any time change your opinion? Does the appeal of small weekly payments deceive low-income customers into thinking they are receiving a bargain?*

Misrepresentation   Agents in the Tampa office of Metropolitan Life Insurance Company earned over $4 million in commissions last year (Steinmetz, 1993). They earned these commissions selling life insurance to registered nurses who thought they were buying retirement accounts, according to Florida regulators. The allegations are that the agents, directed by superiors, used the word *deposit* instead of *premium* and never mentioned they were selling life insurance. *Are such practices deceptive? Who is responsible for these practices in this situation? What monitoring procedures might be established to prevent such activities?*

Honesty in selling goes beyond telling an outright lie. It includes being reliable and responsible for promises made. Salespeople cannot change their minds if the "deal" isn't right. Salespeople, to maintain their integrity, should be loyal to their promises. Therefore, they should be honest in the promises that they make.

Misrepresentation of products or services that is intentional is considered fraudulent behavior. Those customers injured by fraudulent misrepresentation may seek legal damages and can rescind contracts. When misrepresentation is found to be unintentional, the usual result is the rescinding of a contract.

Misrepresentation occurs when salespeople make incorrect statements or false promises about a product or service. In sales, puffing occurs as it does in advertising. But such puffed statements are generally overlooked because they are considered to be such exaggerations that customers are not misled by them.

Although the sales organization is usually considered at fault for misrepresentation, the salesperson can be held legally accountable for all claims in which factual information related to product performance was misrepresented. Salespeople, from a legal standpoint, may be held accountable for statements made to customers. But misrepresentation is unethical because it interferes with the customer's right of free consent to purchase (Cooke, 1990).

When prospects do not recognize the benefits of buying, they sometimes are too embarrassed to tell the truth. But instead of asking questions, they seek a shortcut by fabricating a small lie, some of which are shown in Table 10.1. *Are prospects being unethical when they use such tactics?*

If marketing professionals travel to Afghanistan in an effort to develop business relations, they may run into a particularly tough situation. Lying is pervasive in the Afghanistan society. Some religions even recognize it as an honor to lie to a foreign "devil." Because this is common knowledge, why would any businessperson want to conduct business in Afghanistan? Table 10.2 describes how lying is viewed in several other countries.

Most salespeople will agree that gifts and entertainment play an important role in the selling process. Despite these feelings, gifts and entertainment are two of the most frequently voiced ethical criticisms of salespeople.

Gifts and Entertainment

What happens when a salesperson offers a gift to a customer as an inducement to buy or as a "thank you" for buying? Several thousand years ago it was written, "The borrower is servant to the lender" (Proverbs 22:7). What are the long-term implications of gift giving? If you give a gift to make a sale, have you created the expectation that you will give gifts for every sale? Will the gift expectation become larger? What happens if you decide not to give a gift or if company policy changes and gift giving is limited?

Gifts

It is a tradition with many salespeople to provide small gifts to customers. The sales process is one in which salespeople must build close personal relationships with customers. Salespeople often show their appreciation for their customer's business by providing them with small gifts, particularly at Christmas.

The ethical question surrounding gift giving is, "At what point does the gift become a bribe?" The value of the gift is a frequently used criterion to separate a gift from a bribe. This is not without problems, however. For example, many would argue that gifts such as pen and pencil sets do not cross ethical boundaries. But some would question the ethics of two box seats at a World Series game, even though they may be of lesser value than some pen and pencil sets. Few would debate the ethics of providing call girls, yet the value of such gifts is often less than the value of other gifts that are not as frequently questioned.

The Internal Revenue Service has established $25.00 as the limit on the amount that one can deduct for business gifts given to any one individual. General Dynamics has a strict "no gift giving policy" under any circumstances. Some companies have no such policy. As a rule, company policies place restrictions on the value of gifts, the timing of gifts (e.g., not giving gifts prior to doing business with a customer),

Table 10.1 The Ten Classic Lies Customers Will Use on You	1. Denial I don't need this new product. I would not think of trading in my old machine. There is no reason for changing now.
	2. Alibi I don't have the money to buy. I don't have the authority.
	3. Blaming It's not my responsibility to make that decision. My boss does not like products like that. I want it, but my husband (wife) doesn't like it.
	4. Minimizing This new idea won't do us much good. I don't see what's so great about this. There is little value to spending money on this.
	5. Justification We do have a need, but we are too busy with our reorganization. I would like to go ahead right now, but the budget hasn't been approved. It's no use. As long as business is slow, we can't spend money.
	6. Derogation I heard that these things suffer from frequent breakdowns. When it comes to service, nobody will be around to help us. You don't have a good reputation in this area.
	7. Yes, but It's a good idea, but it won't work here. Yes, it is inexpensive, but we can't afford it. We'd like to buy two, but not right now.
	8. Helplessness It's out of my hands. I cannot do this deal. If I could convince my boss, I'd buy it today. There is no way my wife would agree to that.
	9. I have no choice I tried my best, but I had no choice but to go along with the majority. With the many problems we've had in the past, I had no choice but to cancel the order. Based on the lower offer that we've received from your competitor, I had no choice but to go with them.
	10. Reframing reality Robin Hood was not stealing. He just redistributed the wealth. Our purchasing system is not unfair. We are just limiting the number of suppliers. We may have caused you a minor inconvenience by canceling this order, but believe me, we are saving you a lot of money in the future, because your product would have had a lot of service problems with this type of application.

avoidance of gift giving to spouses, and limitations on the total value of gifts given for a specified time period.

Russia:	Lie, but don't overdo it.	
Denmark:	To find credence, lies must be patched with truth.	
Germany:	A necessary lie is harmless.	
Sweden:	A lie in time of need is as good as the truth.	
Rumania:	A well-turned lie pays better than the truth.	
Czechoslovakia:	Better a lie that heals than a truth that wounds.	

Table 10.2 How Different Cultures Justify Lying

SOURCE: Gschwandter (1992).
NOTE: Every country seems to have its own rules for deception as suggested by these proverbs.

Entertainment

Entertainment, like gift giving, creates ethical problems for salespeople. On the one hand, it seems almost expected that salespeople take customers to lunch and dinner. It is an accepted practice. The prevailing attitude concerning ethics and entertainment is that if entertainment is used to place excessive influence or pressure on the customer, beyond those surrounding the features and benefits of the product or service, ethical boundaries have been crossed. Because the customer's felt pressure is often his or her own, however, it is difficult to determine if entertainment is being used to exert pressure or as a form of appreciation for doing business with the salesperson's company. We do know that entertainment can be influential in a customer's decision to purchase (Zinkhan & Vachris, 1984). Table 10.3 provides a summary of some of the more challenging ethical entertainment issues faced by salespeople.

Many sales organizations have policies that deal with the selling ethics issues discussed here and others, such as those shown in Table 10.4. In Table 10.4, it would appear that the percentage of firms having policies concerning proper ethical sales conduct is quite low. In 1980, when the survey was done, this was, indeed, the case. But today, many more sales organizations have stated policies that concern a wide variety of ethical issues, including overselling a customer—selling that customer more than he or she needs—overpromising on other terms of sales (e.g., delivery, credit), failing to keep confidences, and overstocking customers to meet a quota or win a sales contest.

Such policies do not prevent salespeople from engaging in unethical behaviors. These policies, however, do explicitly let salespeople know the company's position on these issues and the consequences of engaging in specified unethical behaviors. As you can see in Table 10.4, even in 1980, the majority of salespeople favored having policies concerning various unethical behaviors in the marketplace.

Table 10.3 Common Sales Entertainment Activities	Taking a customer or prospect to dinner, lunch, or breakfast.
	Giving a customer or prospect free samples for personal use.
	Playing golf, tennis, or racquetball with a customer or prospect and paying his or her way.
	Paying a customer's or prospect's travel expenses to visit a product demonstration.
	Giving a customer or prospect a work-related gift (e.g., desk pen set).
	Buying a customer or prospect alcoholic beverages at a cocktail lounge.
	Inviting a customer or prospect to your home for entertainment purposes.
	Taking a customer or prospect to a sporting event.

SOURCE: Reprinted by permission of the publisher from "Salespeople's Use of Entertainment and Gifts," by Robert E. Hite and Joseph B. Bellizi, *Industrial Marketing Management,* Vol. 16, p. 281. Copyright 1987 by Elsevier Science Inc.

▧ THE SALESPERSON, COMPETITORS, AND ETHICS

There are a number of ways in which salespeople can act unethically toward their competitors. Some research has suggested that salespeople feel that unethical behaviors that disparage competition are less serious than those that directly affect customers (e.g., DeConnick & Good, 1989; Dubinsky & Gwin, 1981; Dubinsky, Berkowitz, & Rudelius, 1980). This is not the position taken in this book. Let's take a look at some unethical behaviors directed at competitors.

Exclusionary Behavior

Sometimes salespeople can take actions to lessen competition. For example, consider what might happen when a competitor introduces a new brand of product to the marketplace. Salespeople might offer some customers "special deals" to carry more of their brand of the product in attempt to exclude the other brand from the market. Such special deals might include price breaks, unusually large quantity discounts, or the offer of gifts or bribes.

On a company level, some organizations have been known to adopt the "fighting brand" strategy in response to competitive new product introductions. That is, the organization will introduce their own "new" brand to the market, temporarily, in an effort to reduce the market impact of the competitor's new product.

Interfering With Competitive Offerings

There are times when competitive pressures are such that salespeople feel compelled to tamper with competitors' products, shelf facings, or in-store displays. For example, salespeople might sabotage a display by removing parts of it so that it will

Rank	Sales Situations and Practices	An Ethical Question?	Have Stated Policy Now?	Want a Stated Policy?	Table 10.4 Evaluation of Twelve Sales Situations or Practices
1.	Allowing personalities—liking for one purchaser and disliking for another—to affect price, delivery, and other decisions regarding the terms of sale	52	47	57	
2.	Having less competitive prices or other terms for buyers who use your firm as the sole source of supply than for firms for which you are one of two or more suppliers	50	52	61	
3.	Making statements to an existing purchaser that exaggerate the seriousness of his problem in order to obtain a bigger order or other concessions	49	31	44	
4.	Soliciting low-priority or low-volume business that the salesperson's firm will not deliver or service in an economic slowdown or periods of resource shortages	42	34	46	
5.	Giving preferential treatment to purchasers who higher levels of the firm's own management prefer or recommend	41	28	40	
6.	Giving physical gifts, such as free sales promotion prizes or "purchase-volume incentive bonuses," to a purchaser	39	56	60	
7.	Using the firm's economic power to obtain premium prices or other concession from buyers	37	37	42	
8.	Giving preferential treatment to customers who are also good suppliers	36	30	33	
9.	Seeking information from purchasers on competitors' quotations for the purpose of submitting another quotation	34	29	39	
10.	Providing free trips, free luncheons or dinners, or other free entertainment to a purchaser	34	49	55	
11.	Attempting to reach and influence other departments (such as engineering) directly rather than go through the purchasing department when such avoidance increases the likelihood of a sale	29	22	30	
12.	Gaining information about competitors by asking purchasers.	27	29	30	

SOURCE: Dubinsky, Berkowitz, and Rudelius (1980). Used with permission.
NOTE: Numbers represent percentages.

not stand up. Alternatively, salespeople might place their products in front of those of competitors on the shelf. And on occasion, salespeople have been known to remove some of the competitors' products from the shelf.

Criticizing the Competition Many professional salespeople will tell you that there is little to be gained from criticizing competitors. Yet it is common practice. Salespeople may make false or disparaging claims about some aspect of the competitor's organization or products. This activity falls under the same legal requirements as does misrepresentation, and the salesperson is legally accountable for any false claims made about competitors. Most customers view such criticism as unfair, in poor form, and even question the seller's products on the grounds that, if the salesperson has to resort to criticizing competitive offerings, there must be little positive to say about the seller's product.

James Bond Tactics Salespeople use deceptive means to gain information about competitors that is, under legal and ethical circumstances, difficult or impossible to obtain. Such spying techniques include pressing competitive salespeople for information at social gatherings, encouraging customers to let out false bid requests in order to obtain information about competitive strategies, and pretending to be customers at conferences and trade shows. When discovered, such practices are not only considered unethical, but salespeople are held legally accountable for their actions.

The selling process is such that salespeople are often faced with situations in which they must make product comparisons (Dubinsky & Ingram, 1984). So selling situations seem to "invite" salespeople to engage in such activities as puffery, exaggeration, and criticism of competitors. Salespeople take the "high road" when they attempt to base all product comparisons on objective and accurate information. Salespeople take the high road when they attempt to, positively, discuss the merits of their own product, rather than criticizing competitors. Salespeople take the high road when they acknowledge that competition is good and attempt to find a match between their products and services and the wants and needs of customers by legitimately presenting features, benefits, and advantages of their own products.

Another James Bond tactic is insider trading. Most European countries have adopted laws making insider stock trading illegal. But proving insider trading has been difficult. Many complain that the frequency of insider trading is a major reason why relatively few Europeans own stocks. For example, in the United States, about 35% of adults own shares of stock, but in Germany it's 7%; in France it's 14% and in England it's 20% (Whitney, 1993). One Italian analyst, however, stated, "People who make money because they're sly are admired in Italy." But an American fund manager said, "It's clear outsiders like ourselves don't have access to equal information." Comment on the ethical nature of insider trading. *Who gains? Who loses? Would the Italian and American quotes be reversed if the insider trading was taking place in the United States?*

▧ THE SALESPERSON, THE SALES ORGANIZATION, AND ETHICS

Ethical problems can also occur between the salesperson and his or her own sales organization. Some of these ethical problems can have a direct impact on how the salesperson deals with customers. Some, such as unethical recruiting practices, may not appear to affect customers directly, but hiring people under false pretenses can have serious effects on the nature of the salesperson's relationships with customers.

These circumstances are presented not to defend unethical behaviors undertaken by salespeople. Rather, they are presented so that you can see that circumstances beyond the salesperson's control influence behaviors and can lead salespeople to engage in questionable behavior. Although salespeople may not be able to control all of their circumstances, this does not mean they are any less responsible and accountable for their behaviors. But so, too, are sales managers accountable and responsible for their behaviors.

Leadership positions have been entrusted to sales managers. They have the responsibility to give helpful guidance to those they lead. Consider this statement from Proverbs: "For lack of guidance [the people fall], but many advisers make victory sure" (Proverbs 11:14). From another tradition, comes this analogy. In Islam, the body's circulatory system is compared to economic health. Bodily health requires that blood flow freshly and vigorously. If it doesn't, sluggishness and illness occur. Islam does not speak against wealth or reward for performance. It does speak about compassion that is strong enough to pump life-giving blood even to the circulatory system's smallest capillaries. One of the sales manager's tasks is to make sure that salespeople perform at high levels. Just as the human body needs blood, salespeople need management counsel and guidance, and management cannot do this in hypocritical ways—they cannot imply they are taking the salesperson's side to the salesperson and then behave differently when they are dealing with the sales vice president. When sales managers send mixed messages to salespeople (e.g., saying one thing and doing another), they contribute to the uncertainty and anxiety of salespeople and may, indeed, be the catalyst that leads salespeople to questionable behaviors.

Recruiting Salespeople

You may experience some ethical issues as you begin your search for a career. Organizations are prohibited from discrimination in hiring except on the basis of performance. This has been the case since 1964 with the passage of the Civil Rights Act. Despite the law, some companies may have prejudice against others based on race, gender, age, or marital status. Legally, such demographic factors cannot be used to discriminate between employee candidates in the recruiting process.

Should company recruiters tell job candidates about the disadvantages of working for their companies in the job interview? Many would say yes, but many would say no. *What do you think?* One way that this situation is handled is to invite recruits to spend a day in the field so that the recruit can make a personal evaluation of the positive and negative aspects of the job in question.

On another note, the recruit can also engage in questionable behaviors. Recruits have been known to falsify résumés, lie about experiences, and make "puffed" statements concerning their accomplishments. The damage in all these instances is that the recruit may accept a job with a company that has been misrepresented and once that recruit begins to work, his or her expectations concerning the company will not be met if false information has been presented. When employees are unhappy, they tend to engage in questionable behaviors, such as padding expense accounts, falsifying reports, and pressuring customers. On the other side, when an organization hires someone, that person is hired with expectations created in the interview process. Can the person who creates a false impression about himself or herself in an interview meet the company's expectations? Does the company have any right to determine if a person fits with the company? *What do you think? What will be the likely result?*

The Federal Trade Commission (FTC) recently completed an investigation of Subway Sandwiches and Salads (Tannenbaum, 1993). The investigation arose when some franchisers complained that Subway misled them about prospective sales and earnings. Although many Subway franchises are not profitable, Subway has defended its approach to recruiting franchisees. No action was taken by the FTC at the close of its investigation. *What possible ethical issues can arise in recruiting franchisees? How can a franchiser present sales and profit information to a franchisee in a realistic and accurate way?*

Compensation, Promotion, and Evaluation

Salespeople are compensated and promoted on the basis of sales performance. Generally, the top salespeople receive the best compensation. Knowing this, does the pressure to receive higher raises or bonuses or commissions provide incentive to engage in questionable sales behaviors? Unfortunately, for many, such pressure does lead them to such tactics as high-pressure closing, misrepresenting products or competitors' products, padding expense accounts, and offering gifts and bribes.

Promotions represent an ethical dilemma for sales managers. Generally, the best salespeople are the ones who are promoted into management. But if the sales manager is also responsible for "making goal," is that sales manager tempted to not promote the best salespeople so that he or she can ensure that goals will be met? Under such circumstances, do sales managers seek other (not generally accepted company criteria) for making the promotion decision that puts lesser performing people into management positions? *How can such situations be eliminated?*

Complaints about Sears Tire & Auto Centers jumped by 29% in 1990 and an additional 27% in 1991 (Kelly & Schine, 1992). At this time, Sears had implemented a plan of high quotas combined with sales commissions and incentives (e.g., trips) based on sales, offered to the top sellers. The California Consumer Affairs Department made 38 undercover runs. In 34 of them, Sears charged an average of $235 for unnecessary repairs. *Did Sears pressure its employees to sell? How would you determine if Sears' sales goals and reward structure were reasonable?*

Supervision

Lack of supervision or too much supervision can lead salespeople to perform in unethical ways. For example, suppose you were working for a sales manager who rarely communicated with you in any form. How would you interpret this? Would such a supervisory approach represent that manager's implicit way of telling you that "anything goes" as long as the sale is made? Some salespeople would say so. On the other hand, supervision that is so strict can lead salespeople to rebel and seek ways of "beating the system" and "getting back" at the supervisor.

Sales Territories

Most salespeople are paid to sell. But what happens to salespeople who are placed in territories that are so small that they cannot make a fair wage? Or what happens to salespeople whose territories are so large that they cannot possibly cover all the accounts in those territories? In both cases, the salesperson's compensation can be drastically affected.

Salespeople in small territories might respond by trying to oversell customers—selling them more than is needed. Salespeople might use pressure tactics to induce customers to buy when they really have no legitimate need or want for the product. Salespeople might offer unusual deals in an effort to boost sales. Or they might pad expense accounts as a means of supplementing their salaries.

In larger territories, salespeople might concentrate on only a few customers, ignoring many other customers. They might not provide the level of services promised to those customers. They may not provide the routine delivery checks to make sure that products were delivered in the right quantities and with the proper handling. Salespeople might also be led to high-pressure tactics in an effort to reduce the number of calls made to customers. For example, the typical customer might require four sales calls before that customer makes a decision to purchase. In large territories, and under pressure to cover all customers, salespeople may resort to pressure tactics to reduce the number of required calls from four to three or even two.

Coworkers   Salespeople operate with many responsibilities to those with whom they work in their own sales organizations. Salespeople, as you have seen, are part of a team that includes other areas of the organization, such as engineering, production, accounting, credit, and purchasing. Salespeople must also work as a part of a team with their salespeople. For example, to make goal, salespeople can sometimes be tempted to sell products to customers in another salesperson's territory. Such behavior is "encouraged" when a buying organization purchases from more than one location and the origination of sales is more difficult to track.

Salespeople are also driven by the reward systems in their organization that have a strong tendency to favor individual over group performance. Although some organizations do offer group bonuses, these types of rewards are often less than those that salespeople can obtain based on their own individual performance.

In November 1993, flight attendants of American Airlines went out on strike. Thousands of passengers were stranded as a result. At issue were pay, benefits, and work rules. American monitors showed flight schedules with delays, but when passengers reached gates they found out their flights were canceled. American did make efforts to put passengers on later flights and many passengers did, finally, reach their destinations. *Should customers be a consideration in labor-management negotiations? Should a dispute among coworkers cause a company to be unable to deliver on products or services paid for? Is it ethical for employees to use customers as leverage in strikes and negotiations?*

Company Assets   Salespeople must use company resources to sell products and services. For example, many salespeople use company money, in the form of expense accounts, to travel, promote products, provide samples, and "wine and dine" customers. They use company equipment such as portable microcomputers, dictating devices, automobiles, photocopiers, and cellular phones.

The ethical questions concerning company assets tend to revolve around the use of such assets for personal advantage. Padding expense accounts is probably the most well-known example. But salespeople can also use other company assets for a variety of personal endeavors. When one considers that the average cost of a sales call is estimated at $230 ("Survey of Selling Costs," 1992), and that much of this expense is incurred in the company assets category, it is easy to see why companies have an interest in reducing the use of company assets for personal advantage. On the other hand, many salespeople have the attitude that it is acceptable to use company assets for personal gain. One reason is that it is often difficult to account for use differences (e.g., stopping at the grocery store after a sales call on the way home or making a personal, long-distance phone call to a customer). Even when organizations have detailed guidelines concerning the use of company assets, it is often difficult to separate personal from company use.

In this chapter, ethical issues related to selling decisions were discussed. The very nature of the sales position exposes salespeople to ethical problems. Salespeople must serve as customer advocates and advocates of their own organizations. These two sets of needs can be in conflict, sometimes leading salespeople to consider unethical sales activity. This chapter also discussed ethical issues between the salesperson and customers, the salesperson and competition, and the salesperson and the sales organization.

CHAPTER SUMMARY

▨ SELLING SCENARIOS

1. You are a sales representative for a wholesale distributor. Your company has been sponsoring a sales contest, and it is the last day of the contest. You are very close to winning a $3,000 bonus, but your last day must be a good one. Your sales manager calls you early in the morning on the last day of the contest and offers to tell you of a sure sale if you will split the bonus with her. What are the ethical issues in this situation? How would you resolve these issues?

2. You are a sales representative attending a trade show as a representative of your company. During one of your break periods, you pass by a competitor's exhibit and notice that no one is there. To gain an advantage, you take all of the free product samples from your competitor's exhibit. You rationalize that this behavior is acceptable because the samples were free to anyone who wanted them. What are the ethical issues in this situation? How would you resolve these issues?

3. As a sales representative for your company, you are required to travel a great deal. On occasion, you rent a room and a car for an extra day or two at the company's expense. During these times you take a minivacation. You know that this is a common practice among salespeople in your company and your industry. You argue that the leisure time helps you be a more effective salesperson. What are the ethical issues in this situation? How would you resolve these issues?

4. You are a top-notch sales representative. One of the tactics you have used to gain your success is to pose as a prospect for one of your competitor's products. You call these competitors, acting as a prospect. But your real motivation is to secure information about your competitor's product and their sales tactics so that you can use this information in your sales presentations. During these phone con-

versations, you learn about new product introductions, sales strategies, delivery schedules, products under development, and the like. What are the ethical issues in this situation? How would you resolve these issues?

5. Your company holds regular sales contests, most often determining the winner based on sales volume. You have discovered a way to increase the likelihood of winning those contests. When a contest is held, you routinely hold back on orders from several weeks prior to the contest and place them only after the contest has begun. This way you get credit for contest sales plus several weeks of noncontest sales that are included as part of the contest sales. What are the ethical issues in this situation? How would you resolve these issues?

6. You are a sales representative for a large company. It is late December and you are almost at your annual quota. You have little chance of meeting your quota and obtaining a $2,500 bonus unless you sell something to one of your key accounts. To increase the likelihood of a sale, you promise to have the product delivered to this customer within 2 weeks. Your company's normal delivery policy requires you to allow 4 to 6 weeks for delivery of the product. You rationalize your approach by saying that you need the money to put your children through college and when the product is delivered late (as you know it will be) you can easily blame your company's shipping people. What are the ethical issues in this situation? How would you resolve these issues?

7. During your visits to your customers, you often ask them for information about competitor's prices and other elements of your competitor's sales strategy. You justify this by telling your customers that you have their interests in mind. You ask for this information so that you can make sure that you and your company remain competitive so that you can continue to service their needs. What are the ethical issues in this situation? How would you resolve these issues?

8. You have several customers who are in competition with each other. Oftentimes, one of these customers asks you for information about some of your other customers' sales policies, upcoming events, and other information that might be pertinent to effective competition. Occasionally, to gain favor with one of your customers, you let something "leak out" about another customer. You justify this on the basis of the fact that you were not asked directly by the customer for the information that you revealed to that customer. What are the ethical issues in this situation? How would you resolve these issues?

9. You are a sales representative for a large pharmaceutical company. You are responsible for calling on pharmacists and physicians in a large territory, the largest in the company. You are on the road 3 to 4 days each week. Your commission and bonuses net you an annual salary of $46,500, but you have made it a practice of supplementing your salary by about $2,300 per year by padding your expense account. You rationalize this behavior by saying that every other salesperson in your company and your industry does this same thing (Harris, 1990, p. 745). What are the ethical issues in this situation? How would you resolve these issues?

10. You are the sales manager for a local automobile distributorship. One of your responsibilities is to train new salespeople who come into your organization. Your biggest training difficulty lies in working with new salespeople on closing sales. Many of your new salespeople just feel that closing puts too much pressure on the customer. You believe that some customers need to be helped into making decisions to purchase a particular vehicle. Because of this belief, part of your training program involves teaching your new salespeople some high-pressure techniques that you know can be successfully used in closing the sale (Harris, 1990, p. 745). What are the ethical issues in this situation? How would you resolve these issues?

11. You have recently been hired as a sales representative. Your first territory is one in which there are many potential customers. The previous salesperson in this territory has been unsuccessful in sales attempts with the largest prospect in the territory. One reason for the lack of success is your company's policy against providing gifts to any customer or prospective customer. You formulate a plan to make the sale to this customer, and it includes the provision of a nice gift if that is what it takes to make the sale (Harris, 1990, p. 745). What are the ethical issues in this situation? How would you resolve these issues?

12. You are a sales representative employed by an organization that runs frequent sales contests. The winners of those contest receive prizes such as all-expense-paid vacations to desirable locations, television sets, stereos, and other valuable merchandise. You are aware that some of your colleagues hold back on orders and pressure reluctant buyers to purchase so that they can increase their sales during contest periods (Reidenbach, Robin, & Dawson, 1991, p. 84). What are the ethical issues in this situation? How would you resolve these issues?

13. You are a sales representative for an automobile dealer. You are told by a customer that a serious engine problem exists with the car the customer is trading in. Because of your desire to make the sale, however, you do not tell the used-car appraiser of this problem. The result is that the deal is closed, you sell a new car, take the trade-in, and the trade-in value provided to the customer results in a loss for the dealership (Reidenbach et al., 1991, p. 84). What are the ethical issues in this situation? How would you resolve these issues?

14. You sell for a furniture manufacturer. You are working with a new prospect who is in a position to purchase a very large amount of furniture. To ensure that a sale is made, you offer the prospect an unreasonable delivery schedule, about one half the time it normally takes to complete delivery of orders of this size. What are the ethical issues in this situation? How would you resolve these issues?

15. You are in the office of a new customer. You completed your first transaction with this customer on your last visit. But the customer feels that she can trust you, and that is one of the major reasons that she purchased from you in the first place. Today, this customer has asked for your opinion concerning how much product she will need for the next year. You knowingly provide an estimate that is close to twice what her needs will likely be. What are the ethical issues in this situation? How would you resolve these issues?

16. One of the key selling points for the product you represent lies in the product demonstration. Your company's training program has stressed a "seeing is believing" approach to making the sale. You have devised a very clever way to demonstrate the product. But your approach represents a every unrealistic situation and one that tends to overstate the ability of the product to perform. You make no mention of this in your presentation, preferring to allow the prospect to think that the demonstration represents "normal use" for the product. What are the ethical issues in this situation? How would you resolve these issues?

17. During your sales presentations, you make it a habit of stressing the positive aspects of your product. You routinely omit, however, any discussion of the negative aspects of your product, preferring to respond to these only when a prospect inquires about them. Furthermore, when an inquiry does occur, your approach is to say that "all products have weaknesses," and then you proceed to a discussion of the positive elements of the product. What are the ethical issues in this situation? How would you resolve these issues?

18. You are working with a new prospect who has shown some interest in one of the products marketed by your company. It is near the end of the year, Christmas is approaching, and you have not quite made your quota. If you make quota, you will receive a nice annual bonus. You tell this prospect that it is difficult to get this product delivered this time of year because the demand for the product is high and it is sometimes unavailable. You also tell the prospect that you will do your best to get as much of the product as the prospect needs and that you have a special relationship with your delivery people such that they make exceptions for you on occasion. What are the ethical issues in this situation? How would you resolve these issues?

19. You are the floor manager for a large retail store. You have recently hired a college student to sell during the Christmas rush. This college student has been anxious to impress you because he will be seeking permanent employment in the next semester. You discover that, at times, this person has been a little overeager to make sales. He exaggerates the value of certain items or withholds relevant information about certain items trying to make the products look better (Reidenbach & Robin, 1988, p. 873). What are the ethical issues in this situation? How would you resolve these issues?

20. You are a sales representative for an industrial supply company. You sell directly to purchasing agents. Your company has a policy of providing small gifts to purchasing agents as a token of appreciation for their business and as a means of building goodwill. The policy further states that the size of the gift should be consistent with the size of the order. Furthermore, your company has expressly stated not to give gifts to those purchasing agents whose companies have strict policies against receiving gifts (Laczniak, 1983, p. 9). What are the ethical issues in this situation? How would you resolve these issues?

21. A recent experiment reported that the routine habit of ordering sonograms for healthy pregnant women did not make a significant difference in the health of their babies (Winslow, 1993). The procedure is safe, provides comfort, and often results in "baby's first photo." Also, it can help a doctor manage a pregnancy. The procedure's average cost is $200. The results of the experiment suggest that if sonograms were restricted to only high-risk cases, $1 billion from the nation's health care bill would be cut without hurting the quality of the care. Is this an ethical issue? Why do you think so? Do sonograms provide information that satisfies the consumers' right to know? Why do you think so?

SELLING MINICASE

The Speedy Sale

Bernie is very interested in buying a color television. He tells Sam, the sales-person in the discount store where he feels he can get the best buy, that his old color TV recently died and he really misses his favorite shows. The sooner he can buy and get a new TV delivered, the better, he explains. Sam knows that the particular model that Bernie seems to prefer by far to the others will go on sale for 15% off in 3.5 weeks. However, he assumes that Bernie is not willing to wait that long and might look elsewhere. Also, Sam will not make as much commis-sion on the reduced price. Therefore, he reasons that it would make little sense to inform Bernie of the pending sale.

When Sam tells Bernie that the TV set he is interested in is currently out of stock and will not be in for another week, Bernie is clearly disgruntled. Fearing losing the sale, Sam goes out to the back room to ask his sales manager, Michelle, if anything can be done to speed up delivery. Michelle says that this would be impossible, and she suggests Sam could tell Bernie that the store can get the set within 24 hours and simply sell him the demonstration model. Michelle explains that the demo is in as-new condition and Bernie will never know the difference.

Sam feels that selling the demonstration model to Bernie wouldn't be on the level. Knowing that it will take 5 working days to have a new set delivered to the store, Sam thinks of a different sales strategy—tell Bernie he can get a set to him in 2 days, then call Bernie tomorrow to say it will be sometime next week due to a flood of orders at the factory. Sam wonders how he can lock in the sale today.

1. What are the relevant acts?
2. What are the ethical issues?
3. Who are the primary stakeholders?
4. What are the possible alternatives?
5. What are the ethics of the alternatives?
6. What are the practical constraints?
7. What action should be taken?

SOURCE: Lantos, Geoffrey P. (1992c). "The Speedy Sale" (Minicase 16). *Business Ethics Program*. Arthur Andersen & Co. Copyright © 1992 by Geoffrey P. Lantos. Minicases developed by the Arthur Andersen & Co., SC Business Ethics Program. Printed with permission of Arthur Andersen & Co., SC.

11

Ethics and Distribution Decisions

PURPOSE

To present some of the ethical issues that confront marketing professionals as they make distribution decisions.

MAJOR POINTS

Ethical issues related to distribution can arise because organizations that compose the channel of distribution may have differing needs and goals.

Power relationships in the channel can be a source of ethical problems if those channel members with power abuse that power.

Ethical issues related to distribution discussed in this chapter include retailing decisions, direct marketing, gray and black markets, purchasing, and managing the channel.

Distribution decisions concern how a product reaches the final consumer. Figure 11.1 depicts a sample distribution channel and will serve as the basis for the discussion of ethical issues in this chapter. Referring to Figure 11.1, many different organizations may be involved in moving the product down the channel of distribution to the final consumer. There may also be one organization, as in the case of direct channels of distribution.

Each organization in the channel has some vested interest in the product because those organizations must spend some resources to acquire those products and sell them to the next organization in the channel. Therefore, the organizations must have

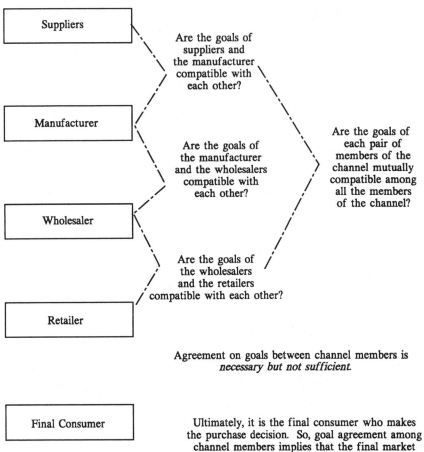

Figure 11.1. Channels
of Distribution:
The Root of
Ethical Problems
in the Channel

solid working relationships with each other. That is, suppliers must be on good terms with manufacturers, who must be on good terms with wholesalers, and so on.

In each of the pairs of relationships, some problems can occur because the goals of the members of the channel of distribution are not always compatible. For example, a retailer might wish to offer a wide selection of products to the final consumer. The wholesaler who supplies the retailer may have one or two "pet" products that he or she wants to push on the retailer. Already, their goals are incompatible. Then, too, the manufacturer, suppliers, and the final consumer may have something to say about what is made available at the point of purchase.

Complicating this picture is that the whole is greater than the sum of its parts. That is, the different organizations that make up the channel can debate about incompatible goals all they want. Recall the example presented in the pricing chapter concerning the pricing goals of members of the channel of distribution. If the end result is one that is not satisfactory to consumers, they will express their dissatisfaction by not purchasing the manufacturer's offering, and none of the goals of the channel members will be met. With this as background, let's take a look at some of the ethical problems that occur in many channels of distribution.

▨ ETHICS AND THE QUEST FOR POWER

Power represents the ability of one channel member to get another channel member to do what that channel member might not have ordinarily done (see Stern & El-Ansary, 1988, p. 302). With power comes leadership and with leadership comes the potential for ethical abuse.

Power is the opposite of dependence. If one channel member has power over another, the latter channel member is dependent, in some way, on the former. For example, if a manufacturer has power over a retailer, that manufacturer might be tempted to exert undue influence over that retailer's business practices. Such influences might include choices of retailer locations, minimum-order sizes, product mix selections, restrictions on alternative sources of supply, and the physical layout of the retailer's location.

Referring to Figure 11.1, exchanges take place between each pair of entities identified. This implies that each has something judged valuable by the other (see Corey, Cespedes, & Rangun, 1989, pp. 281-282). Thus they both have interest in maximizing their individual gains. But such channel relations also carry with them a struggle to obtain a larger share of the profits and control concerning the product or service in question. Also, as noted earlier, the goals of the different members of the channel are likely to be different.

Let's look at suppliers. They must try to enter into partnership arrangements with manufacturers as sources of raw materials. They must build trust with manufacturers as reliable sources of supply and use their influence to ensure that manufacturers continue to use them as sources of supply. The manufacturer must also develop trust relationships with distributors so that distributors will carry the manufacturer's product. But manufacturers must also strive to make their products compatible with the needs of the final consumer, a goal that is not always compatible with those of distributors.

Distributors, on the other hand, act as agents for the manufacturer. They develop marketing programs for the manufacturer's products. They can also build demand for the manufacturer's products. But, often, distributors seek to provide an assortment of products to the final consumer, satisfying the final consumers' needs and wants for convenience and choice. Sometimes, the distributors give preference to certain products because they sell better. Naturally, if these better selling products are not part of our manufacturer's product mix, a conflict occurs.

When such conflicts occur, any or all of the members of the channel can employ means to gain power in the channel—power to influence the decisions of other members of the channel. Sometimes, such a quest for power leads to ethical abuses.

The Federal Trade Commission (FTC) recently sought a court order to block General Electric's planned purchase of Chrysler Corporation's fleet of 4,000 railroad boxcars (Naj & Machalaba, 1993), which Chrysler currently leases out. The FTC action followed intense lobbying by the railroad industry, which opposed the purchase on the grounds that it would allow GE to corner the market on a specially valuable category of boxcars. The purchase would result in GE's owning 90% of all boxcars exempt from federal rate reduction orders. In general, boxcars are in increasingly short supply. *Would allowing such a purchase lessen competition in the boxcar lease market? Would the transaction result in higher lease prices? Would smaller railroads, who could not afford high rental rates, be driven out of business?*

An exclusive bottler of Orange Crush in several Texas markets received a visit from a Procter & Gamble executive. It seems that P&G now intended to distribute Crush to Wal-Mart. But P&G was going to bypass the bottler and sell directly to Wal-Mart (Winters, 1989), despite the fact that the bottler had a legal contract. *If you were the bottler, what would you do? Why would P&G pursue such a course of action? What ethical implications does this situation have for distributors?*

◨ ETHICS IN RETAILING DECISIONS

A number of ethical issues exist at the retail level of the channel of distribution. These issues concern not only the retailer's interaction with the final consumer; they also concern relationships with distributors and manufacturers.

Buying　　Retail buyers operate in a business environment that is similar to that of salespeople. In the process of buying, they do much traveling and, therefore, are away from the direct supervision available to those who work in an office. Like salespeople, retail buyers engage in negotiations, use expense accounts, develop relationships with suppliers, and provide information to those suppliers. Each of these, as you saw in the chapter on selling ethics, can lead to ethical abuses initiated by the buyer.

A buyer for a large retailer can be responsible for millions of dollars of product volume. Therefore, the selling organization may view the buyer as vital to the sale of their products. When a buyer has that much power, the sales representative, as you have seen, may resort to questionable strategies to build and maintain a relationship with that buyer. The buyer, however, may also abuse the power of his or her position and demand things of the seller that are not within the realm of ethical business practice (Gilman, 1985).

What happens when a buyer engages in unethical practices? No one seems certain, but let's pose a few questions.

1. Does the unethical retail buyer negotiate the best possible deal for the retailer? The final consumer?
2. Does the retailer have access to a best assortment of products when buyers clearly play favorites because of ethical abuses?
3. What effect do buyers' ethical abuses have on competition?

Some organizations attempt to control ethical abuses by placing limits on their buyers. For example, Wal-Mart does not allow its buyers to accept anything from suppliers, including a free lunch (Weinstein, 1989). But like all ethics codes, they do not guarantee that such abuses do not take place, initiated by the seller or by the buyer.

Product Assortment

You have already seen how purchasing practices and slotting allowances can affect the products that are carried by retailers. There are other issues concerning product assortments that present challenges to retailers. One issue concerns the use of "sale" promotions. Sometimes, retailers stock lower-quality merchandise to be used at a "clearance sale." The lower-quality merchandise and the misrepresentation of the term *clearance* are clearly ethical abuses to which many consumers are susceptible.

Price lining is also a common retail practice. For example, a retailer may carry several lines of men's shirts, each priced very differently and each supposedly representing different quality. Such a practice, when used properly is intended to appeal to many consumers and provide consumers with choices. But if the price lines are deceptive in some way (e.g., shirts of little quality difference but priced at significantly different levels), then is the consumer being deceived? Some would argue that deception occurs because consumers regularly use price as a signal of quality.

In 1984, Pillsbury-owned Haagen-Dazs Company refused to allow its distributors to carry Ben & Jerry's ice cream. Ben & Jerry sued and the suit was settled out of court (Friday, 1993). Nine years later, Ben & Jerry's and its largest distributor, Dreyer's, are accused of squeezing two independent distributors out of business. The allegation is that Ben & Jerry's tells distributors what brands it can carry. *Is it ethical for a manufacturer to try to dictate what products an independent distributor can carry? Is it good business?*

Pricing

Some retailers have involved themselves in pricing practices such as bait and switch, low-low prices, and resale price maintenance. All of these pricing approaches are accounted for by law. These were discussed in the chapter on pricing ethics and advertising ethics.

A relatively recent phenomenon concerns the overall price strategy of retailers. For example, Sears promises "everyday low prices" and Wal-Mart advertises "always the lowest price." Then there are local retailers who advertise "the lowest prices in town" and "nobody beats our deals . . . nobody!" One of the ethical difficulties is that the term *sale* has lost its meaning in a traditional sense. The term used to imply that goods, previously offered at certain prices, were now being sold for considerably less than the original price. The term sale, however, as used today, can mean a variety of things, including "there are goods and services here available for sale."

When the FTC complained about six book publishers giving price breaks to larger chains, the publishing industry and small retailers noticed ("FTC Decision," 1989). The focus of the complaint was that the publishers had violated the Robinson-Patman Act by selling at low prices to chain operators and higher prices to independent book sellers. The FTC claimed that publishers treat orders from chains as a single order, even if books are separately packed, itemized, and shipped to different outlets. Thus chain stores can pay lower prices than independent bookstores who may actually receive a larger order than that shipped to individual chain outlets. *Do you think that this practice is ethical? Can you think of ways that the lower prices to chains can be justified? What other industries operate in this way?*

Selling

Retail salespeople face many of the same ethical dilemmas as those discussed in the chapter on ethics in selling. These include the following:

1. Salespeople may be pressured to achieve short-term sales results to achieve goals.
2. The conditions under which retail salespeople should offer refunds to customers on returned items can create an ethical dilemma. For example, are the retail salesperson and the customer working as a team to steal from the retail establishment?
3. Retail salespeople generally receive little sales training other than that associated with how to run the checkout counter.

Charging full price for a sale item without the customer's knowledge
Overcharging the customer when the scanner price has not been changed to accommodate a sale
Giving incorrect change to customers on purpose
Not telling the complete truth to a customer about a product's characteristics
Whether to deal with a customer suspected of damaging the product in the store and then wanting a markdown
Pressure from a friend to give him or her a discount
The temptation to take sales away from another salesperson
Allowing a sales trainee to handle the bulk of the workload

Table 11.1 Ethical Issues Faced by Retail Salespeople

SOURCE: Alan J. Dubinsky and Michael Levy, "Ethics in Retailing: Perceptions of Retail Salespeople," *Journal of the Academy of Marketing Science, 13*(4), pp. 6-8. Copyright © 1985 by the Academy of Marketing Science. Reprinted by permission of Sage Publications, Inc.

Table 11.1 details some of the ethical problems encountered by retail salespeople. As you can see, retail salespeople face many potential ethical abuses in their dealings with the final consumer. One not shown in Table 11.1 is the receipt of *push money*. Some salespeople receive push money as an incentive to promote certain products or brands. Although such a practice is considered a legitimate form of promotion, its misuse occurs when a seller offers push money without the approval of the retail store's management. In addition, the same incentives should be given to all salespeople in an effort to avoid unfair or predatory behavior (Levy & Weitz, 1992).

If a patient accidentally takes an overdose of a prescribed drug, the pharmacist may be liable for damages. And pharmacists in some states can now be sued if they do not recognize that a new drug might interact badly with other medications (Woo, 1993). Traditionally, pharmacists have been viewed as "dispensers" (distributors) of medicine. But a landmark case in 1986 changed that. In that case, neither the doctor nor the pharmacist warned a patient about the maximum safe dosage, and serious side effects occurred. *Did the doctor or pharmacist act unethically? Should a pharmacist be responsible for more than just supplying medications? Should the pharmacist have been expected to correct the oversight of the doctor? How would you rule in the following cases?*

1. A boy who took an asthma drug was prescribed another drug for an infection. The infection drug package had an insert that warned of toxic reactions if combined with asthma medication. The pharmacist issued no warning. Nor did he ask the doctor about changing the prescription. The boy suffered brain damage.
2. A man purchased a prescription for an antidepressant, which was filled correctly by the pharmacist. The man then alleged that because of the antidepressant, he forgot to take money out of the stock market and lost a great deal.

3. A pharmacist called out the name of a customer on a newly filled prescription. Another customer claimed the prescription and then filed a lawsuit because he was given the wrong drug.

Some small manufacturers are avoiding large retailing chains because the small manufacturers cannot control the huge discounts at which large retailers sell their products. Some of these small manufacturers sell only certain lines to large retailers. Still others sell to some large retailers but not to others (Reitman, 1993). *Are these small manufacturers, in essence, imposing minimum retail prices for their products by "selecting" retailers? Are consumer advocates correct when they charge that such pricing arrangements are an attempt to wipe out discount retailers? Or do such arrangements help keep the economy going by creating jobs through the maintenance of adequate profit margins for manufacturers and wholesalers?*

Forward Buying   Retailers sometimes wish to purchase products well in advance of the time they will place them on their shelves. This practice is known as forward buying and is usually initiated when retailers can obtain a "good deal" on a product and the retailer wishes to purchase more than the usual volume. The ethical issue concerns what happens when these "deal" products are placed on the shelf ? Clearly, the purchasing savings can be passed on to the consumer and are often advertised as such (Bishop, 1988). But is it ethical to have any less than the entire amount of the savings passed on to the consumer?

Slotting Allowances   Slotting allowances is a practice in which distributors and retailers require additional compensation from manufacturers to carry a new product. Slotting allowances have become routine business practice, and some estimates suggest that they are responsible for as much as 55% of all promotional expenditures (Dagnoli & Freeman, 1988). Slotting allowances received by distributors and retailers increase the profits of these organizations and are rarely used to lower the cost of goods sold to consumers. One estimate reported that slotting allowances (and other trade promotions) account for 2.5% of total retail sales (Buzzell, Quelch, & Salmon, 1990). This is a very large amount, particularly if these costs are passed on to the final consumer.

Distributors and retailers use the proliferation of products as justification for slotting allowances. These organizations believe they must be compensated for handling, storing, shelving, and marketing products. They feel justified in having manufacturers cover these expenses. For example, a retailer might charge a manufacturer $100 per store slotting allowance for the carrying of a new product. Some retailers are even assessing manufacturers a fee if the new product fails (Therrien, 1989).

Critics of slotting allowances have used such terms as *ransom, bribery,* and even *extortion* to describe them. Often, such fees are assessed to lesser known brands, driving up their cost of sale. This can be interpreted as a form of price discrimination from a legal perspective. Slotting allowances are usually negotiated in private and are usually agreed on orally. Such a practice opens retailers to the criticisms that they are treating manufacturers differently. With no tangible evidence, the accusation is easily made, and the retailer has no written proof of equal treatment of manufacturers.

Another concern with slotting allowances is their effect on innovation (Gibson, 1988). If new companies have to pay more than established companies to have retailers distribute their products, are the new companies receiving unfair treatment? Because slotting allowances are accepted business practice, what effect does the existence of these added costs have on the entrepreneurial spirit of those who invent new products?

Finally, another ethical concern revolves around consumers' access to products. Are consumers being denied potentially superior market offerings because slotting allowances prevent those offerings from ever reaching the marketplace? Some retailers charge "annual fees" for products and this practice may, indeed, eliminate some products from the marketplace, or drive up the price of some products to the point where they are no longer competitive (Donahue, 1989).

▧ ETHICS AND DIRECT MARKETING

By the mid-1980s, marketing organizations began spending more money on direct marketing than on network television advertising (see Roberts & Berger, 1989, pp. 11-15). One reason for this growth is that direct marketing offers the ability to measure the effect of the marketing effort. Does advertising create sales? This is a very difficult question to answer. Does direct mail create sales? The answer to this question can be obtained by measuring the returns on the direct mail piece. A second reason is that more and more consumers are shopping direct—by catalog, telephone, and other forms of direct mail. A third reason for the use of direct marketing lies with computer technology. Available technology now allows marketers to create databases that are very accurate. These databases are also comprehensive in that they contain a variety of information about those individuals listed in the database, including past purchase behavior.

Ethical issues raised by direct marketing include those of privacy, confidentiality, and intrusion (Cespedes, 1993). Issues of privacy include the following:

1. The receiving of millions of programmed telemarketing calls daily by consumers
2. The use of data by credit bureaus to create new databases that are sold as mailing lists
3. The use of information collected by banks, by other types of marketing organizations

One other issue concerns the lack of availability of information to consumers. Direct marketing techniques allow marketing organizations to target specific groups of individuals. With such specific targets, many consumers may not ever receive information on the availability of products and services. Under such circumstances are consumers' choices being restricted? Some would argue that they are. Consumers' income levels, zip codes, and other criteria used to develop targeted databases may prevent others not in that target from receiving various marketing information targeted only to a specific audience.

From the marketing decision maker's perspective, being able to target specific audiences helps reduce one of the key problems associated with advertising—waste. Marketers are always concerned with how many consumers exposed to a promotion are not in their specified target market. In the future, we may see marketers become concerned that their ability to target certain consumers is so precise that they will add some "waste" into the process to counter the criticisms of consumers' restricted choice.

Technological advances in information access, database management, and tele-communications are making it easier for direct marketing companies to reach potential customers. *What ethical problems might occur as a result of technological advances in the areas of consumer privacy, sale of customer lists, and protection of personal information? What guidelines would you develop?*

▧ GRAY AND BLACK MARKETS

Gray markets involve the sale of products through unauthorized (by the manufacturer) channels of distribution. Other terms for gray markets include *diverting*, when unauthorized distribution occurs in packaged goods, and *parallel importing*, when unauthorized distribution occurs in international markets. In both cases, goods are diverted to an unauthorized intermediary either in the same market area (diverting) or in another country (parallel importing).

Gray markets and counterfeit markets, also an ethical issue, are not the same. Counterfeiting involves the making of imitation products that are often inferior and do not carry the manufacturer's name. Counterfeit goods are illegal and covered by the Lanham Act. In the case of gray markets, the product is not in question. It is the means by which the product reaches the marketplace that is of concern.

Gray markets pose several difficulties for the manufacturers and the legitimate distributors of products. These include the following:

1. There may be difficulties with pricing policies because the same product delivered from two distinct sources can create price conflicts.
2. If profit margins erode, manufacturers often find that relations with distributors erode with them.
3. Manufacturer's warranties are generally applied only to those products sold through the legitimate channels of distribution. When after-sale service is a prime source of revenue, those products delivered through unauthorized channels are not serviced and do not serve as sources of revenue. Furthermore, if warranties are not honored, consumer dissatisfaction can become a severe problem. (Duhan & Sheffet, 1988)

Although there are many detractors of gray marketers, there are some who view gray markets as an alternative form of competition and a means of cutting channel costs and lowering prices to the final consumer. Those who argue for lower prices do so on the basis that competition lowers prices and allows distributors to set prices that appeal to those segments of the marketplace that are more price sensitive and more price elastic. But most channel members point out several ethical issues associated with gray markets (see Smith & Quelch, 1993, pp. 482-484).

Gray markets and black markets can hurt companies that are trying to set up legitimate, long-term distribution. In Korea, there is a strong black market built on a foundation of Korean entrepreneurs selling imported goods taken from U.S. military bases (Darlin, 1991). Prices at military commissaries average about 25% less than those at American supermarkets. Legitimate Korean distributors pay an import duty of about 15%, taxes, and distribution charges. So black marketers have a decided advantage, even after adding substantial profit margins to the commissary price. *Is the Korean tokebi shijang, or goblin market, a legitimate alternative distribution system?*

Free Riding Problems

Authorized distributors are placed in the position of having to educate consumers about product features' benefits and use and then see those consumers purchase those products from unauthorized distributors. Authorized distributors often offer service such as advertising, demonstrations, and postsale maintenance, all of which involve time and expense. Gray marketers enjoy a "free ride" on these expenses, courtesy of the authorized distributors.

Consumer Protection   Most gray marketers do not offer products warranties. Furthermore, because consumers do not fill out warranty cards, they are often not included in subsequent product recalls and other notices from the manufacturer. If consumers do learn of a recall or a product ceases to work properly, they may find that authorized dealers refuse to honor the recall request or the product warranty because these consumers purchased from unauthorized dealers.

Effect on Channel Relationships. Channel relationships often involve long-term contractual obligations on the part of the two parties involved. Personal relationships and trust relationships naturally result from such long-term commitments. With gray markets, such relationships do not exist. Rather, the tendency is "shadow marketing," a series of short-term arrangements that can become so prevalent that Gresham's law (the bad drives out the good) holds (Levy & Zaltman, 1975). What often happens is that authorized dealers, because of certain responsibilities and costs built into long-term relationships, find themselves at a price competitive disadvantage vis-à-vis unauthorized distributors.

▨ ETHICS AND PURCHASING IN THE DISTRIBUTION CHANNEL

Members of the channel who deal with suppliers engage in a variety of purchasing activities. Large organizations often have purchasing staffs whose primary responsibility is to purchase the right products at the right prices and in the right quality and quantities. For these purchasers, many of the ethical issues discussed in the selling ethics chapter are applicable. That is, these purchasers work with salespeople and other supplier representatives and may be confronted with ethical abuses, such as deception, misrepresentation, high pressure, bribery, and so on.

However, unlike you and me as consumers, purchasing department people are susceptible to other ethical pressures. For example, others in their organization may require that they implement purchasing polices that lead to discriminatory pricing practices (e.g., reciprocity with a supplier). Furthermore, as you saw earlier in this chapter, purchasing organizations can have power in the channel, and that power can lead them to initiate their own ethical abuses. For example, a purchasing manager can offer a bribe just as can a salesperson. Indeed, purchasing people are willing to accept gifts from vendors, and the trend is toward fewer policy statements concerning such gifts being enacted (Forker & Jansen, 1990).

◪ ETHICS IN MANAGING THE CHANNEL OF DISTRIBUTION

Without a doubt, those who provide something of value on credit have the first right to any available income from the customer. Of course, this statement runs counter to the "accepted" practice of stringing out payments in times of tight money, loose money, or any other reason the debtor deems reasonable. The Bible speaks about the dangers associated with lying (see Proverbs 12:22). When someone orders something with an implied promise to pay for it, but does not, that someone has simply lied. In Leviticus 19:13, we are warned to pay our debts promptly.

As you have seen, many ethical issues occur in the management of the channel of distribution. In the past, manufacturers seemed to have the power in the channel for consumer products. But recent developments such as scanner technology have led to a shift in that power. For example, today, retailers control tremendous amounts of information about the marketplace collected through scanner technology. You have probably heard the expression, "knowledge is power," and that seems to be coming true in the power relationships between manufacturers and retailers. We'll close this chapter and this book by referring you to Newsline 11.1. *What do you think? Are there channel-related ethical issues associated with the use of ATMs as a service channel of distribution?*

Newsline 11.1

"Scrip" ATMs Appeal to Growing Number of Retailers, but Noncash Machines Also Attract Some Questionable Entrepreneurs

It sounds like something plenty of retailers would love to offer: the convenience of an automated teller machine at a fraction of the cost and risk.

Instead of spitting out cash, machines placed in stores issue receipts known as "scrip." The scrip, drawn against a customer's checking account, can be used to buy merchandise or can be redeemed for cash at the checkout counter.

Some retailers think the devices have a great future—and so do some entrepreneurs with questionable backgrounds and practices who are promoting the devices.

Retailers view the scrip machines mainly as a means to boost business. "We added one as a convenience to customers," says Lori Silkwood, co-owner of Silkwood Marketing Inc., a gas station and convenience store in Tucker, GA. Ms. Silkwood says she believes the machine, which handles about 30 to 40 transactions a day, has helped increase her business.

Scrip machines are much less tempting to criminals than cash machines. And because they don't need the security features to handle cash, scrip dispensers tend to be much cheaper to build and maintain than traditional ATMs. A typical scrip machine costs about $2,000 to $3,000, compared with $15,000 or more for a cash ATM, according to industry officials.

Prohibitive Cost

The cost of a cash ATM machine is "prohibitive to smaller merchants," says Michael Ellis, vice president for sales of BankCard Services Corp., a Norcross, GA, manufacturer of scrip machines.

To be sure, scrip machines have drawbacks. As they don't spit out dollars directly, they can be less convenient to use. Besides some bank card networks that do the electronic processing of ATM transactions prefer to stick with cash machines and have been unwilling to hook up scrip terminals.

But scrip ATMs have been around for several years, and can be found in several thousand locations around the country, mainly retail outlets. Scrip advocates say the potential market is tens of thousands of locations, and they say they are gearing up for a big sales push.

The industry is pushing business opportunities servicing the machines, essentially computer-age variations on vending-machine routes. An entrepreneur buys a string of ATMs and collects a fee of about 50 cents every time someone uses one of the machines.

Several such business-opportunity ventures have started up in recent months. They have begun advertising in newspapers, including this one, and holding seminars to recruit entrepreneurs.

Hopes to Sell 6,000 Machines

BankCard Services, one of about half a dozen U.S. manufacturers of these devices, hopes to sell up to 6,000 scrip ATMs over the next 18 months. Manufacturers say they have dozens of independent sales companies trying to sell or lease the machines.

At least a few ventures are also promoting the machines as business opportunities that can earn returns as high as 200% a year with virtually no risk. Such assertions have already started attracting attention from some regulators.

"You should always be wary" of anyone who offers or guarantees a high profit," says Robert K. Hooks, director of business regulation at the Georgia secretary of state's office. Mr. Hooks says his office has received copies of the promotional literature of one

Georgia ATM firm and is looking into whether the firm's activities are subject to state regulation.

Another concern offering scrip ATM machines is called American Shearson ATM Inc. Besides selling its device directly to retailers, the Boca Raton, FL, firm is laying plans to sell franchises early next year to entrepreneurs who want to market its device, called "The Money Machine," according to company President Randy Prefer. "We haven't begun to scratch the surface of the market yet," he says.

No American Express Connection

When asked, Mr. Prefer concedes that his company doesn't have any connection with American Express Co. or to Smith Barney Shearson Inc., a unit of Primerica Corp. (American Express previously owned Shearson.) Mr. Prefer, who operates about a dozen companies from the same Boca Raton office suite, insists that his company's name wasn't chosen to be misleading. "It was simply a name I liked," he says.

An American Express spokeswoman says the New York company is looking into whether its trademark rights are being violated by the Boca Raton firm. A Shearson spokesman says he never heard of the Boca Raton firm. He didn't have any immediate comment about the use of the Shearson name.

Another recent entry in the scrip ATM business is Atlanta-based Business Motivations Inc., which has come to the attention of Mr. Hooks at the Georgia secretary of state's office. Business Motivation's owner, Fred Donahugh, is known to federal criminal authorities in connection with a continuing investigation of a series of suspected business-opportunity frauds. Mr. Donahugh was co-owner of one of the suspect ventures.

Federal Investigators

Mr. Donahugh says federal investigators have interviewed him about some of those ventures and about his ties to John Williamson. As previously reported, authorities believe Mr. Williamson was the mastermind of the ventures. Mr. Donahugh says that as far as he knows, he isn't a target of the federal probe and did nothing wrong.

A spokesman for the U.S. attorney's office in Atlanta, which is directing the investigation, declines comment. Mr. Williamson couldn't be located for comment, although in the past, through an attorney, he has denied wrongdoing.

In June, Business Motivations ran an ad in this newspaper touting the scrip ATMs, at $5,000 each, as a "virtually risk free" way to earn 18% a year. Promotional material mailed out by the company said the 18% return would be "guaranteed" by a bond from an oil company, Cherokee Oil & Gas Inc. It turns out that Mr. Donahugh owns the oil company, which is based in the same office suite as Business Motivations.

When questioned, Mr. Donahugh steadily backs away from the guarantee. First, he drops any idea of a Cherokee bond, saying it might run afoul of securities regulators. But he says he will personally guarantee the 18% return. Later, he changes his mind. "[Investors] can take the same risk as I take," he says.

Mr. Donahugh says he is thinking of quitting the ATM business, saying he can't match some of the offers being made by his business-opportunity competitors. "If I put in the paper that you could make a fortune in 90 days, I could sell. But that would be baloney," he says.

SOURCE: Emshwiller, John R. (1993, September 1). " 'Scrip' ATMs Appeal to Growing Number of Retailers." *Wall Street Journal,* p. B2. Reprinted by permission of the *Wall Street Journal,* © 1993 Dow Jones & Company, Inc. All rights reserved worldwide.

CHAPTER SUMMARY

This chapter presented ethical issues that confront marketing professionals as they make distribution decisions. Although each organization in a channel has a vested interest in the product or service being marketed, these organizations have differing needs and goals. These differences can lead to ethical problems. The abuse of power by channel members can also lead to ethical problems. Channel ethical issues discussed in this chapter include retailing decisions, direct marketing, gray and black markets, purchasing, and managing the channel.

▧ DISTRIBUTION SCENARIOS

1. You are the purchasing vice president for a major grocery retailer. You oversee the purchases of the baby food division. You have received a proposition from a manufacturer of apple juice concentrate. One of the features of the proposition is that the price of this firm's concentrate is 20% lower than that of any other brand of any other supplier. Generally, your industry considers it risky to accept a product on the basis of lowest price. Furthermore, you know that this supplier has been found guilty, at least once, of selling products that are in violation of FDA standards. But you also know that your grocery chain has been operating very close to margin and that if the financial picture does not improve, many employees might lose their jobs (Nelson, 1992, p. 318). What are the ethical issues in this situation? How would you resolve these issues?

2. Your company manufactures jigsaw puzzles and has just lost a $2,500,000 order from a catalog company that has national distribution. You are a regional sales manager, and you discover that the order was lost because one of your salespeople did not offer the catalog company's buyer an "agency commission." You are in line for a promotion to sales vice president and you know that this lost sale will hurt your chances. You know the catalog company buyer very well and know that you can obtain the sale if you pay the "agency commission" (Nelson, 1992, p. 318). What are the ethical issues in this situation? How would you resolve these issues?

3. You are the distribution manager for a grocery chain that operates 22 stores in a large city. Your company's policy is to charge the same prices for all the items in all the stores. You knowingly send poorer cuts of meat and the lowest quality produce to your stores in the lower-income sections of the city. You justify this by citing the fact that these stores have the highest overhead because of such factors as employee turnover, vandalism, and theft (Laczniak, 1983, p. 9). What are the ethical issues in this situation? How would you resolve these issues?

4. You are the marketing manager for a publicly held electric power company. Your company is faced with rapidly escalating costs of low-sulfur coal, which you purchase from several suppliers. Your company's forecasting group indicates that this price increase trend will continue for at least the next 6 years. Normally, such price increases from suppliers are routinely passed on to the final consumer, but you are concerned about customer reaction to 6 years of price increases. You know that lower cost, high-sulfur content coal is available, but the use of such coal will increase your emission of pollutants by 40%. You opt to buy the high-sulfur coal so that you can save your customers from the price increases (Harris, 1990, p. 745). What are the ethical issues in this situation? How would you resolve these issues?

5. You are key distributor for a large direct-selling organization. Normally, when one of your independent contractors sells a product, it takes about 3 days for that product to be shipped to that sales representative. Company policy requires those products to be delivered to the customers by the next day. At a Wednesday sales seminar, one of your sales representatives promises to have the merchandise to the customers by Friday. One customer wants delivery by Friday, 2 days from now and probably would not have spent the $200 without the promise of a Friday delivery. The sales representative assured this customer that you were an outstanding distributor and would see to it that she had the product on Friday (Reidenbach, Robin, & Dawson, 1991, p. 84). What are the ethical issues in this situation? How would you resolve these issues?

6. You are the regional sales manager for a supplier of electrical components. You deal with one customer whose purchasing manager has as one of her responsibilities the making of the final decision concerning the suppliers for the various products that her firm purchases. She controls several million dollars in purchases. Because of this responsibility, and because she feels she is underpaid compared to others in her firm, she has let suppliers know that, all other things being equal, her decision will be based on the receipt of an appropriate gift. Your firm has a "no gifts" policy, and because one of your sales representatives abided by that policy, he lost a large sale and considerable commission when the purchasing agent chose another vendor. What are the ethical issues in this situation? How would you resolve these issues?

7. The minister of a foreign nation, where extraordinary payments to lubricate decision making are common, asks you for a $200,000 consulting fee. In return, he promises you special assistance in developing relations with suppliers of raw materials needed by your firm to manufacture its products. Your firm uses over $75 million of these raw materials, and relationships with suppliers in this country would afford your organization a significant cost advantage versus your competitors. What would you do (Vitell & Festervand, 1987, p. 115)? What are the ethical issues in this situation? How would you resolve these issues?

8. You are a purchasing manager for a large company. The vice president of purchasing visits with you and tells you that the company is implementing a new policy. You are now to give preferential treatment to current suppliers when soliciting bids for raw materials used in your manufacturing process. Soliciting quotes from new sources is to be done only to make sure that a sufficient number of bids is received so that top management is satisfied that a proper supplier evaluation has taken place. How would you handle this situation?

9. You are a purchasing manager for a retailer. You have been informed that you are now supposed to tell your current suppliers that you are considering other sources of products. The reason for this is that top management wants to obtain lower prices from its suppliers so that the retail store's profit picture improves. Top management has no intention of changing suppliers and no intention of passing on the savings to customers. Would you implement such a policy? If yes, what would you say to your suppliers? If no, what would you say to top management?

10. You are the vice president of purchasing in your firm. Your president tells you to do everything you can to work with a new supplier. The president tells you

that this supplier has high-quality products at competitive prices. You are told to tell your entire purchasing staff to "do what they can" to develop a relationship with this supplier. After you have told your staff, you learn that the president's brother-in-law is the sales vice president for this supplier. What course of action would you take?

11. You are the regional director for a chain of restaurants. On a visit to one of your most profitable locations, you learn that the manager is taking money without ringing up sales. You send a few friends to act as customers to verify this and learn that it is true. But you also learn that the manager is using the unrecorded payments as a means of offering monetary incentives to restaurant personnel. Such a practice is against company policy. Does high-level performance justify the restaurant manager's actions? Would you confront the restaurant manager? Suppose sales in the location decline because the restaurant manager quits. How would you explain this to your supervisor (Erickson, 1992)?

12. You are the product manager for a large cigarette manufacturer. You have been presented with the marketing plan for the Southeast Asia division of your firm. The plan calls for doubling the advertising budget for three countries in Southeast Asia. The plan also calls for increasing prices to distributors in those three countries. The rationale for the plan is that your company will be able to share in the profits of the high-volume "black market" for cigarettes that exists in these three countries. The advertising will also help increase the sale of cigarettes to children in these countries. Should you approve the plan (Miller, 1992a)?

DISTRIBUTION MINICASE

(Black)Marketing "Primo" in Rohanda

Freshly promoted to International Tobacco Products Manager for U.S. Tobacco, Suzanne Thompson finds herself at the cutting edge of the firm's growth strategy for the next decade. Faced with declining volume sales and systematically increasing taxes on tobacco products in the United States, U.S. Tobacco has targeted for growth in volume sales. Furthermore, the prestige image of American cigarettes in many foreign markets permits higher prices and margins on tobacco products. This is particularly true of the "Primo" brand, whose symbol of a sophisticated, urban, professional male is recognized virtually worldwide.

In Rohanda, UST's plans have run afoul of a government policy that formally bans the import of cigarette products. Although the health ministry supports the ban, the major beneficiaries of the policy are the government-owned cigarette monopoly and the country's tobacco farmers. The monopoly is required to buy the crops of these farmers at above-market prices. Intense pressure from U.S. tobacco companies and the U.S. Department of Commerce has failed to convince the government of Rohanda to repeal the ban on cigarette imports. Ironically, American brands have traditionally controlled about 20% of Rohanda's cigarette market as the result of black market sales by established distributors in neighboring Kalanda. Rohanda's government has not enforced the ban in the past, nor has it made any effort to stop UST from spending $8 million a year to advertise "Primo." Apparently, the government is convinced that the high prices for black market cigarettes are sufficient protection for the brands offered by their monopoly.

Disgusted by what he considers a duplicitous policy, Suppakorn Rachinda, "Primo" brand manager in Southeast Asia, has submitted to Suzanne his first ever marketing plan for Rohanda. He proposes to double the advertising budget in Rohanda to $16 million and increase prices to Kalanda distributors by 20%. He argues that this plan will allow UST to capitalize on its premium position in Rohanda and share in the lucrative black market profits. He asserts further that the plan will not produce higher prices in Kalanda because the smuggling distributors will not have to raise prices, thus ensuring that the nonsmuggling distributors will be unable to do so. Finally, he maintains that the plan is consistent with the established practice of Rohanda's government, if not its formal policy.

Suppakorn's proposed marketing plan is now on Suzanne's desk, awaiting her approval for implementation in the coming year.

1. What are the relevant facts?
2. What are the ethical issues?
3. Who are the primary stakeholders?
4. What are the possible alternatives?
5. What are the ethics of the alternatives?
6. What are the practical constraints?
7. How does the American Marketing Association Code of Ethics apply here?
8. What actions should be taken?

SOURCE: Miller, Fred L. (1992a). "(Black)marketing 'Primo' in Rohanda" (Minicase 3). *Business Ethics Program.* Arthur Andersen & Co. Copyright © 1992 by Fred L. Miller. Minicases developed by the Arthur Andersen & Co., SC Business Ethics Program. Printed with permission of Arthur Andersen & Co., SC.

References

A hard decision to swallow. (1986, March 3). *Time*, p. 59.

Akaah, I. P. (1989). Differences in research judgments between male and female marketing professionals. *Journal of Business Ethics, 8*, 375-381.

Allison, G. T. (1971). *Essence of decision: Explaining the Cuban missile crisis*. Boston: Little, Brown.

Anderson, E., & Weitz, B. (1992). The use of pledges to build and sustain commitment in distribution channels. *Journal of Marketing Research, 29*, 18-34.

Andrews, K. R. (1989, September-October). Ethics in practice. *Harvard Business Review*, pp. 99-104.

Ansberry, C. (1987, March 22). For these M.B.A.s class became exercise in corporate espionage. *Wall Street Journal*, p. 37.

Artz, N. (1992). I SPY: A case of competitive intelligence (Minicase MKTG-20). *Business Ethics Program*. Chicago: Arthur Andersen.

Atkinson, J. W. (1974). Motivational determinants of intellective performance and cumulative achievement. In J. W. Atkinson & T. O. Raynor (Eds.), *Motivation and achievement* (pp. 185-214). Washington, DC: Winston.

Baechler, M. (1993, October 25). Tom Peters ruined my life. *Wall Street Journal*, p. A18.

Bandura, A. (1977). *Social learning theory*. Englewood Cliffs, NJ: Prentice Hall.

Barnett, J., & Carson, M. (1989). Managers, values, and executive decisions: An exploration of the role of gender, career stage, organizational level, function, and the importance of ethics, relationships, and results in managerial decision-making. *Journal of Business Ethics, 8*, 747-771.

Barrett, A. (1993, September). A wonder offer from Herbalife. *Business Week*, p. 34.

Barry, V. (1979). *Moral issues in business*. Belmont, CA: Wadsworth.

Bartlett, R. C. (1989, August 4). *Quickly take the high ground*. Commencement address given at the University of Dallas Graduate School of Business, Dallas, TX.

Baumhart, R. C. (1961, July-August). How ethical are businessmen. *Harvard Business Review*, pp. 6-9, 156-157.

Belasco, J. A. (1966). The salesman's role revisited. *Journal of Marketing, 30*(2), 6-11.

Bell, D. (1984, June). Practical implications of the Data Protection Act. *Personnel Management*, pp. 27-30.

Bennett, S. J., & Snell, M. (1988, February). A corporate spy on your own team. *Sales & Marketing Management Magazine*, p. 60.

Benson, G. C. S. (1989). Codes of ethics. *Journal of Business Ethics, 8*, 305-319.

Bettman, J. R., Payne, J. W., & Staelin, R. (1986). Cognitive considerations in designing effective labels for presenting risk information. *Journal of Public Policy and Marketing, 5,* 1-28.

Bishop, J. E. (1993, November 9). TV advertising aimed at kids is filled with fat. *Wall Street Journal,* p. B1.

Bishop, W. R., Jr. (1988, May). Trade buying squeezes marketers. *Marketing Communications,* p. 52.

Blair, E. A., & Landon, E. L., Jr. (1981). The effect of reference prices in retail advertisements. *Journal of Marketing, 45*(3), 61-69.

Blakey, B. G. (1987, September). Coupon fraud capers. *Security Management,* p. 139.

Boedecker, K. A., Morgan, F. W., & Stoltman, J. J. (1991). Legal dimensions of salespersons' statements: A review and managerial suggestions. *Journal of Marketing, 55*(1), 70-80.

Bok, S. (1979). *Lying: Moral choice in public and private life.* New York: Random House.

Bommer, M., Gratto, C., Gravander, J., & Tuttle, M. (1987). A behavioral model of ethical and unethical decision making. *Journal of Business Ethics, 6,* 265-280.

Borys, B., & Jemison, D. B. (1989). Hybrid arrangements as strategic alliance: Theoretical issues in organizational combinations. *Academy of Management Review, 14*(2), 234-249.

Bowie, N. E., & Duska, R. F. (1990). *Business ethics.* Englewood Cliffs, NJ: Prentice Hall.

Bradley, F. N., & Hatch, M. J. (1992). General causal models in business ethics: An essay on colliding research traditions. *Journal of Business Ethics, 11,* 307-315.

Brady, F. N. (1985). A Janus-head model of ethical theory: Looking two ways at business/society issues. *Academy of Management Review, 3,* 568-576.

Brenner, S. N., & Molander, E. A. (1977, January-February). Is the ethics of business changing? *Harvard Business Review,* pp. 57-71.

Broome, T. H. (1983). New developments in engineering ethics: The AAES plan. In V. Weil (Ed.), *Beyond whistleblowing* (pp. 228-242). Chicago: Illinois Institute of Technology.

Brown, P. L. (1989, November 13). An environmental rating for product packaging. *South Bend Tribune,* p. A7.

Burkett, S. R., & Jensen, E. (1975). Conventional ties, peer influence, and the fear of apprehension: A study of adolescent marijuana use. *Sociological Quarterly, 16,* 523-533.

Butcher, W. C. (1978, November 6). The stifling cost of regulations. *Business Week,* p. 22.

Buzzell, R. D., Quelch, J. A., & Salmon, W. J. (1990, March-April). The costly bargain of trade promotion. *Harvard Business Review,* pp. 141-149.

Cadbury, A. (1987, September-October). Ethical managers make their own rules. *Harvard Business Review,* pp. 69-73.

Calvin, J. (1987). *Institutes of the Christian religion* (T. Lane & H. Osborne, Trans.). Grand Rapids, MI: Baker. (Original work published 1536)

Camenisch, P. F. (1991). Marketing ethics: Some dimensions of the challenge. *Journal of Business Ethics, 10,* 245-248.

Carman, J. M. (1972-73). A summary of empirical research on unit pricing in supermarkets. *Journal of Retailing, 48*(4), 63-71.

Carr, A. Z. (1968, January-February). Is business bluffing ethical. *Harvard Business Review,* pp. 4-10.

Cavanaugh, G. F., Moberg, D. J., & Velasquez, V. (1981). The ethics of organization politics. *Academy of Management Review, 3,* 363-374.

Center for Business Ethics at Bentley College. (1986). Are corporations institutionalizing ethics. *Journal of Business Ethics, 5,* 86-91.

Cespedes, V. (1993). Ethical issues in distribution. In N. C. Smith & J. A. Quelch (Eds.), *Ethics in marketing* (pp. 474-477). Homewood, IL: Irwin.

Chewning, R. (1991, April 17). Action, not wisdom, determines ethics. *Waco-Tribune Herald,* p. 8A.

Chewning, R. C. (1984, April). Can free enterprise survive ethical schizophrenia. *Business Horizons,* pp. 6-11.

Chonko, L. B., & Hunt, S. D. (1985). Ethics and marketing management: An empirical investigation. *Journal of Business Research, 13,* 339-359.

Christie, R., & Geis, F. L. (1970). *Studies in Machiavellianism.* New York: Academic Press.

Churchill, G. A. (1991). *Marketing research: Methodological foundations*. Hinsdale, IL: Dryden.

Churchill, L. R. (1982). The teaching of ethics and moral values in teaching some contemporary confusions. *Journal of Higher Education, 3,* 296-306.

Cody, J. (1993, October 20). AT&T keeps rein on midlevel defector. *Wall Street Journal,* p. B6.

Cohen, J. (1992a). Green earth (Minicase MKTG-23). *Business Ethics Program.* Chicago: Arthur Andersen.

Cohen, J. (1992b). Social impacts of marketing (Minicase MKTG-22). *Business Ethics Program.* Chicago: Arthur Andersen.

Cohen, W., & Czepiec, H. (1988). The role of ethics in gathering corporate intelligence. *Journal of Business Ethics, 7,* 199-203.

Coleman, L. (1992, May 15). ESOMAR hits selling disguised as research. *Marketing News,* p. 1.

Conte, S. O. (1990, September 10). . . . Or tax excess profits. *New York Times,* p. 23.

Cooke, R. A. (1990). *Ethics in business: A perspective.* Chicago: Arthur Andersen & Company, Center for Professional Education.

Cooke, R. A. (1991). Danger signs of unethical behavior: How to determine if your firm is at ethical risk. *Journal of Business Ethics, 10,* 249-253.

Corey, E. R., Cespedes, F. V., & Rangun, V. K. (1989). *Going to market: Distribution systems for industrial products.* Boston: Harvard Business School Press.

Cox, R. (1965). *Distribution in a high-level economy.* Englewood Cliffs, NJ: Prentice Hall.

Crain, K. (1991, November 4). More than just price. *Automotive News,* p. 12.

Crandall, R. (1973). The measurement of self-esteem and related constructs. In J. P. Robinson & P. R. Shaver (Eds.), *Measures of social psychological attitudes* (pp. 45-167). Ann Arbor, MI: Institute for Social Research.

Crawford, M. C. (1970). Attitudes of marketing research executives toward ethics in marketing research. *Journal of Marketing, 34*(2), 46-52.

Critics call cuts in package size a deceptive move. (1991, February 5). *Wall Street Journal,* p. 17.

Crossen, C. (1986, February 26). Tamperproof packaging: Inventors say it can't be done—But they keep trying. *Wall Street Journal,* p. 27.

Cummings, G. F. (1979, September 24). Are purchasing ethics being put to the test. *Iron Age,* p. 35.

Dabholkar, P. A., & Kellaris, J. J. (1992). Toward understanding marketing students' ethical judgment of controversial personal selling practices. *Journal of Business Research, 24,* 313-329.

Dagnoli, J., & Freeman, L. (1988, February). Marketers seeking slotting-fee truce. *Advertising Age,* p. 12.

Danger is lurking in small packages. (1992, November 21). *USA Today,* p. D4.

Darlin, D. (1991, July 19). Korean black market stymies U.S. firms. *Wall Street Journal,* pp. B1, B8.

Davidson, D. L., & Goodpaster, K. E. (1983). *Managing product safety: The case of the Procter and Gamble Rely Tampon* (Harvard Business School Case #383-131.) Boston: Harvard Business School Publishing Division.

Day, R. L. (1975). A comment on ethics in marketing research. *Journal of Marketing Research, 12,* 232-233.

Dayton, E. (1979, October). Utility maximizers and cooperative undertakings. *Ethics,* pp. 130-141.

DeConnick, J. B., & Good, D. J. (1989). Perceptual differences of sales practitioners and students concerning ethical behavior. *Journal of Business Ethics, 8,* 667-676.

De George, R. T. (1986). *Business ethics.* New York: Macmillan.

Delaney, J. T., & Sockell, D. (1992). Do company ethics training programs make a difference?: An empirical analysis. *Journal of Business Ethics, 11,* 719-727.

Dickson, J. W. (1978). Perceptions of risk as related to choice in a two-dimensional risk situation. *Psychological Reports, 44,* 1059-1062.

Direct Selling Education Foundation. (1989). *Code of ethics.* Washington, DC: Author.

Donahue, C. (1989, September). Conflict in the aisles. *Adweek's Marketing Week,* pp. 20-21.

Donaldson, T. (1970). Moral change in the corporation. In W. M. Hoffman (Ed.), *Proceed-*

ings of the Second National Conference on Business Ethics (pp. 83-90). Washington, DC: University of America.

Donaldson, T., & Werhane, P. (1988). Ethical issues in business: A philosophical approach. Englewood Cliffs, NJ: Prentice Hall.

Driver, R. W. (1987, September). A communication model for determining the appropriateness of on-product warnings. IEEE Transactions on Professional Communication PC-30, pp. 157-163.

Drucker, P. (1969). Preparing tomorrow's business leaders today. Englewood Cliffs, NJ: Prentice Hall.

Dubinsky, A. J., & Gwin, J. M. (1981). Business ethics: Buyers and sellers. Journal of Purchasing and Materials Management, 17(4), 9-16.

Dubinsky, A. J., & Ingram, T. N. (1984). Correlates of salespeople's ethical conflict: An exploratory investigation. Journal of Business Ethics, 3, 343-353.

Dubinsky, A. J., & Levy, M. (1985). Ethics in retailing: Perceptions of retail salespeople. Journal of the Academy of Marketing Science, 13(4), 6-8.

Dubinsky, A. J., & Loken, B. (1989, December). Analyzing ethical decision making in marketing. Journal of Business Research, 19 pp. 83-107.

Dubinsky, A. J., Berkowitz, E. N., & Rudelius, W. (1980). Ethical problems of field sales personnel. MSU Business Topics, 28(3), 11-16.

Duhan, D. F., & Sheffet, M. J. (1988). Gray markets and the legal status of parallel importation. Journal of Marketing, 52(3), 75.

Dwyer, F. R., Schur, P. H., & Oh, S. (1987). Developing buyer-seller relations. Journal of Marketing, 51(2), 11-28.

Emshwiller, J. R. (1993, September 1). "Scrip" ATMs appeal to growing number of retailers. Wall Street Journal, p. B2.

Enscoe, D. (1990, March). Sweepstakes are addictive. Target Marketing, p. 14.

Erickson, G. S. (1992). Robbing Peter to pay . . . Peter (Minicase MKTG-24). Business Ethics Program. Chicago: Arthur Andersen.

Ethics Resource Center. (1979). Codes of ethics in corporations and trade associations and the teaching of ethics in graduate business schools. Princeton, NJ: Opinion Research Corporation.

Executive arrested in Japan's probe of bribery scandal. (1993, September 21). Wall Street Journal, p. A16.

Fairweather, V. (1980). $80,000 in payoffs. In R. Baum (Ed.), Ethical problems in engineering: Cases (2nd ed., pp. 50-51). Troy, NY: Rensselaer Polytechnic Institute.

Falls, R. (1993, September 17). It's hard to be a customer. Waco Tribune-Herald, p. 15.

Farmer, R. N. (1967). Would you want your daughter to marry a marketing man? Journal of Marketing, 31(1), 1-3.

Farmer, R. N. (1977). Would you want your son to marry a marketing lady? Journal of Marketing, 41(1), 15-18.

Farnham, A. (1991, January 14). What comes after greed? Fortune, pp. 43-44.

Ferrell, O. C., & Gresham, L. G. (1985). A contingency framework for understanding ethical decision making in marketing. Journal of Marketing, 49(3), 87-96.

Ferrell, O. C., Jr., & Weaver, K. (1978). Ethical beliefs of marketing managers. Journal of Marketing, 42(3), 69-73.

Finn, W. (1988, August). How to make the sale and remain ethical. Sales & Marketing Management, pp. 18-19.

Ford, Chrysler move to correct glitches in two new products. (1993, November 8). Wall Street Journal, p. A2.

Forker, L. B., & Jansen, R. L. (1990). Ethical practices in purchasing. Journal of Purchasing and Materials Management, 26(4), 19-26.

France aims to regulate, limit markdown sales. (1990, January 9). Women's Wear Daily, p. 10.

Frankel, M. S. (1989). Professional codes: Why, how, and with what impact? Journal of Business Ethics, 8, 109-115.

Frazier, G. (1983). Interorganizational exchange behavior in marketing channels: A broadened perspective. Journal of Marketing, 47(4), 68-78.

Freedman, A. M. (1993, September 22). A marketing giant uses its sales prowess to profit on poverty. *Wall Street Journal,* p. A1.

Freeman, R. E. (1984). *Strategic management: A stakeholder approach.* Boston: Pittman.

Frey, C. J., & Kinnear, T. J. (1979). Legal constraints and marketing research: Review and call to action. *Journal of Marketing Research, 16,* 295-302.

Friday, C. (1993, July 5). Cookies, cream 'n controversy. *Newsweek,* p. 40.

Friedman, M. (1962). *Capitalism and freedom.* Chicago: University of Chicago Press.

Friedman, M. (1970, September 13). The social responsibility of business is to increase its profit. *New York Times Magazine,* pp. 32-33.

Fritzche, D. J. (1992a). Elite furniture (Minicase MKTG-18). *Business Ethics Program.* Chicago: Arthur Andersen.

Fritzche, D. J. (1992b). Inside information (Minicase MKTG-2). *Business Ethics Program.* Chicago: Arthur Andersen.

Fritzche, D. J., & Becker, H. (1983). Ethical behavior of marketing managers. *Journal of Business Ethics, 2,* 291-299.

Fry, J. N., & McDougall, G. H. (1974). Consumer appraisals of retail price advertisements. *Journal of Marketing, 38*(3), 64-74.

FTC decision may affect price-breaks, take-backs. (1989, February). *Chain Store Age Executive,* pp. 18-19.

FTC guides concerning use of endorsements and testimonials in advertising, 16 C.F.R., § 255 (1982).

FTC to decide whether to sue RJR tobacco for Old Joe ad. (1993, May 10). *Marketing News,* p. 6.

Fulmer, R. M. (1979, May-June). Ethical codes of business. *Personnel Administration,* pp. 49-57.

Gallup Poll. (1983). *Honesty and ethical standards* (Report No. 214). (Available from the Gallup Organization, Inc., 47 Hulfish Street, Princeton, NJ 08542)

Gatty, B. (1993, May). FTC cracks down on "green" pretenders. *PROMO,* p. 47.

Geis, G., & Stotland, E. (1980). *White-collar crime: Theory and research.* Beverly Hills, CA: Sage.

Gellerman, S. (1986, July-August). Why "good" managers make bad ethical choices. *Harvard Business Review,* pp. 85-90.

Gerlin, A. (1993, September 15). Learning a language this way is as easy as one, three, two. *Wall Street Journal,* p. B1.

G.I. Joe surrenders. (1993, July). *Consumer Reports,* p. 413.

Gibson, R. (1988, November 1). Supermarkets demand food firms payments just to get on the shelf. *Wall Street Journal,* p. A1.

Gilman, H. (1985, April 1). Bribery of retail buyers is called pervasive. *Wall Street Journal,* p. 6.

Goldhaber, G., & De Turck, M. (1988, Spring). Effects of consumers' familiarity with a product on attention to compliance and warnings. *Journal of Products Liability,* pp. 29-37.

Goldman, K. (1993, December 2). Spy service rapidly delivers rival TV ads. *Wall Street Journal,* p. B8.

Goldsmith, W., & Clutterbuck, D. (1984). *The winning streak.* London: Weidenfeld & Nicholson.

Goodpaster, K. E. (1970). Morality and organizations. In W. M. Hoffman (Ed.), *Proceedings of the Second National Conference on Business Ethics* (pp. 91-101). Washington, DC: University of America.

Gorman, C. (1991, May 15). The fight over food labels. *Time,* pp. 52-56.

Gowans, C. W. (1984). Integrity in the corporation: The plight of corporate product advocates. *Journal of Business Ethics, 3,* 21-28.

Grasnick, H., & Green, E. (1980). Legal punishment, social disapproval, and internalization as inhibitors of illegal behavior. *Journal of Criminal Law and Criminology, 71,* 325-335.

Grimm, P. F., Kohlberg, L., & White, S. H. (1968). Some relationships between conscience and attentional processes. *Journal of Personality and Social Psychology, 3,* 239-252.

Grisez, C. (1970). *Abortion, the myths, the realities, and the arguments.* New York: Corpus.

Gschwandter, G. (1992, May/June). Lies and deceptions in selling. *Personal Selling Power,* pp. 58-64.

Gupta, U., & Tannenbaum, J. A. (1993, November 9). Clinton plan may lead some to flout flaws. *Wall Street Journal,* pp. B1, B2.

Hall, R. T. (1968). Professionalization and bureaucratization. *American Sociological Review, 33*(1), 92-104.

Hansen, D. P. (1991, Winter). Managing for ethics: Some implications of research on the Prisoner's Dilemma Game. *SAM Advanced Management Journal,* pp. 16-20.

Hansen, R. S. (1992). A multidimensional scale for measuring business ethics: A purification and refinement. *Journal of Business Ethics, 11,* 523-534.

Harrington, S. J. (1991). What corporate America is teaching about ethics. *Academy of Management Executive, 5*(1), 21-30.

Harris, J. R. (1990). Ethical values of individuals at different levels in the organizational hierarchy of a single firm. *Journal of Business Ethics, 9,* 741-750.

Harvey, M. (1988, July-August). A new way to combat product counterfeiting. *Business Horizons,* pp. 19-28.

Heide, J., & John, G. (1988). The role of dependence balancing in safeguarding transaction-specific assets in conventional channels. *Journal of Marketing, 52*(1), 20-35.

Henthorne, T. L., Robin, D. P., & Reidenbach, R. E. (1992). Identifying gaps in ethical perceptions between managers and salespersons: A multidimensional approach. *Journal of Business Ethics, 11,* 849-856.

Hickson, D. J., Hinings, C. R., Pennings, J. M., & Schneck, R. E. (1971). Contingencies and conditions in intraorganizational

power. In A. R. Negandhi, H. Aldrich, G. G. Darkenwald, D. J. Hickson, C. R. Hinings, J. M. Pennings, R. E. Schneck, & L. R. Pondy (Eds.), *Conflict and power in complex organizations: An interinstitutional perspective* (pp. 73-91). Kent, OH: Kent State University Press.

Hirsch, J. S. (1993, September 15). "Do-not-rent" lists tag bad drivers. *Wall Street Journal,* p. B1.

Hisrich, R. D., & Peters, M. P. (1991). *Marketing decisions for new and used products* (2nd ed.). New York: Macmillan.

Hite, R. E., & Bellizi, J. B. (1987). Salespeople's use of entertainment and gifts. *Industrial Marketing Management, 16,* 278-284.

Hoffman, W. M. (1984). Ethics in business education: Working toward a meaningful reciprocity. *Journal of Business Ethics, 3,* 259-268.

Hoffman, W. M., & Moore, J. M. (1982). What is business ethics? A reply to Peter Drucker. *Journal of Business Ethics, 1,* 293-300.

Hoffman, W. M., Moore, J. M., & Fedor, D. A. (1986). Are corporations institutionalizing ethics. *Journal of Business Ethics, 5,* 191-198.

Hofstede, G. (1980). *Culture's consequences: International differences in work-related values.* Beverly Hills, CA: Sage.

Honomichl, J. (1991, June 24). Legislation threatens research by phone. *Marketing News,* p. 16.

Horton, C. (1986, September 15). Ethics at issue in Lotus case. *Advertising Age,* p. 9.

Hosmer, L. T. (1988, July-August). Adding ethics to the business curriculum. *Business Horizons,* pp. 9-15.

Houston, M. J. (1972). The effect of unit pricing on choices of brand and size in economic shopping. *Journal of Marketing, 36*(3), 52-69.

Hunt, S. D., & Chonko, L. B. (1984). Marketing and Machiavellianism. *Journal of Marketing, 48*(3), 30-42.

Hunt, S. D., Chonko, L. B., & Wilcox, J. B. (1984). Ethical problems of marketing researchers. *Journal of Marketing Research, 21,* 309-324.

Hunt, S. D., & Vitell, S. J. (1986, Spring). A general theory of marketing ethics. *Journal of Macromarketing,* pp. 5-16.

Hyman, M. R., Skipper, R., & Tansey, R. (1990, March-April). Ethical codes are not enough. *Business Horizons,* pp. 15-22.

Information thieves are now corporate enemy No. 1. (1986, May 5). *Business Week,* p. 120.

Ingersoll, B., & Barrett, P. M. (1993, November 11). U.S. investigating S&L chief's '85 check to Clinton, SBA-backed loan to friend. *Wall Street Journal,* p. A3.

Jackall, R. (1993). Moral mazes. In K. R. Andrews (Ed.), *Ethics in practice* (pp. 167-183). Boston: Harvard Business School Press.

Jackson, G. C., & Morgan, F. W. (1988). Responding to recall requests: A strategy for managing product withdrawals. *Journal of Public Policy and Marketing, 7,* 152-165.

Jacobs, R. M. (1988, December). Products liability: A technical and ethical challenge. *Quality Progress*, pp. 27-29.

Jacoby, J., & Hoyer, W. D. (1989). The comprehension/miscomprehension of print communication: Selected findings. *Journal of Consumer Research, 15*, 434-443.

Janis, I. (1972). *Victims of groupthink*. Boston: Houghton Mifflin.

Janis, I. L., & Mann, L. (1977). *Decision making: A psychological analysis of conflict, choice, and commitment*. New York: Free Press.

Jansen, E., & Von Glinow, M. A. (1985). Ethical ambivalence and organizational reward systems. *Academy of Management Review, 10*(4), 814-822.

Johnson, R. (1987, January 9). The case of Marc Feith shows corporate spies aren't just high tech. *Wall Street Journal*, p. 1.

Johnson, R., & Koten, J. (1988, June 28). Sears has everything including messy fight over ads in New York. *Wall Street Journal*, p. 1.

Jones, E. E. (1985). Major developments in social psychology during the past five decades. In G. Lindzey & E. Aronson (Eds.), *The handbook of social psychology* (pp. 47-107). New York: Random House.

Jones, T. M. (1991). Ethical decision making by individuals in organizations: An issue-contingent model. *Academy of Management Review, 16*, 366-395.

Kahneman, D., Knetsch, J. L., & Thaler, R. H. (1986). Fairness as a constraint on profit seeking: Entitlements in the market. *American Economic Review, 76*(4), 728-741.

Kamm, T. (1993, October 28). Brazil is tested by fresh graft scandal. *Wall Street Journal*, p. A14.

Karr, A. (1993, December 30). FDA bans unproven health claims by makers of some diet supplements. *Wall Street Journal*, p. B4.

Katz, D., & Kahn, R. L. (1966). *The social psychology of organizations*. New York: John Wiley.

Keichel, W. III. (1979, January 29). The crime at the Topic Frewhaul Corporation. *Fortune*, p. 35.

Kelley, C. A. (1992a). Justifying price increases (Minicase MKTG-08). *Business Ethics Program*. Chicago: Arthur Andersen.

Kelley, C. A. (1992b). Lottery mania (Minicase MKTG-11). *Business Ethics Program*. Chicago: Arthur Andersen.

Kelly, K., & Schine, E. (1992, June 29). How did Sears blow this gasket? *Newsweek*, p. 38.

Kennedy, J. F. (1962). Kennedy recommends consumer protection. In *Congressional Quarterly Almanac* (87th Congress, 2nd sess., p. 890). Washington, DC: Congressional Quarterly Service.

Kerr, S. (1975). On the folly of rewarding A while hoping for B. *Academy of Management Journal, 18*, 269-283.

Kodak announces it won a round over Fuji paper. (1993, October 13). *Wall Street Journal*, p. B5.

Kohlberg, L., & Candee, D. (1984). The relationship of moral judgment to moral action. In W. M. Kurtines & J. C. Gerivity (Eds.), *Morality, moral behavior, and moral development* (pp. 52-73). New York: John Wiley.

Kotler, P., & Mantrala, M. K. (1985, Summer). Flawed products: Consumer responses and marketer strategies. *Journal of Consumer Marketing*, 27-36.

Krugman, D. M., & Ferrell, O. C. (1981). The organizational ethics of advertising: Corporate and agency views. *Journal of Advertising, 1*(1), 21-30.

Laczniak, G. R. (1983, Spring). Framework for analyzing marketing ethics. *Journal of Macromarketing*, pp. 7-18.

Laczniak, G. R., & Murphy, P. E. (1993). *Ethical marketing decisions: The higher road*. Boston: Allyn & Bacon.

Lans, M. S. (1993, May 23). Protecting trade secrets helps maintain marketing edge. *Marketing News*, p. 13.

Lantos, G. P. (1992a). The competitive and combative toilet tissue campaign (Minicase MKTG-5). *Business Ethics Program*. Chicago: Arthur Andersen.

Lantos, G. P. (1992b). Incredible shrinking potato chip package (Minicase MKTG-4). *Business Ethics Program*. Chicago: Arthur Andersen.

Lantos, G. P. (1992c). The speedy sale (Minicase MKTG-16). *Business Ethics Program*. Chicago: Arthur Andersen.

Laroche, M., McGown, K. L., & Rainville, J. (1986). How ethical are professional marketing researchers? *Business Forum, 11*(1), 21-25.

Lawless, M. W., & Fisher, R. J. (1990, March). Sources of durable competitive advantage in new products. *Journal of Product Innovation and Management,* pp. 35-44.

Leiser, B. (1979). Beyond fraud and deception: The moral uses of advertising. In T. Donaldson & P. Werhane (Eds.), *Ethical issues in business* (pp. 59-66). Englewood Cliffs, NJ: Prentice Hall.

Levenson, H. (1974). Activism and powerful others: Distinctions within the concept of internal-external control. *Journal of Personality Assessment, 38,* 377-383.

Levitt, T. (1958, September-October). The dangers of social responsibility. *Harvard Business Review,* pp. 41-50.

Levy, M., & Weitz, B. A. (1992). *Retailing management.* Homewood, IL: Irwin.

Levy, S. J., & Zaltman, G. (1975). *Marketing, society, and conflict.* Englewood Cliffs, NJ: Prentice Hall.

Lewin, T. (1984, April 1). Putting a lid on corporate secrets. *New York Times,* p. C1.

Lewis, P. V. (1989). Ethical principals for decision makers: A longitudinal study. *Journal of Business Ethics, 8,* 585-597.

Lewyn, M. (1991, February). Does someone have your company's number? *Newsweek,* p. 90.

Luthans, F., & Kreitner, R. (1985). *Organization behavior modification and beyond: An operant and social learning approach.* Glenview, IL: Scott Foresman.

Maccoby, M. (1978). *The gamesman.* New York: Bantam.

MacIntyre, A. (1977). Why are the problems of business ethics insoluble? In W. M. Hoffman (Ed.), *Proceedings of the First National Conference on Business Ethics* (pp. 318-327). Waltham, MA: Center for Business Ethics at Bentley College.

MacIntyre, A. (1981). *After virtue: A study in moral theory.* Notre Dame, IN: University of Notre Dame Press.

Mason, R. O., & Mitroff, I. I. (1981). *Challenging strategic planning assumptions: Theory, cases, and techniques.* New York: John Wiley.

May, L. (1987). *The morality of groups: Collective responsibility, group-based harm, and corporate rights.* Notre Dame, IN: University of Notre Dame Press.

McGuire, E. P. (1972). *Evaluating new product proposals.* New York: Conference Board.

Meier, R. F., & Geis, G. (1982). The psychology of the white-collar offender. In G. Geis (Ed.), *On white-collar crime* (pp. 34-40). Lexington, MA: Lexington Books.

Merton, R. K. (1957). The role set. *British Journal of Sociology, 8*(2), 106-120.

Miles, R. H. (1977). Role-set configuration as a predictor of role conflict and ambiguity in complex organizations. *Sociometry, 4*(1), 21-34.

Miller, F. L. (1992a). (Black)marketing "Primo" in Rohanda (Minicase MKTG-3). *Business Ethics Program.* Chicago: Arthur Andersen.

Miller, F. L. (1992b). The pizza puzzle (Minicase MKTG-6) *Business Ethics Program.* Chicago: Arthur Andersen.

Miller, T. J. (1989, May-June). Food advertising and health claims: Everything you read is not always good for you. *Journal of State Government,* pp. 107-110.

Mitchell, J. (1991, May 29). GM is accused on way it used Baldridge Award. *Wall Street Journal,* p. B1.

Monroe, K., & LaPlaca, P. J. (1972). What are the benefits of unit pricing? *Journal of Marketing, 36*(3), 16-22.

Muncy, J. A., & Vitell, S. J. (1992). Consumer ethics: An investigation of the ethical beliefs of the final consumer. *Journal of Business Research, 24,* 297-311.

Murphy, P. E., & Enis, B. M. (1985). *Marketing.* Glenview, IL: Scott Foresman.

Murphy, P. E., & Laczniak, G. (1981). Marketing ethics: Review and implications for managers, educators, and researchers. In B. M. Enis & K. J. Roering (Eds.), *Review of marketing* (pp. 251-266). Chicago: American Marketing Association.

Murphy, P. E., & Wilkie, W. L. (1990). *Marketing and advertising regulation.* Notre Dame, IN: University of Notre Dame Press.

Myers, R. (1993, November 5). Angry customers say Dauphin Deposit reneged on high-yielding IRA accounts. *Wall Street Journal,* p. B3.

Naj, A. K., & Machalaba, D. (1993, September 30). FTC to try to block GE plan to buy Chrysler boxcars. *Wall Street Journal*, p. A6.

Nash, L. (1981, November-December). Ethics without the sermon. *Harvard Business Review*, pp. 79-90.

Neiman, J. (1984, June 25). Cookie makers deny swiping P&Gs secrets. *Advertising Age*, p. 2.

Nelson, J. (1992). The market ethic: Moral dilemma and microeconomics. *Journal of Business Ethics, 11,* 317-320.

Nelson-Horchler, J. (1988, January 4). Safety: A tough sell. *Industry Week*, p. 24.

Niebaur, H. R. (1963). *The responsible self.* New York: Harper & Row.

Niebaur, H. R. (1970). *Radical monotheism and Western culture.* New York: Harper & Row.

Nielson, R. P. (1987). What can managers do about unethical management? *Journal of Business Ethics, 6,* 309-320.

Oakes, G. (1990). The sales process and the paradoxes of trust. *Journal of Business Ethics, 9,* 671-679.

O'Brien, B. (1993, July 12). Predatory pricing issue is due to be taken up in American Air's trial. *Wall Street Journal*, p. A1.

Ortega, B. (1993, October 13). Wal-Mart loses a case on pricing. *Wall Street Journal*, p. A3.

Ortmeyer, G. K. (1993). Ethical issues in pricing. In N. Craig Smith & J. A. Quelch, (Eds.), *Ethics in marketing* (pp. 393-394). Homewood, IL: Irwin.

Owens, J. (1982, April). Business ethics in the college classroom. *Journal of Business Education,* pp. 258-262.

Pandya, A. M. (1992). Green acres promotion (Minicase MKTG-29). *Business Ethics Program.* Chicago: Arthur Andersen.

Pattan, J. E. (1984). The business of ethics and the ethics of business. *Journal of Business Ethics, 3,* 1-19.

Patzer, G. L. (1992). Falsification of data (Minicase MKTG-10). *Business Ethics Program.* Chicago: Arthur Andersen.

Penn, W. Y., & Collier, B. D. (1985). Current research in moral development as a decision support system. *Journal of Business Ethics, 4,* 131-136.

Peters, T. (1987). *Thriving on chaos: Handbook for management revolution.* New York: Knopf.

Petrick, J. A., & Manning, G. E. (1990, March). Developing an ethical climate for excellence. *Journal for Quality and Participation,* pp. 84-90.

Petrick, J. A., Manning, G. E., & Curtis, K. (1989, September-October). Teaching business ethics in a business education program. *The Balance Sheet,* pp. 11-15.

Petrick, J. A., Wagley, R. A., & Von der Embse, T. J. (1991, Winter). Structured ethical decision making: Improving the prospects of managerial success in business. *SAM Advanced Management Journal,* pp. 28-34.

Pincoffs, E. (1986). *Quandaries and virtues: Against reductivism in ethics.* Lawrence: Kansas State University Press.

Preston, I. L. (1975). *The great American blow-up: Puffery in advertising and selling.* Madison: University of Wisconsin Press.

Preston, I. L. (1993). Relating research on deceptiveness law to ethics in advertising. In N. C. Smith & J. A. Quelch, (Eds.), *Ethics in marketing* (pp. 664-665). Homewood, IL: Irwin.

Prosser, W. (1971). *Handbook of the law of torts.* Minneapolis, MN: West.

Pruden, H. O. (1971). Which ethics for marketing? In J. R. Wish & S. H. Gamble (Eds.), *Marketing and social issues* (pp. 98-104). New York: John Wiley.

Quinn, J. B. (1992, July 13). Buyers beware. *Newsweek,* pp. 46-47.

Rachels, J. (1986). *The elements of moral philosophy.* New York: Random House.

Raelin, J. A. (1984). An examination of deviant/adaptive behaviors in the organizational careers of professionals. *Academy of Management Review, 3,* 413-427.

Reich, R. (1987). *Tales of a new America.* New York: Random House.

Reidenbach, R. E., & Robin, D. P. (1988). Some initial steps toward improving the measurement of ethical evaluations of marketing activities. *Journal of Business Ethics, 7,* 871-879.

Reidenbach, R. E., Robin, D. P., & Dawson, L. (1991). An application and extension of a multidimensional ethics scale to selected marketing practices and marketing groups. *Journal of the Academy of Marketing Science, 19,* 83-92.

Reilly, P. M. (1993, October 11). Several major music companies face FTC probe of alleged CD price fixing. *Wall Street Journal,* p. B3.

Reilly, R. J., & Hoffer, G. E. (1983). Will retarding the information flow on automobile recalls affect consumer demand. *Economic Inquiry, 21,* 444-447.

Reitman, V. (1993, November 30). Manufacturers start to spurn big discounters. *Wall Street Journal,* pp. B1, B2.

Rice, D., & Dreilinger, C. (1990, May). Rights and wrongs of ethics training. *Training and Development Journal,* pp. 103-107.

Richards, J. I. (1990). A "new and improved" view of puffery. *Journal of Public Policy and Marketing, 9,* 73-84.

Roberts, M. L., & Berger, P. (1989). *Direct marketing management.* Englewood Cliffs, NJ: Prentice Hall.

Robin, D., Giallourakis, M., David, F. R., & Moritz, T. E. (1989, January-February). A different look at codes of ethics. *Business Horizons,* pp. 66-73.

Robin, D., & Reidenbach, R. E. (1986). A framework for analyzing ethical issues in marketing. *Business and Professional Ethics Journal, 2*(1), 3-22.

Robin, D. R., & Reidenbach, R. E. (1987). Social responsibility, ethics, and marketing strategy: Closing the gap between concept and application. *Journal of Marketing, 51*(1), 44-58.

Robin, D. R., & Reidenbach, R. E. (1989). *Business ethics: Where profits meet value systems.* Englewood Cliffs, NJ: Prentice Hall.

Robinson, J. (1973). General attitudes towards people. In J. P. Robinson & P. R. Shaver (Eds.), *Measures of social psychological attitudes* (pp. 587-727). Ann Arbor, MI: Institute for Social Research.

Rokeach, M. (1968). *Beliefs, attitudes, and values: A theory of organization and change.* San Francisco: Jossey-Bass.

Rotter, J. B. (1966). Generalized expectancies for internal versus external control of reinforcement. *Psychological Monographs: General and Applied, 80,* 609.

Sack, S. M. (1986, December). Some words on warranties . . . *Sales & Marketing Management Magazine,* pp. 52-54.

Sandberg, J. (1993, November 1). Computer "cracking" is seen on the rise. *Wall Street Journal,* p. B5.

Santilli, P. C. (1983). The informative and persuasive functions of advertising: A moral appraisal. *Journal of Business Ethics, 2,* 27-33.

Saul, G. K. (1981). Business ethics: Where are we going? *Academy of Management Review, 6*(2), 269-276.

Schlender, B. R. (1992, January 27). The values we will need. *Fortune,* pp. 75-77.

Schlossberg, H. (1991, October 23). Right to privacy issue pits consumers against marketers, researchers. *Marketing News,* p. 14.

Schneider, K. L. (1982). Ethics and marketing research. In J. E. Nelson (Ed.), *The practice of marketing research* (pp. 591-617). Boston: Kent.

Schrank, J. (1975). *Deception detection.* Boston: Beacon.

Schroeder, M. (1991, August 12). Did Westinghouse keep mum on PCBs? *Newsweek,* pp. 69-71.

Schubert, R. (1979, Summer). Is dishonesty good for business? *Business and Society Review,* pp. 39-44.

Schwartz, J., Washington, F., Fleming, C., & Hamilton, K. (1993, February 22). No scandal—No story. *Newsweek,* pp. 42-43.

Schwartz, V., & Driver, R. W. (1983). Warnings in the workplace: The need for a synthesis of law and communication theory. *University of Cincinnati Law Review, 52*(1), 60.

Selz, M., & Emshwiller, J. R. (1993, March 3). Selling items to deal with disaster jumps to fever pitch. *Wall Street Journal,* p. B2.

Senn, J. A. (1990). *Information systems in management.* Belmont, CA: Wadsworth.

Sethna, B. N. (1992). Washing dirty laundry (Minicase MKTG-28). *Business Ethics Program.* Chicago: Arthur Andersen.

Shah, A. (1994, February 28). FDA cites evidence of cigarette makers keeping nicotine at addictive levels. *Wall Street Journal,* p. B4.

Shapiro, E. (1993, September 27). Cigarette makers outfit smokers in icons, eluding warnings and enraging activists. *Wall Street Journal*, pp. B1, B4.

Sheridan, P. J. (1990). FCC sets children's ad limits. *Information Access Company, 119*(20), 33.

Sherwin, D. S. (1983, November-December). The ethical roots of the business system. *Harvard Business Review*, pp. 183-192.

Simon, H. (1973, June). Technology and environment. *Management Science*, p. 1110.

Sims, R. R. (1992). Linking groupthink to unethical behavior in organizations. *Journal of Business Ethics, 11*, 651-662.

Smith, A. (1971). *Wealth of nations.* London: Everyman. (Original work published 1776)

Smith, A. (1976). *The theory of moral sentiments.* London: Oxford University Press. (Original work published 1759)

Smith, H. (1991). *The world's religions.* San Francisco: HarperCollins.

Smith, H. R., & Carroll, A. B. (1984). Organizational ethics: A stacked deck. *Journal of Business Ethics, 3*, 95-100.

Smith, K. J. (1992, December). Coupon scam uncovered in Detroit. *PROMO*, pp. 1, 45.

Smith, N. C., & Quelch, J. A. (1993). *Ethics in marketing.* Homewood, IL: Irwin.

Sonnenberg, F. K., & Goldberg, B. (1992, April 6). Business integrity: An oxymoron. *Industry Week*, pp. 53-54.

Spekman, R., & Salmond, D. J. (in press). *Consensus and collaboration in industrial marketing rela-*

tionships. Boston: Marketing Science Institute.

Stead, W. E., Worrell, D. L., Spalding, J. B., & Stead, J. C. (1987). Unethical decisions: Socially learned behavior. *Journal of Social Behavior and Personality, 1*(1), 105-115.

Steiner, G. A. (1975). *Business and society.* New York: Random House.

Steinmetz, G. (1993, October 12). Former agents draw a picture of Met Life's sales practices. *Wall Street Journal*, pp. B1, B5.

Stern, L. W., & El-Ansary, A. I. (1988). *Marketing channels.* Englewood Cliffs, NJ: Prentice Hall.

Stern, L. W., & Eovaldi, T. L. (1984). *Legal aspects of marketing strategy: Antitrust and consumer protection issues.* Englewood Cliffs, NJ: Prentice Hall.

Stevens, A. (1993, October 29). S&L lawsuits fail to answer questions on ethical standards. *Wall Street Journal*, p. B5.

Stipp, D. (1993, September 16). Some question extent of lead's risk to kids, need to remove paint. *Wall Street Journal*, pp. A1, A10.

Stout, H. (1991, June 22). U.S. may bring civil charges over Retin-A. *Wall Street Journal*, pp. B1, B4.

Sturdivant, F. B. (1985). *Business and society: A managerial approach* (3rd ed.). Homewood, IL: Irwin.

Survey of selling costs. (1992, June 22). *Sales and Marketing Management*, p. 8.

Sutherland, E., & Cressy, D. R. (1970). *Principles of criminology.* Chicago: Lippincott.

Taking the scare out of auto repairs. (1993). Washington, DC: Federal Trade Commission.

Tannenbaum, J. A. (1993, December 8). Subway sandwich chain investigation by FTC is closed. *Wall Street Journal*, p. B2.

Taylor, R. E. (1984, May 27). White collar crime getting less attention. *Wall Street Journal*, p. A27.

Therrien, L. (1989, August 7). Want shelf space at supermarket? Ante up. *Business Week*, pp. 60-61.

Thorelli, H. B. (1972). A concept of consumer policy. In *Proceedings of the annual meeting of the Association for Consumer Research* .

Tocqueville, Alexis de. (1956). *Democracy in America* (Vol. 2). New York: Knopf. (Original work published 1840)

Trevino, L. (1986). Ethical decision making in organizations: A person-situation interactionist model. *Academy of Management Review, 11*, 601-617.

Trevino, L. K., & Youngblood, S. (1990, August). Bad apples in bad barrels: A causal analysis of ethical decision making behavior. *Journal of Applied Psychology*, 378-385.

Tsalikis, J., & Fritzche, D. J. (1989). Business ethics: A literature review with a focus on marketing ethics. *Journal of Business Ethics, 8*, 695-743.

Tybout, A. M., & Zaltman, G. (1974). Ethics in marketing research: Their practical relevance. *Journal of Marketing Research, 11,* 357-368.

Udell, G. G., & Laczniak, G. R. (1981). *Marketing in an age of change: An introduction.* New York: John Wiley.

Unger, S. H. (1982). *Controlling technology: Ethics and the responsible engineer.* New York: Holt, Rinehart & Winston.

Urbany, J. F., Bearden, W. O., & Weilbaker, D. C. (1988). The effect of plausible and exaggerated reference prices on consumer perceptions and price search. *Journal of Consumer Research, 14*(1), 95-110.

Vandivier, K. (1980). Engineers, ethics, and economics. In R. Baum (Ed.), *Ethical problems in engineering: Cases* (2nd ed. pp. 136-138). Troy, NY: Rensselaer Polytechnic Institute.

Van Fleet, D. D. (1991). *Behavior in organizations.* Dallas, TX: Houghton Mifflin.

Velasquez, M. (1982). *Business ethics: Concepts and cases.* Englewood Cliffs, NJ: Prentice Hall.

Velasquez, M. G., & Rostankowski, C. (1985). *Ethics: Theory and practice.* Englewood Cliffs, NJ: Prentice Hall.

Victor, B., & Cullen, J. (1988). The organizational bases of ethical work climates. *Administrative Science Quarterly, 33,* 101-125.

Vitell, S. J., & Festervand, T. A. (1987). Business ethics: Conflicts, practices and beliefs of industrial executives. *Journal of Business Ethics, 6,* 111-122.

Vitell, S. J., & Grove, S. J. (1987). Marketing ethics and techniques

of neutralization. *Journal of Business Ethics, 6,* 433-438.

Vleeming, R. G. (1979, February). Machiavellianism: A preliminary review. *Psychological Reports,* pp. 295-310.

Wall, S. (1977, January-February). What the competition is doing. *Harvard Business Review,* pp. 32-34.

Waters, H. F. (1990, January 8). Watch what kids watch: New legislation hopes to channel children's TV in a healthier direction. *Newsweek,* pp. 50-52.

Waters, J. A., & Bird, F. (1989). Attending to ethics in management. *Journal of Business Ethics, 8,* 493-497.

We woz sugged! (1991, June 14). *Investor's Chronicle,* p. 27.

Weaver, M., & Ferrell, O. C. (1977). The impact of corporate policy on reported ethical beliefs and behavior of marketing managers. In B. A. Greenberg & D. N. Bellenger (Eds.), *Contemporary marketing thought* (pp. 477-481). Chicago: American Marketing Association.

Weeks, W. A., & Nantel, J. (1993). Corporate codes of ethics and sales force behavior: A case study. *Journal of Business Ethics, 12,* 105-112.

Weinstein, S. (1989, June). Changing values in changing times for business. *Progressive Grocer,* p. 36.

Werner, S. B. (1992). The movement for reforming American business ethics: A twenty-year perspective. *Journal of Business Ethics, 11,* 61-70.

Whenmouth, E. (1992, March 16). A matter of ethics. *Industry Week,* pp. 57, 62.

White, L. P., & Wooten, K. C. (1983). Ethical dilemmas in various stages of organizational development. *Academy of Management Review, 8*(4), 690-697.

Whitney, G. (1993, November 4). Europe moves to curb insider trading. *Wall Street Journal,* p. A13.

Williams, O. F. (1982, Summer). Business ethics: A Trojan horse. *California Management Review,* pp. 14-24.

Wines, W. A., & Napier, N. K. (1992). Toward an understanding of cross-cultural ethics: A tentative model. *Journal of Business Ethics, 11,* 831-841.

Winslow, R. (1993, September 15). Study indicates fetal sonogram is overused aid. *Wall Street Journal,* p. B1.

Winter, G. (1966). *Elements of social ethic.* New York: Macmillan.

Winters, P. (1989, July 10). Crush fails to fit on P&G shelf. *Advertising Age,* p. 1.

Wise, J. (1989, October 23). On a wing and a prayer. *Adweek's Marketing Week,* p. 45.

Woo, J. (1993, October 29). Suits against pharmacists are on the rise. *Wall Street Journal,* pp. B1, B5.

Wotruba, T. R. (1990, Spring). A comprehensive framework for the analysis of ethical behavior, with a focus on sales organizations. *Journal of Personal Selling and Sales Management,* pp. 10, 29-42.

Zeithaml, V. A. (1982). Consumer response to in-store price information environments. *Journal of Consumer Research, 8*(4), 357-369.

Zey-Ferrell, M. K., Weaver, M., & Ferrell, O. C. (1979). Predicting unethical behavior among marketing practitioners. *Human Relations, 32*(7), 587-604.

Zinkhan, G. M., & Vachris, L. A. (1984). The impact of selling aids on new prospects. *Industrial Marketing Management, 13,* 187-193.

Author Index

Subject Index

Organization Index

About the Author

Lawrence B. Chonko is the Holloway Professor of Marketing at Baylor University in Waco, Texas. He is also the Director of Educational Programs for Baylor's Center for Professional Selling. Born in Jersey City, New Jersey, he received his Bachelor of Science in Business and Economics from Lehigh University (1973). He received an MBA (1975) and PhD (1978) from the University of Houston, where he was the recipient of the university's Teaching Excellence Award. He has also taught at Texas Tech University (1978-1985), where he was the recipient of the President's Award for Teaching Excellence and the Outstanding Teacher Award presented by Mortar Board and Omicron Delta Kappa. He has also received recognition for outstanding teaching by the Order of Omega Society at Baylor University.

Professor Chonko served as editor of the *Journal of Personal Selling and Sales Management,* the only academic journal devoted exclusively to the field of professional selling and sales management. He also served as editor of *Winning Traditions,* a monthly sales newsletter. His research interests include professional selling and sales management, business-to-business marketing and business ethics. His scholarly work has appeared in a number of journals having to do with marketing, management, selling, ethics, advertising, business, banking, and education as well as in edited volumes. He is also the recipient of several research grants.

Professor Chonko has coauthored four books, *Direct Marketing, Direct Selling, and the Mature Consumer; Managing Salespeople; Professional Selling,* and *Business, the Economy, and World Affairs.* He is currently working on *Introduction to Marketing Strategy.* Throughout his career, he has been a consultant to organizations in the industrial products, consumer products, services, and nonprofit industries. His work has contributed to the growth and development of a variety of organizations.

He and his wife Barbara have two children—Paul, who is 14, and Christy, who is 11. His hobbies include softball, racquetball, bowling, golf, and photography.